D0611915

Working Lives

THE *SOUTHERN EXPOSURE* HISTORY OF LABOR IN THE SOUTH

EDITED BY
Marc S. Miller

WITH AN
INTRODUCTION BY
Herbert Gutman

PANTHEON BOOKS
New York

Library of Congress Cataloging in Publication Data

Main entry under title:

Working lives.

   Bibliography: p.
   Includes index.
   1. Labor and laboring classes—Southern states—
History—Addresses, essays, lectures. 2. Trade-
unions—Southern States—History—Addresses, essays,
lectures. I. Miller, Marc S. II. Southern exposure.
HD8083.A13W67   331'.0975   80–7720
ISBN 0–394–50912–9
ISBN 0–394–73965–5 (pbk.)

*Grateful acknowledgment is made for permission to use the following previously
published material:*

"Cotton Dust Kills, and It's Killing Me," Copyright © 1978, 1980 by Mary M. Conway.
Reprinted by permission of the author.

"Davidson-Wilder Blues," by Ed Davis, from *American Folksongs of Protest,* by John
Greenway. Copyright © 1953 by the University of Pennsylvania Press. Reprinted by
permission of the University of Pennsylvania Press.

"In Egypt Land," from *Collected Poems, 1924–1974,* by John Beecher. Copyright ©
1960, 1974 by John Beecher. Reprinted by permission of the author and the Macmillan
Co., Inc.

"Puttin' Down Ol' Massa," by David Moberg, from *In These Times,* September 5–11,
1979. Reprinted with revisions by permission of *In These Times.*

Excerpts used in "Strike at Davidson-Wilder, 1932–33," reprinted by permission of the
Knoxville News-Sentinel.

All other articles first appeared in Southern Exposure *or were previously unpublished.*

Designed by Clint Anglin

First Edition

Manufactured in the United States of America

Contents

Editor's Preface

SINCE ITS EMERGENCE IN THE seventies out of the civil rights and antiwar movements, the Institute for Southern Studies has been deeply concerned with the struggles of working people in the South. In 1973 the institute founded its unique journal, *Southern Exposure,* to spread awareness of the past and present work of progressives throughout the South, and to expose the power structure they confront.

The record established by *Southern Exposure* made the task of assembling this book a pleasure. Most of the articles first appeared in the magazine, especially in two issues devoted entirely to labor: "No More Moanin'," edited by Sue Thrasher and Leah Wise in 1973, and "Here Come a Wind," edited by Bill Finger in 1976. This core guaranteed a book to be proud of. Collecting new articles was similarly rewarding: thanks to the institute's reputation, people who were asked to update old articles or write new ones responded with twice the expected effort. In fact, trying to squeeze all the available material into one book of manageable length brought sleepless nights and thoughts already for volume two.

The high standards of *Southern Exposure* have been built by the dedication of its editors over the years and the variety of viewpoints they bring to the journal. The collective influence of these editors made this book more than either an amorphous grouping of articles or a dry historical narrative. Everyone at the institute contributed time, concern, and support, but Bob Hall and Jim Overton provided the criticism that gave structure and substance. Chris Mayfield lent a well-appreciated editing hand when 400 pages proved too much for one person to handle in a few short months. Several previous editors of *Southern Exposure* and a great many friends of the institute commented on various drafts, materially changing our conceptions of what we should be doing in a book on labor in the South. Among these people were Tom Terrill, Sue Thrasher, Leon Fink, Chip Hughes, Len Stanley, Brenda Bell, Fran Ansley, and Jim Sessions. Wendy Wolf, our editor at Pantheon, gave crucial support and criticism throughout.

Lastly, *Working Lives* was assembled not by a few people in 1979 but by ten years of writers, activists, institute staff members and volunteers, and by generations of Southern workers.

—Marc S. Miller
Durham, November 1979

Introduction

HERBERT GUTMAN

SOUTHERN EXPOSURE IS A VERY special American magazine, the best of its kind now being published. Less than a decade old, it relentlessly and imaginatively focuses on the ways class and racial privileges—regional and national—continue to undermine democratic processes and distort opportunity in the American South; it also brings to light how Southern black and white popular movements seek to alter those constraining and oppressive structures. The magazine is visionary. It is democratic and egalitarian in outlook. Privilege and injustice are regularly exposed; at the same time, the folk beliefs and popular culture of ordinary rural and urban men and women are recovered. The many, many varieties of experience that shape their everyday lives, and the strategies the oppressed use to confront inequality, find a prominent place in the magazine. So too, not surprisingly, does their history.

The essays in *Working Lives* restore to all Americans a little-known and frequently misunderstood part of this nation's history: that of Southern workers, white and black, in our own century. First-person accounts of everyday experience add a moving personal dimension to detailed descriptions of collective struggles to sustain and improve life. The essays shift across the region, from rural Tennessee and Kentucky to urban Charleston; across work settings, from chemical and auto plants to the more familiar textile mills and coal mines; and across time, from Louisiana's isolated piney woods at the turn of the century to today's corporate headquarters in downtown Greenville, South Carolina, and New York's Wall Street. Most of the pieces in *Working Lives* first appeared in *Southern Exposure;* taken together, they give an authentic voice to men and women otherwise silenced by what British historian E. P. Thompson castigates as "the tremendous condescension of posterity." This is popular history at its best.

But the Southern working-class history recovered in these pages is popular history of a special kind,. and for a special reason. The writing of most popular American history continues to be dominated by "achievement" and "assimilation" models. These models invariably distort the true experiences of working men and women, compressing history by emphasizing only what "worked." Such models treat the everyday as little more than an extension of conventional domestic drama, and exaggerate those aspects of working-class historical experience that have encouraged the replication of mainstream ("middle class") cultural beliefs and practices.

An emphasis on achievement and assimilation as "the" American story does more than distort and homogenize working-class history: it alienates working people from their past. The essays that fill these pages restore the connection. They simultaneously redefine and deepen our understanding of Southern working-class history, and they enrich our historical memory about the Southern poor.

But an enlarged understanding of the events chronicled here has even broader consequences. It alters our understanding not merely of Southern working-class history but of Southern history as a whole—and of American labor history itself. Such shifts in historical consciousness are important. They allow us, not necessarily to predict the future, but to redefine our relationship to the present. Describing similar popular historical writing in Great Britain, David Caute observes: "Groups who lack a sense of their collective past resemble individuals without knowledge of their parents—stranded, half-invalidated, insecure. The rediscovered past furnishes us not only with heroes, famous and unknown, but also with a diachronic pattern which provides an alternative context for thought and action."

A NEW YORK CITY SEMINAR FOR LABOR LEADERS WHICH I directed in 1977 well illustrates just why this rediscovery and deepened historical memory are so critical to American workers— Northern and Southern—in the late twentieth century. Fifteen union leaders, both black and white, participated, none of national stature but all holding responsible positions. The unions they led served building-trades, service, white-collar, and industrial workers.

The oldest participant came from northern Alabama, where his father had been a mill worker. The son had become a factory worker in the late 1930s and spent his adult years building an Alabama industrial union, supporting integration within the labor movement, and serving the state labor movement as an elected official. He was now in his mid-fifties, a quiet, dignified, largely self-educated Southern white trade-union leader.

The seminar members studied changing patterns of work over 350 years of American history. They read about and discussed such topics as the introduction of clocks, the origins of slave labor, the decline of household manufacture, the erosion of artisan crafts, and the mix of corporate reorganization and "scientific management." The discussions centered on the causes of changing work processes and the struggle for control over these processes.

One session was devoted to the "New South." We focused on the spread of industrial capitalism and the emergence of a white and black industrial working class in the South between 1880 and the First World War. We read an essay by Paul Worthman entitled "Black Workers and Labor Unions in Birmingham, Alabama, 1897–1904," published in *Labor History* in 1969. A very original study filled with information about miners, iron and steel workers, craftsmen, and unskilled labor, the essay examines in particular the relations between black and white workers, their unions, and their employers. Worthman describes the fiercely oppressive and violent setting within which new corporations imposed their power on the region. He shows how racism often divided the workers—but also explains why interracial trade unionism triumphed for a brief moment. He points out that the Birmingham Trade Council increased from 31 locals with about 6,000 members in 1900 to more than 60 locals with more than 20,000 members in 1902. "The state's labor movement," Worthman concludes, "struggling to overcome both craft-union exclusiveness and racial conflict in Alabama, organized more than 8,000 black workers and challenged the industrialists' ability to use racial hostility to discipline the class antagonisms of the New South."

Worthman's essay provoked a vivid discussion, during which the Alabama union leader remained noticeably silent. Later, he praised the work, but explained that every single item of information in it was new to him. This was an educated man; he knew more about the differences between the American Federation of Labor and the Knights of Labor than most college teachers of introductory United States history. The northern Alabama labor struggles of the 1930s and 1940s were etched deeply in his mind. But he knew nothing about northern Alabama's (and especially Birmingham's) working-class history before that period—or about the thwarted efforts by white and black workers to build democratic and protective class institutions in his own father's youth. He was a direct descendant of an experience which had been totally closed off to him.

In *Working Lives,* that man might read of efforts to organize across racial barriers by timber workers in Louisiana and Texas as early as 1911. He could hear 85-year-old Dobbie Sanders recount his own experiences in Birmingham's steel mills in the 1920s. But until he read Paul Worthman's essay, neither these nor any other of the events that shaped the environment in which he had lived and worked for over forty years had "happened."

The social closure that denied this man access to his immediate working-class past was not a distinctly Southern phenomenon. A similar shrinkage of social memory occurred in Lawrence, Massachusetts, as journalist Paul Cowan discovered while studying the 1912 textile strike. Thirteen-year-old Camella Teoli (the daughter of Italian immigrants) was scalped by a cotton-twisting machine at the Washington Mill and hospitalized for several months in 1911. She returned home as the strike was beginning and was one of the Lawrence workers who testified at a Washington congressional hearing. Her testimony, Cowan writes, "had the same shocking effect as Fannie Lou Hamer's would when she talked about her years as a sharecropper before the Democratic Party Platform Committee in 1964. The girl's story became front-page news all over America." Cowan sought out Camella Teoli in 1967 but learned that she had died a few years before. She had lived with her daughter, a telephone operator and the wife of a welder.

When Paul Cowan met Camella Teoli's daughter in 1976, Mathilda (not her real name) was a grown woman. Cowan describes his experiences with her:

The accident at the Washington Mill had left Camella Teoli with a permanent scar—a bald spot toward the back of her head that was six inches in diameter. Practically every day of her life Mathilda had combed her mother's hair into a bun that disguised the spot. . . .

Mathilda knew nothing at all about Camella Teoli's political past—nothing about her trip to Washington . . . nothing about the sensational impact her mother had made on America's conscience. Neither, it turned out, did her brother. The subject had never been mentioned in her home. . . .

I was carrying two books that contained descriptions of Camella Teoli's testimony. Standing in . . . [a] huge parking lot, she read her mother's account of the old days in the Washington Mill. She wanted to know more. So I drove her to the Lawrence library where there was a two-volume record of the 1912 hearing. She read her mother's full testimony, enraptured. "Now, I have a past," she said. "Now my son has a history he can be proud of."

Both Mathilda and the Alabama union leader had discovered a new past—a working-class past denied them by the ways in which mainstream American culture had come to celebrate "America" by narrowly identifying it with achievement and assimilation. That socially destructive process occurred between 1910 and 1940, and stretched across the nation to alter the perceptions and self-perceptions of working men and women in the North and South. The essays in *Working Lives* begin to restore the fullness of the twentieth-century American working-class experience. They do so specifically for the South, but what they reveal is just as meaningful to Camella Teoli's grandson as it is to the descendants of early twentieth-century Southern white mill hands and black sharecroppers.

VERY SPECIAL HISTORICAL PROCESSES HAVE SHAPED THE SOUTH'S history, giving it a truly distinctive character within the broader American context. The experiences and events recounted in *Working Lives* illustrate ably some of the factors that have distinguished the lives of Southern workers from those of other American workers through time, and which cannot be ignored when we consider American history as a whole.

Two and a half centuries of racial slavery and an even longer history of racially determined class subordination shaped that distinctiveness. That legacy of slavery was paralleled in the existence of large numbers of nonslaveholding whites who toiled for generations outside the market economy and who formed the core of the labor force in early Southern factories. The memories recorded both in "Farm to Mill" and in the scrapbook of the Southern Summer School for Women Workers provide eloquent testimony to the roots of a working class as men and women began to be moved off the land and into industrial situations.

Outside its coastal and river cities, the South knew relatively few European-born laborers. Extractive industries that supplied industrial raw materials such as lumber and minerals drew largely on local workers, although racial exclusion closed off certain working-class occupations to Southern blacks for decades. Many blacks simply abandoned the South altogether and sought jobs elsewhere, brought north by men like the Reverend D. W. Johnson, profiled in "The Recruiter."

The development of factory labor and a wage-earning class outside the growing Southern cities was especially important. State-sanctioned and privately sponsored violence against popular rural and urban lower-class movements occurred more commonly in the South. The history of the Southern Tenant Farmers' Union is filled with such turbulence, as are the more familiar experiences of strikers in the Gastonia mills in 1929 and in the Davidson-Wilder mines of the Tennessee's Cumberland Plateau in 1932.

Throughout the region and in many industries, the prevalence and influence of absentee capitalist ownership gave rise to cases of a regional "colonial economy," whose existence, for example, led J. P.

Stevens workers to picket in New York the headquarters of a corporation they were trying to organize in North Carolina. This situation made for an environment in which it was extremely difficult for labor self-organization to sustain itself. Over time, that resistance to unionism encouraged middle- and late-twentieth-century Northern capitalist investment in the South and Southwest, and it still gives rise to "runaway" factories such as the auto plant in Hartwell, Georgia, facing tremendous pressures against organizing even now. Antiunion traditions can take hold of an entire city, with wide reverberations in the path of its development, as we see in the profile of Greenville, South Carolina, a major corporate stronghold in today's New South.

Privilege and inequality have clearly taken a different course in the South than elsewhere, given its patterns of economic, racial, and political subordination. How, then, has the Southern worker responded to the pressures of this environment? And what have we still to learn from the separate experience of its labor history?

"THE ESSENTIAL," JEAN-PAUL SARTRE INSISTS, "IS NOT WHAT 'ONE' has done to man, but what man does with what 'one' has done to him." Southern and Northern workers have experienced inequality and oppression in different historical settings, but common social and class processes continue to shape their responses, processes that cut across regional and racial lines. Exploitation creates more than enough despair and hopelessness along with plain misery among the exploited and the unequal. A different culture, however, also emerges in almost every setting. Each of these cultures has its own history. "Rules for living," for example, developed among Southern black sharecroppers as well as among Northern immigrant factory workers. Within these cultures, where the constraints are often severe, working people create institutions and act on beliefs that sustain life without necessarily altering or transforming their condition.

Within each community and its culture, and at all moments of time, there is, moreover, a changing tension between individualist ("utilitarian") and cooperative ("collective") ways of sustaining and improving everyday life. That central tension shaped the history of the Southern working class. The case of the South presented here demonstrates most dramatically how even the intensely individual character traditionally associated with the region also has its collaborative component. The restless and often tentative alliance of two ostensibly opposing energies led, in case after case, to the eruption of rebellion and violence and sometimes to victory, though often to defeat at first. The intensity of the tension suggests why the auto workers' sitdowns of the 1930s began in the South, both the individualism and the cooperation moving Atlanta workers to action while the Detroit-based fledgling union waited for the right moment to act.

The tradition of resistance does not always assume an obvious, dramatic stance. Working-class cultures—even those which reject acquisitive individualism—do not necessarily directly challenge inequality and the structures and belief systems that sustain it, but the existence of these cultures themselves is a form of resistance. Under changing historical circumstances they become the source of oppositional social and political movements. The distinctive experiences recounted in *Working Lives* make clear how such transformations lie at the core of the history of the American working class.

The emergence of such oppositional movements dots the twentieth century from the 1911 Brotherhood of Timber Workers to hospital workers in Charleston in 1969. This emergence is irregular and unpredictable and it attacks on many fronts, visible and hidden. The movements that reveal its presence do not always succeed. Often they take enormous personal tolls, as with Selina Burch ("The Rebel in Me"). They result in limited gains, such as those achieved by workers for health and safety standards against cotton dust or chemical fumes, but still face enormous corporate resources marshaled against them. Some movements lose momentum quickly; others are violently repressed or absorbed into the ongoing social system. In places like Laurel, Mississippi ("Puttin' Down Ol' Massa"), the results still await decision even after a long and difficult siege. Nevertheless, it is the recurrence of these movements that gives vitality to working-class history and that organically relates everyday life to popular struggles.

THE PAGES THAT FOLLOW ARE FILLED WITH RAGE AND PAIN AND despair; they also unfold hope. The oppressive racial and class structures of the American South have changed radically since 1900. Class and racial inequality, however, retains a grip on that region's working class and its hold is strengthened, in part, because of a constricted historical memory. *Working Lives* alters that memory. The tensions over ways of dealing with inequality still exist, but so does the latent capacity for oppositional politics.

There are powerful class structures in the South today that are seemingly resilient and inaccessible to popular pressure. But by examining how several generations of Southern workers have confronted their oppression, *Working Lives* demonstrates that the transformation of working-class cultures into oppositional social and political movements has been a constant theme of Southern history. That fact sustains an egalitarian and democratic vision for the American South.

PART ONE
The Promised Land
1900–1929

INDUSTRIAL WORKERS HAD CALLED THE SOUTH HOME SINCE COLONIAL days, but their numbers had not been large. As cotton rose to king in the century preceding the Civil War, the leaders of the region found it increasingly profitable to import manufactured goods and export the South's prime crop. Consequently, in contrast to the rest of the nation, the Southern work force was focused more and more in agriculture, even into the twentieth century. This trend allowed the South to develop a unique class structure, one that would prove, when the economic tide ultimately turned, extremely well suited to provide the new working class called for by the first advocates of a "New South" eager to catch up with a quickly industrializing nation.

At the top of the order stood the men who, either alone, with neighbors and other Southerners, or with Northern investors, initiated the first large-scale wave of textile-mill construction in the 1880s. Some of these men were planters; others were local bankers, merchants, and entrepreneurs who had gathered enough capital ($75,000 in the case of Tom Lloyd in "Farm to Mill") during or after the Civil War to open a mill.

Soon small textile companies dotted the Piedmont, stretching across Virginia and the Carolinas into Georgia and Alabama. While Northern industry during these years was concentrated in large cities, where immigrant workers formed the base of a new working class, Southern boosters pointed to the virtues of rural men, women, and children as ideal workers. Just as the immigrants, conditioned by a past of poverty in Europe, were expected to accept factory discipline, so too were sharecroppers and tenant farmers thought to be well prepared for a dawn-to-dusk mill routine. And because the Southern mills were scattered among many small communities, the work force could in most cases be drawn from the surrounding countryside, often lending the new mill villages a distinctively rural character. As "Farm to Mill" shows, this blending of agricultural and industrial patterns smoothed the transition from one to the other, helping the new working class adjust to a changed life while letting the mill owners justify low wages to workers who continued to supplement their factory income with food from family farms and gardens in town.

Not all industrial work took place in factories. In the piney woods of Louisiana and Texas, black and white lumberjacks and sawyers played their role in the industrialization of the nation. In contrast to the stereotype (encouraged by the boosters) of the docile Southern worker, thousands of timber workers rose up to do battle with the timber barons, and eventually the Brotherhood of Timber Workers—which affiliated with the revolutionary Industrial Workers of the World— fought the lumber wars of 1911 to 1913. Only a fierce and violent repression by the large corporations, especially the Santa Fe and other railroads that employed the workers and exploited the forests, could finally break the strength of the union. The BTW drew on the tradition   3 of hostility to corporate capitalism previously demonstrated by the Knights of Labor and the Populists, but, even in defeat, it also foreshadowed the new elements of successful organizing that would bring the CIO victories in the 1930s: broad, industry-wide membership; strong community support; cooperation between white and black workers in a single, integrated union.

White and black men worked side by side in the timber industry, but it was more typical for certain occupations to be reserved to each race. The same segregationist logic that led textile mills to employ only white workers also decreed that many tasks in the steel and iron factories of northern Alabama were fit only for blacks—blacks drawn, as were the white textile workers, from the impoverished population of the rural South. In "If I Could Go Back," Dobbie Sanders, who left home in 1922 to work in a United States Steel plant outside Birmingham, tells why he left the farm: "Hell, if you worked all the time and somebody took all you made, you'd leave too."

Some black workers found employment in Southern factories, but many more moved north to escape Jim Crow. There they took the place of the immigrant labor supply that had been cut off by World War I and postwar anti-immigration laws. Most of the new black industrial workers migrated north on the strength of reports by friends and relatives; a few read of opportunities above the Mason-Dixon line in contraband black newspapers. Many were induced and helped by men such as the Reverend D. W. Johnson, who acted as agents for Northern factories looking for workers. Life was highly dangerous for "The Recruiter" as well as for the person migrating, for these agents were unwelcome guests in Southern communities which had erected elaborate mechanisms after the Civil War to tie blacks to the plantation economy.

The Great Depression hit a South far different from that which had entered the twentieth century. While few industrial cities had grown up, countless villages now had at least one factory. The region, though still predominantly rural, now faced the ever-present pull of an industrial economy that lured its workers from the farms. Where racism closed off almost any chance of advancement, the movement of black people out of the South turned into a massive migration that would last for decades; these men and women formed the core of the Northern working class just as poor whites did for the Southern working class.

Workers in the South had never passively accepted the discipline of the new industrial order, and their continued resistance, which included that of the turn-of-the-century timber workers, reached a climax during the turbulent years of the Great Depression. Sporadic resistance would move toward collective rebellion as workers—black and white, men and women, Northern and Southern—forged the beginnings of powerful industrial unions.

ONE

Farm to Mill: The First Generation

VALERIE QUINNEY

CARRBORO, NORTH CAROLINA, was in many ways a typical village in the Piedmont section of our country in the first decade of the century. The entire town consisted of a gristmill, a sawmill, and a cotton gin, plus a few scattered houses. It differed from most mill villages, however, in that it was adjacent to Chapel Hill, the site of the University of North Carolina. In fact, the village at first was just a train depot for the university.

The story of the building of the cotton mill is common for the region and the time. Tom Lloyd had returned home to Carrboro after the Civil War. He took up farming on his family's land, gradually accumulating enough money to build the gristmill and the cotton gin. He branched out into other small enterprises, such as supplying the university students with firewood. In 1898, when he was 60 years old, he issued $75,000 worth of capital stock and began building the Alberta Cotton Mill beside the railroad tracks. He couldn't read or write and knew little about cotton mills; but he knew a lot about cotton and the trade, having raised it, ginned it, and sold it. The two-story brick mill was finished in 1899.

At first Lloyd's mill, which manufactured cotton yarn for stockings, occupied the first floor only, and he rented the second floor for use as a knitting mill. Lloyd built houses around the mill to attract workers, and he sent agents out to other mill towns and to farms to persuade families to come in to Carrboro to work in his mill. He himself worked in the mill

5

Exterior of mill, Carrboro, North Carolina, ca. 1913

every day in his overalls with white suspenders. He knew all the workers well and many were his cousins, nieces, and nephews. In 1909 Lloyd sold the mill to Julian Carr of the Durham Hosiery Mill Company, but the operation of the mill changed little, with a close paternal relationship between mill owners and mill workers.

Workers came from farms in the same county or adjoining counties or from nearby mill towns, rarely from more than fifty miles away. They were of English, Scotch, Irish, or German descent. Some had owned land, but the generous land grants of 1776 had since been subdivided among sons, grandsons, and great-grandsons so often that plots were usually too small to support a family. Most were now tenant farmers and rented land from the fortunate few who had accumulated more land than they could cultivate. The farms grew principally cotton and tobacco, neither of which was a secure way to make a living. Prices on both crops fluctuated; and both deplete the soil, require considerable expense for fertilizer, and can easily be ruined by bad weather conditions. Cotton can be devastated by pests, while tobacco barns often burned during curing. All too often a farmer would be wiped out, and his family, left with nothing, came into the village. Families with a number of children and a parent dead, or aged parents, also came into the mill village; there the children could find work.

The first generation of Southern mill workers used their agricultural skills to survive in the mill village. The village itself was hardly an urban environment: although the mill houses were close together, land and woods were near and no one seemed to know or care who owned them. Still independent from a money economy, they could tolerate the low mill wage by providing for themselves. They knew how to grow food and preserve it; how to raise and butcher hogs; how to keep chickens and cows for milk, butter, and eggs. They learned thrift on the farm and practiced it in the mill village.

Resourcefulness also continued as every family member—man, woman, and child—sought ways to supplement the family income.

To be honest, sober, and hardworking was their way. Both mill and church—in the country and then the town—enforced this moral code. Both Methodists and Baptists rejected the union church provided by the mill owner and built their own churches. The independent stance regarding ownership of the churches suggests that they did not identify church with mill.

Life went on in the village in much the same way through World War I and until 1930, when the Carrboro mill, like many other small mills, went bankrupt. The Carrboro mill owners had stocked up on long-fibered, expensive cotton when the market was good, only to find they could not compete with cheaper yarn when the prices for cotton knitted cloth dropped during the Depression. The small mill chain just didn't have the capital in reserve to survive, and large companies such as Burlington Mills bought them out. The new managers were bent on streamlining operations, cutting costs, getting as much out of each worker as possible, and maximizing profit. They didn't know their workers, and they refused to be concerned with individual needs.

The only alternatives left to the Carrboro workers were to commute to factory jobs in other cities or to take low-paying service jobs or construction work with the nearby university. Many of their children, with the advantages of education and geographical mobility, moved away. Those who stayed entered white-collar jobs, became professionals, or opened small businesses. Where the first generation blended two life-styles, the second generation is wholly urban: they buy ready-made clothing, packaged foods, and services that their parents would have taken care of themselves.

The small community of mill workers vanished as Carrboro itself, growing more populated and congested, ceased to be rural. With it vanished the life in the mill described in the voices recorded here, a man and a woman talking about their experiences during the early movement in industrialization.

These autobiographies come from a collection of first-generation life stories compiled and edited by a sociologist, Hugh Brinton, and two historians, Brent Glass and Valerie Quinney, under the auspices of the Chapel Hill Historical Society in 1974 and 1975. Costs of transcribing thirty of the interviews were borne by a grant from the North Carolina Bicentennial Commission. Tapes and transcriptions are located under the title "Families of Carrboro" in the archives of the Chapel Hill Historical Society in the town library of Chapel Hill, North Carolina, and in the Southern Historical Collection in the library of the University of North Carolina.

FRANK THOMPSON WAS BORN IN CHATHAM COUNTY, NORTH CARO-
lina in 1889. His father tried to support nine children as a tenant
farmer, but the whole family left farming for mill work in 1909. Mr.
Thompson talked about his work in the mill in Carrboro until it closed
in 1930 and then his work in a mill in Durham in the forties—a span
of more than thirty years. During that time, management techniques,
machines, and organization of labor changed drastically. This comes
from oral history interviews conducted by Hugh Brinton.

We didn't own a farm. We just rented. It was a small farm: we'd make
about seven or eight bales of cotton a year, raised tobacco—a little of
everything. We always kept two or three cows, enough to have our milk and
butter. We raised chickens and raised everything we ate, just about. We raised
hogs, just enough for our own use.

In 1909 we went to a mill up on Haw River. And then we moved to
Carrboro in 1910. I would say there were maybe 125 or 130 people in the
mill; some men and some women—about equal parts. Years ago in the cotton
mill, a woman's job was mostly spinning or winding or spooling. Women's
hands are smaller. For a man, there was a lot of cleaning up to do. Men
would do most of the heavier work—run the heavy machines, card.

Young boys doffed and swept. On the spinning frame there are 224 spinners
and there's a bobbin on each one. When that would get full, they'd have to
pull it off and put another one on. That's what you call doffing. That was done
by boys mostly, just young boys.

The girls ran the thread off the little wheel onto the spool, to put it in a
bigger package. They could sell those. Then later on they put in what you call
a winder, a cone winder. It'll make a cone of a couple of pounds of yarn.
That'll go to the knitting room to a knitting machine (we were making hosiery
yarn).

They couldn't work children under 14. There was some people, though, that
just didn't care whether they went to school or not. They'd take their Bibles,
you know, and change their name [*laughs*] and try to fool you, make it seem
like they were 16 years old or 14.

You could catch on to the work in two or three weeks. With a spinner now,
we'd put them on maybe four or five what we called "sides." A spinner thing
has two sides and we'd start them off. As soon as they got so they could put
up an end, they'd have about two sides, then to four and on up. About eight
sides was considered a good day's spinning. Maybe the first two or three
weeks you'd make 25 cents a day. Then maybe two more sides and you'd get
up to eight sides—a dollar a day.

It went on that way until 1918 or something like that. Then they began to
raise wages a little bit.

When I went there, I went to work in the card room. I worked at what you
call drawing and they paid me 75 cents a day. Then I worked there for a little
while and I didn't like it and I got a job in the spinning room oiling machinery.
I worked at that for a while and they paid me $7½ a week. I worked at that
for three or four years and then I learned how to fix the machinery—what
they call a section man. I finally got up to around $15 a week. Then they had

a second hand, the assistant to the overseer. They paid him $12½ a week and the overseer got $18 a week. He was the highest in the department. Workers got $7½ on up to $10 or $12.

You worked by the hour. If you were sick, you didn't get a thing; and if you lost time—[if] the power would go off—you'd have to make that up. You were working 10 hours a day then, and if the power went off, it would take some time to get started back up. You'd have to get Duke Power Company in there. It got so you'd have to stay 12 hours to work 10. [*Laughs*]

Anybody that wasn't used to the noise couldn't talk much, but after you stayed in there a good long while, you could talk just about as good as you could anywhere.

When I first went to work, it was 60 hours a week, and they finally put it down to 55. We'd go to work in the morning about 6:30. We'd work 10 hours a day for five days and a half day on Saturday. We'd sit down for about thirty minutes for dinner. Shut the machinery down. Most of them would go home. If they lived a little ways out, they would bring their lunch.

The mill rented houses by the week. Twenty-five cents a room at that time. Most of them were three- or four-room houses. There would be one well for four or five families. And just a little house out in back.

They built a three-room house for $350. It was just sealed—weatherboarded and sealed. They put up two-by-fours and weatherboard on the outside and sealed it on the inside. Had pine floors, just one-board thickness. Fireplaces and a chimney. Sometimes the company would sell you coal. At that time you could get coal for $5 a ton and then burn coal in the fireplace. Some people burned wood. Farmers would haul it in there and sell you wood for around $3½ or $4 a cord. They usually had wood cookstoves to cook with.

We bought just meat, coffee, and some groceries. Now, we had some kin people lived on the farm. They'd come maybe once a week, and they'd bring things like beans, and anything that they raised. If you wanted to give a little money, they'd bring it around and peddle it around. And you could get vegetables that way all right. And some of the stores would buy a lot of it. They'd buy eggs and chickens. Have chicken coops out there full of chickens. They'd pick you out a chicken, weigh it, and you'd pay about 15 cents a pound for it. Have a chicken dinner.

We always tried to have a little garden. Always have. Raised snap beans and potatoes and cucumbers, tomatoes, most anything.

For a school, they had an old wooden building. The county paid for it. It took time to find out, though, that they didn't have enough room, and the help was so bad, the situation was so bad, they decided to build a new school. And the Durham Hosiery Mill did put some money in the building up there. But they had to go to Chapel Hill for high school. Very few went.

We never locked our door there. Everybody seemed to behave themselves all right. Better than they do now. Once in a while there'd be somebody'd get drunk and get locked up. They'd fire them if they got drunk. I never heard of any stealing.

People had to dig everywhere they could for a living then. A man would go and ask a farmer to let him cut some cross-ties on his land. Pay him so much. Farmers, when they couldn't work on the farm or on the land, they'd work at cross-ties. They'd go down, cut them white oaks just about the right size and then split it off that way. It had to be hewed, though. They didn't want sawed. All over in Chatham County there would be wagons bringing a load of cross-ties, and there was an old fellow by the name of Tad Williams working for the Southern Railroad, and he'd grade them, first, second, or third. Fifty cents a piece for first class, 45 cents for second, and 40 cents for third.

There wasn't much recreation for the young people. Some of them would play on the baseball team. A lot of people—a lot of the boys—would love to hunt a whole lot. They'd just go down on the creek or go down on the river and fish some.

What would the men do for recreation? Well, they'd just walk right down the street, walk down to the post office and stand around the corner of the street and talk.

Occasionally a family would have a piano, or one of the old kind of organs. I had a brother had a guitar, and he was good.

They did put up a little old movie house out there, but at that time they didn't have no power to run it. Had a little old gasoline engine and there was a thing that popped, popped, and the picture faded out. They'd have to go and start the engine again. And so it didn't amount to anything. It was 15 cents.

During the year 1918, the flu broke out there. Of course, at that time they had no water in the mill. They had an old colored fellow to pump water. His name was old Ed Jones. His job was to pump water and clean out the outside toilets, and various other stuff. We had a bucket of water and a dipper for drinking.

And I had a woman by the name of Maggie Crabtree. She come in there one morning and she told me, said she had a bad headache, and she wanted off. And I told her, I said, "Well, I don't have anybody anywhere to put on the job. If I could give you a little aspirin, reckon you could make it?" And she said, "Well, I'll try." Well, I went and got her some aspirin, and she worked on that day, but every once in a while she'd go and take a dip and drink part of it.

That was along about the middle of the week. Along on Saturday morning I got up sick. I was just about to die. And I went on to the mill. Well, I had to go, because there was nobody to take my place and you had to pay off there. And I was so bad off when I got away from the mill about one o'clock, I just went home and I went to bed—shoes, clothes, and all. I didn't remember a thing in the world from that time till Monday morning about eight o'clock. The manager of the mill lived in Chapel Hill. He come out there and he came walking in my room and woke me up and said, "What in the world is the matter with you? Half of the mill is out sick. We ain't got enough to blow the whistle this morning." I told him I didn't know. I says, "I reckon I've got what they call the flu. I've got something I've never had before." "Well, I don't see how you expect me to run with everybody out." And I said, "Well, I ain't a-thinking. I—" It made him mad. He went out the door. And by George, they shut the mill down. And it was in both mills.

No, sir, you didn't get no pay. You didn't get nothing if you didn't work for it. And if you didn't have the money, some of the stores there would trust you a little bit, a week at a time. And, I expect, overcharge you for it.

Just Dr. Lloyd would come and see you. But he was so busy, he didn't have much time. Couldn't do very much. So that was on a Monday morning, and I reckon it was about Thursday, Dr. Lloyd come walking in and told me, he said, "Now, I'll tell you, I think that the best thing you can do is to get out of that bed in there and sit in the sunshine. Get up and sit in a chair there. Put your head back there and sit away in the sunshine awhile." He said, "You're so weak you'll have to gain your strength." So I told him I didn't see how I could get to the chair. And he said, "Well, just stand. I'll help you to get up."

He walked out of my room and told me, "Now you sit there in the sunshine an hour or two, and then you go back to bed." There was a man lived right across the street from where I lived. He had just come and told him the same thing, and as he went out they called and told him the man had fallen out of his chair. He come back in there and told me, "You better get back into bed."

And they hired a nurse. She'd go around, and anybody report sick, they'd call and she'd visit them and see what was the matter with them. She'd go and take their temperatures and get them taken to the doctor.

There was what they called the soup house. Soup was available there for the sick. Go down there and make soup, and carry it to people. Sometimes a whole family would be down. It helped a little while they were sick till the time we got to the place where we could take part of the help at Number Seven and part at Number Four and run one mill. And they run that way three or four weeks till it finally passed over. Kept the soup house going awhile as a clubhouse. They decided to keep the nurse there and let her come to her office every morning, and we would turn in our reports, who we had out. The nurse would come in and obtain the names of the ones that reported sick. And she would visit the home and see whether or not they were sick. And it helped a lot. I married the nurse.

The Carrs, they was always looking for new ideas and things like that. And there was a woman in Durham by the name of Miss Shaw. Miss Shaw was the one who started that industrial democracy. They had the clubhouse up there. Made a office and reception room in it for her.

Miss Shaw would come through the mill, and she'd tell the people, "Now, if there's anything you think that we could help you with, let us know," she says, "just most anything. And if you feel like you're not being paid enough, let us know and we'll see what we can do."

Maybe some things she done was pretty good. A good thing they did was to have a basketball court fixed up. And they had teams organized and they'd play games.

Miss Shaw would visit and mingle with the people. And she got the idea that they thought there could be a great saving in waste, you know, where the people were not being real particular with the work. Now there's what you call the spools. What they'd do, they'd take a bobbin of yarn and wind off some of it and hide it, and they'd always tell a little went to waste. They'd put it in their pocket, you know. Well, they decided there was too much of that, and they wanted to put a little bag at each machine and made the woman put her waste in there, and if she saved, they'd give them a bonus. Well, they'd put it in the weigh box and weigh it and then they would sell it to some mill. They paid the workers once a month or something like that. It didn't amount to much—maybe they'd get 50 cents or 75 cents for a month's work.

When they'd weigh up the waste every night and some of them would have mighty little, I knew there was something going on there because there weren't enough to worry about. [*Laughs*]

And lo and behold, now, the sewage line run across town—there was a pond over on the other side of Number Seven there. That new mill emptied into there. Went in there one day and went to start up, and the sewage was stopped up and had run all over the floor. And they had to get the men over there and dig up that sewage line and there was enough waste in that pipe to stop anything. The water couldn't go through. They'd put that waste in their pocket in place of putting it in the bag like they were supposed to, then take it to the commode and toss it down. It went on out in the pipe. I don't know how large the pipe was, but they worked there for two or three days unclogging that pipe. And that was the end of industrial democracy. It cost them no telling what.

The Depression come on, and it kind of got pretty tight. They had to just cut down on anything they could, and they thought they could get along without the nurse. When they got rid of the nurse, that just done away with the clubhouse.

The mill closed down in 1930. Some people tried to get jobs in Durham. They'd have to go on the bus. Some of the families would board over there. Some of them rode the bus just anywhere they could pick up a job. A few of them got on down at the university working at the laundry there. They'd just drift around out there and find it.

Well, the company just left people living in the houses after we closed down for a while, and then they sold the houses. That upset a lot of people who were living in the houses; they didn't charge them any rent at that time. They told them they might have to sell the houses, and they did. They were going to sell the houses just real cheap. Some men who owned stores bought several.

Finally, they sold the machinery for junk and to some other mills that needed it. They had some good machinery but some of it was getting pretty old.

Durham Hosiery Mills offered me work over there in Durham, but I was one of the foremen in Carrboro, and there was no opening at that. They told me if I'd come over there and just take a job, if a foreman's job come open, why, they'd give it to me, but that's all they could do. But in the meantime, I went up to West Durham to Erwin Mills.

In the forties, when I worked for the Durham Hosiery in Durham, they wanted to organize a union, and the company didn't want it, you know. They felt like it would be a whole lot of trouble. But they kept a-working and finally they got enough—they kind of forced it on them. They voted to have a union.

Well, in Durham they began to say that they had to put a minimum wage on. Up until that time, if a superintendent or a manager, if he come in and he saw a machine standing, why, he thought that was terrible. But after the government put a minimum wage on, they didn't want to see *anybody* sitting down.

So they thought the thing to do now, said, "If we got to raise the wages, we've got to get more work out of them." And so they had a committee go around and figure it out and stretch it out that way. Well, people just swore they wouldn't take it. They just weren't going to do it. So they struck. And closed that mill up, and they didn't turn a wheel in six months. Well, finally they agreed to it. They said they'd just have to go to work.

I don't know how many strikes we did have. Then Burlington Mills bought out Durham Hosiery. And the first little inkling that they had that they was going to have trouble, the manager called a meeting. He got up and told them, "Now, I'm going to tell you, we bought this mill and paid for it and we're going to run it or shut it down." He said, "Now, we're going to run this mill and pay you fair wages and if there's any trouble or any strikes going on, we'll make trouble for Durham." And I haven't heard of any more trouble.

WHEN I INTERVIEWED VIRGINIA PARSONS IN 1974 AND 1975, SHE lived alone in a large white house on a lane in Carrboro. Her husband had been dead nine years. Grandchildren who worked in the village came over to her house for lunch every day. Her children who lived near stopped by, and a loved niece lived just across the street. She had an erect, spare frame and walked with quick, light steps. Her hair was pure white, drawn back in a bun, and her eyes were black and dancing. Her chief interests those summers were canning and social gatherings with her Sunday school class, whose members had been close friends of hers for sixty years.

She was born in 1899, a middle child in a family of nine children. Her father and mother had been raised on farms. Her father had been a tobacco farmer in Person County and had brought his family to Roxboro in 1910 to work in a mill. The next year the family was working in a mill in Burlington; Virginia, 12 years old then, was a full-time mill worker. They moved to Carrboro in 1913 and rented a five-room house from the mill. She often began our conversations with stories from her childhood in Roxboro, Burlington, and Carrboro just before World War I.

There was thirteen of us in the family: there was nine children, and my mother and father, and my two aunts that lived in my home with us. And we used to be so thrilled when come time to go strawberry picking, and blueberry picking or blackberry picking. And, oh, we would walk, and we'd walk, and walk, and pick berries and just get so hot we wouldn't know what to do, and just get eat up with red bugs. And, you know, after I got grown I never did go back blackberry picking; I couldn't stand the red bugs. But we just had more fun.

And then our games around the house. We played ball, jumped rope, and, of course, played "jack rocks." But we didn't have the kind that the children buy now. We just hunted all kinds of pretty rocks. And that's what we played with. And we would sit for hours playing jack rocks.

And then it wasn't all play because we all had something; each one had little jobs that they did back home. But after we were through with them, then we got out and played. We made play houses and one would have a house in one place in the yard and the other in another place. And then we'd all visit each other. And if we had a baby to die, or anything, we had a burying ground. Anything that died, we would have funerals. I mean we really had the funerals. And one of the neighbors, he always done the preaching. [*Laughs.*] And we really cried.

And the woods was right close to where we lived, so we would all go. We'd get these big oak leaves, and we would see which one could make the prettiest hats. And the broom sage that grows out in the field, you could break it off and make straws out of it. And we'd break it off about as long as a toothpick. And that's what we could glue this together with. And we made beautiful hats and decorated them with daisies and just the leaves that grew in the field. Well, we'd just spend our whole afternoon up there.

And I never will forget the first day that I went to school. Every time I saw my mother come to the well, I raised my hand to be excused. I wanted to go out and see her because I hated to leave her so bad that I didn't know what to do. I wanted to go to school, but if she hadn't had to come to the well, and I hadn't seen her, I would have been all right. But I was in the first year of school. I just couldn't stand it unless I went out and talked to her a little bit. Then she would go on back to the house with her bucket and I'd go on back in school. And the teacher, she caught on to what it was. So she always pretended. She knew where I was going.

When people used to roll their own cigarettes, they bought sacks of tobacco. The sacks were in little squares, you see. They were bagged up in these great big sacks and piled up in the sack house, and then we would go and get them. And, now, we had to clip those little squares—every one had to be clipped—and then we had to turn them. We had a wire fixed on a board. We had to turn them, and then we had to string them. And that meant going in from one side and turning it around and going in from the other, so you could pull the ends of the string to make the drawstring. Then after we strung them, we would have just a lot of them, just in basketsful, and then we would have a party, a sack time, and invite all of the neighbors. This was the different families; it wasn't just us that done this. And in that way, we helped each other with the sacks. They had to be tied. Then they had to be stacked, twenty-five to a stack, and then they had to be packed through. And then after we'd got that done, we'd carry them back to the sack house and get our pay.

My aunts would tell me, "Now, if you will be right smart and help us out and help us get this bag of sacks ready in time, then when we get our money, we'll pay you." Well, in what time I wasn't a-playing, I would help. And so I never will forget, one summer, whenever they got the money, they said, "Well, you made a dollar." And I'll never forget what I done with that dollar. I don't reckon I was over 7 or 8 years old. But I went with my mother to town. I told her that I wanted to spend my dollar for something that I really wanted. And I bought me a pair of Mary Jane patent leather shoes, because I wanted a pair so bad. So that's what I bought. They were a dollar.

I had a good mother and daddy, and they wasn't strict with us, but they taught us right from wrong, and they always taught us that, regardless of what anybody had, a good name was better than anything in the world to have. And they always wanted us to live up to it.

My two aunts that lived with us was two of the family. Back then you never heard tell of nobody going to the rest home; there was no rest home. We heard tell of a poorhouse: that's what it was called. And later on, a county home. But there was none of my people ever went to one because when something happened—like, my two aunts, when their husbands died, my daddy, their brother, took them in. We had one big room—three beds in there. I slept with one of the aunts. My two sisters slept in the other bed. And the other aunt and my little brother—he was about 5 years old—slept on a bed together.

There at my home was the meeting place for the young people all together, to hear Aunt Bea and Aunt Susan tell ghost stories. They would sit and tell about things that happened back when they were growing up. We would be sitting there so scared we could hardly be still. And if they stopped, we'd say, "Go on, go on. Don't stop!" Then they would all be afraid to go home. We would have to get up and go with each one, but they would be right back up there the next night.

I was 6 years old when the youngest child of the family was born, and I had an aunt that came, and she came with her suitcase. She came before to stay until it was time for the baby, and then she was going to stay afterwards till my mother got able to get up. Well, I thought all the time that she brought the baby in that suitcase. I believed that for a long time after that, because we just didn't know things back then.

I remember going to see an aunt of ours, and when we got there I can remember her cooking the meal on the fireplace, and that was the best meal that I think I have ever eaten. It was all cooked on the fireplace. And we didn't live but about ten miles from them, and so whenever we got ready to leave, she packed a basket of food for us to eat.

At our house, for Sunday dinner, there was always a meat on the table. And then, if it was summertime, it was all fresh vegetables. And if it was wintertime, it was canned or dried. And I can remember drying apples to make apple pies in the winter, and my mother used to make the best apple dumplings I ever ate. I used to cut the dried apples with the sugar into little pieces. And she would make the apple dumplings, and they would just bubble in their juices, with the butter and all in them. And then we'd pour sweet milk over them. And she used to put up what they called their woods grape. It's a tiny grape, just about the size of the end of your little finger, and she would pack those grapes in sugar, and that's the way she kept them. And then in the winter she'd make pies out of them, and they were delicious. And then they would can. Oh, we had a brass kettle—I can see that brass kettle now—and there's no telling how many preserves was ever made in that kettle. And we had rows and rows of jars of preserves and jellies and brandied peaches and kraut.

My mother cooked three full meals every day because she always had boarders. She'd bake biscuits or else make corn bread at every meal. My mother and daddy had a garden, chickens, a cow, and hogs. Nothing went to waste. What was throwed away, we had hogs and chickens to eat it. We bought cabbage, flour, coffee, and sugar at the store.

I went to work in Burlington when I was 12 years old. I stood up on a stool in what they called the warp room and tied knots on the warp that came down from the machines. I made 50 cents a day and I was the proudest thing that you ever saw. When I came to Carrboro, I worked in the spool room.

And I worked in the winder room, and then my last work was in the knitting room. When I was 14, working in the spool room, I made about $10 a week. It seems to me that I worked from six until seven. And also, we worked on Saturday until one. We quit at twelve and then it was always one when we left, because we had to clean up our own machines that we worked on.

There was lint everywhere in the mill, but you didn't get it in the spool room or the winding room like you did in the spinning room. And you know, way back then, most of the time, we made what you called dust caps. They were made round and we would run elastic in them. There was a little ruffle and we wore them on our heads to keep it out of our hair.

Oh, we had the best time. We knew everybody. Carrboro was a very small place and we knew everybody. We would get caught up with our work and then we'd go around in each other's alley in the room and talk.

I am terrified of thunderstorms and they are very bad inside of a mill, you see, with all the transformers in there. So, I would quit. I'd just stop. And I never will forget, a thunderstorm came up one morning, so I went home. I was living on Weaver Street, right up on the corner. It was still raining, still looking like the thunder was going to come. And D. A. Johnson, my boss man, come after me. And my mother told him, "Mr. Johnson, I don't think that she will go back. She's scared to death of thunderstorms. She said that she don't think that you like for them to quit." And he told me, he said, "If you will just come back and go to work and if another thunderstorm comes up, you can quit and sit down and, just as long as it takes, I won't expect you to work." And so, I got up and went on back with him. And he told me, going on back, "If you weren't so darn mean, you wouldn't be afraid of a thunderstorm."

You see, Jane Harrison and I were very good friends, and we were always cutting up with Mr. Johnson. He would wear his Sunday shoes to the mill and then he would have an old pair that he would put on after he got there. Well, we got his old shoes, one morning we got there before he did and we nailed them to the floor. We got back behind the machine to watch him, you know. And he pulled off his Sunday shoes and he put his feet in them, and he moved this way and that! [*Laughing*] I can see him now. And then one night, it was real cold and we went and got his coat sleeve, where he had hung his coat up, and we turned it wrong side out and tied the lining in the coat and then we hung it back. Then we got behind the door as everybody was coming out of the mill in order to see him when he took his coat down. It was freezing cold. [*Laughing*] So, we did dumb things like that all the time. And he thought the world of us.

The Carrs in Durham, Julius Carr and the rich folks owned the mill. So, on the Fourth of July, they put on a big barbecue and everything for the employees. Some of the people around would get up a program for the Fourth of July and have all the young people in it and that went on all day.

We had the old church [Baptist] and there was never a Christmas that there wasn't a Christmas program. They started a month before Christmas getting it up and we would go two and three times a week to practice our parts. The church was real close and everybody knew each other. We were just like a family. Everyone was in the program. There was nobody left out.

On Sunday, we would go to Sunday school and preaching. And in the afternoon, we would all get together and go walking. A spring was down there and it was called the Drip Spring. We would all go for a walk there and then walk down the railroad to the old mine. But we had to get back in time for BYTU [Baptist Youth Training Union].

I met my husband when I was working in the mill. He worked in the winding room, too. I worked on one side of the machine and him on the other. And back then, we weren't in cars in the night. We dated two years before we were married, and I went with him in a car one night with another couple out to Damascus to a school closing. Old Man C. B. Anderson went with us. [*Laughing*] We were going, the two couples, and Old Man C. B. wanted to go, so he went with us. But we would go to a movie and walk to Chapel Hill. And I don't mean just one couple, several couples, we would all get together and walk.

We married in 1917. I was 18. He was one year older than me. He had got a job and was working in Durham, and so he had got us a place to live and everything. We ran away. That night, I was 18 years old, but that was the first time that I had ever left home without asking my parents. We didn't go home for a week.

Four months after Clifton and me was married, we took his family in and looked after them. His daddy died during World War I when we had the influenza epidemic. We all got it, every one of us was down at the same time. One of us wasn't able to hand the other one a drink of water. And so, the Carrs, that I told you owned the mills, they really was good to their employees. They turned a dwelling house into what they called a soup house. They had people down there making soup and carrying it out in cartons to the sick. Oh, I can't tell you the people in Carrboro that died then. And they sent to Durham and got a colored nurse. I never will forget. Her name was Mary, I can't think of her last name, but her name was Mary and she was wonderful. And she looked after us until she come down with it and then she had to leave. But Clifton and me, we really got up before we were hardly able to. But we felt like we were younger and we just felt like we had to get up and look after his mother and daddy. So we looked after both of them. That was an awful time. The dead—one girl that I had known for years and just thought the world of, lived not many houses above me, and a man and his wife, our neighbor right next door, he died right beside of me. It was just all awful.

My first child was born in 1919 and I worked for two years after that. Clifton's mother was living with us and she kept him. But after that, I just didn't want to put that responsibility on her. I had been transferred from the spooling and winding room to the knitting room, and so they put a machine in my house so that I could still work and be at home with the baby and Clifton's mother.

Clifton looked after the outside things and worked in the mill from six to six. We had a garden, a cow, and raised our own hogs. He trapped, too. He would come home from the mill and then he would go all over. I don't reckon that there is a stream for miles around that he didn't trap muskrats. There was a man that always came around and bought the pelts and that's where we got our Christmas money. I helped him skin them. And we had stretchers. After you skinned them, you would put them on that and adjust the stretcher to the size that you wanted and hang them up and let them dry. And we would have stacks of them when the man came.

During the Depression, when the mill started short-time, then he worked as a meat cutter at the stores. I got up early in the morning, got my children off to school, sat down at the sewing machine, and sewed for people.

Then the mills all shut down and that was a pathetic time. The mill sold the houses here for two and three hundred dollars. Well, we were living in one and so we bought the house. You can imagine what you save on working at the mill, but my husband had worked two jobs.

We had seven children. One night, just before I went in labor, I went out on the back porch. They didn't have a bathroom inside the house. They put water in the houses, but they made the pantries into bathrooms. And you had to go out on the back porch to go to the bathroom. I could see the doctor coming up the hill. I could see him lots of times through the night, way in the night, coming home. He drove a little one-seated car. That night he had just gotten home when I went into labor. One of the two oldest girls went and told him, and he came and stayed the rest of the night. And my mother was what you would call a midwife, and he never went to a place that he didn't have her with him. So, she was with me with all of them except the last.

Back then we never heard tell of birth control. The people had their children —they done the very best they could with them.

Never known Dr. Lloyd to send nobody a bill. I don't know that he even kept a record of it. He might have kept a record of some big bill, but not for just a call. And he lived right in front of me, and if anything happened to one of the children, I just went over there. If he was dirty, if I was dirty, it didn't make no difference. If I was in the kitchen cooking and something happened, I just automatically run over to Dr. Lloyd's. Dr. Lloyd was a wonderful person. It hurt me so bad when he died. It never was the same.

There were a lot of decisions back then to be made because you had to count every penny very carefully. You just didn't have money back then to run to the store and sit down and eat ice cream or drinks or things like that. We didn't go hungry, we ate plenty of food and things like that and we always had enough with as many children as we had. I did a lot of cooking—candy and cookies. I'd make taffy and Martha Washington candy, just lots of things. And I sewed all day. I clothed my children through grammar school and high school. My two boys, I made their shirts and pants until they were great big boys. I made evening dresses—I made three wedding dresses. I sewed for other people and took that money and bought material to make our clothes.

We raised seven children and they all are living, all married and got children, grandchildren. I have eighteen grandchildren, two great-grandchildren. Let me see, how many is there of us? Is it twenty-nine or thirty when they all get together? And we still have the Thanksgiving supper here and the Christmas and Mother's Day.

TWO

We Owed These Children More

MARGARET H. MARTIN

TEACHING SCHOOL HAS NEVER been easy, and possibly the recent years have been the most demanding of all, but sometimes I wonder. Before the turn of the century, my grandmother taught in a one-room school, and her pupils' ages ranged from 6 to 16. A coal stove furnished the heat in winter, flies came in the open windows in the summer, and the scraping of slate pencils was a sound to set one's teeth on edge. While one small group was being heard to recite, the other children had to be kept busy at activities productive and quiet. This called for ingenuity on the teacher's part. Fortunately, children of that era were expected to obey, and any tendency to misbehavior could usually be quelled with a look.

Another challenging situation developed in some North Carolina schools in 1916, when a number of children entered first grade who had heretofore worked in the textile mills. Child labor laws, just then going into effect, freed them to attend school for the first time.

It seems almost incredible now that I, just out of high school, but with a teaching certificate, was asked to teach first grade in a mill town. I had six weeks of teacher training at what was then the State Normal, and had passed the state teacher's examination which "qualified" me. However, the superintendent of schools knew me well, so when one of his teachers resigned in August I was chosen to replace her.

The first day of that school year was something of a nightmare, with its confusion and bustle, compounded by the presence of

19

well-intentioned school board members who felt that it was their duty
to be on hand and observe. My class numbered forty-five, and, as in
the case of my grandmother, their ages ran from 6 to 16. Eight or nine
of my children had worked in the mills, probably for years. The older
they were, the frailer their bodies and the paler their faces: faces that
bore the look almost of old age. It was not that they were wrinkled; it
was more their tired, listless expressions. Their eyes held no childish
merriment. They looked as though they hoped for very little and were
wary of their surroundings. Edna St. Vincent Millay's poems were
widely read at that time, and I was reminded of the one about the
little children looking out of factory windows at the well-to-do grown
men playing golf on a nearby course.

   Whether it was a lack of money or foresight that denied a special
curriculum to these older children, I do not know, but no preparation
of any kind had been made for their needs. They should have had
experienced teachers; larger, more comfortable seats and desks; and
even separation from the younger children. (Times for stretching legs
and backs cramped by the undersized desks had to be allowed rather
frequently.) Reading and writing courses should have been designed
with more sophisticated subject matter for these mill children. Some,
undoubtedly, needed more individual attention than I was able to give
in such a large class. Fortunately, I had a wise and helpful woman
principal who gave me much valuable guidance.

The patience of these older children was touching. They tried hard to apply themselves to studies that must have bored them exceedingly. The reading course dealt with the doings of a little boy and his sister, their dog named Wag, and their cat named Puff. Day after day we read about their unexciting lives, and day after day we cut out pumpkins, arranged scenes in the sandbox, trimmed a little Christmas tree, or colored May flowers. Obviously, it was less wearing than working long hours in a hot, noisy, lint-filled spinning or carding room, but school should have been more than respite.

One boy in particular aroused my concern. He was 16, poorly dressed, his shoes broken, and not very clean. He sat in the rear of the room and was no trouble, but it must have humiliated him when he read aloud or recited, to be outshone by a girl or boy ten years his junior. Another girl who sat across the aisle from her younger brother took an overprotective stance where he was concerned, and looked at me with unconcealed resentment if I corrected him.

To my delight, however, I found that if I read a story, all ages were attentive. Not many mill village homes contained books, and even if a story were familiar, it was welcome.

Even though those days are long gone, occasionally now I meet a former pupil who has reached grandfather status and likes to remind me that I taught him in the first grade. Somehow they all seem to have turned out well.

THREE

The Brotherhood

JIM GREEN

THE PROBLEMS FACING TODAY'S Southern labor movement are not unique. Many of the same difficulties have plagued the region for decades, in fact since industrialization first came to the South. Workers have fought for years, for instance, against the divisive force of racism. And industrialists have fought—usually with more success—to keep the workers racially divided and powerless. But occasionally black and white workers have stood together with community supporters and challenged the big capitalists who controlled the region's people and natural resources. Often these periods of unity ended only when local business interests violently attacked the workers and their allies. The ferocity of these attacks is testimony to the strength of the laborers and of their unions.

One chapter in this violent story occurred in the piney woods of western Louisiana and East Texas in 1911 to 1913. During the "lumber war," thousands of black and white timber workers formed a racially unified industrial union, the Brotherhood of Timber Workers (BTW), in order to battle the "timber barons" and their powerful Southern Lumber Operators' Association (SLOA). The Brotherhood won significant support in an isolated rural region supposedly dominated by conservative politicians and powerful industrialists; it recruited thousands of black and white laborers in an area characterized by increasing social segregation and racist repression.

Eventually, the BTW, an indigenous union of Louisiana workers, voted to affiliate with the revolutionary Industrial Workers of the World in 1912. The IWW provided important support—especially in unifying black and white workers around militant industrial unionism and a radical ideology. But the BTW's strength and solidarity were not created by "outside agitators." The Brotherhood developed as a response of Southern workers to an industry that chewed up workers almost as fast as it did the countryside. This remarkable union was founded and led by Southern-born socialists. And it was Southerners who suffered when the BTW was crushed by the lumber operators in 1913.

INDUSTRIAL CAPITALISM CAME RAPIDLY TO THE TEXAS-LOUISIANA PINE region. The Homestead Act of 1866, which had guarded the virginity of Southern forests, was repealed after only a decade, opening up huge sections of timber to exploitation by Northern speculators. At its peak, in 1910, the industry employed 63,000 lumberjacks and mill hands. Ten years later, the rich stands of yellow pine in the Sabine River area had been slashed to the ground by a handful of large corporations, leaving the region ravaged and depressed.

For forty years, thousands of hill-country whites and Delta blacks poured into the Southern forests, attracted by the relatively high wages offered by industrialists in chronic need of labor. The poor whites generally came from surrounding corn and cotton farms that offered only a subsistence living. In western Louisiana, a large number of the rural refugees were "redbones," a people of "fighting stock," part black, part white, and part Indian who sometimes had a French ancestry like the Cajuns to the south.

Blacks (who formed a majority of the industry's work force, especially in the lower-paying, more dangerous sawmill jobs) usually came from the plantation areas of the Texas or Louisiana Delta, but some journeyed from as far as the Mississippi and Alabama black belts. Many black field hands who fled the plantations of the Louisiana Sugar Bowl and the primitive turpentine camps of Mississippi had experienced gang labor and factory discipline; they also learned about strikes when the Knights of Labor organized in their camps during the 1880s and 1890s. These workers escaped a slavelike status, but others who came to the pine belt were not so fortunate; they were peons and convicts on lease who were forced to toil in the forests and mills to work off their "debts."

The black workers who migrated from the Gulf Coast sugar plantations had an unusual heritage of militancy. Their ancestors were rebellious slaves brought to the Bayou Teche region of St. Mary's Parish to be "broken." According to a Department of Labor study, the sugar workers were of "bad stock"—the "descendants of a particularly vicious lot." These "dangerous Negroes" added to their reputation for militancy in 1886 when they joined the Knights of Labor and struck during harvesttime, provoking a violent response from planters.

But most lumber workers, black and white, came to the pine region from their cotton farms unprepared for the changes life and labor in the industrial uplands would demand. In the face of painful dislocations caused by rapid industrialization, these men clung to older traditions: a leisurely, agrarian attitude toward work and production, a grudging insistence on "squatters' rights" to the land, and a "primitive" respect for nature. Industrial capitalism in the Southern pine region challenged all of these traditions and demanded conformity to rigorous and alien standards of time, work, discipline, and social behavior.

The extreme danger involved in sawmill work made it especially difficult for workers to adjust to the machines. In 1919, even after state safety regulations had been passed, 125 deaths and 16,950 accidents were reported in the Southern lumber industry. Four years earlier the Texas Commissioner of Labor declared that "a large percentage of accidents" in the sawmills were due "to absolute carelessness on the part of the employers."

Sawmill workers, white as well as black, naturally resisted this demanding, dangerous work routine. Many laborers, especially the blacks who usually lacked family ties in the region, simply moved on when they were exhausted or maimed.

Unlike their fellow workers in the sawmills, the loggers were still close to nature. Occasionally work in the forests was suspended in rainy weather. These respites became less frequent, however, as tramlines extended into the forests permitting logging operations even in the wet season. The lumberjacks were no longer agricultural workers. They still worked the soil and harvested its products, but now they were destroying, not creating. Mechanized logging was agriculture in reverse.

Like many workers with agricultural backgrounds, mill hands were very irregular in their work habits. Although Southern workers did not observe religious holy days and national holidays as frequently as immigrant workers, they did seek escape through alcohol and narcotics (mainly cocaine). When they were "hungover," especially on "blue Monday," the men simply refused to go to work. One sheriff in a Louisiana lumber town said that he had instructions from the company superintendent to "be at the sawmill every day, and if enough men did not report to work go to the colored quarters and 'drive' the required number out of their homes or even their beds if necessary." The sheriff explained that unless this was done the sawmills could not "operate at full capacity."

Despite their hatred of the corporations and their work, many poor farmers found the promise of a $1.50 cash wage for a working day of

11 hours irresistible. A few workers, like the skilled saw filers, received as much as $10 a day, but hundreds of sawmill laborers earned as little as 75 cents a day. Comparatively, the Southern laborer received less pay and worked longer hours than any lumber worker in the country. Union organizers did not focus their protests on the rate of pay, however; wages were still higher than those of turpentine and sugar-cane workers and greatly exceeded the income of tenants and croppers. The timber workers complained more frequently about the irregularity of their paydays, the numerous deductions for dubious "benefits," and the control the company maintained through paying in scrip (fake money redeemable only at company-owned facilities). As an employee of the Kirby Lumber Company, largest in Texas, explained, the average worker

is born in a Company house; wrapped in Company swaddling clothes, rocked in a Company cradle. At 16, he goes to work in the Company mill. At 21, he gets married in a Company church. At 40, he sickens with Company malaria, lies down on a Company bed, is attended by a Company doctor who doses him with Company drugs, and then he loses his last Company breath, while the undertaker is paid by the widow in Company scrip for the Company coffin in which he is buried on Company ground.

Historian Herbert Gutman points out that workers, farmers, and townspeople in many American localities at this time opposed the new industrial order because they judged the actions of local capitalists by old agrarian values. The Populists in Louisiana and Texas articulated these values forcefully during the 1890s when they led an attack on the "lumber trust." Conservative Democrats, supported by planters, merchants, and industrialists, had destroyed the People's Party in these two states by the turn of the century, but this powerful agrarian movement laid the groundwork for a more radical kind of opposition to the timber barons that encompassed farmers and workers of both races.

Significantly, the first act of resistance to the industrialists' demands came from the most exploited workers in the Louisiana-Texas pine region, the black mill hands. In 1902, Afro-American laborers struck successfully for a reduction of the working day against a sawmill company in Lurcher, Louisiana; a year later these men founded one of the few "Negro locals" of the Socialist Party. In 1904, black workers, assisted by radical organizers of the American Labor Union, engaged in a strike against a lumber company in Groveton, Texas.

Collective mass action by the timber workers first broke out during the panic of 1907 when operators imposed a 20 percent wage cut and a stretch-out of the working day. Nearly all of the workers in the Sabine pine region walked out in a spontaneous general strike that shut down hundreds of mills. Besides protesting the new demands made by the operators, the timber workers had a list of longstanding grievances: poor wages and hours, "gouging" in company stores, payment in scrip, excessive insurance and hospital fees, inadequate housing and sanitation, and irregularity of paydays. Promised wage increases when prosperity returned, most of the workers went back to work immediately. But the workers around DeRidder, Louisiana (later a stronghold of radicalism), held out for several weeks.

A Louisiana lumberjack

In December 1910, Arthur Lee Emerson and Jay Smith, Southern-born lumberjacks, founded the Brotherhood of Timber Workers at a damp logging camp in Carson, Louisiana, and began recruiting workers—black and white. They knew that black workers held a majority of the jobs in the Southern lumber industry and that these laborers had been the vanguard in the early protest strikes just after the turn of the century.

J. H. Kirby, leader of the area's lumber operators, warned his mill managers that Emerson was a "rank socialist with some attainments as a scholar" and that his comrade Smith was a "desperate fellow with a great deal of natural ability but little education." Kirby's spies warned him about the presence of these organizers in the piney woods, but the company managers could not stop them. Moving through the mills and camps disguised as insurance salesmen and gamblers, Emerson and Smith managed to avoid the spies and company guards.

In June 1911 the union organizers felt strong enough to come out of the woods and into the open. They held a convention in Alexandria, Louisiana, and formed a constitution modeled after the Knights of Labor. Blacks would be invited to join the union and organize their own locals. The membership would be mixed, including women, farmers, friends, and supporters. Most importantly, the new Brotherhood of Timber Workers declared itself an industrial union which would follow the example of the Knights, the United Mine Workers, and the IWW in organizing all lumber workers into one big union and not into separate craft unions like the American Federation of Labor.

Shortly after the convention, the Southern Lumber Operators' Association (SLOA), organized after the general strike of 1907, initiated a lockout designed to destroy the BTW. Employers hired Burns detectives to ferret out union men, but the Brotherhood's umbrella of secrecy frustrated espionage activities. Covington Hall, a BTW leader who wrote an important account of the industrial conflict, recalled: "When the lumber barons began their crushing operation in 1911, they found the Brotherhood everywhere and nowhere. It entered the woods and mills as a semi-secret organization with the usual passwords and grips so dear to Southerners, regardless of race." As the lockout continued into the summer of 1911, the lumber corporations began importing strikebreakers and demanding yellow-dog contracts in which workers pledged not to join the union. And in July, the SLOA closed eleven mills in the "infected area" around DeRidder, Louisiana, laying off 3,000 men.

After a summer of vigilant antiunion activity, the Operators' Association admitted that it had failed to break the back of the BTW. One operator told Kirby that the union had so many organizers in the field (he estimated 500) and had "increased its membership so rapidly" that a more "efficient machine" would have to be designed to combat it. The leaders of the Operators' Association responded by hiring labor spies and by organizing the most efficient blacklist in Southern industry.

Union members who had been shut out and blacklisted managed to survive by picking cotton on the nearby farms of friends and relatives. Manufacturers who were distressed by the lockout's failure to increase demands for yellow pine also worried about the support the Brotherhood received from "lots of merchants, farmers, all kinds of landowners and some officers." They were even more distressed to learn that in September three "redneck" lumberjacks from the BTW attended the Sixth Convention of the Industrial Workers of the World in Chicago.

Late in 1911 many mills in western Louisiana reopened, minus hundreds of blacklisted union men. In the dismal winter months which followed, the BTW went underground and nearly expired. A membership reduced to less than 5,000, a depleted treasury, and an exhausted cadre of organizers led the Brotherhood to affiliate with the IWW in May 1912. "Big Bill" Haywood himself came south from Wobbly headquarters in Chicago to sell discouraged timber workers on the One Big Union. One of the most charismatic figures in the American labor movement, Haywood presented a strong case for affiliation by promising the Brotherhood financial aid, experienced organizers, a union newspaper, and a big injection of confidence and militancy.

The BTW-IWW merger proposed by Haywood was effectively supported by Covington Hall, a remarkably articulate revolutionary. Born in Mississippi and raised in Terrebonne Parish in the Louisiana Sugar Bowl, Hall had witnessed the uprising of the black cane workers in 1877. After helping organize the New Orleans general strike of 1907—where he grew to hate the conservative AFL craft unionists who dominated the Southern labor movement—he joined the Wobblies. When the Brotherhood affiliated with the IWW, Hall launched a union newspaper called the *Lumberjack,* which combined the Wobblies' revolutionary industrial unionism and interracial emphasis with appeals to the Reconstruction legacy of hatred for Northern carpetbaggers and the Populists' legacy of opposition to corporate monopolies. Hall was one of the IWW's most effective propagandists because he could put anticapitalist Wobbly ideas into the language of the poor people of the piney woods. Hall, like the Brotherhood leaders, was conscious of the Sabine region's Populist history; he fully appreciated that many of the timber workers "were some of the most rebellious farmers in the United States."

In the spring of 1912, the Wobblies were on the crest of a rapidly breaking wave. Haywood had come to the South fresh from a sensational IWW victory over textile manufacturers in Lawrence,

Massachusetts. The militant tactics of the IWW seemed to be working and the voice of radicalism was heard throughout the land. "When we entered the Louisiana Lumber War," wrote Hall, "the great majority of militants taking part were convinced that the United States was ripe for a mass upheaval; that 'The Revolution' was just around the corner; and we acted accordingly."

The strategy of "direct action"—strikes, demonstrations, work stoppages, and sabotage—as preached by the IWW appealed to poor white farmers who had seen their Populist candidates "counted out" by Democratic poll watchers in the 1890s. It was also attractive to transient lumberjacks who failed to meet local residency requirements and to black mill hands who were disenfranchised on account of their race. Voting was just another privilege of the white middle class. The Wobblies took a more direct approach to the class struggle, argued Jay Smith, a BTW founder:

It is here on the job, in the union hall, that the working class begins to learn that the broadest interpretation of political power comes through industrial organization. It is here on the job, in the union hall, that the workers will learn that the IWW places the ballot in the hands of every man and woman, every boy and girl who works. It is here that the workers will learn that the IWW re-enfranchises the colored man.

Four days after the Brotherhood voted to join the Wobblies, it presented a list of grievances to ten lumber companies in the DeRidder area of western Louisiana. The operators were aghast at these demands and they promptly responded with a lockout late in May 1912. In a short time, employers began importing black strikebreakers so that they could reopen their mills with nonunion labor. Since armed guards and stockades kept the union men from talking to the scabs, BTW leaders decided to hold rallies outside the mills. Women and children would accompany the male strikers in order to discourage violence.

On Sunday, July 7, A.L. Emerson led a band of 100 strikers and their families to Bon Ami, Louisiana, where the huge King-Ryder mill was operating with scab labor. When the group learned that an attempt had been made to assassinate a socialist agitator in that vicinity, the leaders changed direction and headed for a smaller mill town called Grabow. Arriving at a crossroads near the Galloway Lumber Company, Emerson mounted a wagon and began to speak to his followers and a few bystanders around the town. Almost immediately company gunmen opened fire on the group from concealed positions. As people ran for cover, several armed union men fired back at the gunmen in the Galloway Company office. In the ten-minute gun battle that followed, 300 rounds were fired (largely by the company guards) and four men were killed (two unionists, one bystander, and one hired gunman). In addition, forty people, including several women and children, were wounded. The guards' shotguns "did deadly work," the operator's journal reported, "and the brotherhood members went down in rows." That evening hundreds of angry farmers and workers from Calcasieu Parish armed themselves and gathered at DeRidder; they wanted to avenge those who had been attacked at the Grabow massacre. After a long night of angry talk, A. L. Emerson and other BTW leaders persuaded the people to disperse and "let the law take its course."

Soon after the gun battle, lawmen arrested Emerson and sixty-four other union men and indicted them on charges of murdering a guard employed by the Galloway Company. The defendants remained in the cramped confines of the Lake Charles jail for two months awaiting trial; they took the opportunity to form a unique "branch local" of the Socialist Party. Meanwhile, experienced Wobbly agitators came into the region to help organize defense movements. The IWW press, with Covington Hall's aid, began a national publicity campaign. *Southwest,* the industry's trade journal, denounced "this frantic effort . . . to make it appear as though it were a trial of the 'lumber barons' versus the 'workingmen,' instead of a case of the State of Louisiana against a crowd of rioters." Nevertheless, the New Orleans *Times Democrat* reported that a "dangerous state of opinion" existed in the pine region because so many farmers and workers were outraged by the course the law had taken following the Grabow massacre.

On the first day of the trial at Lake Charles, forty workers in J. H. Kirby's biggest mill at Kirbyville, Texas, walked off their jobs to express their solidarity with Emerson and the other defendants; they were all fired and ejected from their houses on the same day. This act of defiance symbolized the importance of the Lake Charles trial to the workers of the Sabine region. Their sense of outrage increased when prosecution attorneys, led by "progressive" Democratic Congressman A. J. Pujo, rejected all potential jurors who expressed sympathy for unionism.

The prosecution's case collapsed when its star witness admitted that the gunmen at the Galloway mill had been drinking before the BTW marchers arrived at Grabow. At one point, the mill owner told his storekeeper to pour liquor into the guards until the union men came up. Under the circumstances, Congressman Pujo, who was famous for his investigation of the "trusts," closed his case and hoped that his own clients would not be prosecuted.

It only took the jury a few minutes to find the Grabow defendants innocent. When the verdict was announced, the little courtroom erupted with cheers and the audience spilled into the streets of Lake Charles for a victory parade. That night a "jubilation" meeting took place at the Carpenter's Hall that was attended by members

Timber workers in Texas

of all the unions and by all seven of the farmers who served on the jury.

The Wobblies reached the peak of their influence in the pine region at this time, but the BTW's membership (about 20,000 in the early summer) continued to decline as the lockout wore on and the blacklist lengthened.

THE BTW REALIZED THAT THE GROWTH OF INDUSTRIAL UNIONISM IN the piney woods depended largely upon the support of black laborers who held a majority of unskilled forest and sawmill jobs. The Brotherhood's attempt to organize black and white workers came at a time when demands for segregation divided the working class and made contacts between the races less frequent and more violent. The workers lived in separate quarters in most industrial towns. Social and religious activities were usually divided by race, especially in the years after Jim Crow laws were passed to prevent mixed assemblies.

But churches, schools, and clubs were weak and few in number in the chaotic, congested lumber camps. There is no evidence of segregation in places where workers frequently congregated—saloons, houses of prostitution, grocery stores, and barber shops. Jim Crow laws were far more important in cities and county-seat towns, where there were transportation facilities and public institutions to segregate and established patterns of residency to maintain.

The Wobblies knew that employers had the upper hand in dealing with the race question; if the BTW integrated, the operators could "nigger bait" and play on the blacks' distrust of rednecks, but if the BTW stayed "lily white," they could use "black legs" with devastating effectiveness. *Southwest* seemed justified when it predicted the Brotherhood's failure. "Both black and white laborers are employed indiscriminately," the trade journal declared, "and men of wisdom recognize at a glance how impossible it would be to organize the territory under these circumstances." In the summer of 1911, however, *Southwest* reported that "700 or 800 men and women, a good percent being negro," heard speeches by A. L. Emerson and Cajun firebrand W. D. Fussel. The Brotherhood recruited several thousand members in western Louisiana, the article added, "largely negroes" or white "tenant farmers and loafers about the sawmill places."

Emerson and other union leaders realized from the start that they had to organize the black workers, but they could not ignore the obstacle racism presented. The original BTW constitution provided separate lodges for "negroes" and control of all dues by white locals. The blacks were not satisfied with such arrangements and declared at the second convention that they eschewed "social equalities," but could not "suppress a feeling of taxation without representation."

Accordingly, their delegates demanded a colored executive board, elected by black union members and designed to work "in harmony with its white counterpart." But these discriminatory rules against which the blacks protested were later rescinded and eventually overshadowed by the commitment the BTW made to interracial organizing.

The affiliation of the Brotherhood with the IWW in 1912 brought with it the rhetoric of militant egalitarianism. When Bill Haywood arrived at the Alexandria convention of 1912, he immediately complained about the absence of "colored delegates." Covington Hall explained that the black unionists were meeting in a separate hall in accordance with state segregation laws. "Big Bill" boomed his response: "You cannot possibly do business this way. Bring the colored delegates in and hold the convention."

Haywood told the white delegates that since they worked with blacks they could just as well meet with them in convention. "Why not be sensible about this," he asked, "and call the Negroes into this convention? If it's against the law, this is one time when the law should be broken." The white workers responded favorably to this plea which was echoed effectively by "Cov" Hall. "The Negroes," Haywood wrote, "were called into the session without a murmur of protest from anyone. The mixed convention carried on its work in an orderly way and when it came to the election of delegates to the next IWW convention, black men as well as white were elected."

The black union men expressed enthusiasm for the Brotherhood's merger with the IWW and declared: "We have come this far with the Grand Old organization of the B. of T.W. with a true, sincere and loyal intention of going to the end. If she went down as the great ship Titanic did in the Atlantic waters . . . we are willing to go down with her." The blacks had some reasons to be encouraged. They elected a delegate to the IWW convention, D. R. Gordon of Lake Charles, and a black executive board. What is more, their protests led to the organization of mixed locals, which actually formed in many localities even though black and white union men went to jail for meeting together.

For its brief period of existence, the union provided a new form of association for workers and a substitute for social institutions weakened or made irrelevant by rapid economic and demographic change. One account—by a hostile observer—tells us something about the social role the Brotherhood played for workers of both races. A traveler gave the following account of a BTW meeting he had seen at Merryville, Louisiana, in July of 1912:

I was informed that it was the celebration of Negro emancipation, and that the negroes had given a fine barbecue and that the whites had gone in with them to help out in the financial part and also to celebrate with them as the "Lumber Workers" Union. There were about 2,000 or more people upon the ground—about three whites to every two negroes. There was a general mixture of races and sexes, especially when to the sound of the band they collected like a swarm of bees—white, black, male, and female—around the speaker's stand.

Then, according to the observer, a black minister spoke and introduced A. L. Emerson, who related the slaves' struggle for emancipation to the Brotherhood's battle against the lumber trust.

Several conditions prevented racism from destroying the union movement in the piney woods. First, the remoteness of the Sabine region initially created a labor shortage that forced employers to integrate blacks into the work force. Later, this situation hindered the importation of black strikebreakers to a certain extent. Second, the Wobblies could apply industrial unionism to an interracial work force that was not seriously divided into separate crafts or by wage distinctions. Therefore, white workers were not especially concerned with protecting their privileged job status, as they were in the railroad brotherhoods and the building trades. Finally, and most importantly, the militant industrial unionism of the BTW checked the spread of race hatred within the ranks of the Southern lumber workers. The organizers of the union, especially the outspoken Wobblies, effectively urged laborers of both races to join together in resisting the demands of the region's industrial capitalists.

In addition to black support, the Brotherhood depended upon assistance from farmers and townspeople. BTW leaders appreciated the importance of rural support. They knew that the Populist movement created a strong anticapitalist sentiment among many small farmers. They also knew that the lumber corporations forced many of these men and their sons into tenant farming. As one redbone tenant from Calasieu Parish pointed out in the summer of 1912, "There is a great deal of feeling here against the sawmill companies on account of their land-holding policy." Like many tenants, he wanted to force the corporations to open their cut-over lands for purchase.

In addition to this longstanding grievance over their "natural right" to the land, the hill country farmers reacted violently to the mill managers' attempts to prevent them from peddling their produce in the company towns. Near Fullerton, Louisiana, the redbone farmers forced the company to allow them access to the town by sabotaging machinery and sniping at company guards. The superintendent of the Pickering Land and Lumber Company told David J. Saposs, the Industrial Relations investigator, that the redbones (who were a majority of the white workers at his plant in Cravens, Louisiana) were the "backbone of the 1912 strike," and that the farmers in the area, "who came from the same stock, sympathize with them."

Townspeople as well as farmers supported the Brotherhood, especially in the early days of the conflict. Merchants and professionals depended on workers' patronage, and some also shared populist values hostile to corporate capitalism. The BTW in Sillsbee, Texas, an industry agent reported, included "farmers, merchants, and small men of trade who naturally sympathize with working masses." Community solidarity helped the merchants as well as the workers. In Merryville, Louisiana, shopkeepers "met and protested against a 10 percent discount on their checks turned in at the American Lumber Company's office." The company refused to pay the vouchers at par. "The Union Lodge has backed the merchants," wrote one observer, "and claim they will shut the mill down before they will submit to any further discount." The lumber company backed down in the face of worker-merchant demands.

The workers received most of their middle-class assistance in established towns not controlled by large corporations. In these older agricultural communities—unlike the newer company towns—the merchants remained free agents, farmers peddled their vegetables in the streets, and professionals served the community rather than the corporation. The workers could preserve ties with their agrarian past and defend themselves against the dislocations caused by industrialization. In some of these towns the people elected officials openly hostile to the corporations.

As industrial strife increased, the corporations supplemented their antiunion tactics with campaigns to undermine the BTW's community support. Company guards and mill managers organized "law and order leagues" to fight the union. These "homespun storm troopers" soon recruited the "best citizens" in the town—doctors, lawyers, merchants, and the like—and began to attack the BTW. For example, E. I. Kellie, a candidate for Congress and the leader of the citizen's league, wrote to J. H. Kirby from Jasper, Texas, that he and some of the "boys" had driven Wobbly speakers out of town. "We told them" he said, "this was our town" and that we "were the law and we would not allow no one to speak here that preached their doctrine. Kellie's 'old Ku Klux Klan' are not dead, they were only sleeping and were thoroughly aroused the other night." Moved to eloquence by Kellie's deed, Kirby responded: "The American manhood which your act typified is the sole reliance of their Republic for its perpetuity."

In DeRidder, a BTW stronghold, the lumber companies used economic pressure to change the prounion editorials in the local paper late in 1912. Early in the next year, socialist mayor E. F. Presley withstood the efforts made by the Good Citizen's League to oust him, but at about the same time this organization of merchants and businessmen successfully drove BTW organizers out of the town. The participation of the "best citizens" in the law-and-order leagues of the pine region, as well as in the Councils for Defense and the Ku Klux Klan which followed later, demonstrated that the middle classes of this region had a greater propensity for authoritarian activity than the workers.

THE CONFLICT BETWEEN THE BTW AND THE SLOA REACHED ITS CLIMAX at a strike in Merryville, Louisianá, in the winter of 1913. A large corporation, the Santa Fe Railroad, moved into this prounion town and drove a wedge between workers and their white middle-class supporters.

The American Lumber Company dominated Merryville, but the workers did not live in a typical company town. Sam Park, the mill manager and part owner, accepted the Brotherhood and most of its demands. He made his mill at Merryville into a model plant which attracted workers from all over the pine region. The *Times Democrat* estimated that 90 percent of Park's 1,300 employees were members of the Brotherhood in 1912. It also reported that "public sympathy is decidedly with the B.T.W." and that "many of the business men in Merryville are members of the Union and display B. of T.W. flags in their windows."

The SLOA denounced Park for treachery because he refused to follow Association orders to shut down his mill during the lockouts of 1911 and 1912 and because he "treated with the union." The Brotherhood was so successful at the American Lumber Company that the SLOA resolved to do away with Park. The Operators' Association kept applying pressure on the Santa Fe, which owned the controlling interest in the American Lumber Company, and in the autumn of 1912 the railroad corporation forced Sam Park out and assumed control of the Merryville complex.

On November 10, 1912, only a week after the celebrated Grabow trial, the new management attempted to precipitate a strike for which the union was unprepared by firing fifteen union men who had appeared as witnesses for the defense in the Lake Charles court. Jay Smith assembled the Wobblies of Merryville on the tracks of the Kansas City Southern and told them that the Brotherhood could not sustain a long strike because of the losses it had suffered since the Grabow massacre. Smith put the question to a vote and the most militant workers in the pine region moved to the left side of the tracks. The next morning 1,200 union men struck against the American Lumber Company and the BTW began its last battle.

In the first months of the struggle at Merryville the workers held their own; they even formed a communal organization (Hall called it the "first American Soviet") that attracted considerable attention in radical circles throughout the country.

Phineas Eastman, a Wobbly who helped to organize black workers, claimed that racial solidarity in the Brotherhood reached its strongest point at Merryville. "Although not one of the 15 men fired by the company was a Negro," he wrote, "our colored fellow workers showed their solidarity by walking out with their white comrades and no amount of persuasion or injection of the old race prejudice could induce them to turn scab or traitor."

In the strike's third month, after the mill had reopened with scab labor, the corporation mobilized its community power to crush what was left of the union. On February 10, 1913, the Merryville Good Citizens' League struck. Organized by the "leading citizens" in the town, led by the company doctor and staffed by Santa Fe gunmen, the league destroyed the union headquarters, attacked and "deported" several Wobblies, and burned the soup kitchen staffed by female BTW members. The *Lumberjack* screamed "Class War at Merryville" and charged:

Men born and raised in Louisiana have been beaten, shot and hunted down as though they were wild beasts. Our fellow women workers were driven away from the soup kitchen, the only place where hungry children could be fed, at the point of guns. All of the houses of union men were searched without warrant by agents of the capitalist class.

Hall's paper explained later that "about 300 men had guns," and paraded in the streets up and down the Santa Fe railroad tracks. "Some asked about the law in Louisiana." Dr. Knight, the leader of the league, "pounded his chest and said this is all the law we want." Knight and his league had indeed taken "the law in their own hands" as the Lake Charles *American Press* reported. And by midwinter of 1913 the American Lumber Company had exerted enough pressure in Merryville to completely isolate the small number of Wobblies who were still on strike. Having stripped radical workers of their civil rights and separated them from their white community supporters, employers easily crushed the timber workers' last revolt.

By 1914, when open hostilities abated, nearly all of the Brotherhood's members had been fired and blacklisted. Union leaders like A. L. Emerson, who was severely beaten by Santa Fe guards at Singer in 1913, had been driven from the region. The companies even harassed blacklisted union men who remained in the area and were "suspected" of being socialists or IWW sympathizers.

More importantly, the operators succeeded in polarizing the lumber towns and isolating the workers from their community supporters. Peddlers (especially redbone farmers who were known to be very sympathetic to the radical movement) were shut out of the company towns, and independent grocers were prevented from delivering goods.

The black workers, including a large number of strikebreakers, were put in guarded compounds within the mill towns. At Fullerton, Louisiana, where the "colored quarters" had been fenced in, a black cook said that "the colored people know that if they talked unionism they would be fired on the spot." Ultimately, the corporations' ability to polarize the lumber towns and isolate the workers (especially the blacks) from the surrounding community was more fatal to the union movement than the more direct and violent attacks their guards made on radical leaders.

ALTHOUGH CORPORATION REPRESSION COMPLETELY DESTROYED THE Brotherhood in 1913, the history of the timber workers' struggle should not be written solely as one of defeat. In fact, as the BTW was being crushed by the region's businessmen and their vigilante henchmen, "some of the most obnoxious causes of dissatisfaction, such as payment in scrip, forced use of company stores, and monthly payments were modified and small wage increases and shorter hours were granted," says Vernon Jensen in his *Lumber and Labor*. The three-year struggle of the black and white timber workers against the powerful timber barons had not been waged in vain.

The history of the Brotherhood of Timber Workers conflicts with the conventional stereotypes of passive, racially divided Southern workers. Despite the lack of support offered from official AFL unions, Southern lumber workers took on the most powerful industrial capitalists in the region and organized their own union. As an industrial union, the BTW broke from the pattern of exclusionary AFL unions and opened its membership to women and blacks. The leaders of the Brotherhood— primarily native Southerners—forced the membership to confront the race question and to abandon segregated locals, though AFL union leaders said they were inevitable in the South.

The Brotherhood of Timber Workers stands in a bold tradition of Southern interracial industrial unionism that goes back to the Knights of Labor and the UMW. But the BTW advanced beyond the nineteenth century trade unionism by adopting the IWW's disciplined, guerrilla warfare tactics and the revolutionary vision of industry controlled by the workers. Drawing upon the deeply rooted hostility to corporate capitalism initially expressed by the Knights and the Populists, the Brotherhood won wide support for a broadly class-conscious attack on the alien lumber trust. It threatened the corporations with a brand of unionism that went beyond limited concessions. Blacks and whites, skilled and unskilled, even sympathetic townspeople and farmers—all were brought together in "one big union." A unified movement of this kind presented a radical threat to the industrial capitalists of the region and their allies. It had to be destroyed. But even in defeat, the Brotherhood's indigenous brand of interracial, industrial unionism leaves an important legacy to the modern struggle against a corporate elite that still exploits the South's people and resources.

For notes on sources, see page 371.

FOUR

If I Could Go Back

GROESBECK PARHAM
AND
GWEN ROBINSON

FAIRFIELD, ALABAMA, IS A COM-
pany town, one of seventeen
residential areas near Birmingham
built by the United States Steel
Corporation. Nearly everyone who
lives here works—or has worked—
in U.S. Steel's local mills or mines.

Dobbie Sanders is one of those
former employees. Now 85 years
old, Dobbie spent more than a
quarter century working for U.S.
Steel, and the years have reshaped
his body. His eyes are blurry; his
feet, covered with callouses; his
fingers, thick and rough—one with
a tip missing.

Sanders lives in a small house on
the corner of Fairfield's Sixty-first
Street and Avenue E. Each day, he
walks slowly about his yard,
dressed in a pair of greasy overalls.
A passerby may see him squatting
on the ground repairing a broken
lawn mower, or leaning underneath
the hood of a car, or fixing some
electrical gadget. Sometimes he sits
for hours looking through one of
the trunks in his yard, searching for
objects that take him through his
past: his baby sister's dress from
their family farm, a pair of his
brother's old gloves, records of
outdated wage rates at U.S. Steel,
flyers from the International Labor
Defense and various unions, his
retirement papers, old insurance
policies.

The objects that still fill Dobbie's
life are many and various, revealing
his journey from a Mississippi farm
to Alabama's steel factories, from
Birmingham to Chicago and back
again. Like many black sharecroppers, he left the farm for
higher wages and independence

near the turn of the century. He found the company bosses instead. He went north looking for a means to advance himself, and enrolled in a school of electronics. He could make good money in the North, he says, but he felt he had to come home. And in Fairfield, he couldn't find a job that met his new skills. He stayed, though, and persevered.

Today he sits on a yellow quilt, beneath a thin aluminum boat propped up by a single oar, and reads again the papers of his youth.

"Yessir," he says as he rises from his quilt. "I'm a Mississippi man."

Born in Bigbee Valley, Mississippi, near the Alabama line, Dobbie grew up with nine brothers and three sisters. They all began working at an early age.

My whole family sharecropped on the land of P. Q. Poindexter, a big white millionaire down in Bigbee Valley. I worked from the time I first remembered myself. My father died when I was one year two months old, but Mama told me he was a ditchdigger. He dug ditches around the big farm to drain off the water.

Mama raised us all. She was a mama and daddy too. She did a good job 'cause we didn't have nothing. We did all the work and got nothing in return. Poindexter would credit us the tools, hogs, mules, cotton, corn seed, and a

Dobbie Sanders at home in Fairfield, Alabama, 1976

pair of brogan shoes and jean pants. At the end of the season when it came time to add up, we would always owe him more money than we had to pay him, no matter how big the crop. We would always end up in the hole. We grew and raised everything, but he took it all. Course we had enough food 'cause we raised it. But that's all we had.

Every morning when the bell was rung, we had to get up and go out to the barn. Mr. Poindexter had hired a black man as the bell ringer; he was a wage earner. When we got out to the barn to get our tools and stuff, it would still be dark. We would take our plows out to the field, and when the sun started rising, we were supposed to be sitting on our plows ready to work. The sun was the sign. And we would work and work and work until it got dark.

Mr. Poindexter had hired a white overseer who rode through the fields on a horse telling us what to do. He never beat us, but Mama used to tell us how, when she was coming up, that the white overseers would beat the people with a whip. Sometimes we'd be out in the middle of the field working, and Mama would just bust out and start cryin' and hollerin'. She'd say, "If Bill was here, I wouldn't have to be doin' all this hard work." Bill was my daddy. I was small then, and didn't understand why she was crying. But after I got up some size I understood.

Lots of times people thought about leaving the farm, but if you tried to, the owner would take away everything you had. Your tools, mules, horses, cows, hogs, clothes, food, everything. But things were so bad that people still left.

My oldest brother left home in 1919 and came to work in Fairfield at the U.S. Steel Wire Mill. On May 8, 1922, I left. Mama had died, and I just wanted to wear good clothes like some of the rest of the boys. Hell, if you worked all the time and somebody took all you made, you'd leave too.

After I left, I went and worked in the Delta at a levee camp as a wheeler, helping to pile dirt on the river bank to make a dam. I was paid about $1.75 a day. I stayed there a little while and then left. I hoboed, caught rides, and walked my way to North Carollton. That's near Yellow Dog, Mississippi. I worked there for a while laying Y-shaped tracks at the end of railroad line until they laid me off. Then I hoboed on trains and walked until I got to Sulls, Alabama, working my way on up to Fairfield.

In Sulls, I worked in the mines with my brother Jim. I only worked for a month and had to quit 'cause I was too tall for the mines. My head kept hitting up against the roof. I told my brother I was going up to Fairfield to get a job in U.S. Steel's Wire Mill and stay with another one of our brothers, William. Jim said OK, but told me, "Make sure you work enough to feed yourself."

And I did. When I got to Fairfield I stayed with William and his wife in Annisburg, next to Englewood.* I started working in September 1922. William's wife would go down to the company store and get food, and the company would deduct it from my paycheck every two weeks.

---

*Annisburg and Englewood were the first areas built for black families working for U.S. Steel. Although now a part of greater Fairfield, the areas were originally separated from the white neighborhoods by a row of bushes that Dobbie Sanders calls the "Iron Curtain."

When he first entered industry, Dobbie Sanders followed a path beaten by thousands of black Southern workers before him. Even before the Civil War, blacks played a crucial role in Southern industry, and especially the iron business. As far back as 1812, 220 slaves were owned by the Oxford Iron Works of Virginia. In the Tennessee Cumberland River region, one iron company owned 365 slaves in the 1840s, and twenty other establishments in that area worked more than 1,800 slaves. In 1861, the Tredegar Iron Company of Richmond employed the third-largest iron-working force in the United States, and half of the 900 men were slaves. Altogether, an estimated 10,000 slaves worked in the South's iron industry.

Before the Civil War, Selma had been the major site of Alabama's iron works, but in 1865 the city fell and its plants were destroyed. Other coal and iron plants were soon constructed throughout the state and began to grow and merge. In 1871, Birmingham was founded as the ideal location for an industrial steel complex, which required easy access to coal, iron, water, and transportation. Eventually the Tennessee Coal & Iron Company (TCI) became the uncontested leader in Alabama's steel business, and in 1892 it moved its headquarters to the "Magic City," a name Birmingham soon earned for its phenomenal growth. Fifteen years later, J. P. Morgan absorbed TCI into his U.S. Steel empire.

In 1910, 13,417 blacks were employed in U.S. blast furnace operations and steel-rolling mills, the vast majority in the lowest-paying, dirtiest, most tedious jobs. At this time, almost three-quarters of all common laborers in the steel and iron industry were black, though they were only 8.2 percent of the skilled work force and 10.7 percent of the unskilled workers. Of those few skilled black workers, almost 40 percent were employed in Alabama—635 men.

Like Sanders, many of these workers had recently come from nearby farms in search of freedom from their hard times. Most didn't find it.

When I started working at U.S. Steel's Wire Mill, the company owned the houses, food and clothing stores, hospitals, schools, churches, everything. And they deducted everything out of your paycheck—food, clothes, rent. Sometimes we'd work the whole pay period and time come to get paid, and we'd draw nothing but a blank slip of paper. That mill was rough. When I started working there in 1922, we were doing 10-hour shifts at $2.45 a day, as many days as the man told us to come in. Later, they went on the 8-hour day at $3.10 a day, but we still had to work 10-hour shifts. We had no vacation, no holidays, no sick leave, no pension, no insurance, no nothing. It was rough.

I went ahead and got married in 1927. Most of the women in town did cleanup work. A lot of them worked in the basements of Loveman's and

Pizitz's department stores shining shoes and scrubbing floors. No dark-skinned women drove the freight elevators even.

Dobbie Sanders had come to Fairfield frustrated with working long hours and getting nothing for it. Now he found himself in the same situation.

One day back in '27 or '28, I just got tired of the whole thing and quit work. I enrolled in the L. L. Cooke School of Electronics in Chicago. L. L. Cooke was the Chief Engineer of Chicago. Even though I had only finished the third grade, I was a good reader. I used to read all of my brother's books. I'm a self-educated man.

When I was in electronics school, I learned how to make and fix door bells, wire up burglar alarms, wire houses and everything else. I'll even wire you so if anybody touches you, you'll ring. I wired up that old dog pen out there just so it would touch the old dog up lightly when he tried to step over the fence. It'll touch you up lightly too if you try to git in.

Sanders points with pride to a thick, dusty electronics textbook printed in 1927 by L. L. Cooke Electronics School, Chicago, Illinois. Many sentences in the book have been underlined, with numbers from 1 to 10 marked beside them.

You see, at the *end* of each chapter there are ten questions. The *answers* are in the chapter. I put the numbers of the questions next to the answers. Then I underlined the answers. I made everything in that book, and I read and studied every page of it. That's why I can fix so many things.

I can fix everything except a broken heart. Can't fix that.

After I left Chicago, I went on to Detroit. I was making good money there, too, just fixing things. But I came on back to Fairfield. You know how it is 'bout home. You know everybody and everybody knows you. Plus, when I was away I was living with other people. You know how it is.

So when I got back here, the head of the school in Chicago called the people at U.S. Steel and told them what I could do. But they said they wasn't hiring no colored electricians. They still made me do electrical work sometimes, but they just didn't pay me for it.

If the working people of this country would ever get together, they could run the whole thing. That's why I like that worker/farmer form of government.

While working in Fairfield, Dobbie Sanders became involved in a number of groups fighting for black and working people's rights. One was the International Labor Defense (ILD), organized by the Communist Party in 1925 to fight extralegal organizations such as the Ku Klux Klan. ILD members had become active in highly publicized campaigns to free Tom Mooney, Warren Billings, Nicola Sacco, and Bartolomeo Vanzetti. In 1931 the ILD came south as the main organizers of the Scottsboro Boys' defense in Birmingham. Over the next few years the ILD was able to turn national attention to the South and to the trial of the nine young blacks facing the death penalty on charges of raping two white women. Blacks and a few whites throughout the South supported the ILD and the Scottsboro Boys, contributed money from church offerings, and attended rallies. At one Birmingham meeting 900 blacks and 300 whites turned out.

Yes, the ILD was in here with the Scottsboro Boys, and I was right along with them. I used to pass out leaflets for them down at the plant. I would stick 'em in my lunch bucket and tie 'em round my waist and ankles. On the way inside the gate, I would open up my bucket, untie the strings and let the wind blow the leaflets all over the yard. I'd just keep steppin' like nothin' ever happened. There's always a way, you know.

But he is reluctant to talk much about the organization's problems. He laughs, "You go ahead and talk some. I done already gone too far. Why, I been seventy-five miles barefoot, and on cold ground, too. But I'll just say this: it was all about obtaining a higher standard of living."

Sanders was also a member of the United Steelworkers of America, which began organizing in Alabama in the late 1930s and joined the state's long tradition of integrated unions. That tradition started with the United Mine Workers before the turn of the century. By 1902, the UMW had organized about 65 percent of all miners in the state, a majority of them black. Racism and social segregation were continual problems for the union, but even in 1899 a few blacks were able to hold the presidency of locals that included white members. A series of long strikes took place in the first decades of the century, one from 1904 to 1906, which weakened the union immensely. But the UMW kept returning—in the teens, in the twenties, and again in the thirties.

Throughout this period, attempts were made to organize the steel industry, but that feat was not accomplished until the birth of the Congress of Industrial Organizations (CIO) in 1936. Under the leadership of UMW president John L. Lewis, one of the top priorities of the CIO was the organization of the steel industry. The CIO established the Steel Workers Organizing Committee (SWOC) for that purpose, which later grew into the United Steelworkers of America (USWA).

Dobbie Sanders joined USWA in its early years. He explains:

Before the union came in here in the 1930s it was rough. We didn't have any say in anything. I was one of those who helped get people signed up. We had to slip and sign our cards and pay our dues. When the Steelworkers ran into trouble, they'd just call in the Mine Workers. Them boys would come in here from Walker County with snuff running down their chins, both black and white. And they didn't take no stuff. If it wasn't for Ebb Cox and the Mine Workers, we never would have got a union.

Cox was one of the steelworkers' most determined leaders, encouraging workers to join the union wherever he could—in churches, in the bars, and on the streets of Fairfield. Tall and light-skinned, with no formal education, he became one of the staff. He was the object of much antiunion and antiblack violence in Mississippi and Georgia as well as Alabama, but he continued his relentless fight for the union. He was eventually elected the first black member of the Alabama CIO Executive Board.

Dobbie Sanders was also a union leader in Fairfield.

I put food in a lot of women's and babies' mouths by writing out Step One-and-a-Half in the promotion line in the wire mill. Step One was on the broom. Step One-and-a-Half was classified as the "helper," even though you'd actually be doing the work [of the person on the Step Two job]. This was so the company could get away with paying Step One-and-a-Half wages even though you'd be doing Step Two work.

After the union had come in, I wrote a provision that said that after so many hours on the job, a man had to be given a chance to bid for the job and be paid the right wages. I took it to my supervisor, and he couldn't do nothing but accept it. Hell, before this thing was written up, they'd keep a man in Step One-and-a-Half for a hundred years. Yessir, that mill was rough.

And we had a lot of people working against us, too. Not just the company, police, and sandtoters [informers], but most of the preachers. Man, them preachers is a mess. Most of 'em ain't no good. Brainwashing, that's what they all about. They should have been race leaders, but instead they are race hold-backers. And the people who support them are crazy, too. Does it make any sense to pay somebody to hold you in the dark? These preachers go around here charging people to keep them looking back. Goin' around here tellin' people 'bout heaven. How you gon git to heaven after you die, and you can't even get to 19th Street in downtown Birmingham when you are alive. When you die you can't even go to the undertaker, they have to come and get you. So how you gon go to heaven?

Dobbie stayed at the mill for more than twenty-five years, doing the same work at the end that he did when he started. "I retired on March 31, 1959," he remembers with the precision that he has for only a few significant facts of his life.

Since then he has lived at the corner of Sixty-first Street and Avenue E in Fairfield, surrounded by the memories of his life. "I tell you," he says softly, looking up from his boxes, "if I could go back through the whole thing again, I'd git me one of them easy shootin' guns, the kind with a silencer on it. And I'd be a killer."

EBB COX WROTE THE FOLLOWING MESSAGE TO HIS BROTHERS IN District 36, USW, in 1945.

The point I would like to clarify is what our civic, social, economic, and political situation was in 1934. And what is the condition on these problems today.

1. The company was owning all the villages, schools, churches, recreation, and controlled all food and clothing stores. The company was issuing nonnegotiable checks. Wages were $2.33 for 10 hours per day. Wages today here in the South are the same as they are in Pittsburgh, Pennsylvania.
2. There was no sanitary service at all. No streets were paved. The alleys grew up with weeds and were filled with ashes and cans. Nothing was done to protect the health and safety of the people.
3. The law completely separated whites from Negroes.
4. Less than 2 percent of the Negroes could qualify to vote.

But now, what is the answer? The county controls the schools. The people own their homes. Wages are paid in American money, the streets are paved. The whites and Negroes are meeting together and working out their common problems.

In 1936, no company would let me sit in a conference, but today I am servicing twenty plants alone. I was disowned by my brothers and father and my race. My service the first three years was given free, but today we have improved our race relations greatly.

All my effort was through the United Steelworkers of America, C.I.O. My objective was to build a union and through the union we could solve all problems.

FIVE

Work Like the Devil for My Pay: Mobile, Alabama, 1900-1929

MELTON MC LAURIN
AND
MICHAEL THOMASON

ALTHOUGH ITS PORT DOMINATED the economy, Mobile's general overall development reflects a pattern common to most Southern cities. In the years following the Civil War, the construction industry and emerging industrial firms provided employment for the large majority of Mobile's work force that was not employed in commerce or the retail trades. Except for a few textile mills, such firms were small, and they sold their products in local or regional markets. Not until the late 1920s did Mobile begin to develop a truly significant industrial sector.

By the end of the twenties, the city's excellent transportation facilities, low taxes, and bountiful supplies of cheap labor and fresh water had attracted the attention of national firms. But the plants they established in Mobile produced low-value-added products with unskilled or semiskilled labor. This gradual development of an industrial base had little impact upon organized labor, for most union members remained in the old skilled trades. The industrial work force was completely unorganized. Throughout the period blacks performed menial labor; whites held the "better" positions, including the better-paying and less strenuous industrial jobs. Women entered the work force in positions reserved for their sex, such as textile workers and telephone operators, but were unable to obtain traditionally "male" jobs.

The following photographs were all taken in the Mobile, Alabama, area.

49

LEFT ABOVE: Packing strawberries for shipment north: a truck crop raised by agrarian day labor rather than prevalent tenant farmers, 1910

LEFT: Interior of sawmill, ca. 1900

ABOVE: In the sawmills that ringed the city, black and white workers cut logs with unguarded saws, ca. 1910

BELOW: International Paper, the first large corporation to establish a plant in Mobile

ABOVE: Longshoremen awaiting the call to work, ca. 1928

RIGHT: Whites supervising black laborers loading cotton and lumber for export and unloading crates of sugar and bananas, ca. 1925

RIGHT BELOW: Unloading sugar, ca. 1928

BELOW: Whites manned the fishing and oyster fleets; blacks processed the catch

ABOVE: City employees laying water lines, ca. 1912

RIGHT ABOVE: International Paper upheld the traditional racial and sexual employment patterns

RIGHT: Small industrial firms used mostly white labor, as in this gutter factory, ca. 1900

BELOW: Cotton compress, Alabama State Docks, ca. 1930

SIX

The Recruiter

CLEMENT T. IMHOFF

BEFORE WORLD WAR I, AMERICAN industry—which was almost entirely in the North—had an abundant labor supply to draw from. For fifty years, an annual average of 500,000 new immigrants had offered their services to the expanding U.S. economy. Few blacks worked in Northern industry; they continued to live in the South, most still fastened to the land by the sharecropper system.

The war and new restrictive immigration policies changed that. A major source of laborers suddenly dried up and industrialists actively recruited Southern black men for their factories. Some of these workers moved to jobs in Southern cities, but a larger stream began a migration to Northern cities such as Chicago and Detroit. For example, according to one estimate, blacks entered Chicago at a rate of 2,800 a month during 1917–1918. A few found their way to smaller Northern towns like Beloit, Wisconsin, where 19-year-old D. W. Johnson moved in 1919.

The new policy of hiring black laborers such as Johnson fit conveniently into the antiunion efforts of many industrialists. Business leaders discovered that a labor force divided along ethnic and racial lines poses great difficulties for union organizers; by importing blacks, a cheap work force could be gained and unionization efforts weakened at the same time. In the two decades 1910–1930, more than one million blacks left the six Deep South states, compared to only one-fourth that number during 1890–1910.

Most of the new, black industrial workers migrated northward on the recommendation of friends and relatives. Some responded to the powerful, persuasive voices of contraband black newspapers such as the Chicago *Defender,* which persistently urged black workers to take advantage of opportunities in Northern industries. Others were persuaded by the covert inducements of labor agents who were hired specifically for the dangerous work of penetrating Southern states to recruit blacks. Reverend D. W. Johnson served as one of these recruiters.

Johnson was born in Macon, Mississippi, in 1900 to sharecropper parents. He first left home to work for the Gulf, Mobile & Ohio Railroad when just 17. About a year later, he returned to Macon as a labor recruiter. He made several more trips to Mississippi and neighboring states to offer black men opportunities as line workers for the railroad.

In 1919, he left the South for Beloit, Wisconsin, and the foundries of Fairbanks, Morse & Company, a corporation which aggressively recruited black workers from north-central Mississippi during and after World War I. After two years in Beloit, Johnson returned to Murphysboro, Illinois, where he resumed his responsibilities as a labor agent for the GM&O. Railroads were among the most active recruiters of black labor at this time; the Pennsylvania Railroad alone brought 12,000 blacks north to maintain tracks and equipment.

Agents like Johnson were unwelcome guests in Southern communities. Elaborate legal and quasilegal mechanisms had arisen in the post–Civil War South to keep blacks tied to the region's plantation economy. In *The Emergence of the New South,* George Tindall cites a licensing regulation in Macon, Georgia, which required each labor agent to pay a $25,000 fee and to obtain recommendations from ten local ministers, ten manufacturers, and twenty-five merchants. Many Southerners were even more direct, however, and used guns and gallows to eliminate suspected recruiters.

Johnson and scores of other labor agents for Northern corporations radically altered the development of industry, unions, and especially the South. Yet they have often been invisible characters. Stories of them have been told, references made to their accomplishments, but very rarely have labor agents explained in their own words their actions and adventures. D. W. Johnson is one of the first.

The following recollections have been taken from an interview conducted by Clement T. Imhoff on February 29, 1976, at Johnson's home in Beloit.

My father was a devout old man. He meant to do good. He was a meek man, could just take it on both sides. You could say something to him that could be awful nasty, but he'd have a kind word. And I love him for that today.

Fortunate enough for us, Dad would tell us when we left home how to conduct ourselves. First thing, his word was, "Keep your head up." He meant, stay level. Try to meet people as you want to be met, talk to them as you want to be talked to. And then sometime you have to go a little further. He would always try to teach a method that we could get along and be thought of as a human. We loved Dad for that, 'cause now that he left us, none of us have to beg for bread.

My mother was a clean old lady. She taught her children to go straight. If I acted up some way—maybe it was just a rumor—she'd take me in and set me down beside her and begin to read the Bible to me. I believe that Bible, 'cause Momma taught it to me. Dad was the same way, but Momma was closer to me in a way.

I grew up like other boys. I was tryin' to get away from them; but that was the awfulest thing I could do—try to run away. I'd get into somethin' every time. I'd get hurt or somethin' would happen to me. I'd find myself runnin' back there just like a little old lamb.

Well, I do appreciate it now. My parents taught me to be honest. That old lady would tell me, "Son, your behavior will get you where your money won't. Your money'll be counterfeited, but if you practice livin' a good life, you'll have a way when you get there."

My father was a minister in Macon, Mississippi, never fortunate enough to have a church large enough to furnish much finance. So, that required all the scufflin' that we could do to help him to get along.

As soon as I was about 8 or 9 years old, I would work for the different people in the little town, whatever I could do to bring in a little somethin' to the home. I would get to go to school part-time, not too much. I always saw that my sister would stay in school, 'cause I knew that someday she would appreciate an education.

I WAS BORN WITH A LOT OF DRIVE AND AMBITION. WHEN I GOT 17 years old, I were workin' then as a man. I was workin' for this old man, Asa Lever, drivin' a team of mules. This job was to haul wood to the light plant. They burned wood in those days.

He'd be out in the woods cuttin' it, and then I hauled it in and ricked it up at the light plant. He paid me $5 a week. That was 1912.

One day he said, "You know as hard and good a worker as you are, you'd be an awful good railroad Negro."

I said, "Is that right?"

He said, "Yeah." Well, he give me an idea.

I had some threats, too. I had some threats. Previous to workin' for Asa Lever, I'd worked for another one, name o' Charlie Bonds, for $2 a week.

When I drove into town that next Saturday after I quit at Bonds', I ran into this fella's son, Henry Bonds. He was a big stout guy—wanted to know why I leaved his dad. I told him, "I can get more money."

He said, "If you don't come back to Dad by Monday, we'll do away with you."

I knew what that meant. He and his brothers were gonna get me if I drove for Asa Lever on Monday. I didn't dare argue with him 'cause maybe he'd got me right then.

There was a recruiter, a fella by the name of Will Parlot, happened to be in town the same time. He'd grown up in Macon, then he went to Selmer, Tennessee, with the GM&O. He would come back and get men.

I got in touch with him. He explained what it was and what they paid, the livin' conditions and all. I was encouraged to go, because it were more than I were gettin'. So we left Sunday night for Selmer, Tennessee. I didn't go back to Macon for quite a little while, until I eventually went back as a recruiter.

Quite a few left to come into Tennessee. From there they'd go to St. Louis, Murphysboro, some to Detroit, in fact all over the East. None went as fast as I did though.

I was in danger of my life when I left Macon. It seemed like it was a period when white folks was angry. The Negroes were leavin' out, and they were leavin' out by numbers. They were comin' north because jobs were open. They may not have been the best, but they were far better than we had there.

They were very rough in that period. They beat up a lot of our people, left 'em out on the road. The flies got in some of 'em before the people found 'em. Just because they were tryin' to better their condition. It was awful rough in that time.

When they began to leave, if you owed these fellas a quarter, you daren't talk about leavin'. They'd say, "You owe me money." And they'd make it whatever they want to, and you dare not leave. So, I beat the rap by gettin' out of there that Sunday night.

The Neely family, DeKalb, Mississippi, ca. 1900 (The little girl in the center came to Beloit twenty-five years later and brought this photo with her)

Foundry workers in Fairbanks, Morse & Co., Beloit, Wisconsin, ca. 1925

I never made contact with the Bonds family. I never even had to swap words with 'em. I guess that's a blessin' from the Lord, 'cause he took care of me.

But I did know the outcome. The Bonds didn't get to be very old men. When I went back, one of those fellas was blind. The other son was crippled up—he couldn't walk. They were kind of a rude family. They didn't come out good. It didn't pay off.

I got acquainted with a foreman, Jim Raymond, in Selmer. After I learned the way around, I would go to the foreman or the roadmaster and ask for a book of passes. They'd give me as much as thirty-five—men I could bring back, you know. So, I was very successful, but I run into a problem back in Macon.

When I got to Macon, I told the fellas there was a man goin' to Meridian—course it were me, but that keep me in the clear—he had passes for thirty-five men. He'd pick 'em up if they would have a quarter to buy their ticket to Brookville, Mississippi, which were ten miles from Macon. Then this man had the passes—which were me—but I told 'em the man was goin' to Meridian. They took my word for it.

That night there was others there who had passes at this little old Jim Crow station waitin' to go to Brookville. There must have been forty or fifty men. Train gonna run at 12:30 to bring us out of there.

But about midnight that door swung open, and there were three great big red-faced guys—one was Mac Henry, a farmer, and another was Swans, and I can't remember the other. Now they had a bullwhip on their shoulder, and a rope, and each one a big gun. They said they gonna kill every so-and-so Negro they found that had a pass.

They searched us one by one. Got to me. Said, "Where you goin'?"

"Goin' to Selmer, Tennessee, sir."

"How in the hell you gonna get there?"

"Well, sir, my partner's goin' to Meridian. He got the pass for two of us. When he get back, he'll check me up here in Macon."

"You better be damn sure you're tellin' the truth. We gonna kill the son-of-a-bitch we find with a pass tonight."

"Yessir."

And they searched me, all but pulled off my shoe where the pass was. Had they pulled off my shoe, that would've been it for me.

And this Will Parlot, he in there the same night. One of 'em said, "Anybody here know Will Parlot?"

Will said, "No, sir!" And he swallowed that pass! Boy they wanted that fella that night.

IN 1922 I WENT BACK TO ILLINOIS, TO MURPHYSBORO. THAT'S WHEN I did most of my recruitin'. I didn't get into nothin' as serious then as the first time.

I was just like a little mole. I'd get in there, get a bunch, and get out. I had to use a little chicanery, I would say. Maybe a snake. You had to get through without gettin' caught. I had a pretty good hitch on it. I could do a good job now.

I'd get in there and I'd tell 'em that there's a man goin' to such-and-such with a pass. And I got the pass in the toe of my shoe. They wouldn't take that shoe off. But they'd search every part of you. Oh, my God. They'd turn down the cuffs of my pants.

They'd say, "Where ya gonna go? How ya gonna get there?"

I'd say, "I got a man gonna pick me up. He got a pass for two of us." Biggest lie I ever told, but I'd get away with it.

You got to know what language to use. You got to tell a little white lie.

You got to make a guy believe there's one thing, to get him you got to tell him the facts about it. I told the men there would be jobs for them in Tennessee and Murphysboro, Illinois. Now Murphysboro was a railroad center and there was quite a bit of work there for laborin' people. They hired all that would come.

But gettin' out of there with him, you got to find your own method to do that. 'Cause if he go tell somebody that Johnson's in here with a pass, that's all for you.

You got to tell him some kind of fairy tale about somebody gonna come from here or yonder, and he'll be there at a certain time. Don't ever let it be you! That's what I'm talkin' about. You got to tell a little fair lie! You never let it be you in person. You got to always have a dummy over there somewhere. You got to always figure out some way to keep yourself in the clear.

The minute they find out it's you, they may not get you this time, but maybe next trip they'll be all set for you. And they didn't care what they'd do to you. They'd just as soon kill you as see you come out alive, if you were takin' the Negroes out of there. It was pretty dangerous, but I got by.

I go all the way in on the GM&O Railroad. I just liked to ride anyway. I had a lot of fun on the trains.

Then maybe I'd go into Mobile. I'd loaf around all day. I'd walk up to a guy and say, "What do you do?" I'd question him—get all I can out of him.

Then I'd say, "I'll tell you what. There'll be a fella on that train. He'll pick you up." And I got him! I did that a lot of times. I'd pick up from one to ten and bring 'em in. I could never tell 'em it were me. But all the time I was goin' down there, I never did get trapped.

The white guy dare not go in there to recruit either. They'd kill him quicker than they would a rattlesnake. Damn Yankee comin' down here gettin' these niggers. No strange white man go to get nobody.

There was another thing. There was a number of people in Macon that I'd known all my life. They was farmers. Some of 'em had sons my age. All those fellas I was acquainted with. I would tell them a story about better conditions, they would believe it. Only thing they had to do, they couldn't dare tell those fellas they was gonna leave. They'd get in trouble. They'd do 'em some harm somehow.

Macon was a mean little town. I could tell you some things that didn't seem like human. There was some, they called 'em the mob crowd. Brother, them guys had blood in their eyes. There was Ku Klux I guess too, but these fellas was known as the mob crowd.

When you say, "The mob crowd will get you," that meant they comin' in for you. Shoot you full of holes. Burn your house or do anything to get you. Nothin' too bad for those fellas to do in those days.

I had experienced some pretty mean times, but it seemed that this time they were determined that the Negroes wouldn't leave. If they found a group thinkin' they was gonna leave, they were in danger. They might beat 'em up or even kill 'em. And that lasted a long time.

I recruited white people to work, too. It was the same. You still had to be a shadow or somethin'. Then you could check 'em on your pass. I didn't bring any of the whites out of Mississippi, but out of Kentucky and Tennessee.

I only got my regular money, $3 or $4 a day. Once in a while I'd get a little bonus. But all I was doin' was ridin', so that wasn't too bad.

I did it for the benefit of those fellas, if I could help them to get better. I risked my life to help somebody. I still do. If I can help somebody to have better conditions, I think he's entitled to it. If you don't help the people, maybe they'll never get an opportunity.

Well, I came the hard way. My past experiences have been pretty rough. But all the time I managed to have a clear glass of water, and one I could share with somebody else. Therefore, I'm very happy.

PART TWO
No More Moanin'
1929–1945

AS THE FIRST GENERATION OF SOUTHERN INDUSTRIAL WORKERS SETTLED into a new life-style and gradually lost contact with their agrarian past, Southern capitalists made fewer and fewer paternalistic efforts to attract and hold workers. Mill owners and other employers took advantage of the approaching Depression to exploit their employees to human limits and beyond; unable to survive on their own off the land, workers were forced to accept what the boss demanded in the factory —or revolt in desperation.

Perhaps the most shocking example of this economic blackmail occurred in the hills of West Virginia; the victims, as so often in American history, were almost all black. When the New Kanawha Power Company could convince no experienced local workers to build a tunnel through a mountain of silica at Gauley Bridge, the company imported black men from outside the county who knew nothing of the dangers of silicosis. Two thousand died within a few years of a disease that usually takes decades to kill. At the same time as the almost unimaginable massacre at Gauley Bridge, coal miners in Appalachia were suffering slow and tortured deaths in hazardous mines and company towns.

But rather than putting the last nail in the coffin of organized labor in the mountains, the work speedups and employment cutbacks of the 1930s initiated an era of rebellion. In a war that had begun in the mid-nineteenth century, coal miners again and again fought the owners in some of American labor's bloodiest battles, each a step toward the eventual formation in the 1930s of a solid United Mine Workers of America. The whole world knows of "Bloody Harlan," but miners in other counties and other states faced the same kinds of bosses and died defending the same principles.

America tried to ignore the workers at Davidson-Wilder, Harlan, and the other towns and camps that dotted the mountains, but the miners and their neighbors preserved history, both in their memories and in songs and stories generated by the heat of conflict. When company thugs murdered her father, 12-year-old Della Mae Graham wrote "The Ballad of Barney Graham" and traveled to Washington a week after the murder to raise money for the Davidson-Wilder strikers. Tom Lowry, a miner, put the strike to music in "Little David Blues." In Harlan, Florence Reece asked "Which Side Are You On?" in a song that continues to inspire activists in and out of the coalfields.

While the nation fumed at the supposed greed of John L. Lewis's miners, Russell Lee's 1946 photographs of Harlan prove that World War II had not eradicated poverty in the mountains. Despite their poverty, the spirit and warmth of the people remained strong, although the lure of jobs in Cincinnati, Detroit, Cleveland, and elsewhere pulled thousands out of their homes. Russell Lee stayed with Blaine and Rhoda Sergent during his visit to Harlan during the 1940s. When his   **65**

photographs appeared in *Southern Exposure* in 1976, the Sergents wrote us from Dayton, Ohio: "Me and my wife were raised in Harlan County, Ky. Left in August 9, 1960. It is a good place to be from, but a Hell of a place to go back to." In 1979, Blaine wrote:

My wife died May the 23, 1979. And I went back with her and buried her where me and her was raised up as children and in later years we were married at the Harlan County Court House on a Saturday, July the 31st. Few more days and we would have been married 39 yrs. . . . I am counting on leaving here [Dayton] just as quick as I hear from my Black lung. I draw $275.00 miners pension a month. But you can't live on that now days. But I guess I can make it, nobody but me now. And you could give me the world and everything in it, but nothing can take the place of my wife. . . . I will give you my address when I go to Harlan, Ky. For I won't be back here.

Historically, coal and textiles have been the two major Southern industries, but others have also found a home here—oil in Texas and Louisiana, steel in Alabama, automobiles in Atlanta—and workers from these industries made their contributions to the national struggles of organized labor. The Flint, Michigan, sit-down strike in 1937 is widely recognized as the opening of the CIO's drive to victory, but the path was actually prepared by General Motors workers in Atlanta, who sat down in December of 1936 and held out for three months while the fledgling UAW in Detroit got ready to join their fight against the automobile companies.

The wave of worker rebellion in the 1930s inspired Americans from other classes to join the fight for justice. Support groups, political organizations, and labor-oriented schools sprang up throughout the nation. In Virginia and then North Carolina, middle- and upper-class women established the Southern Summer School for Women Workers. Here, working-class women learned how to record and use their own life experiences toward leading class struggle. In teaching these valuable skills, the Southern Summer School provided one model for people outside the working class who want to make that struggle their own.

"No More Moanin' " ends where it begins—with the poorest, most-exploited workers in the South and the United States. The difference is that by the end of the Depression and the Second World War, many of these men and women had successfully organized themselves. In Arkansas, Mississippi, Alabama, and Louisiana the Southern Tenant Farmers' Union brought together thousands of agricultural workers in an interracial union whose line of descent extends into today's United Farm Workers. During the war, the inspiration and strength of the CIO, combined with a government desire for uninterrupted production, toppled several major industrial giants that had held out during the thirties. In 1943 black workers at Reynolds Tobacco took the initiative themselves, actually leading CIO organizers in a week-long strike which won a union.

As the Second World War ended, the labor movement in the South appeared to stand on solid ground. Unions existed to one degree or another in every major industry; and some, like the UMWA, had organized virtually an entire industry. Fifteen years of crisis in depression and war brought strength to working people in the South, and victory finally seemed within reach.

SEVEN

Massacre at Gauley Bridge

ERIC FRUMIN

THE HARDSHIPS OF THE GREAT
Depression are generally thought
of as simply widespread, intense
manifestations of the "ordinary"
evils always suffered by poor
people: unemployment, hunger,
loss of shelter. But in the first years
of the Depression—until the New
Deal provided some relief and
workers themselves organized to
fight back—America's industrial
giants had a free hand to exploit
the situation; characteristically,
some industries chose to operate
solely for profit, and the workers
be damned. For one group of
largely black workers in a tunnel
construction project in Gauley
Bridge, West Virginia, between
1930 and 1932, the results
amounted to damnation on earth—
under conditions later described as
"slave labor," "concentration
camp," and "genocide."

The company that employed
them was Rinehart and Dennis, a
large Virginia construction
contractor working for the New
Kanawha Power Company, a
subsidiary of Union Carbide. Union
Carbide established New Kanawha
Power to supply hydroelectric
power to another Union Carbide
subsidiary, the Electro-Metallurgical
Corporation, a metal refinery. New
Kanawha found it necessary to
divert water from the New River
by building a tunnel four miles long
through a mountain. In 1927 it
chose Rinehart and Dennis to do
the tunneling, thereby setting the
scene for one of the most
abhorrent tragedies in American
labor history.

Before building the tunnel, the

company did exploratory drilling to determine the content of the rock. Surprisingly, the rock turned out to be silica, in a purity of up to 99.4 percent. Since silica is an important and expensive constituent in metal-refining, plans for the tunnel width were increased from thirty-two to forty-six feet.

Silica is also famous for its harmful effects on human lungs. People who inhale sufficient quanties of the dust, usually over a period of years, develop silicosis, a seriously disabling, progressive condition which causes large scars to form in the lungs, reduces breathing capacity, and eventually suffocates its victims. The fatal process takes up to twenty years; the last two to five years are generally a period of total disability and great suffering. Silicosis was first recognized by Hippocrates in the fourth century B.C., and was quite familiar to coal miners in the vicinity of Gauley Bridge; it is fair to assume that Rinehart and Dennis engineers, who themselves used masks whenever they went into the heading to collect rock samples, knew the dangers of digging big tunnels through pure silica.

With construction ready to begin in 1930, the company sent out a call for workers. While there were many unemployed miners—about 75 percent white and the rest black—in the immediate area, the dust conditions in the tunnel were so bad that the miners who began working there either became ill much quicker than they had expected or knew enough about mining to sense that further work meant certain death.

Rinehart and Dennis needed workers who would accept the conditions, and they turned to inexperienced black workers from outside the county. According to the 1936 congressional testimony of Philippa Allen, a New York social worker who investigated the events there, the new workers were

poor, ignorant men with no standing in the community, and there was no friendly organization to which they could protest. . . . They had come in droves from states up and down the Atlantic seaboard, from Pennsylvania, Georgia, North Carolina, South Carolina, Florida, and from states as far inland as Alabama, Kentucky, Ohio. Most of them had been recruited by scouts of the company who went through the states giving glowing accounts of "steady work" in Fayette County. The steady stream of cheap labor enabled the company to reduce the hourly wage to a low of 25 cents.

George Robison, a black miner, described the conditions under which the men worked:

I went to work there on September 1, 1931, as a driller. I drilled on the bottom bench. The drilling there had to be day drilling, because otherwise they couldn't drill fast enough. It was at the head that they drilled with water. We put the holes from one to twenty feet, straight down. A fellow could drill three holes dry to one wet. . . . The boss was always telling us to hurry, hurry, hurry. When the rocks were in danger of falling at any time the foreman kept telling us that everything was all right and that we should keep right on. . . .

Me and my buddy drilled only four feet from two other fellows drilling, and those two fellows got killed by falling rock. They were only about four feet from me and my buddy. The boss himself was up there about the time, and he got tangled up with the equipment on the ground, and he saved himself only by retreating. The two fellows that had been drilling near me and my buddy never knew what hit them. They got crushed beyond recognition. . . .

When they would bring in water to drink, the dust would settle on top of it and one would have to drink that dust, too. When drilling, the hole would go straight down and the air would then force the air back into one's face. As dark as I am, when I came out of that tunnel in the mornings, if you had been in the tunnel too and had come out at my side, nobody could have told which was the white man.

Emma Jones, wife and mother of several white miners who had died from silicosis, gave this account of the treatment of the blacks: "They was treated worsen if they was mules. The foreman would cuss at them bad and run them ragged. He would run them right back into the powder smoke in the tunnel after a shot, instead of letting them wait thirty minutes like the white men do."

These horrors did not affect the plans or budgets of Rinehart and Dennis. But the company was amazed at the rapid appearance of the disease. Silicosis, they knew, usually took years to make itself felt, and a few more to kill. But these workers were dying on the job, or within months of quitting work. Philippa Allen told in her testimony of these deaths:

Almost as soon as work was begun in the tunnel the colored men began to die like flies, because the percentage of silica in the dust they inhaled was so large.

The ambulance was going day and night to the Coal Valley Hospital. As soon as a man died, they would bury him, we were told. One colored boy died at four o'clock in the afternoon and he was buried at five o'clock the same afternoon without being washed. Why? Because the company did not want an autopsy to be made, which autopsy would have uncovered the cause of his death. Had word of the terrible disease killing the men reached their ears, do you think they would have stayed on the job? The tunnel must be finished quick, quick, quick—we want our profits, profits, that was all that interested the company. We heard of cases where mothers took the clothing of their husband to bury their sons in.

Why do you think the contractors from Charlottesville, Virginia, dared not furnish their workers with safeguards of masks and wet drills? Because they thought they would finish the job and be out of the state before the men began to die. Silicosis usually takes ten to twenty years to develop in one's lungs. Lies [purchasing agent for the company] spoke for the company when he said to Hawkins, the assistant superintendent, "I knew they was going to kill these n———— within five years, but I didn't know they was going to kill them so quick."

By the time of the congressional hearing in 1936, 476 workers at Gauley Bridge had died from silicosis, and 1,500 more were dying fast.

The living conditions provided for the workers matched the working conditions. Allen described for the hearing what she and a local deputy sheriff, Horless Gibson, saw when they visited the places where the workers lived:

As high as twenty-five to thirty Negroes used to sleep in a shack no larger than ten by twelve feet. They were made of Jerryline stripping with a half a window in the side and a homemade door. There were two bunks stretched across the side of the room, and [Gibson] said, "I have observed as many as fifteen men piled in a heap on the bunk."

When we said we would like to talk to some of the men who had worked in the tunnel, Mr. Gibson called to a colored man who was passing, "Come here, George, and tell these ladies your story." We asked George how much rent he had paid for sleeping space in one of the boxlike hovels Mr. Gibson had described, and this is what he said: "Fifty cents a week. They furnished only a little old shack. We paid shack rent every Friday. There was nothing in the shack. The men had to buy bedclothes, coal, a stove. They used to bring old dynamite boxes up from the workings to set on. Men, women, and children were crowded up together. Some of the women were married, and some wasn't. Families had four, five other men sleeping on the bunks with them. . . . At first, we had to pay 25 cents a week for coal, then they raised it to 50 cents. Every year they raised it."

Every man who worked paid for coal, whether he used it or not. Wages were cut from the 50 cents an hour that men were paid in the beginning in 1930, to 40 cents and then to 30 cents an hour.

They had a shack rouster named McCloud, who carried a gun. He was a deputy sheriff licensed by Fayette County, the license having been given on recommendation of the New Kanawha Power Company, and every morning he went up to the shacks and made the men go to work. McCloud threatened to jail men who would not work. When George's partner in the drill had his head cut off by falling rock, George did not want to go back into the tunnel; therefore, Deputy Sheriff McCloud arrested him. . . .

In #1 camp for colored people McCloud ran a club for men, a place where they could drink and gamble. "It was a skin game," Mr. Gibson said. The cut for the house was 25 cents when betting on cards. He chased the "n————" in from the hills if he found them throwing dice and made them gamble in the clubhouse so that he would get a percentage of their winnings. He would take all their money away from them and give it back to the company.

What had become of McCloud, we asked. The religious people in Gauley Bridge complained about the gambling, and C. A. Conley, head sheriff of Fayette County, after he had warned McCloud several times to stop the gambling, went up and closed the clubhouse. He took McCloud's commission away from him at the same time.

Another black worker told the hearing of the same sorts of harassment:

The camps of the colored men were not close to the camps for the white men. If a colored man was sick and really couldn't go to work in the morning, he had to hide out before the shack rouster came around. That fellow had two pistols and a blackjack to force the men to go to work. He was a fat man and we called him what we called most of the other white men around there, "Cap."
We couldn't resist him. If we didn't go with him or go to work he would club us and make us go, and if we resisted him he would shoot us.

These abuses created veritable ghost towns, inhabited by workers and their families starving to death while the workers were waiting to die. In 1934, the Federal Emergency Relief Administration sent an investigator named Leon Brower to the village of Vanetta, West Virginia. Brower sent back a description of the town with a set of recommendations undoubtedly unique in the history of American social welfare activities:

Upon completion of the project in September 1932, Vanetta reverted to the status of an abandoned village. In 1932 there were 101 persons in residence, occupying 61 tumbledown hovels: 14 children, 44 adult females, and 43 adult males. Of the latter all but 10 have silicosis. Support for the community comes from the earnings of 15 of the males, but 14 of whom suffer from silicosis. Thirteen are engaged on a road-construction project eighteen miles away and are forced to walk to and from work, leaving them but five hours a day for labor. Moreover, many, because of their illness, must lay off work every other day and are frequently too weak to lift a sledgehammer.
Coupled with all these hardships is starvation. Relief has always been spasmodic and irregular, and more irregular than is warranted. Every family related the lack of food, and for days at a time during the last winter they had nothing to eat. One white person living in Vanetta kept many from starving. Many of the Negroes went to Gauley and begged for food and work. Several white families in Gauley contribute regularly to the support of some families. Clothing was always inadequate, and there were numerous cases of slightly frozen limbs; also several families were evicted during the winter, and nearly every family was served with eviction notices. . . .
It is inadvisable socially to keep a community of dying persons intact. Every means should be exerted to move these families, so that they may be in communities where they will be accepted, and where the wives and children will find adjustment easier.

Since West Virginia's workmen's compensation law did not then cover occupational diseases, the only recourse available to those workers who didn't die immediately was to sue Rinehart and Dennis for monetary damages. In 1933 several trials were held in the county seat of Fayetteville, West Virginia, but in each case one or two jurors refused to make an award to the workers. Finally, the company decided to settle the whole group of suits out of court for $130,000 (of which the lawyers would get at least $30,000). Fortunately for history if not for the workers, lawyer James Mason, who represented 96 of the 100 plaintiffs, exposed the corruption and obstruction of justice to congressional investigators and pointed the finger at Union Carbide's political power:

In May or June of 1933 I was called to Fayetteville, where these cases were tried, and told that a settlement had been reached. I asked the terms of the settlement and was advised that Rinehart & Dennis agreed to pay $130,000 in settlement of all the cases. I demurred, thinking the amount was not sufficient, and asked why the sum of $130,000 had been reached. I was told that such was the best figure Rinehart & Dennis had offered or would offer; it was the largest sum that could be obtained.

I refused to settle on behalf of my clients, and I was told that unless I did, all papers, all evidence, would be destroyed, and that, of course, meant a helpless situation so far as the clients I represented were concerned. I finally agreed to settle and releases were obtained and the cases were closed in August 1933.

In October 1933 I was advised that Rinehart & Dennis, the tunnel contractors, had paid some of the attorneys for the plaintiffs $20,000 in order to effect that settlement. I later found that there was a contract entered into between Mr. Perkins, then general manager of the Rinehart & Dennis Co., tunnel constractors, and two of the attorneys representing the plaintiffs under the terms of which contract Rinehart & Dennis agreed to pay the attorneys $20,000 for effecting the settlement.

In May 1934 that contract was a basis upon which to proceed, and I wrote to Mr. Falconer, president of the Rinehart & Dennis Co., tunnel constractors, Charlottesville, Va., and demanded an accounting of that money. I sent a copy of the letter to those representing the defendants and the attorneys who had received the $20,000. I received a letter from Falconer stating that the money had been paid in good faith. One of the two attorneys came to my office and stated that the money had been paid, and that he was in a position where he could raise half of the money that had been paid over, and if we would accept that, the money would be paid. In a few days he brought to us a check for $10,000, and that money was distributed to the clients who had participated in the settlement.

In the final settlement, black workers received from $80 to $250 each, and whites from $250 to $1,000.

Union Carbide took no responsibility for the slaughter and injustice it had countenanced, to the point of denying "that there had been a single death directly attributable to silicosis." They boasted to the *New*

York Times that "they were 'very proud of our safety record everywhere.'"

In December of 1935, after the *People's Press,* a small radical weekly in Chicago, exposed the Gauley Bridge massacre, a young socialist congressman from East Harlem, Vito Marcantonio, started an investigation by a subcommittee of the House Labor Committee. Unfortunately, the subcommittee did not have subpoena power, and the companies refused to testify. However, several miners, relatives, and friends did testify, including West Virginia Senator Rush Dew Holt.

Most newspapers imitated the reaction of the *New York Times* to the hearings. On January 28, 1936, after the completion of the subcommittee's hearings, the *Times* editorialized:

All this seems to be based on mountain gossip and an article in a Midwestern radical weekly. What the facts are will no doubt be brought out by the investigation. Meanwhile, the defense of the contractor . . . deserves as much publicity as the accusations. In the 30 months required to drive the tunnel, 165 [*sic*] laborers died. . . . Considering the number employed on the entire contract was 4,948 and that a total of 2,500 worked underground, the accident record is better than what engineers expected in tunnel work. The death rate is said to be less than half that of the county in which the tunnel lies.

A month later an article in the "Travel and Resorts" section of the *Times* commented:

It is hard to believe, as the tales from West Virginia have it, that 476 died of silicosis and that 1,500 are suffering from the disease. The casualty list is too high for a contract on which 4,948 were employed—2,500 underground—too high to be readily believed.

Time magazine blamed it all on the irresponsibility of a few leftists:

Some relicts won [their lawsuits]. Some derelicts won, too. Many lost or sued too late to accomplish anything for themselves. But as a result, West Virginia passed its silicosis compensation law, which in turn prompted the radical press to dig up the Gauley Bridge skeleton, to rattle its bones. . . .

[Gauley Bridge was an] unholy industrial condition from which the U.S. radical press last week was belatedly trying to distill national bitterness.

In 1935, additions to the West Virginia workmen's compensation laws were finally passed so that workers suffering from silicosis would receive protection. However, the workers from Gauley Bridge were completely excluded because of the statute of limitations and other technicalities. The congressional hearing brought publicity for the miners' cause, and not much else. The final House subcommittee report did denounce Rinehart and Dennis, characterizing the tragedy as "a condition that is hardly conceivable in a democratic government in the present century." Unfortunately, the whole committee refused to support Representative Marcantonio's call for full subpoena powers and a complete investigation. The companies got off scot-free. No one was ever prosecuted for murder or racism or genocide, because where workers are concerned—particularly black workers—these crimes were not illegal.

It is an open question whether conditions have changed significantly since 1936. Between 1954 and 1970, over 1,500 workers in New York State alone were awarded compensation for death or total disability due to silicosis. Those partially disabled were legally excluded from coverage, but would have added additional thousands if they had received compensation for their illnesses. In 1977, the Occupational Safety and Health Administration inspected the U.S. Steel Corporation's foundry in South Chicago and found silica levels twenty-one times the current (and woefully inadequate) standard for silica exposure. Seventeen out of sixty-eight workers examined were found by the government to have advanced, incurable cases of silicosis, and an additional sixteen were found to have suspected cases. The company announced its intention to close the foundry.

In 1979, the National Institute for Occupational Safety and Health revealed an additional thirty-one cases of confirmed silicosis among ninety-one workers at two other Illinois workplaces. Six had severe, complicated silicosis after having as little as two years exposure. However, the *New York Times,* on May 27, 1980, in an article entitled "Disease of Lungs Stirs New Concern," conceded the accuracy of the earlier statistics on the death toll at Gauley Bridge. It pointed out the continuing high incidence (30 percent) of fatal silicosis among sandblasters in the Gulf Coast oil-rig fabrication yards, and compared it with the situation in Great Britain, where silica has been outlawed in abrasive cleaning operations since 1949.

Finally, in 1972, the U.S. Secretary of Labor declared silica one of five national "target health hazards." Unfortunately, the federal bureaucracy took an additional three years to do the research necessary to even begin to set a standard under the Occupational Health and Safety Act of 1970 for workplace exposure. As of this writing, the U.S. Department of Labor has not even announced an intention to propose—much less finalize—a new, stringent regulation to protect silica-exposed workers.

And what about the special risks suffered by black workers in American industry today? In the steel industry, racist hiring practices put grossly disproportionate numbers of black workers in coking plant operations, particularly in the most hazardous jobs around the ovens. These workers are exposed to the highly cancerous coal-tar derivatives in the smoke from the ovens, and kept in those jobs by the now defunct departmental seniority system in the collective bargaining contract. As a result, black workers in coke plants have a lung cancer rate three times higher than that of white coke plant workers. In jobs on the "top side" of the ovens—the work site for one-fifth of the blacks but only one-thirtieth of the whites in the coke plants—the rate of lung cancer among black workers is eight times the rate for steelworkers in general.

In central North Carolina (including Winston-Salem), where black workers have suffered tremendous discrimination in all industries, but especially the tobacco industry, blacks have the highest rate of death due to skin cancer in the United States.

For notes on sources, see pages 371–72.

EIGHT

Strike at Davidson-Wilder, 1932-1933

BRENDA BELL
AND
FRAN ANSLEY

DAVIDSON AND WILDER IN 1932 were sizable mining camps of the Cumberland Plateau region of Tennessee. They were strung like beads on a string with two other camps, Crawford and Twinton, in a gorge ("the hollow") cut by the East Fork of the Obey River in Fentress and Overton counties.

The coal miners' strike on the Cumberland Plateau began in 1932. It was a long, hard, bloody strike, fought to preserve what was at that time the only recognized coal miners' union south of the Ohio River. It ended in the defeat of the union workers in 1933.

We first heard about the strike at Davidson-Wilder on a record by Hedy West. In the beginning, that was the only thing we had to go on. Later, we found that a few things were written about the strike. But primarily we have talked to many people who were involved in the strike: strikers and their families; people who left at the beginning of the strike and became farmers; outsiders; and scabs.

In the pages that follow, the people who were involved in the strike tell the story themselves. We tape-recorded our conversations with fourteen people, and we made notes about talks we had with about ten others. We have changed the names of the people who appear in the story except for those who are recognizable anyway from their position, or from something they did.* No one

*The people who appear in the story under their real names are the following: Commander Boyd, W. D. Boyer, Captain

77

asked us to hide their identities, but there were so many people mentioned, we knew we could never locate them all to ask their permission.

In putting the story together we didn't try to be "neutral." We believe that working people and poor people need to get together to gain a better living and a say over their own lives. So we felt on the side of the strikers when we began, and the things we learned since then have made us feel that way all the more. But even though we had our own point of view, we tried to get everybody's side of the story.

Sometimes, of course, people disagree on exactly what happened or what certain events meant. Especially people from Fentress County and nearby may disagree with some versions given here, or may know something else that's not told. We want to share with others what we have learned so far, as an encouragement to other people to try this way of learning history, and as a tribute to the people who shared their story with us.

BEFORE THE STRIKE, THREE MINES WERE BEING WORKED: BRIER HILL Collieries at Twin, owned by a New York company, which had already worked out an earlier mine at Crawford; a second at Davidson owned by the Patterson brothers, E. W. and Hubert; and the third and largest at Wilder, owned by the Nashville-based Fentress Coal and Coke Company. General manager W. D. Boyer and superintendent L. L. Shivers ran the Wilder mine.

The people who lived and worked in the mining camps, almost all native mountaineers, had until recently made their living by farming in the area and working in the timber woods or sawmills of the lumbering industry. Some had been coal miners in other places before.

I was something around 15 year old, the first work I done in the mines. I went to work chalk-eyeing* for another fellow for a dollar and a half a day and my board. . . . Worked seven months that way, then I got myself a room of my own and went to digging and getting so much a ton myself.

I went to school to the sixth grade. And then I went to carrying water up there around the tip. The war broke out . . . and the foreman come in and said, "How old are you?" I said, "I'm going on 17." I was big for my age. He

---

Crawford, Billy Garrett, Barney Graham, Della Mae Graham, Jack "Shorty" Green, Henry Horton, Myles Horton, Bill Jacobs, H. S. Johnson, Howard Kester, Governor McAllister, Pat Officer, E. W. Patterson, Hubert Patterson, L. L. Shivers, Dr. Alva Taylor, John William Thompson. All other names are fictitious.

*A "chalk-eye" helped a coal digger and usually got the lowest pay. Young boys often chalk-eyed for an older relative. We don't know the origin of the word.

said, "How old are you?" I said, "I'm going on 17." I was big for my age. He took me in the mines and I mashed my fingers half off on the tailchain. I was 13. I stayed in there from then on. I had a big old mule and I had to get somebody to help harness it. I couldn't reach up to it.

Used to, you'd go in the mines and take a place, a room neck, and you'd widen that out to forty feet wide, and you had that, that was your place. You set the timbers and you laid your track, and pushed your car in and pushed it out. And what coal you took out of that place, why, that was your living, that was all you made. If you didn't load any, you didn't make nothing. So if you made a living, you had to get in there and work, and work hard all day. There wasn't no stopping. If you could get cars, you didn't even take time to eat. I've went many a day, the only time I took a drink of water is when I put water in my lamp. I never touched my bucket all day. But if you didn't get cars, why you'd sit there worrying because you weren't going to make nothing.

Well, it was pretty rough. They didn't know nothing about safety and didn't care. We had two or three men burned up in explosions. We had a state mine inspector, but he turned his back when he saw some of the dangers. You was just on your own when you went in there. If it was going to cave in on you, go ahead and do it. Nobody cared. They'd hire farmers from around here to come in, when they first opened the mines. They didn't know anything about mining. They'd soon better learn if they lived long! The graveyard down there is full of men killed in the mines.

Miners were paid every two weeks. The company kept daily records of how much each man made, and if he ran out of money before payday, he could go to the company office and draw scrip (if he had any credit in his account, that is). Scrip was only good at the company store.

You see, if you had to buy groceries, you'd have to go to this office, and you'd tell them you wanted $2 or $3 in scrip and they'd give it. But you didn't dare overdraw, because if you did, you wouldn't get a penny. You were turned down. But if you made over that, if you had money coming to you, you could get it.

Most folks just had scrip all the time. Money, why I didn't see no money till I was 25 years old.

Before you got that money, the company had to have their take-outs on the first of every month—house rent, your coal, light bill, doctor bill. And they held that out whether or not you made anything. The miners had to buy their powder, their fuses, and everything, to shoot that coal down with.

The superintendent was the head man in town; his wife was the head woman in town. The foreman didn't have any status. It's like on a plantation, driving slaves. Everybody lived in shacks except the superintendent's family and they lived in a house. A company town.

Well, you take the company doctor back then, he would just as soon tell you coal dust was good for your lungs. And it wasn't bad for you if you got a leg broke! If he could set it, it was all right. You were just as good as you ever was. You take it at Wilder, the older kids raised there could have had black lung easy. You take sulphur smoke, over by the slate dumps and sulphur in it and it burning. You could hardly breathe in town back when I was a kid there. My wife's got a sister, and the doctors gave her medicine for black lung. She said it wasn't anything except breathing that old sulphur smoke. They lived close to the mines.

The mining camps, they didn't even have electricity. You couldn't buy a washing machine. And they washed on rub boards most of the time. No running water, you carried water.

The women, most of them, just went on about their business and let the men do what they wanted to do, and they stayed at home. At union meetings, the men would go, and the women didn't have anything in it—they stayed at home.

I don't see how miners' widows lived at all. Because their folks didn't make enough to make a living for theirselves, much less anybody else. My uncle died and he had two kids, and I don't know how she got by, she'd just come to our house for a while and go to her daddy's awhile, and finally she got married again. But a woman with a big bunch of kids, I don't see how she did it.

Well, women had a bunch of influence in the union more and more. Now, if a woman's strong for the union, why her husband will be strong. And if she's against it, it's hard for him to do anything. My wife was behind me all the way though.

MINERS AND THEIR FAMILIES HAD NEVER JUST SAT BACK WITHOUT trying to improve the conditions of their lives. Whenever times were good, miners pressed for a better share. During World War I coal was in great demand and the industry boomed. The War Labor Board supported the right of defense workers to have unions. So when many Southern miners went on strike in 1917, the government helped pressure the coal operators into an agreement which the Chattanooga *Labor World* called "the greatest victory ever won in any union coal field in this country." The miners won shorter hours, better pay, the right to a committee, and other things as well. In 1918 the United Mine Workers of America campaigned throughout eastern Kentucky and East Tennessee, signing up more and more mines under the new agreement. Wilder, Davidson, and Twinton were among them.

When we started organizing, I know the first time I joined the union, I was up in Twin City up beyond Davidson about two miles. They signed me up out under a bluff in the woods, hid out. It was in about '18, I guess.

It would crop up from somewhere or another. You had to keep it kind of secret till you got a majority. You just signed the card and you kept your mouth shut until you got enough men together. It'd be some union organizer, but he would start with the man he thought he could trust, that could work through the men. And that one, after he'd signed the card, maybe he'd work on his best friend to get him to sign a card, and just keep working that way until they got a majority of the men and then they'd call a meeting for to talk to the company and have a committee.

This first organization didn't last long, though. As soon as the war was over, the companies started trying to cheat on their agreement and cut corners wherever they could. In 1921 and 1922 depression hit the coal fields, and the unions lost many of the gains they had made. By 1924, coal companies felt strong enough to make their move:

So in '24, the company just shut down. We didn't come out on strike, it was just the company shut down in order to break the union. It lasted up till '25. Sometime in '25 we had to go back to what they called the 1917 scale, $3.20 a day for just ordinary labor.

I was married then and our first kid wasn't born, soon it would be. And they got an injunction against us and came and notified me we were going to have to move. And in about a month our kid would be born. I told them I wouldn't move until after we had that. And I didn't.

From 1924 till 1930 the miners in Wilder were without a union. To get a job, they had to sign a yellow-dog contract, swearing that they would never join a union or go out on strike. Conditions went from bad to worse.

If you belonged to the union, the law and the county officials and everybody was against you. There wasn't too many miners in the county, and we wasn't very popular in the county. They thought the work was good. They didn't understand the trading at the company store and not having a place for a garden. So we lost that strike.

It just kept gradually going down, down, down. The companies would keep fightin' us with West Kentucky, West Kentucky. That's all we could hear. West Kentucky would cut the prices on the coal, and they had to come cut us in order to compete with them. And so it was gettin' ridiculous.

The companies, squeezed by the Depression and engaged in cutthroat competition with other coal producers, cut the Davidson and

Wilder men's pay twice during this time. Soon the mines were only running two or three days a week. The miners were destitute.

In 1930 the company tried to cut the miners' wages a third time. The men decided they had to try to organize. And incredibly enough, with no other mine anywhere in UMW's District 19 organized, they

won contracts with the three companies in the hollow. This contract prevented the third cut.*

*District 19 of the United Mine Workers of America includes coal miners in Tennessee and eastern Kentucky.

The way we got it, we struck Twin and Davidson. Wilder was the biggest. So the men come on strike at Davidson and Twin. The policy committee decided we'd strike them two, and then go in and talk to the company at Wilder. We had a policy committee of fifteen men, five from each mining camp.

We worked together all over. We'd have meetings and decide on what to do. We struck them at twelve o'clock noon one day, and all the men come out. And I was the one selected to go and see the management, me and Ray Smith, another man on the committee. Ray was supposed to be the spokesman. He got in there and he couldn't talk to save his life. He agreed with the president of the company, and we come out and I told Ray, "Now we've got to face them other thirteen men up there when we go back, and you never have told him nothing." He said, "Well, you go in and tell him." I said, "All right, let's go back," because I wasn't wanting to go back up there and tell them fellows we hadn't told him nothing. I went back in and told the president we'd heard his side of the story, and that the miners had struck the two mines above there, and he'd either sign a contract with us, or we'd go on strike, one. "And if you want to do any business, then we'll talk the thing over. If you don't, why, there's nothing else to do only just close this one down."

So the president said, "We'll talk to you about the weather, and the date, but that's all." So I went back and told the committee if we'd wait a while, a week or two, maybe he would come around. So we went back to him again and told him what we thought. It would be a good idea for him to do it; we wouldn't try to even get a living out of it, but just get along till times got better and maybe we could get a raise later on. And he agreed to talk to us.

Why the men were able to get the contract is still something of a mystery. Fount Crabtree, who used to teach school in Wilder, wrote in 1937 that one of the mine officials told him that the management of the three mines had tried to get together and agree on a lockout, but that the agreement had broken down, and the miners were able to take advantage of the split. A striker told us that there was a union sympathizer close to the management who convinced them to sign.

The miners in the hollow worked for the next year under a contract. On July 8, 1932, that contract expired. Before it did, the Brier Hill Collieries at Twin signed again to renew it. But before the new contract had even begun, the company shut down indefinitely, saying it would try and wait out the bad times, throwing hundreds of men out of work. Meanwhile, the mines at Davidson and Wilder refused to sign unless the men would accept the cut in wages that they had fought off the year before.

The president of the union at Davidson explained it this way to a newspaper reporter from the Knoxville *News-Sentinel:*

We had a union contract, but it wasn't satisfactory because the company didn't live up to it. The contract was to expire July 8. Before that time a committee from each of the locals got together and decided on changes we would ask in the new contract that would take care of our grievances. We provided in that contract that miners wouldn't have to work knee-deep in water and would be paid for removing rock falls.

On July 8 our joint committee met with the operators and presented the contract. The operators turned it down flat and asked us to meet again the next day. We met and they offered a new contract that provided for a 20 percent wage cut.

We told them that we had bummed and begged for food, had run an aid truck every week, that some miners went into the mine without breakfast or lunch, worked all day, and then at the end of the day couldn't get a dollar to buy food with because the money earned was held back to pay for house rent and other expenses. We told them that we had to issue orders on our local treasury to buy things for the miners' families to live on, and we said that under such conditions we could not take a 20 percent wage cut.

The operators said that they had no other proposal, and they posted a notice at the mine that those who wanted to work at the wages offered could do so. Not a miner went to work, and the mines closed.

Other men remembered:

I think I was maybe making 36 cents a ton. Loading a whole ton for 36 cents. It was a tossup. You didn't know if you were going to win or starve to death. You was going to starve to death with work!

When they put on that last cut at Wilder, the mine foreman come in and told us they told him they was putting on a cut, and I said, "What are you trying to do, organize the mine?" He said, "I'm just passing the word on." And he give me 5 cents a ton, they cut 5 cents to a ton.

If the committee recommended a strike, they'd work weeks and months to avoid it. 'Cause it hurt us worse than it did anybody, the strike did. There wasn't anybody wanted a strike. But it was necessary. The union would be broken up if we just went back to work.

FOR THE REST OF THE SUMMER, THE MINES STAYED DOWN. SUMMER was a slack season anyway, and the miners just waited, hoping that the companies would come around, but knowing that probably they would try to reopen the mines with scabs. Sure enough, in October, the Fentress Coal and Coke Company in Wilder announced that they would reopen on a nonunion basis. Boyer, the general manager, told a newspaper reporter: "We offered them a union contract at a 20 percent cut in wages. They refused. Now we won't have anything to do with the union. We tried it out a year and it didn't work."

Wilder was tense before the reopening. At first the company could find almost no one willing to work, as most people either sympathized with the striking miners or were afraid of them. But gradually they were able to find more men who would go to work.

When the company saw the miners weren't going back, they scraped the hills and hollers and took farmers out of potato patches and put them to work in the mines.

Chalked signs had appeared on train cars around Wilder before the mines reopened. One read: "No scabbing—but there may be blood and lives. We understand the mine company is to fire up. We will make it so damn smoky that they can't see to fire up."

About a week after the mines at Wilder opened, the Patterson brothers at Davidson followed the lead of the Fentress Coal and Coke Company. They posted a notice that they would reopen in a matter of days. That night their $20,000 tipple burned to the ground. They postponed opening.

Before long though, back in Wilder, the company had managed to accumulate enough coal to be hauled away. On November 15, a train pulled out of Wilder carrying the first load of coal to leave the county since July 8, the day the miners first walked out. The following day one end of a steel railroad bridge, over which that train had traveled, was destroyed by dynamite. At that point Tennessee Governor Henry Horton ordered in the National Guard.

The company had pressured the governor to take this step. They had circulated a petition in the county in an attempt to obscure the fact that practically all the miners backed the strike demands. Superintendent Shivers said, "In asking the Governor for troops, the people were only expressing the desire to protect themselves until a handful of radicals were finally disbanded."

During the next seven months, until the following June, the hollow was the scene of much violence. Strikers and scabs alike were shot at, wounded, or killed; company property was damaged, as was some people's personal property. There was then, and is now, a lot of disagreement as to who did what. For instance, whenever any piece of company property was destroyed, the company and the law immediately blamed it on the strikers. Union leaders, however, often told a different story. The president of the local at Wilder told a news reporter:

I know that the bridges were burned and blown up after the coal had been taken out. If some of the disgruntled miners were going to do such a thing, it seems to me they would have done it before, not after, the coal had been taken out.

I also know that after the mine's substation was blown up, they got out bloodhounds, and the dogs tracked down two strikebreakers. I don't know why strikebreakers should do such a thing unless they were working with the company's private guards. You know these guards get $5 a night, and when the trouble dies down they lose their jobs. So it's up to them to keep the trouble going.

Some others thought that it was union men who did at least some of the damage. And they thought there was a good reason for it:

They went to blowing up bridges, railroad bridges, because they were hauling out coal, you know. The union people did it. And they'd blow them piers out from under the railroad so they couldn't haul any coal. They slipped in the mines and blowed up fans inside the coal mines.

Every time there would be some scab shot at, or blowing up coal trains, or beating up scabs, or that kind of thing, they'd say "the ganders" did it. You know: "I don't know anything about it. I was in the potato patch." "Well, who do you think did it?" "I don't know. I think the ganders did it."

It was nerve-racking for everybody. Even the ones working.

My children would be playing marbles out in the front yard and the bullets would be whizzing over them. Shooting at somebody going up the little hill right out on the road, you wouldn't know who it was. And them bullets would just whiz.

On a Sunday night, I believe it was, I never heard such a blast go off and all, and I just felt so sad over it. I didn't know who'd done it or nothing about it, and I think they'd blowed up some of the front of the mines, wasn't it? But we don't know who done it, or nothing. But what I worried about, didn't make no difference if he was a scab or whatnot, I didn't want nobody killed.

They [the National Guard] had orders not to take sides, to try to keep peace, but I wouldn't doubt but that they took sides.

People were glad that they sent the militia. They thought that they would have peace if they brought them. But it seems to me like it made it worse.

Troops remained in the hollow through the better part of the winter, but they were the least of the strikers' worries. Pretty soon the company got the county court to grant an injunction against the strikers. This injunction said that 104 men specifically named could be arrested for being on company property, for having a picket line, or for eight other offenses including "jeering or sneering" at scabs.

Soon after the injunction they began using another tactic that was common enough in the coal fields: they hired what the miners called "gun thugs," had them deputized, and set them to guarding the mines.

Oh, they got them anywhere they could get them. In '24 I know of one of them they got out of the penitentiary.

Jack Green was the head thug of the strike. He never worked in the mines a day in his life, and nobody knew where he was from or what he had done or anything. He had a good education. He'd never done nothing in that county except bootleg and make whiskey. He had killed a few men in the county, I guess a lot of men in the United States. And he was tough, so they put him in as the head of it. He kept all the guards and the thugs keyed up with moonshine.

I've heard one of the thugs tell about how a man jumped into the air when he shot him. "Jumped high as a brush pile," he said, "and fell as pretty as ever you saw."

I didn't feel too bad about the men that had gone back to work, 'cause I knowed what they'd been through. But these that come on in, now them was the real ones—like Shorty Green and the thugs. Just working, that was all right, that wasn't so bad, but trying to kill everybody else because they didn't go back to work . . .

In the strike, the thugs would get paid $5 a day for guarding and stuff like that. And free whiskey, free drinks. That was a whole lot of money then.

The company tried dozens of harassing tactics during the course of the strike. They tried to evict strikers' families, but the union men fought that one and won. Once they took the electric lights out of the homes of thirty-three strike leaders. Sometimes they tried to bribe people. One man told us they had tried this on him the first time in 1931:

The general manager told me one time, that was when we made that contract, "Now you're getting $5 a month from the union, and you worked harder for the union than Shivers did for me, and I paid him $250 a month, furnished his house. If you'll work for me like that, I'll have your pocket full of money all the time." I said, "When I get ready to be sold, I'll get on a block and let them bid on me, and let the highest bidder get me. Some of them might pay more than you would."

When bribery wouldn't work, the companies sometimes tried framing people:

One day Captain Crawford told me that somebody fired at some of the guards up there. I had an old gun. It was used in the Spanish-American War. It shot a great big bullet, a .4570. And he said somebody shot at one of the boys last night with a .4570. I said, "How did you know it was a .4570?" He said, "Well, it hit a bracket on a light pole." It was glass, you know, and he could tell what size bullet it was! [*Laughing*] Hit glass—as if you could tell anything from that! So I just got shut of the gun. I knew what they was up to.

The companies also tried to keep people in the camps cut off from the outside. If outsiders did get to Wilder, then the company tried to keep them from hearing the miners' side. Captain Crawford said that newspaper reporters should come only to him to find out what was going on. Myles Horton, from the Highlander Folk School, was trying to organize support for the strikers. The first day Horton went into the hollow, he found this out about Crawford the hard way:

I went over and I started talking to some strikers, you know, like I'd do anywhere. They told me they weren't getting any relief, Red Cross stuff was going to the scabs. So I checked it out with a bunch of people around, asked how the National Guard was treating them, and women said they were always shooting around and they were afraid they were going to kill their kids.

So, I talked to them awhile, convinced them I was on the level, told them about Highlander. They believed me. I told them what I wanted, asked them to send somebody with me to talk to some of the people. So they did. That way they could keep tabs on me and at the same time help me out. There was a bus that left about four o'clock, and I was going to take that bus back to Crossville.

I think I was on my way to the bus, and by that time the grapevine had not only worked its way to the miners but to the National Guard, and they had seen me going around talking to the miners and had decided, I guess, that I was a dangerous person. The head of the National Guard, Boyd from Cleveland, was away. But they stopped me and asked me where I was going. I told them I was going down to catch the bus. They said, "Well, you're under arrest." I said, "What?! Under arrest for what?" They said, "You're just under arrest." They had their bayonets all punching me, and I knew damn well I was under arrest. They were just young kids, you know, and they'd like nothing better than to push hard, and I didn't want any of those damn bayonets in me. I was just surrounded. I said, "But you have to have a charge, you can't just arrest somebody. You have to say what you arrest them for." And they muttered among themselves, they hadn't figured that out. One of the guys said, "You're under arrest for coming in here and getting information and going back and teaching it." So they knew what I was doing, they knew about Highlander. They were from Cleveland, so they knew about Highlander, and they thought Highlander was the hotbed of communism, you know, dangerous place. And here was a big conspirator here in their midst and they were going to be great patriots and arrest him.

They said when Colonel Boyd comes in they were going to turn me over to him. So they took me down to the Shivers's house, a big fine—it had kind of a club atmosphere. I think it was a company house, but they lived there. The Shiverses weren't there; it was the headquarters of the National Guard then. At night they had a big fire and they had some good books there, and a big comfortable chair. So they brought me in and nobody was there. So they said, "You wait here," and they put guards around me. I looked around and I found a book, so I settled down in front of the fire in the comfortable chair and I started reading. There wasn't anything else I could do, I couldn't run away.

Then it started raining, just pouring down rain. And they got fidgety. Boyd hadn't gotten back; it was ten o'clock and Boyd wasn't back. They kept looking at me; I was the only one that was comfortable. So Boyd came in, and they told him. He said, "Oh my God, you shouldn't have done that." So he came up and he said, "This is a mistake, you aren't under arrest." I said, "It certainly was a mistake, but I'm under arrest. When people point bayonets in your belly and tell you you're under arrest—you're under arrest. They've been sitting here guarding me all this time." He said, "Well, you look pretty comfortable." I said, "I am comfortable. I made myself at home. I've been sitting here reading. I couldn't catch my bus." He said, "Well, it's all a mistake. I apologize. You can go." I said, "Go? Go where? It's raining. I'm not going anywhere. There are no buses. I haven't got anyplace to go. I'm not going to get out in this rain." He said, "But you can't stay here." I said, "I'm not going to go out in this rain. I've been forcibly detained, and whether I was under arrest properly or not, I was under arrest, and I'M NOT GOING TO LEAVE." He said, "There's a little hotel down the way." "Yeah, but that's a quarter of a mile away. That's your problem. I would have been gone." He said, "We'll pay for your room and everything." I said, "I appreciate that but I'm not going to go out in this rain. I don't have any other clothes to wear, and I don't want to get wet. I'll just stay here. I'll sleep on that couch." "No, you can't stay here. This is our headquarters."

So he called a little huddle. Now the railroad track ran right to the back door or the front door of the hotel—right to the edge of the porch. And he made a couple of these cusses that arrested me, or some others just like them, get out on a handcar and hold an umbrella over me, and they got out and pumped the handcar up to the hotel and took me in. I knew I had him, because he knew that I would expose it, he knew I'd publicize it, and he was really concerned. That's why he didn't push me around. I knew when he came he'd be upset.

THE COMPANY HOPED THAT THE FEAR AND THE ISOLATION AND THE plain hunger would starve the union out. The miners fought back with everything they had—which wasn't much. Even before the strike, the union had run an "aid truck" around the surrounding farm country, begging for food for the miners. When the strike came, they needed it all the more.

They run a commodity truck for a while. They'd go through the country and pick up food, you know, and deliver it to the people that didn't have no work or nothing like that. They'd have potatoes and cabbage and all kinds of such food. Flour and lard and meal. Meat. It might do you for a week or two at a time that way.

People all over this country give us loads of potatoes. They were in sympathy with us. They knowed we was just nearly on starvation. Well, we was. You just couldn't get nothing to eat.

I don't know what to tell! [*Laughs*] There were some people got hungry. I know sometimes that the last bite we had was cooked and put on the table and eat. No job, no money, nothing. But somehow or another when the next mealtime came, we had something to eat. It weren't no steak and stuff like that.

I'd go with my wife and the other women, picking wild sallet. I believe, I'll say to the boys, I believe every kind of weed that grows makes good sallet. This woman would say, "This weed makes good sallet, but you've got to mix it with something else." And another one would say, "This makes good sallet, but you've got to mix something else with it." So about every weed that grows makes good sallet, but you've got to mix something else with it! [*Laughs*] It was something to fill up the empty places. And we survived on it.

There was a bunch of men who stole for other people's use, from people who were fighting the union or from a store that wouldn't give credit. Then they would put the stuff on the porches of needy union families.

They had a bunch down there in that holler called the Meat Committee. They'd get out and kill a man's cow or hog, and all the strikers would get up the next morning and there'd be a mess of meat at their door. They'd divide it up with everybody. And anybody that had a big corn patch or anything, you'd go out and get roasting ears, and there'd be a big pile of roasting ears on the porch.

It wasn't that the men didn't want to work. They would have jumped at the chance. Some of the union men managed to get jobs with the state working on the roads, though it was never full-time. Some tried to get work at neighboring coal mines but found that they were blacklisted.

Now I went over there at Petros to look for a job, and they told my daddy-in-law if I stayed all night down there that he'd lose his job, and I walked all the way from Petros plumb through Wartburg, and camped out under that old bridge over there, and then walked into Monterey and took back down this railroad, and walked twenty-one miles to Davidson, and I was just about dead.

I went to work making whiskey! [*Laughs*] It's hard work. You could pack yourself to death, but I was young then, I could take it. I couldn't wrassle no barrel in the woods now! I'll tell you the truth, girls, I believe I made as good a whiskey as I ever drunk in my life.

People found many ways of battling the hunger and of surviving the threats and violence, too:

Our kids slept on the floor. 'Cause they would shoot through the house a lot of times. We'd take the springs and the mattress off the beds and put it on the floor, so they'd shoot over them.

But at the same time that each striker's family was fighting to defend itself and simply to survive, the miners were organizing to try and beat the companies together. They didn't have to try to solve all their problems individually. They had a Policy Committee.

It had been the Policy Committee that originally recommended strike rather than taking a 20 percent cut in wages, and it was the Policy Committee that was responsible for leading the strike. Along with the Policy Committee, each local met regularly.

The union members had confidence in the Policy Committee. Five from each camp. We'd get together in twenty-five minutes, any time day or night. There'd be runners going from each man's house. And any striker that wanted to come to the Policy Committee would meet so and so at a certain time, and they'd go. Night or day. We had the best-organized people; I bet they don't have any now. I mean everybody was together. But it was so long. And we didn't have anything to start on.

The president of the local and the head of the mine committee, they was on the Policy Committee. And then they elected two others. The mine committee was the bunch that'd take up any grievance.

We had a regular meeting out at the Davidson schoolhouse about once a week. And Wilder had one down there. All of us had a meeting place, and sometimes they all met at Wilder, or all met at Davidson. We've had so many people down there in that holler a time or two that we could hardly get them in there.

Supposedly the Policy Committee and the three locals had the backing, help, and good advice of their union, District 19 of the UMW of A. But the UMW itself was in a rough period. It had few resources and had come under vicious attack in Harlan, Kentucky, a fact that Tennessee miners were very aware of. But in Harlan when the going got too rough, the UMW had pulled out. (It was the communist-led National Miners Union that stayed and tried to win the fight.) And many Wilder miners felt that the UMW didn't stand by them in Tennessee the way it should have either.

Ben Williams was the field worker then, and Turnblazer* sponsored it. They come in and met with the Policy Committee.

They didn't help us—they didn't turn their hand. All they done over there was make a speech. They said, "Stay in the boat, fellows. We're going to win." That's what they'd tell us—stay in the boat. They didn't care, the big guys, the organizers.

---

*William Turnblazer, then president of District 19 and the father of the William Turnblazer who was later president of that same district and who was implicated in the murder of Jock Yablonski.

We asked them what was happening to that money we were paying in there for the last four or five years. It was supposed to be in the treasury. They said it went into international dues money. And they didn't offer to buy anything or do anything to help us. Just told us to take that $400 and buy a truck.

Of course, the Mine Workers were very weak; they didn't have no treasury built up then, and they didn't have nobody to help them strikers, and they just had to do the best they could.

But with what small backing they did have, the Policy Committee tried to find support for the men and settle the strike.

Members of the Policy Committee had a lot more contact with and knowledge of outside supporters than most of the rank-and-file miners. They worked with a "Wilder Emergency Relief Committee" that was formed by socialists and others in Nashville to bring food and clothing into the hollow. They also worked some with Myles Horton and others from the Highlander Folk School, though they weren't always sure how they felt about this connection with people who were labeled as radicals.

Well, we met some of the people from Highlander. They tried to give us some publicity for the mines. I don't know whether it helped or hurt. Their intentions were good, I would say at that time. And the things they was for was good, but it hurt us, because they had a background that the majority of the people didn't agree with. They felt like it was somewhat on the red side.

As the strike wore on into the late winter and early spring, the company's tactics began to take their toll. More and more miners began trickling back to work:

You know, there's one of the best bunch of union men ever been in the country here at Davidson, but we did go to work. We was forced to. We didn't have nothing to eat. We stayed out as long as we could bum anything. We went just as far as we could go without starving plumb to death.

There were some people who went back to work, people they called scabs. But there's two sides to anything. Just like, I don't blame no man for taking care of his family. I just had one child, we raised a garden, we owned our own house, and we didn't have no rent to pay or nothing like that. And there's other families there that had eight or ten kids (them miners, they had to raise big families), and some of them had seven or eight kids. I don't blame them for not letting their kids go hungry.

There are a lot of real good union men that worked, went to work at the last, because it was just too, well, they lived in a company house, they seen the mines were going to be scabbed anyway, so they just went to work. Couldn't make a living, but they could live there, in a company house.

ONE MAN, ESPECIALLY, SEEMED TO STAND FOR THE SPIRIT OF DETER-mination among those who still wanted to fight until they won. That man was Barney Graham, the president of the union local at Wilder. Barney had come to the hollow in the twenties, some say from Alabama, others say Kentucky.

Well, I think he was a pretty good union leader. What I mean, what he was in for, he stood for it. Now he was in to try to get the men more to live on. I don't think he'd do anything unless you tried to hurt him. He was high-tempered, all right, but unless you raised a ruckus with him, I don't think he'd bother anybody. But he was high-tempered.

Barney Graham died for the union. He wasn't afraid of anybody, and anybody that'd try to run over him, because he was actually one of the union leaders. He wasn't a man that got up there and talked and abused someone else. He didn't have too much to say. There's a lot of people that were afraid —the companies were afraid of him, and they hired him killed.

Just a regular mob—just mobbed him. Blood just a-running in the road where they killed him. They said they were on top of the storehouse building with a machine gun and killed him. And the blood now was just a-running in the road. I seen it myself. They had gun thugs there that was working for the company. And they were wanting to get shut of Barney. He was president of the local and they figured if they got shut of him, that would put us all back to work.

A bunch of us was watching our houses that night. We was expecting thugs to come through. They'd shot in a fellow's house a little bit before that—the stove was hot and the bullets, lead bullets, would just hit the stove and stick on it. So we was kind of watching our houses then. And we heard the shots where they killed Barney. It sounded like a machine gun except there was some big guns and different sizes. So we figured about that time Barney was going home, and we went over there and John William Thompson—he was one of the thugs—had a machine gun, and he waved it at us to stop. I told Ed and Melvin to not put their hands about their pockets. And so we went on up to where Barney was shot. And his gun laying under him. He'd managed to get his gun out. He was shot. He had eleven bullet holes in him, with his brains leaking in three places. And there was a gun there with the handles off of it where they had beat him.

We asked who killed him, and Thompson said he didn't know, there was so many shooting. And I said, "Well, we'll just let him lay here till we find out. 'Cause he's dead, so we'll just let him stay here till we find out." He said, "There ain't no use in starting anything." I told him we wasn't starting anything, they had started it. So he talked to somebody and he come back and said, "The man that killed him is in the office. He won't talk to you, but he'll talk to Ed and Melvin." We decided to let them go on down there. And Green told them he killed him. Self-defense! That Barney was standing up fighting when he shot him the last time! And him with his brains leaking in three places.

Myles Horton recalled:

We told Barney he was going to get killed. I told him who these people were and that they were brought in to kill him. He knew they were going to kill him.

He was that tough kind that wouldn't quit, you know. So I went to work to try to get pressure to expose this before it happened, thinking that might bring enough pressure on the company and on public opinion that it might save his life. And that's when I tried—tried everything I could, put everything in the paper, the names of these guys, their history, said they were going to kill Barney Graham, and I couldn't move anybody.

That just killed me. That just killed me. That kind of thing is a traumatic experience, I tell you. You get involved with death of people, know it's going to happen, and you can't do anything about it. Society's so cruel. If I hadn't already been a radical, that would have made me a radical right then. Didn't do anything to make me less radical, I'll tell you that.

Nearly a thousand people attended Barney's funeral. Six hundred were in the march that went from Highland Junction to Wilder to the spot where Barney was killed and back again. The speakers at the funeral were William Turnblazer, president of UMW District 19; Howard Kester, head of the Wilder Emergency Relief, who had run for senator on the Socialist Party ticket the fall before; and H. S. Johnson, a union coal miner and Methodist minister. The Nashville *Labor Advocate* reported their speeches at the funeral. Kester said:

I knew Barney Graham intimately. I had no better friend. I loved him as a brother, not alone for his own worth, but for his place in the leadership of America's toiling millions. Those who say that Barney was a "bad man" never knew him. Barney Graham was a true son of the mountains, straight, fearless, and honorable in his dealings with men. He never hunted trouble and when possible went out of his way to avoid it. He never thought of his own comfort. When his family was in desperate need of food and clothing, I have known Barney to refuse all aid and to give it to others who he thought needed it worse than he did. I could not keep him clothed because he gave away whatever clothing I gave him.

Meanwhile, Shorty Green was loose on $2,000 bail, with Bully Garrett, the company lawyer, by his side. The trial was in September. The UMW had been promising to send down a good lawyer to handle the case. Two days before the trial, Turnblazer had assured the union miners over the phone that someone would be there. The lawyer never showed up.

They tried Shorty Green out here for that killing. Of course, the company had the money and politics all mixed up in it—you know how it works—and they got out of it.

It was a sick sort of a trial, and of course it was a farce. Bully was a big ol' fat guy; I hated his guts.

Shorty Green had plenty of witnesses. He could have proved anything he wanted to. He proved in court that Barney was standing up fighting when he hit him in the head the last time. Our lawyer told them, "Why, an elephant couldn't have stood up under that." Brains leaking in three places. A .45 bullet going through his lung, besides ten other bullet holes. But it went through. We didn't have no witnesses there at all. Of course the whole thing was set up, the witnesses and everything.

When Barney was killed, that broke the strike. They didn't get scared, they just . . . you know, their leader was gone. They had to go back and get them somebody else they thought would be trustworthy.

It was lost before they ever killed that man. That man was killed for . . . I don't know why. Because two-thirds of the men were working and the others were just on the verge of starving. Most of them was getting just anything they could find to steal.

THAT FALL STRIKE LEADERS AND SUPPORTERS TURNED THEIR ATTENTION to trying to find jobs for those men who were still holding out.

Eventually, through the efforts of union people, politicians, Highlander staffers, and sympathetic agency people, jobs were found for practically all the union men who wanted them. Some went as laborers to work on Norris Dam, first dam in the TVA system. Others went to the Cumberland Homestead, a federal resettlement project designed to put poor people on subsistence farms, where they built their own homes and tried to develop cooperative industry. The younger men went into the manual labor camps of the Civilian Conservation Corps. How these jobs were found and how the mining families reacted to their new situations is a story in itself. For the strike at Davidson-Wilder, it meant that most of the remaining leadership found ways to leave. They had decided there was no hope of winning.

Ben Williams, our organizer, come in here. Up at Highland he made a little talk. "Boys," he said, "I'll tell you. If you can get jobs, you better just get them, for this union is shot all to hell." That's the way he spoke it.

Ben Williams, he said, "We'll come back again one day." Which they did. This whole holler went union when these mines finally got organized in the forties. And Monterey, too.

But mining is not what it was in Fentress County. Union success in the forties, too, is long ago now. Since then, working and retired miners have watched many things happen to their union. Many of them complained to us about favoritism in the handling of pensions, about men having their hospital cards taken away, and about corruption in the leadership. But most of them still get the UMW *Journal* and are following with interest the progress of the union under Arnold Miller and Sam Church.

There are no more deep mines in the hollow now. They were worked out long ago. There are some truck mines hauling coal stripped off the steep mountainsides. There are small settlements at Davidson, Twin, and Crawford, and at Davidson there is a friendly and thriving community cooperative store. But at Wilder—as in so many old mining camps in the mountains—there is nothing at all.

People come through here now and they can't believe it when we tell them there was a whole town down there. There was thousands of people there. They had streetlights and everything. If people never saw it then, they don't believe it.

The railroad come through here in 1900. We lived down that road in a log house behind the schoolhouse. I stood in the door watching them lay that track. In 1970 we sat here and watched them take that track up. I seen the first train go in and the last one go out.

The young folks don't stay around here anymore. They leave, hunting jobs.

I've worried a lot about my kids, if another depression comes. What they'd do. 'Cause a lot of them wouldn't know how to even make a garden.

Children, I'll just tell you, you don't know what you're going to go through with in life, nor what you're going to have to put up with. You sure don't. But this is the awfulest times I've ever experienced. We ain't fighting war, we're fighting everything! We're fighting starvation, and we're fighting all nations, and everything else. Back in the Depression, people was honestly living good to what they're living now. They've got plenty of money and plenty to eat and plenty of everything, but look at the crimes and everything that's going on. The United States is in the worse shape it's been in my history. If anybody would have swore, I wouldn't have believed it. I wouldn't, really and truly.

Yeah, my children don't like to talk about it or even think about it.They like to forget those times. But, anyway, I'm kind of proud of it, that I went through it, and helped them out a little.

For notes on sources, see pages 372–73.

NINE

Davidson-Wilder Blues

ED DAVIS

MR. SHIVERS SAID IF WE'D BLOCK OUR COAL
He'd run four days a week.
And there's no reason we shouldn't run six,
We're loadin' it so darn cheap.
It's the worst old blues I ever had.

CHORUS:
I've got the blues,
I've shore-God got 'em bad.
I've got the blues,
The worst I've ever had!
It must be the blues
Of the Davidson-Wilder scabs.

He discharged Horace Hood
And told him he had no job;
Then he wouldn't let Thomas Shepherd couple
Because he wouldn't take the other
     fellow's job.

Mr. Shivers he's an Alabama man,
He came to Tennessee;
He put on two of his yeller-dog cuts,
But he failed to put on three.

Mr. Shivers, he goes to Davidson,
From Davidson on to Twin;
And then goes back to Wilder
And then he'd cut again.

Mr. Shivers told Mr. Boyer,
He said, "I know just what we'll do;
We'll get the names of the union men
And fire the whole durn crew."

We paid no attention to his firing,
And went on just the same;
And organized the holler
In L. L. Shivers' name.

Mr. Shivers, he told the committeemen,
He said, "Boys, I'll treat you right."
He said, "I know you're good union men,
And first class Campbellites.*"

*Members of the Christian Church (Disciples of Christ),
founded in 1810 by Thomas and Alexander Campbell,
or members of the Church of Christ, a group that
separated from the Disciples of Christ in 1906. **99**

I felt just like a cross-breed
Between the devil and a hog;
And that
And that's about all I could call
  myself
If I sign that yeller-dog.

There's a few things right here in
  town
I never did think was right;
For a man to be a yeller-dog scab
And a first-class Campbellite.

There's a few officers here in town
And never let a lawbreaker slip;
They carried their guns when scabbing
  began
Till the hide come off their hips.

Phlem Bolls organized the holler
About a hundred strong;
And stopped L. L. Shivers
From putting the third cut on.

Mr. Shivers got rid of his nigger,
And a white man took his place;
And if you want me to tell you what
  I think of that,
It's a shame and a damned disgrace.

Dick Stultz is for the union men,
And Bully Garret against us all;
Dick kicked Bully in the stomach,
And you'd oughta heered Bully
  squall.

Paw Evans has got a 'tater patch,
Away out on the farm;
Alek Sells guards that 'tater
  patch
With a gun as long as your arm.

I'd rather be a yeller-dog scab
In a union man's back yard,
Than to tote a gun for L. L. Shivers,
And to be a National Guard.

TEN

The Ballad of Barney Graham

DELLA MAE GRAHAM

ON APRIL THE THIRTIETH,
In 1933,
Upon the streets of Wilder
They shot him, brave and free.

They shot my darling father,
He fell upon the ground;
'Twas in the back they shot him;
The blood came streaming down.

They took the pistol handles
And beat him on the head;
The hired gunmen beat him
Till he was cold and dead.

When he left home that morning,
I thought he'd soon return;
But for my darling father ,
My heart shall ever yearn.

We carried him to the graveyard
And there we lay him down;
To sleep in death for many a year
In the cold and sodden ground.

Although he left the union
He tried so hard to build,
His blood was spilled for justice
And justice guides us still.

DELLA MAE GRAHAM WAS ONLY 12
years old when her father was
killed. At Barney's funeral, the
newspapers said, there was a single
mourners' bench—and she was the
only one sitting on it. Her mother
was too sick with pellagra to come.
Della Mae held her composure
until almost the end, when she
finally broke into tears. At that
moment, they say, most of the
crowd broke down with her.
    The week after her father's
death, the Nashville *Tennesseean*
reported:

In the hope of securing funds for the
strikers' aid, Graham was to have gone   **101**

with [Howard] Kester and other labor leaders this weekend to Washington to attend the Continental Congress for Economic Reconstruction, which has been called by labor, farm, and political groups for Saturday and Sunday. After Graham's death, Mr. Kester decided to take the oldest child to the meetings. Della Mae is in the national capital today, seeing sights she never saw before, and telling the story of her father's death so as to secure aid for the miners whom he had imbued with the idea of fighting on.

In 1976, Della Mae Graham wrote:

I was real sad when I wrote that song because we were having a hard time and I was a kid that loved to sing, and I loved to try to play the guitar. I just decided that I would try to put some words together and I did. You know, the people just really wanted to hear it everywhere I went, wanted me to sing it, you know. I really felt just like the words I put in the song. I felt that very way.

The song was published and I didn't even know that until one day my son was up in the shopping center and he found this book. He came in and said, "Mom, did you know that they've got that song you wrote in here when you was a kid?" I said I didn't know anything about it. Sure enough, there it was—in an old-time song book. They had took it upon themselves to publish it and just taken for granted that it was all right, but I wouldn't have had that done for nothing.

They paid me for the song, though. They paid me $50 for the song, two publishing companies did—*after* they had published it. But I said, $50 is $50. I signed a contract that I wouldn't do anything about it. I didn't want to get revenge on anybody; I just wanted what was coming to me, that's all. That's what I feel I should have.

ELEVEN

Little David Blues

TOM LOWRY

TOM LOWRY COMPOSED THE "Little David Blues" in his head, and that's the only place he thought the words and tune were. He was amazed to learn from us that someone had written down the song during the Davidson-Wilder strike, and that it was published in *American Folksongs of Protest.* No one even bothered to tell him.

We had found out about Tom from some friendly people in the Davidson community grocery store. They were looking over the songs we showed them, explaining verses to us, and someone said, "Why Tom Lowry, he lives right up here in Roanoke!"

One late summer morning Fran Ansley, Florence Reece, and Brenda Bell sat on Tom's side porch and talked with him about his song and about coal mining. Florence also wrote a song during a mining strike—she was in the thick of the Harlan battles with her husband Sam and young family when she wrote "Which Side Are You On?" Tom and Florence had never met.

TOM: I hadn't thought of that song, hadn't thought of that holler . . . I hadn't thought of none of that in years!

FRAN: When we first came over in Fentress County, we didn't know anybody. We knew your song—that's what got us off on this whole wild goose chase. We wanted to hear the story of the strike.

TOM: You mean that song got you people started on this?

FLORENCE: Look what you done and didn't know it. You done a lot of good and didn't know it. I'm so proud! I'm glad they brought it back to memory. Sing it for us!

103

TOM: I swear, I never would have thought of that no more! [*Laughing*] I don't know if I can sing it, but I'll try. You know, that takes me a way back, buddy. I can just see me setting on that old big front porch over there . . . let's see . . . Little Cowell . . .

There is a pause, while Tom studies his song, talking to himself, trying to get up his nerve to sing for us. Then he starts singing, hesitantly at first, the tune wavering, but then getting steadily stronger. He chuckles at the words as he sings, and we laugh and sing along some. He's good.

Little Cowell worked for John Parish
For 35 cents a day;
He ate so many cheese and crackers
He fell off a pound a day.

   REFRAIN
   It's all night long,
   From the midnight on.

Then he came to Davidson a-working
For Mr. Hubert and E. W. too,
And Cowell knows just exactly, boy,
How to deny you.

You go in the mines and find water
It's right up to your knees;
You surely don't like to work in it,
But you don't do as you please.

They'll take you by the collar,
They'll maul you in the face;
They'll put you in the water hole,
It's right up to your waist.

You come out by the office
After working hard all day;
Your sheriff dues and your doctor bill
You surely got to pay.

Men go through the office
They go through one by one;
They'll ask you for two dollars in
   scrip
And "Oh, gee! Make it one."

You get your handful of scrip,
And you go right in the store.
You find a fellow with a black
   mustache,
Writing it down on the floor.

You ask for a bucket of lard
And "What's meat worth a
   pound?"
"We sell it to you at any price,
'Cause we're spizwinkin' now."

You ask for a sack of flour,
And then you'll ask the cost.
It's a dollar and a quarter a sack
And fifty cents for cloth.

I went into the store one day,
Mr. Cowell was frying some
   steak;
I warned it would give him
Scab colic and the bellyache.

TOM: Now I don't know if that's any way *near* the way I used to try to sing that.
BRENDA: Tell us how you came to write the song.
TOM: I don't know, you'd have to know the situation of that song before you know what it was. It all had to do with the circumstances that come up around me. The strike started it. The little fellow in there had been like a daddy to me. I mostly made that song about that one man. That was Little David Cowell. He was a little bitty fellow and they brought him in there in that strike as a bookkeeper. "Oh gee, oh golly"—that was about as rough a language as I ever heard from him. One of the finest men I ever got to know in my life.

Well, of course, the miners worked hard. Some of them, like when you "go through the office one by one," I've heard many a man go through there after $2 in scrip, they'd ask for $2 and Cowell'd look at what they'd done that day. You see, when you load your turn of coal that day it comes by telephone from the mine and they call it down to the office before the miner comes in. Cowell'd say, "Gee golly." Maybe you loaded so much and you'd ask for $2 and he'd say, "Oh gee, can't have two, just make it one."

But Mr. Cowell, see, he went on and done different things that I didn't like at the time. He was against what I was believing—I thought he was anyway. I thought he was agin the Mine Workers, agin everybody that was striking, which he wasn't. He worked down there for that company, and he lived on a dime's worth of cheese and crackers, that was all a person could eat. He worked for so little, well, that's what he lived on. It just come out of the top of my head, I just started remembering it. I don't know, I hadn't thought no more about it since then.

I was thought very little of, myself, now I'll just tell you. My wife, even she thought I was a regular smart aleck. Even in that song, now, I was trying to do my bit, I guess. I was going to tell them how I felt, anyway. I didn't just tell it in that song, I'd tell it to anybody who would listen to me. I was a hundred percent for the union.

FLORENCE: When you was writing that song, you was organizing. You should have written down those songs, and you should now. Why don't you just study when you're by yourself? Just think, think, think—and when you think, write it down. It'd be good for the people.

TOM: As Snuffy Smith says, "When your schoolhouse is as weak as I am, you don't write too much." You see, I didn't get through the third grade. Back then, when a boy got big enough, and come out of a big family, he'd go to work. Of course, I did, too. I had two full sisters and they was twin, and me, and there's eight more.

FLORENCE: Coal miners, they raise big families. And when their sons would get up, they'd take them in the mines with them to help them load up coal to feed their families. And as soon as they'd get old enough, they'd get married, and it'd start revolving all over.

TOM: Back then it was nothing strange for a 12-year-old boy to be working in the mines. So they'd do that, and they growed up like anything else—like a boy raised on the farm out here.

Of course, I did a lot of other things besides mining, but that's what I knowed. I worked at Oak Ridge, I worked on construction work, I drove a school bus for some time, I worked for the state highway department and the county. Just little jobs in between. But until I got crippled in the mine over here, I'd go right back in the coal mines.

But that strike and all that, that was a rough deal. That song I wrote, I didn't call it a song. I didn't call it anything. As I said, mine was mostly about old man David Cowell and how he'd turn people down. I tell you what, it's pitiful, you take a man that goes in the coal mines and works real hard all day working in that—I've seen men in water up to their knees. They couldn't get the company to furnish the pumps to pump it out, and they just walked right in there and worked all day long, buddy. Then you got in that office to ask for your scrip, and your family maybe had a little flour, a little gravy. It may sound like a lie, but I swear it's true. My mother would take a biscuit and put sugar between the biscuit and a little chew of fat meat, and I've loaded twenty tons of coal on that.

FLORENCE: My daddy faced the same thing, and my husband faced the same thing. So, when coal miners get together, they know when the truth is told!

TOM: And came back home for supper and you know all there will be for supper is pinto beans and corn bread.

FLORENCE: Exactly! That's what we had. That's what I raised my children on. But here's the thing. You know all these things, and your children face this same thing. You can tell them what will happen to them. You say, "Now, when these demonstrations come, they'll probably ban them and say, "Oh, don't get in that demonstration, ain't going to do no good—communist.' " It's no such thing. It's people wanting a decent wage. And they'll kill you for less than that.

BRENDA: Where did "All night long, from midnight on" come from? Did people always work night shift in the mines?

TOM: I guess where I got that "midnight on" in there, a lot of fellows would go in the mines and work all day, then they'd come out and go back to prepare for the next day. They'd work half a night. I've done that. I doubt at that time there was a night shift except people who fired the boilers. Very little night work, except preparing for the next day. Later on, when I worked at Horse Pound, we worked straight around the clock. Quick as one shift come off, another went on.

BRENDA: There's a verse in here about the fellow with the black mustache.

TOM: They brought him in there from Livingston. Store manager, and he got rich off them coal miners. They paid him a salary and he got a percentage. Of course, they do that a lot now. He was a big dark-skinned fellow and wore a mustache. I wrestled with him a lot. He wore white a lot, and I'd waylay him. See, there wasn't nothing around there but coal dust, sulphur balls, and ashes, and I went without a shirt a lot. He'd sneak around and try to get back in the store before I could find him. I'd hide from him and I'd just run out. All I wanted to do was black up his clothes. He was all right. He was a good boy.

BRENDA: He'd write down how much scrip you'd bring in?

TOM: "Writing down in the floor." Where I got that, you see, everything back then had to be weighed. Back then you had to cut it and weigh it. Pinto beans, you'd have to weigh them. Before draw day, you'd weigh it and have it all ready. Well, they wrote down when you went in there to trade. The store manager always had a ticket book or something and he'd write that down. Of course, he wasn't writing it down on the floor. Floor just rhymed with store.

As for the other people in the song, John Parish was the fellow Mr. Cowell started to working for. He had an old sewing machine. Seems to me like he was a notary public, or a lawyer maybe, a little jack-legged lawyer. Then during the strike, there were two brothers, E. W. and Hubert Patterson. They bought the Davidson mine and Mr. Cowell went to work for them as a bookkeeper, under a contract. And the miners struck. Then I took my spite out on him, and them others.

FRAN: Well, I guess you all had a rough time of it! Sometimes it's hard to understand how people could come through it.

TOM: Since me and Edna married, I've come in so tired that I'd have to lay down a while before I could take a bath. Of course, you took it in an old tub.

FLORENCE: Yeah. Eyes so black—you couldn't get all that coal dust out.

TOM: That's right. And I'd work on a motor. I've went to work many a morning at five o'clock, and they'd turn the lights on at the tipple. I mean in the summertime like this weather right now, you can just guess how many hours we'd work. They'd turn the lights on to dump the last trip, and we only got the same price—it didn't make any difference. Never heard of overtime or double time.

FLORENCE: And no vacation with pay.

TOM: Only time I can ever remember getting off in my life back then was at Christmas. They would give you Christmas off. Didn't have no holidays.

FLORENCE: The men used to tell my husband, he'd tell them about they'd get so many days with pay. "Who ever heard of getting paid for not working?" He said, "If you got sense enough you'll stand up there." Now they're getting it. They say now, "Sam, you know a long time ago you told me about that and I thought you was a liar."

TOM: There's been a lot of sacrifices for that Mine Workers.

FLORENCE: I say there has.

TOM: I actually guess the biggest part of that started in Harlan, Kentucky.

FLORENCE: That was something awful. They's a man up there, and he'd just shoot them men, I don't know how many. But finally they killed him. Said the man's wife went over there after he was shot, and he wore a breast-flint, and said he had something on his face, and they just raised that up and spit in his face, after he was a-dying. Because he killed so many people. He was worse than Hitler, it could have been.

At first I just went to church and thought, "It's bad, it's bad," until them thugs started. Then I thought, "You stand up and be counted or you're going to be killed and your children will starve to death." They's one woman, they arrested her husband and put him in Harlan jail, she had little twins, and she had pellagra, you know, scaled all over and starving. She took her two little girls and went to see her husband. Old John Henry Blair said, "We'll turn you out of jail if you'll leave the county." "I ain't going to leave the county," he said, "I live here; I want to stay here and go back to work." And he give them two little girls a dime apiece. That dirty old high sheriff.

Florence Reese, author of "Which Side Are You On?"

TOM: They didn't care about life. Now that part of that there song there, "Don't kill that mule, you be careful with that mule, because we can't buy that mule. We can get men, but you can't go out here and buy a mule." But dad-gum that man. I've heard the mine foreman, "If you don't like it, barefooted man waiting outside the door there waiting to take your job."

FLORENCE: Exactly! And that's what my husband—boy, you could hear him cussing. One old superintendent said, "I hope that these miners' kids had to gnaw the bark off the tree." And, boy, they was a-looking for him. They said they was going to kill him. I told my husband, "Don't you do that, it ain't worth it, don't do it."

FRAN: Florence, why don't you sing your song for Tom?

FLORENCE: Used to, I could sing, but now I can't because I'm too old. My throat's always grooveling. We'd always sing in church and everything, you know. See, I wrote this song in 1930; they had the Harlan strike then.

TOM: Yeah, lord, I read and heard about that.

FLORENCE: Did you hear about "Which Side Are You On?"

TOM: No.

FLORENCE: That's the name of the song. Because you see, the gun thugs were coming down to help them search our house; my husband was an organizer with the United Mine Workers. And they'd put him in jail, and turned him out, and all that stuff. And he had to kindly stay out to go on organizing. And the thugs would search our house and I said, "Well, what are you here for?" I had a bunch of children. They said, "We're here for IWW papers and high-powered rifles." I never had heard of IWW papers. My husband did have a high-powered rifle because it belonged to the National Association of Rifles, or something like that, and him and the miners would go into the mountains and hunt with his old rifle. He didn't have it for no bad purpose. When I found out they was wanting that, I knowed these thugs were dirty—hired by John Henry Blair to come in there and break the strike. I said, "All these miners wants is a right to live in decent ways." And the miners had their hands and their prayers —that's all they had. But the coal operators hired these gun thugs. They buy them good whiskey to drink, they rent them good hotels, they give them high-priced cars to drive, and pistols, high-powered rifles, and one had a machine gun.

   They could give that to beat the miners back. But to give the miners more to raise their children, they couldn't do it. And then my husband and me finally left. But I'll not go into the whole story, but, anyway, it was just like Hitler Germany. It was the worse thing I was ever in and I never will forget it. I'd stay there by myself, and I'd say to myself, "There's something I've got to do." They wouldn't let the newspaper come in there, you know. And people would send in truckloads of clothes or food or something, but the thugs would meet them and if they wanted anything, they'd get it, turn it over so the miners couldn't get it. They were trying to force them back to work.

   Now, my daddy was killed in the coal mines in 1914, and he was loading a ton and a half of coal for 30 cents. After they got the unions they wouldn't have done it. So, the union was the only thing stood by the men, but the coal operators didn't want the union 'cause the miners would have a say—but anyway—I'll try to sing this song.

"Which Side Are You On?"*

Come all of you good workers,
Good news to you I'll tell
Of how the good old union
Has come in here to dwell.

Which side are you on?
Which side are you on?

With pistols and with rifles
They take away our bread
But if you miners hinted it,
They'll sock you on the head.

They say they have to guard us
To educate their child.

Their children live in luxury
While ours is almost wild.

They say in Harlan County
There is no neutral there;
You'll either be a union man
Or a thug for J. H. Blair.

Oh, gentlemen, can you stand it?
Oh, tell me how you can.
Will you be a gun thug
Or will you be a man?

My daddy was a miner
He's now in the air and sun†
He'll be with you fellow workers
Till every battle's won.

TOM: That's right. Your song, see, that come out of experience. It was right there happening.

FLORENCE: I was trying to get some of the thugs to answer which side they's on—what're you doing over there being a gun thug and shooting down your fellow men.

I've seen little children walking along the road down there, and their little legs would be so little and their stomachs would be so big. They didn't get anything to eat. I've seen some of our good neighbors just staggering. Well, they put up this soup kitchen, think it was in Harlan or right below—two men, both of them killed same night. The thugs done it—pretended it was somebody else to get the miners. And they'd find bones up in the mountain where they had killed the miners.

TOM: They called 'em "deputies," them thugs for the company, they had their deputy badges and papers and everything. They'd walk around here, I've seen them, they'd lay a hand on them guns many a times over dad-gum crazy little old fights, lord have mercy. You'd stand around there innocent and just get shot down. But I didn't think about it then.

Actually I was around there part of the time hoping it would start, because they was men out there then, at that time, that I had it in my heart that I wouldn't have cared to see them killed. Boy, I tell you what, when you get hungry and you go to bed hungry, and you cry and you know who's crying because, of course, kids will, and there ain't nothing to eat, and you don't know where the next meal's coming from, and you look at the next fellow out there and you know he ain't in no better shape than you are. Then a dad-gum bunch of people running around there with a bunch of guns on, and if you look cross-eyed at one of them, they'd kick you or they'd knock you. If you don't think it'll make you mean—it shore will. I sure don't want to go through that again.

TWELVE

Day by Day, 1946: The Sergent Family

PHOTOGRAPHS BY RUSSELL W. LEE

JOHN L. LEWIS WAS NOT IN THE habit of being pushed around by anybody. Not even the President of the United States. At the height of World War II, when the whole country mobilized to fight the Nazis, John L. pulled his miners out on strike and threatened to stop the engines of America's war production. The Bituminous Coal Operators Association (BCOA) would not renew their contract with the United Mine Workers, and, war or no war, Lewis was not about to be denied the greatest weapon organized labor (and particularly industrial unionism) has against recalcitrant employers—the ability to withhold in unison the workers' labor and shut down an industry. The pressure against Lewis was enormous, but not even the pleadings of President Roosevelt that the strike jeopardized the war effort would change Lewis's position. He was determined that this national crisis would not, like the Depression, cripple the union that so many had fought to build. Finally, in mid-1943, the federal government used its powers to seize the nation's mines and force the operators to sign an agreement with the UMWA that, with a series of further strikes, brought the wage changes Lewis wanted. It was an impressive victory that Lewis would not let the industry or the government forget.

In the spring of 1946, the short postwar contract with the BCOA expired and again the owners refused to sign an agreement with the UMWA. They considered outrageous Lewis's demand for an **111** unprecedented industry-sponsored Welfare and Retirement Fund. But to Lewis, the fund's ability to provide miners with adequate medical care and pension benefits was a long-overdue necessity in the nation's most dangerous industry. In his typically florid style he lambasted the coal operators: "You aver that you own the mines," he told the operators. "We suggest that, as yet, you do not own the people. . . . We trust that time, as it shrinks your purse, may modify your niggardly and antisocial propensities."

The confrontation that resulted dwarfed even the 1943 skirmishes. The miners remained on strike for fifty-nine days, until the government again chose to intervene on the grounds that "basic industries, such as steel and electric power, were threatened with paralysis" and that the war recovery effort was being jeopardized. Again Lewis had timed his move perfectly, winning a tremendous victory for the union. Under the novel agreement between the United States and the United Mine Workers (which the industry eventually signed), union-appointed safety committees and the Welfare and Retirement Fund were established as vehicles for the protection and health care of the miner and his family.

As a part of that unique contract, the government agreed to undertake a massive survey of existing health and welfare conditions in the mining towns from Wyoming to West Virginia. The study lasted ten months and involved teams of doctors, engineers, social service specialists, and photographers in exploring everything from outhouses to churches. The end product appeared as a 300-page collection of charts and commentary entitled "A Medical Survey of the Bituminous Coal Industry." What brought the report to life was the photography of Russell Lee.

RUSSELL W. LEE HAD ALREADY MADE A NAME FOR HIMSELF WHEN THE government commissioned him to photograph the coal camps of America. With Dorothea Lange, Walker Evans, Arthur Rothstein, and Marion Post Wolcott, Lee had documented the nation in the Great Depression for the Farm Security Administration, perfecting in the course of his work a style of photography that lets the details of simple life express its deepest meaning.

On the suggestion of historian Barry O'Connell, we traveled to Washington, D.C., to explore Lee's photo files in the National Archives. What we found was truly astounding. Some 8,000 photographs took hold of the miners' lives, moment by moment, revealing the anxieties, the harshness, the easygoing humor, the hard work, the hopes and needs, the good times with friends, the bonds of brotherhood that would make a union strong. There seemed no better way to dispel the monotonous character conveyed by the Bloody

Harlan stereotypes than to present in these pages Russell Lee's portrait of one family.

BLAINE AND RHODA SERGENT LET LEE STAY WITH THEIR FAMILY FOR several days in Harlan County. They lived in the camp of the PV&K Coal Company, shopped in their company store, worked in their mine. The Sergents' oldest son worked in the same mine and lived with his wife and son just next door to his parents. Another married son lived in the coal camp in Verda and worked in the mine there. Rhoda Sergent spent her days doing chores around the house, handicapped by the lack of running water, refrigeration, or electricity. The children all had daily responsibilities but always managed to find time for the simple games their dirt front yard would allow.

The life of the Sergent family contrasts sharply with the excitement and glamor of John L. Lewis's high-level negotiations. But without them, Lewis was nothing. His power depended on their everyday dreams and devotion to his judgment about the way to achieve them. John L. Lewis might be able to face down the President of the United States, but ultimately it was up to miners like the Sergents to create the means of surviving day to day, generation to generation.

The Sergent family: (*l to r*) Franklin D., Louis, Lucy, Mr. Blaine Sergent, Bobbie Jean, Mrs. Rhoda Sergent, Wanda Lee, and Donald

ABOVE: Breakfast is the family's healthiest meal: a slice of fried ham or chicken, plenty of biscuits and potatoes and hot coffee

LEFT: Rufus Sergent and his son

RIGHT: There is no company bath-house, so Blaine must remove the head-to-toe coal dust at home with water heated on the stove

LEFT ABOVE: Bobbie Jean, age 4, plays on the front porch with a friend

LEFT BELOW: Franklin brings up coal for the household stove

RIGHT: Some of the Sergent children at school

BELOW: Donald draws up water from the camp well

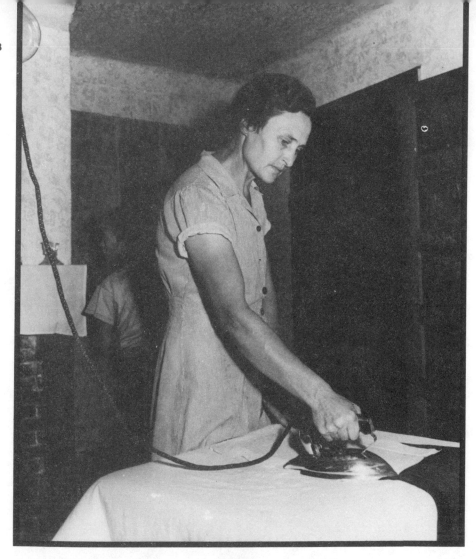

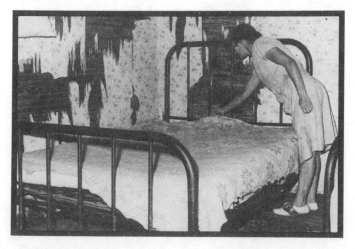

ABOVE: The company-owned house has only one electric outlet for a light bulb and the all-important radio

LEFT: Work around the house is full-time for all the family

RIGHT: A quiet moment between mother and son

THIRTEEN

The Southern Tenant Farmers' Union

LEAH WISE
AND
SUE THRASHER

IN THE SUMMER OF 1934, ELEVEN white men and seven black men met in a one-room schoolhouse on the Arkansas Delta and organized themselves into a "tenants' union." For the croppers, already living on subsistence wages from one "furnish" to the next, the decline in cotton prices brought on by the Depression had been disastrous. The New Deal's answer to the crisis, the Agricultural Adjustment Administration's (AAA) acreage reduction program, pushed sharecroppers off the land while it rewarded the planters with parity payments. Thousands of tenants and sharecroppers were evicted and forced to find work as day laborers or go on relief programs.

By the time the croppers met at the Sunnyside School, other forces were in play throughout Arkansas that were to reinforce and interact with the newly formed union. Coal miners were striking in the northwest section of the state and fighting with the United Mine Workers for control of their local union. In the Ozark Mountain town of Mena, Commonwealth College was training labor leaders. Nearby in the town of Ink, refugees from the Llano Cooperative Colony in Louisiana had established still another cooperative venture. In Paris, Claude and Joyce Williams were using the church to organize the unemployed, to hold classes in political education, and to aid the striking miners. The Socialist Party, organized earlier in the Tyronza area, had already held one state convention, boasted a sizable membership, and had brought Norman Thomas into the area to speak.

Uppermost in the minds of those planning the union was the memory of what had happened in Arkansas fifteen years earlier when black sharecroppers in Elaine had attempted to organize. Issac Shaw recalled that event, known as the Elaine Massacre, and gave a moving plea as to why the union had to be integrated: black people couldn't do it on their own without inviting racial slaughter.

It is probable that at least some of the organizers in the room that evening were aware of a similar attempt at sharecropper organizing in Alabama. The Alabama Sharecroppers Union (SCU) had been organized in 1931 by the Communist Party in response to requests from black croppers and day laborers who complained that the landlords had set day wages at 50 cents a day for men and 25 cents a day for women. The union organized around several demands including food advances through settlement time, the right for the sharecroppers to sell their own time, day wages paid in cash, and a nine-month school term for black children. A skirmish outside a union meeting one night at Camp Hill ended in a gun battle, and the subsequent repression quieted activity in the area and sent the nascent union underground. The following year the union emerged in Reeltown and ended in another gun battle, recorded in John Beecher's poem "In Egypt Land" (see pages 151–52) and in participant Ned Cobb's oral account, *All God's Danger: The Life of Nate Shaw,* compiled by Ted Rosengarten.

Although it was not the first attempt by sharecroppers to rebel against the viciousness of the plantation caste system, the organization of the Southern Tenant Farmers' Union (STFU) would bring the plight of the sharecropper to the nation's consciousness. Subjected to continuous harassment and intimidation by the landed gentry and their hired lawmen, the union nevertheless continued to grow in both membership and mass appeal. Throughout the thirties and into the early war years it spread to six Southern states. Stubbornly maintaining its union structure despite rebuffs by both the CIO and AFL, the STFU became a mass movement—a movement that people joined with the enthusiasm they normally saved for their religion, a movement that gave common people the means to organize and fight for the right to live decent and productive lives.

In September of '35, the union called its first major strike. Nearly 5,000 cotton pickers responded by staying out of the fields. No written contracts were gained, but most of the planters eventually agreed to pay higher wages. More important than the wages, however, was the boost to union membership. Following the strike, chapters were spontaneously organized in Oklahoma, Missouri, Tennessee, and Mississippi. By the end of the year, the union claimed a membership of 25,000.

What we present here are first-person accounts by six people who were active participants in the union as organizers, national and local officers, and local members. Not all were sharecroppers. George Stith was a young man when he joined the STFU and was quickly made secretary of his Cotton Plant local because he could write; he became vice-president of the union in 1947. Clay East, a service station owner, was converted to socialism when he read *Letters to Jud* by Upton Sinclair: "It just made sense." He took in the first members of the union when it was organized at the Sunnyside School and remained active in the union for the next year; Mrs. Naomi Williams was a member of an STFU local in the Gould area; J. R. Butler taught school for a while near his hometown of Pangburn, but was working for his brother at the sawmill when he attended the first state socialist

The STFU'S first handbill

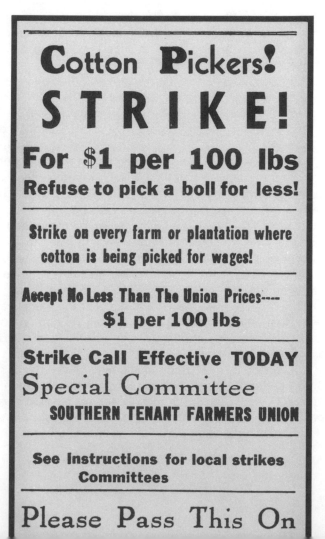

Cotton Pickers!
STRIKE!
For $1 per 100 lbs
Refuse to pick a boll for less!

Strike on every farm or plantation where cotton is being picked for wages!

Accept No Less Than The Union Prices----
$1 per 100 lbs

Strike Call Effective TODAY
Special Committee
SOUTHERN TENANT FARMERS UNION

See Instructions for local strikes Committees

Please Pass This On

convention in Arkansas. He was president of the union from 1935 to 1942, the union's most active and productive years. H. L. Mitchell, who ran a dry cleaners, was co-founder of the union and served in an executive capacity up through the time the union was known as the National Farm Labor Union, until its affiliation with the Amalgamated Meat Cutters and Butcher Workmen. Carrie Dilworth, from a well-off black landowning family, served as secretary of the Gould local, helped the union raise money by speaking nationally, and coordinated the transport of labor to work in the canneries during the war years.

STITH: When my father got down sick and couldn't work, then I had to quit school and take over. I barely finished what we called elementary and that's all the schooling I got, and the most anybody got in the family.

People asked me, "What you gonna do with the fourteen acres of cotton?" I said, "I'm gon' work it," and lord know, I don't know how I figured I was gonna work it. I just figured I had it to do. I was the only one to work and that was just it. So I dropped out of school and went out and got the crop ready, planted it. When it come time to chop, the owner of the plantation said, "What you gon' do about the cotton?" I said, "I'm gon' work it, I'm gon' try." He looked at me and he said, "You got more nerve than any boy I ever seen. I'll tell you what to do. You get a pair of mules in the lot. You plow your crop and after that I've got a hay crop you can plow for me. I'll see that the cotton is chopped and what's left over I'll charge it to the crop." So that's the way we worked it. We worked on through hay season, which at that time was all done by mules. When we finished with hay season I had enough money coming to buy me a suit of clothes. It was the first long-pants suit of clothes I ever had.

When I wasn't working the crop I worked out on farms, baling hay and cutting timber as a day laborer. I made more money by working than we did out of the crop. I don't remember how much it was we made from the crop; you never was told that. But I know the money from the crop wasn't too much, because we bought winter groceries. I know, I went with my parents when they went to trade. They bought a barrel of flour, a fifty-pound sack of sugar, beans, and rice. That was it.

In the last part of '34, after the crops were harvested, we came to Arkansas. The man we moved with sent a truck to move us from southeast Missouri to Augusta, Arkansas, and we paid that out of the next crop. So we didn't have much money.

In Arkansas, I worked on the plantation of A. L. Cole and Son. It was about twelve square miles. They really didn't want you to go to work off the plantation unless you got permission from them. They wanted to keep you busy, and you didn't get any money out of it. But they would say, "Now look, if you need a little grocery money come up and I'll give you a half book." When you borrowed money to make a crop, you didn't get cash money; you got a coupon book. A book looked pretty much like food stamps today. It wasn't good anywhere except at the company store.

The owner, Cole, he had a mint of his own called "brozeen." When he paid you off and credited your money, you got his money called brozeen. There was a lot of plantations, large ones, like the Wilson plantation up near

Blytheville and Ozone which had five plantations I think. Now each plantation had a different brozeen, but you could spend Wilson brozeen only at a Wilson store. The coupon books stayed for a long time, but the brozeen disappeared, and I'm not sure whether it was helpful or not. When brozeen disappeared there still wasn't any money; they went totally to the coupon book.

The plantation was actually like a state. It had its own government and they even held their own courts on certain plantations. Many times the agent on the place where I worked went to trial for me. I didn't go; he was my representative. It was the owner's own court. They had a judge, and the plantation owner actually appointed the justice of the peace.

Now back in those days Negroes didn't vote too much, and the justice of the peace was elected by very few people. If the plantation owner went to all agents and all the white people who lived on the place and said, "Look, Mr. So-and-so is running for justice of the peace, vote for him," he got the votes. So he was a legal justice of the peace. Many plantations were broke up into units, often miles apart. So, no matter what unit he was on, the justice of the peace had jurisdiction over whatever his court area was. The plantation I lived on didn't have it, but a lot of the large plantations even had their own penal farms.

EAST: Times were so bad that people over at one of those small towns over there stopped a bread truck and took the bread off the damn thing, a bunch of these damn working people out there. Couldn't get nothing to eat. And that happened over quite a bit of the country.

There was a world of credit done at that time—everything was done on credit. The small farmers back at that time all had to borrow money every year to make a profit. So, if they had a bad crop year, a lot of them, that's the way they lost their farms. The bad times back there was 1920, and you just can't imagine the number of people then that was big men the year before who had lost everything they had.

They had no control whatever over what their cotton sold for. They were paid what the cotton buyer wanted to pay them. The supply-and-demand deal didn't work out so much. In a way, it did, but if they had a big supply and the demand for cotton went down, then the price of cotton went down. I've seen cotton sell for 4 cents a pound.

Well naturally this country was made up of those small farms to begin with —people who had come in there and bought small farms for themselves. Ritter and Emrich furnished a world of people. They had the largest store there [Tyronza] by far and had the gin and everything. Well, when a man went broke and lost his farm, they got it. So first thing you know, there's a few big businessmen who was getting ahold of all the land. The small farmers practically all lost their farms.

About the acreage reduction program, all of that was very much in favor of the man that owned the land, the producer—it didn't make a damn whether he did any work or not. The government contract also stated that the way this was divided up should be decided between the producer and the tenants. And the check went to the producer, so he's sitting now with the check in his hand. Well, he can say, "You guys didn't have to pick this cotton. All you did was to plow it up, so you're not entitled to half of it." And a lot of them never did get anything.

Well, since I was what in that section they called the law, because I was the only officer in that section, these people would come to me and tell me their troubles, see. Tell me that Mr. So-and-so got the check and he hadn't given them anything. The way I saw it, they started out on the shares, and after this farmer had agreed to plow up this cotton, well, I figured that the sharecropper had carried out his part of the contract and I thought that he was entitled to half of it. And a good many of the farmers did; all of them didn't have trouble. Mostly the bigger ones and the crooked ones would only give them a third. As I said, a lot of them never did get anything out of it. I don't know just what the sharecropper could do. The owner is setting there with the check and the money and he can go down and cash it. This guy doesn't have to sign it or anything, he goes down and cashes it and he's got the money in his hand. That was the way the government contract read, that this tenant has to make a deal with the producer.

WILLIAMS: During the Depression I had a crop of my own. And if I had a little leisure time to get off, I'd go over there to the boss's place and pick cotton. And that was for 35 cents a hundred. I was a good cotton picker; and I picked 300 pounds in one day to get me a dollar and a nickel. I'd go out there in the early morning just so you could see a row of cotton. It was hard, but I made it. I tried to keep my own account at the commissary store. But now where the cheating came in was on this stuff you put on the cotton, fertilizer and all that kind of stuff, and in the seeds. When they sell the cotton, they wouldn't give me what the cotton was worth. They put it there and I had to pay it all. I was renting but I wasn't supposed to pay it all. But I had all that to pay. Yes, I owed them at that store everything. I gathered crops so much. And then when I'd get enough crop gathered, then I'd pay him. I had got all my groceries and that would leave me with nothing.

I usually made forty and forty-five bales, more sometimes, and I had enough money to run me through the winter, to buy new children's clothes for school and to buy groceries to last till the next time they start to furnish over in the spring. They didn't never give us nothing until the first of April. But I was wise. I'd buy enough of what I couldn't raise to last till April or May. I was raising hogs, had cows, and made my own garden and put up dry food, beans and peas and all that. I done worked myself to death.

And another thing, they didn't allow no colored children to even go to school but seven months, and they made them stay in the field and the white kids was going to school all kind of every way. I wouldn't stick for that now. I taught school until I got so many children I couldn't get nobody to take care of them and it took all I made. But I taught before I had the three little children. And when I got the fourth one I had to quit and take care of them. You know, in them days you had to know how to teach everything, from the first to the eighth grade. But I wasn't getting nothing but $35 a month. They raised it to $45 about a month after I quit. But I had to pay somebody to keep my babies. And them people charged me $2, $3 each kid a month. That's $10. And then I had to feed them and go get them, bring them home, had to do this and do that, and when I'd get finished with all that I wouldn't have $10. And I just quit teaching. My husband say, "Go 'head and quit teaching and sit down and maybe you'll get some peas and okra."

BUTLER: Those were terrible days for everybody—Depression days that made for a lot of people thinking about trying for something better. More and more people got to thinking socialist, you know. Well, I had been a socialist for a long, long time. When I was about 16 years old, I began to read about Gene Debs and began to see how things was really beginning to work, so I became somewhat of a socialist then, and I still am. I couldn't be anything else and be honest with myself.

My father was a farmer from the time before I was born. In fact, I guess he was born a farmer over in Alabama. And then he did move to Arkansas a while before I was born. Then I never was out of the state of Arkansas until after I was grown. I never went to what you would call a high school or anything of that kind. We had a little country school, way out some eight miles from Pangburn where I grew up and went to school in a little one-room country school where one teacher taught everybody, and believe it or not, kids when they'd get through what they would call eighth grade knew more than the kids that get through high school today.

MITCHELL: I have always said that my family came down the agricultural ladder. My father was a tenant farmer who owned his team and farming tools. My grandfather owned his own farm and lived near Halls, Tennessee. He was also a Baptist preacher. From the time I was 8 years old I worked for wages on the farm. I worked for 50 cents per day upwards. I made my first sharecrop about 1919.

EAST: TYRONZA WAS A LITTLE TOWN, I'D SAY AROUND 500. JUST BEFORE we came back from Texas, a mule bogged down there on Main Street and they couldn't get him out and he died in there.

The town at one time was built, all of it, right along the railroad track, facing the railroad track with a road between the buildings and the railroad track. And that's the way most towns back there were built at that time, built right up to the railroad track because all their supplies came in by rail and they wanted to be as near to that as they could, because they had to haul all that stuff by wagon.

On Sunday everyone would meet the train and get a paper. Not much other place to go and they was always a big crowd at the depot on Sunday morning.

I was from an old-time Tyronza family. My dad had a nice grocery store and farmed on the side. I had a hell of a reputation as a boy. I was one of the worst in town, always into something, even when I was in school.

I couldn't say definitely, but I probably had been running a service station for a couple of years when I first knew Mitch—when he came in there and started that dry cleaning outfit. He traded with me and I looked after his cars.

Mitch didn't have much to do with other people. As far as us talking about politics or anything, I never had any conversations with him at all until I got to setting around over there doing nothing and figured me out a system I thought we should be operating under, and when I went over and talked to Mitchell, he said, "Why, you're a socialist." And of course I was kind of smart-alecky and I told him, "Hell, my hair's not long enough." About the only thing I at that time knew about socialism was calling them Bolsheviks; some people said Bolshevikii and we'd see cartoons in the paper about Russians and my granddad always called them "Roosians." But that's about as much as I knew about them.

Mitch told me that he'd bring down a book for me to read. I told him then that if it was about socialism, he needn't bring it down to me. So, Mitch said, "You don't have to be so damn narrow-minded, you can read it and if it's no good, forget about it." I guess maybe that day or the next day he come by there and pitched me out a little paper book, *Letters to Jud,* by Upton Sinclair. Well, I never had heard of Upton Sinclair. I didn't know nothing about him. And I started in reading that thing and the more I read, the more sense it made. After that, I knew there was something wrong and everyone else did too.

See, the Socialist Party was what we started first. The only thing that I could tell you about that was Mitch, my brother, and Nunnally had about twelve or fourteen that went in together and got a state charter, the first socialist charter issued in Arkansas. It must have been in 1931. I wasn't in on that because I was running for constable at the time; but as soon as the election was over I joined the party and got a card.

At that time, we was instructed about how to hold meetings. They said to get a group together at home and discuss these things and talk them over. After we got this going, we got the Odd Fellows Hall and had regular meetings in there. And anywhere from 50, I'd say, to 100, 150 maybe, would come to the meetings. Quite often we'd have people from some other surrounding town or something, but most of them were local people. Mixed meetings weren't held back there until we started up with the union. So this was before the union, and I just don't remember any black people being in there at all.

I'd make a lot of talks. I always made a practice of telling stories that showed a comparison between socialism and capitalism and I'd always make fun and show how stupid and silly the capitalist system was, and how much more sensible the socialist movement was. At that time, they had the WPA [Works Progress Administration], which was put out by the government, see. And we always had suggestions or criticism about the way it operated.

That had to be in the early part of 1932, and Thomas was campaigning. He was traveling over the country, he and his wife, driving from city to city in an old Buick. We had this meeting at the Tyronza schoolhouse and had Thomas in there to speak. People were there from all over the state.

The way I remember the union getting started—see, in the South we call twelve o'clock "dinner." When Norman Thomas was there to speak we had dinner at my home, and during the meal Norman was the first one that planted that idea in our heads. He told me at that meeting, "What you need here is a union." In other words, the Socialist Party wasn't going to be any help to these tenant farmers. This was after we had taken him out and shown him the conditions in the country and all. And that is where the idea originated, when Thomas told us that. So, after he left, we talked the thing over. Mitchell was actually the big planner in this deal. There was Mitch and myself and two other guys, I think probably Ward Rogers and possibly Alvin Nunnally.

I can't remember just how many there was at the first meeting, but as I remember, it was about fifty-fifty, about half white and half black. We had to have an understanding among the union members, and you couldn't have much understanding if you had two separate unions. So we didn't have any complications to amount to anything about that. I got up and I was pretty hot by that time, and it was, as I said, getting up pretty late and I told them we'd come down here to decide what or whether we was going to have a union or not, and if we was going to have one, well, let's make up our mind and get some members in here. So I took in the first members. They started signing some cards, we had some cards and all there, and these guys joined up.

BUTLER: I got this letter from Mitchell and they told me that they were going to have a state Socialist convention at Tyronza, and invited me over, and I went.

After I had gone back to my sawmill job I got a call from Mitchell, and he told me that they were ready to start building a union there. In fact, I think they had already had a meeting at which they sort of got together on some ideas. So I went back over again, and we worked out a constitution and started organizing. It wasn't long before we had an organizer or two in jail because the plantation element in that part of the country absolutely did not want them "niggers" organized, and they didn't hesitate to say it in just those words. The whites were niggers, too. There was no difference, and some of 'em was beginning to see that there was no difference. Of course, there was still a lot of prejudice among white people in those days, but hard times makes peculiar bedfellows sometimes, and so some of them were beginning to get their eyes open and see that all of them were being used. So it was easy to get a start on organizing.

None of us who were really interested in getting the work started would agree to having a separate union or separate meetings or anything of that kind. A lot of the Negro people agreed with us because they knew that if they had a meeting with just black people there, they wouldn't have any protection whatever, but a few white people might have protective influence, so it was to their interest really to have all of it together.

Of course we had opposition on every hand, the law enforcement officers and the plantation owners and a lot, even, of the white sharecroppers themselves were opposed to an organization that took in both races. But we overcame all of that to some extent and we were ready. As soon as we began to tell people what the situation was and what might be done about it, well, they could see that the white people were being treated just the same as the Negroes, they were in the same boat and they all had to pull together. That's about the best way that I know to express it.

STITH: The population in the area [Cotton Plant] was about 90 percent black, and all black on the plantation. Around Tyronza and Marked Tree where the union started, it must have been around 40 to 60 percent more Negroes than whites. The northeast part of Woodruff County was virtually all white. That's where we got a large part of our white membership from. This whole section north of McCrory, around South Bend, over as far as Martin, until you get up near Wynn, was mostly white. At one time Negroes wasn't allowed to go through these places north of McCrory, unless they was a white person with them. But overall, the cotton-growing area was about 75 percent black.

Racial makeup of a local depended a lot upon the area where you organized. Agriculture labor, especially in the cotton fields, at that time was about 85 or 90 percent black, so your membership normally ran just like your area. In Arkansas in the early days of the union, I think our white support was an over-average percentage compared to their population at large. Our white membership at one time ran higher than 15 percent whites, much higher, especially in certain areas. And it increased as the union spread into other states. In parts of Alabama there was nothing but whites.

When we first started there was no integrated local. Even though white and black organized together, it was set up on the basis of race. It was a community thing. Naturally the communities were segregated. That's why we had segregated locals, because whites and blacks usually didn't live on the farm together. Let me tell you this. When I went to Louisiana in 1953 down in the sugar-cane fields, we had the same situation there. Certain plantations were all black and certain plantations were all white. The first time I went to a place called Raceland to make a talk to a group of sugar-cane workers, I was the first Negro, except the janitor, that had his foot in the American Legion Hall. The workers were all white, and I went in there that night, and they looked at me sort of funny and said, "Is this who gon' talk?"

Later when we had our district meeting to bring our locals from the whole sugar-cane area together, you had the whites and the blacks. And when they sat down and talked and thought of the situation, they decided we were all in the same boat. So they said, "Well, when are y'all gonna meet, we want to come over. When we're gonna meet, we want y'all to come over." This was a thing that just happened. They couldn't see segregation.

Usually we held it in a church or a country schoolhouse. A lot of time they were held without authority, but we could always get in. But the whites had a problem. Where they belonged to a church, the higher-ups also belonged, and they couldn't get the church to have a meeting. So they had to come to a Negro place in order to have a meeting.

MITCHELL: EVICTIONS OCCURRED CONTINUOUSLY. WE ESTIMATE SOMETHING like a half a million or a million as a result of the cotton plow-up program. Dr. Calvin Hoover, who was doing a survey with Howard Odum, estimated a little higher—900,000 evicted as a result of the cotton plow-up in 1933 and the reduction in the cotton program in 1934.

In the beginning, if a union family was evicted and the family wanted to, we'd put them back in the houses. This was done now and then. Usually the plantation owner didn't want them and most of them didn't want to stay. We did that continuously in 1935 because there just wasn't any place for them to go and many people had come back from the city. The relation between the farms and the cities wasn't as close as it is today.

In the beginning, we were trying to get a section of the law enforced providing that sharecroppers should not be evicted from the land because of the operation of this AAA [Agricultural Adjustment Administration] program. We were trying to get that enforced, but of course they didn't pay any attention to the law, any more than they do now when poor people are concerned. We filed a lawsuit in the courts, and about the time the lawsuit was being thrown out, we sent a delegation to Washington to see the Secretary of Agriculture, Mr. Henry Wallace, the great liberal. As we always did, we had representation of both whites and blacks; there were two other whites besides me and two blacks [Reverend E. B.] McKinney [vice-president of the STFU] and another minister, Reverend N. W. Webb, a union organizer from Birdsong, Arkansas.

Arkansas sharecroppers at STFU meeting

We got up early in the morning. Because of the interracial composition of our group, we drove day and night, as there was no place for us to stop and we didn't know what else to do.

Soon after nine o'clock we went back to the Department of Agriculture. We marched up the stairs, the guard had told us the Secretary's office was 204. We went right into the Secretary's office, and the receptionist asked who we were and we told her we were a delegation from the Southern Tenant Farmers' Union and we wanted to see the Secretary. She asked if we had an appointment. Of course we did not. I never heard of having to make an appointment to "see" anybody before. I hesitated and didn't know what to say. McKinney stepped up and said, "Ma'am, we will just sit down here. If Mr. Wallace is busy, we'll just wait until he gets through and we can talk to him then." The receptionist didn't know what to do with a group of people who intended to sit in the office and wait for Mr. Wallace. About that time I remembered a letter I had, addressed to Paul Appleby, the Undersecretary of Agriculture, and I asked her if she would deliver the letter to Mr. Appleby. Paul Appleby came out and soon he got Henry Wallace out there to see us.

Wallace promised to send an investigator down to investigate the displacement of people under the AAA. We evidently put up a rather convincing story to him.

STITH: The first meeting I went to was at a private home on the plantation that I worked on. However, there were three plantations in that one union local and we rotated. We were a little bit afraid to meet at one place too long because they had been beating up and killing a few to try to break the union. We would rotate our meetings, and we had outside guards with shotguns.

So I guess there were about fifty people at that first meeting. At one time that union local had a hundred and forty or fifty members, and there were many locals that were larger than that. About 95 percent of the families on the three plantations joined the union.

And that very night the friend that brought me got up a motion that I would be made secretary of the union local. He was secretary but he wanted to give it up because he didn't think he could write good enough. None of the others could write too well, not so far as writing letters and communications. They could write their name and put down some figures. But when it come down to writing or communicating in a business manner, they didn't. And I hadn't never either, but for some reason I was just able to do it. Actually, my job was really only to keep minutes, read communications, and to record and hand down whatever decisions was made by the local. When the local was called on for meetings in Memphis, I usually went. They usually tried to send the person who was thought could get the best understanding and bring it back. Sometimes that would be the local president and/or the secretary. Of course, in the local I was in, it would always be me that was the one. I guess that give me a lot of courage. They thought I could do it so I always tried. I remained secretary until I moved to Gould in 1947.

I believe the president of our local at the time I joined was Will Curry. Although our local was all black, it had been organized by a white fellow—I can't think of his name—along with a colored man by the name of Farrish Betton from south of Cotton Plant. Betton was later made vice-president of the organization. Betton wasn't a sharecropper. He was what was known as a tenant. He rented. He lived in this community I call Dark Corner; it's in Monroe County. And he was a justice of the peace in that community. It was about 70 percent black. The white man who was justice of the peace had died. Before his death he requested from the quorum court that they make Betton justice of the peace because he was the only other qualified person in the area then. He had a high school education, which was at that time good. And he stayed justice of the peace until he left there. Of course, he had some trouble—out of both races, in fact. And he had all kinds of threats, even after he got in the union, not for being justice of the peace, but because he was in the union. I remember him telling me that from time to time some of the white people—and I use the word because he used it—would come to him and tell him, "Look, Betton, you're justice of the peace and you're too good a man to be mixed up with these low-class people. So the best thing for you to do is just get out of it."

They tried to separate people by class, and they tried to do it by race. Whichever was best to use, they used it. It worked on a lot of people, and some people it just didn't work on. For instance, the agent on the plantation where I lived wanted to join the union because he knew the problem, but he was afraid to. And he says to me, "Now George, look, I know you. Anything y'all need that I can give you, just tell me. Information or anything else, I'd get it."

Our local had all kinds of committees for whatever we thought was necessary—program committees, committees to make decisions on strikes. When we elected the first strike committee, it was made standing. Anytime we decided on a strike, this committee was consulted and told what the problem was. Strikes were talked about all the time, all the time. Strikes was actually voted on by a local at the STFU headquarters in Memphis. The union would call in the locals and say, this is what we have in mind. The secretary would tell the local to decide whether it was a good thing. Then they would send their representatives over to Memphis. Somehow we got them there, a lot of times I don't know how. But when we got to Memphis, a decision was made. Because legal procedures and very little of the law was on our side, a strike was always decided in Memphis. It were talked about by the executive committee, which usually involved a person from almost every area, at least from every state. Where unions was heavy, we had it broke up into areas or districts. For instance, this area local was in Pine Bluff, and the executive committee would decide which would be best. They would report their decisions back to the locals. Sometimes the idea for a strike would come from the local. The local would write in and say, well, this is what is happening here; we believe if we could have a strike, it might could do some good. The executive branch of the union would look into it. If they thought it feasible, they'd say go ahead and have a "local." This was known as a local strike. But most of the time we tried to do it on a larger basis because it was more effective. Plantations used one against the other. For instance, if we struck on this plantation and the other two around didn't strike, they would be used against us. The owners would say, "Look, such and such a thing is happening over here, go over and help him out."

At that time we had a family membership. Where there was a widow involved, she was the head of the family, so she took out a legal membership. But where there was a man and his wife involved, she was a member too. She had a voice when it come down to talking or voting on.

Women were very active and made a lot of the decisions. Women decided to do things that men felt like they couldn't do. We had several locals around Cotton Plant and I believe in one of the locals all the officers were women. This was because men were afraid. Owners never bothered women. They never beat up any women. Oh yes, I think they did in Mississippi and maybe one place in Arkansas. But usually they would pick on the men. They was a little bit slow about bothering women.

Yes, we had some women, and especially there was one that could make just about as good a speech as any of the men could. Henrietta McGee was her name. She went with us on trips to New York and Washington and made speeches before groups and was a big help in getting contributions, because she got right down to earth with the things that she had to say.

She was a widow from over there in eastern Arkansas somewhere, I don't know which town she was from, but she was as active as any other union member that we ever had. And, to give you an idea of her character, she went with some of us to Atlantic City to the first convention of the CIO as a separate organization from the AFL. While we were there, I remember all of us went to a restaurant for a meal one time. Mrs. Roosevelt was there. Several of us went in and set down at the same table and Henrietta was in the group. She was black. Well, this waitress wouldn't serve her at all and Mrs. Roosevelt saw that the waitress wouldn't serve her. So Mrs. Roosevelt went over and invited Henrietta to come over and sit at her table. The same waitress came along and she didn't dare refuse, because of Mrs. Roosevelt, you know. So she tried to apologize to Henrietta. She said, "You know, a while ago, I didn't know that you were a Puerto Rican." "Well," she said, "I'm not. I'm a nigger, nigger sharecropper from down in Arkansas." All that the waitress could do was turn her head and not say anything. She went ahead and served her.

IN 1935, NORMAN THOMAS AGAIN CAME TO ARKANSAS AND attempted to speak in the community of Birdsong. The meeting was broken up by a crowd of angry planters and lawmen, and Thomas was assured that no "gawd-damn yankee bastard" was welcome in Arkansas. Union organizer Ward Rogers had been arrested earlier when he threatened "to lead a group that would lynch every planter in Poinsett County." In the "reign of terror" that followed, union meetings were banned and union members were arrested on the slightest pretext. The union moved its headquarters to Memphis, and its officers depended on dark nights, fast cars, and back roads to get them in and out of the state safely. Acting under pressure, the Agricultural Adjustment Administration sent an attorney, Mary Conner Myers, into the state to investigate the massive evictions and wave of repression. Mrs. Myers was considered an "impartial" observer, but the report that she subsequently wrote for the department was considered too controversial to be released.

STITH: After what happened at Tyronza, where they beat up a few and maybe killed some of them, we decided on a local basis that we had to put up some kind of defense if we were going to meet. We were not just going to let people come in. And this is what I heard a lot of: "We're not gonna let them do us

Norman Thomas speaking in Bay Bridge, Arkansas, September 1937

like they did in Elaine, just come and kill us out. So we gon' be prepared." I didn't know too much about the Elaine riot, though my father was there. But we never had cause to use our guns.

MITCHELL: We decided that under no circumstances would the union retaliate, no matter what happened. We would try to influence public opinion and attempt to get the public on our side. If we had fought back it would have been our Negro members who suffered most. We were sure of that fact and we didn't want another Elaine Massacre.

In the records of the union there is a set of instructions we sent to members about attending union meetings. We advised them not to go in groups of more than two or three at a time. They were to go quietly to the meeting place and to have their outer guards and inner guards watching. If the planters came, the guards were to notify the members to disperse. If they wanted to sing, that was all right, but they should keep their voices low. We had this all worked out.

EAST: We went over in a different section to a Negro church and Butler was there and Mitch was there and myself and possibly another speaker or so, I don't know. We had a good turnout, possibly a hundred, a hundred and fifty tenant people in there. And just before we got the meeting started, here come one of the big planters from over there, Mr. Sloan.

He came in with a couple of big deputies, see, with their pistols buckled on them, and he just came marching in there. He wanted to see what was going on. Well, you don't know how a lot of those colored people felt back there when the boss man comes in and sees them at a union meeting. They was a little bit shaky, but I'll say this, that the colored guys back there, if anything, were more solid than the whites. They'd go ahead and sacrifice and get killed or beat up or anything else before they'd give up.

I had a big six-shooter on and a reputation, not a bad reputation, but they knew that I wouldn't do to fool with. So, I got up and told them that "if you folks are going to be scared because your boss has walked in here and so forth, just quieten down, now this thing is perfectly legal. We've got corporation papers and we got our constitution." Well, he wanted a copy of this, Mr. Sloan did. So Mitch says, "Well, if you've got 10 cents, you can have one." So he sold him a copy of the constitution. And then Mitch proceeded to tell him, "Well, you folks are not eligible for membership in this, so we'll ask you to leave." And I have often wondered what he would have done if Sloan had refused. But at the time, he got up and walked out. He and his men went trudging out of there with his six-shooters and all, see.

We got a raft of members signed up at that meeting. You didn't need much. Those folks were in a bind and they was being mistreated, and when you got up and pointed these things out to them, why you didn't have much trouble signing them up. Practically all the people that came to meetings signed up.

BUTLER: One little incident occurred during the time of the union, over at Earle, Arkansas. A plantation man that was also a deputy sheriff needed some work done on his farm, so he got around and arrested, I believe, eleven members of the union and threw 'em in jail. When they had their trial the judge turned them over to him then to work out their fines, and he put them out on his plantation under guard, and had them working out there. We found out about it and we got some pictures by a man crawling around through cotton rows and making pictures and so on. Well, we brought charges against them in the Department of Justice.

The Department of Justice sent two lawyers down to Memphis to check. Well, old Peacher had got scared enough that he'd turned all these people loose. When these Department of Justice investigators came down there, they said, "Now we will not go into Arkansas to make any investigation, but if you can get some of those people and bring 'em here to Memphis, we'll question 'em." So I went to Earle, and ran across one or two of the fellows that had been enslaved. They gathered up others, and they had about seven of them around my car, telling me about what had been done and how and all that, and here came a deputy sheriff. His name was Graham, he rammed his car up close to mine, jumped out, grabbed a .38 out of his holster, slammed it down across the door into my ribs, and said, "What the goddamned hell are you doing over here?" Well, I knew I had to tell him something, so I said, "Well, I'm over here getting the evidence that's gonna send you and Paul Peacher and a few more of you to the penitentiary for the rest of your lives." I said, "The FBI knows exactly where I am. They know exactly what I'm doing, and they know exactly when to expect me back in Memphis, and if I'm not there, they're gonna find out why." He jerked the gun down, slammed it back in his holster, and said, "All right." He got back in his car and pulled out.

Well, when that happened, all of the fellows that had been around talking with me just disappeared except for three, and those three stayed with me and were still talking, and we saw a car go down the road towards Memphis that was loaded with about a half a dozen men with rifles and so on. One of these guys said, "They're going down to waylay us." But we went to Highway 70 so we could go into Memphis on a different road. I told the fellow, "Now, get down in back and stay quiet because we're going in. If somebody gets in our way, we're still going in." Well, I opened up my big old Hudson and we went. We expected—I expected really—that they would try to block me at West Memphis, but they didn't. I think some of them might have been parked around there, but they didn't try to block the highway. So I went on through and I got the men over there and the Department of Justice men asked them enough questions to get enough for an indictment and we got Paul Peacher indicted and convicted of peonage.

EAST: This guy from the Workers Alliance, Dave Benson, and a bunch of colored folks had been put in jail over at Forrest City for inciting to riot. Benson was in for no driver's license, and they had a bunch of trumped-up charges against him. We couldn't get a lawyer in Memphis to take the case and I went and got this lawyer from Little Rock. I had a fast automobile, a '35 Tereplane, and I still wasn't scared to go into Arkansas. When a union man went into Arkansas, he was taking a good chance of getting killed or at least beat up. I don't remember the lawyer's name, but his father was one of the attorneys that defended the Scottsboro boys.

When we got to Forrest City, he went into the courthouse and the men came up for trial. It was so tense. I was setting in the back of the courtroom myself and an old colored guy passed by and there was this old cripple man setting there with a damn walking cane and he hit at him just as hard as he could. That thing was so tense you could just feel it in the air. I knew it was bad.

Well, when this attorney left the courthouse, a damn mob followed him down to my car. I started down there, and this guy took off and the mob turned on me. The lawyer went down to a café to get something to eat and the boys went and took him out of that damn café and I understand beat him up and put him on a bus and told him, "Don't you ever come back into Forrest City or we'll kill you."

Well, this man led this mob on me, telling them all I had done. He had that mob ready. Well, they was backing me up, they was on me and they was hollering, "Kill the son of a bitch," and all this kind of stuff. I backed into a kind of ditch and fell on my back, and when I fell I had my head up against a hedge and these guys was trying to get ahold of me. I was just laying on my hips and I'd wheel and kick one, and every time one would get close to me I'd kick the hell out of him. And some big guy—never did know who he was —got right straddle of me and told these guys, said, "Get the hell off of him. Leave him alone." Well, I got up and they was hollering, "Kill him!" and all that kind of damn stuff and I told them, "Now listen. If I've violated any kind of law or done anything, then put me in jail." I could see that they didn't have much of a leader and the jail was just right up there behind the courthouse.

They put me in jail and then they was just marching through and saying, "Goddamn, we'll hang you tonight. We'll break your neck," and all this kind of stuff. And they was calling me "nigger-lover" and all that stuff.

Well, Sheriff Campbell come in there. Of course, he knew I was the deputy sheriff over in Poinsett County, knew I was from a good family and all and he didn't want this damn thing. He was afraid he might be getting in a little trouble about that. He come in there and asked me, "East, would you like to get out of here?" And I told him, "Why sure, I haven't done a damn thing. I haven't violated any law. They got no right to put me in jail." So, he said, "Well, we're gonna take the state rangers and take you out." I told him, "Well, OK." Well, that's when this boy spoke up and said, "Clay, you're a damn fool if you go out of here. They're just laying a trap for you. If you go out of here, they'll get you just sure as the world." And I told him, "Well, I'll take a chance on that. I'm going out." I still wasn't scared, I didn't believe that any damn guys would get me, somehow. So, that's what I'm telling you, that ain't bravery, you've got nothing to be brave about. The only time that I was afraid was when I walked down there with that damn lawyer, because I knew these guys was fixing to nail me.

Well, anyway, we got in the car and started out toward Memphis. By that time, two or three carloads of guys was already on the road after us. So I told this guy, "Now, if those guys catch up with us, there ain't a damn bit of use of you getting hurt. You either give it to me or give me a chance to get that damn gun of yours and I'll get out and get away from you and you won't get shot." Those guys was really gonna shoot us up.

They couldn't get a Memphis lawyer to go over there for nothing. Man, they wouldn't cross that river. Not for the union. But Mitch—I'm quite certain that it was Mitch—contacted someone and found out about this guy from Helena, Arkansas, and he said, hell yes, he'd take the case. And he took it and went to Forrest City and this damn gang ganged up on him and he told them, "You men are a bunch of fools. I'm an attorney, I'm working for a living. I don't care nothing about them niggers and croppers in there. All I'm interested in is the money. I've put in a lot of time in school and been out a lot of expense in order to make a living being an attorney. I don't care nothing about these people." And they let the damn fool go ahead and plead the case and he got these guys out.

STITH: THE STRIKE OF '35 WAS ONE OF THE MOST UNIQUE THINGS EVER happened. It was well planned.

After meeting several times beginning in the early fall, I think it was, and working on this thing for another year, we decided upon a cotton picking strike. Cotton is perishable to a certain extent; it's got to get out of the field and ginned up before the weather gets bad or you take a loss on your cotton; the quality of it goes down.

So we had decided a general strike would be the thing. But it taken a lot of planning to figure out how we were going to do it. The executive committee finally got together and had all these handbills printed up, brought them in and made packages to go to each area according to what they thought their needs would be. Then we set a strike date. All the representatives came in and got their strike handbill with strict instructions. They didn't put them out until that night, eleven o'clock was the time. And that night at eleven o'clock they was all over Arkansas, Missouri, part of Tennessee, part of Mississippi, and Alabama.

DILWORTH: On Sunday night everyone, all over Arkansas where there was an organization alive, had to be on the job at eleven passing out leaflets. Oooh, I don't know how many we passed out. We spread them handbills saying, "Don't go to the fields and pick no cotton," over every street in this town.

I was riding in my car. Marie Pierce, a student from Memphis, was riding in the back seat with Mr. Bolden. Mrs. Burton and I sat in the front. I was laying down on my stomach holding the door cracked open, and I'd push the leaflets through the crack and spread them out in the street. You pick up speed and that'd just make them things go flying all over the yards.

By the time we got down by Mr. Dean's house, we had done the whole route. Then this car came swooping by us. I said, "Cut the lights off and let's go right into these woods." We got down in a little curl and cut the motor off. If they had caught us, I don't know what they would've done to us. But they couldn't tell where we was. They went out there where they was fixing the levee and got stuck in the mud. Water was up to our knees in the car. It was three o'clock that next morning when we got home and it was still raining. It wasn't no easy job.

White folks thought a plane had flown over there and spread all them leaflets. They were all over the state.

MITCHELL: There was a kind of unofficial bargaining. They wouldn't recognize the union as such, but they'd watch to see what the union was going to demand, particularly after that cotton picking experience of 1935. We'd call a wage conference every year, maybe twice a year, with several representatives from each local union, and they would decide what we were going to ask for. Often, we'd make a survey of our members and have a ballot to see what they thought the union should ask. We'd do this before the wage conference. Then we'd tabulate all of the returns and say, here's what the members think that we can get. The conference would determine we can get a dollar per hundred this time, and we would announce that the union was demanding a dollar per hundred pounds for picking the cotton. We'd invite all plantation owners to meet with us to work out a contract and an agreement, but of course they never did. This had the same general effect as a wage contract. It was kind of the old IWW idea.* If you didn't have a contract, then you take action on the job. If the boss didn't pay the union rate, the people quit work and went somewhere else—where the union scale was paid.

We thought in terms of a trade union. I don't know if we really ever expected it to happen. At least we used all of the usual union terms. We didn't just go out and say, this is the way we're going after it. We always wanted a contract signed by all of the plantation owners. We would work out model contracts. We had proposed contracts for sharecroppers and contracts for tenants and wage workers and we had circulated them around. Sometimes the fellows on the plantation would take them to the owner and ask him to sign the union contract. Sometimes they got thrown off the land as a result of doing that.

The nearest thing that we ever had to such a contract was at the end of 1935. The lawyer for the union, whose name was Herman Goldberger, had been meeting with a plantation owner by the name of C. H. Dibble. Mr. Dibble was fair and liberal for that area. He'd come from some other area of the country and owned a medium-sized plantation. He had, as I recall, thirteen families, which meant 500 or 600 acres of cotton. Word got out that Dibble was negotiating a union contract. He was told by his banker that if he signed a contract with the union they would foreclose his mortgage and that he had to get rid of the union members. He served them notice about Christmas that they were going to be evicted if they did not move by the first of the year. Maybe we made a mistake, I don't know, but we laid down the law to Mr. Dibble at our convention that if he tried to evict these people, we were going to put them back in their houses. We said we were going to put a picket line around his plantation. It became a question as far as the entire community was concerned. I mean, the upper-class part of it, the guys on the right side of the tracks had Mr. Dibble do what he had threatened to do—evict all these families, which he proceeded to do. He threw them out in the middle of the winter.

STITH: THE PROBLEM WAS THAT BLACKS IN THE AGRICULTURE FIELD DIDN'T have leaders with enough education to do what was necessary. That's number one. And number two, a black man wasn't recognized enough to get into the places where he needed to go, even if he had enough education. Even at that time, government organizations didn't look at a black man too much. So a black person as president could not have been too successful in getting a lot of outside help. It was the major role of the union to bring in outside support, money, etc. It had to be. It was the only way we could survive. We had no funds. The members didn't have enough money to pay dues to the

*Industrial Workers of the World, see "The Brotherhood," pages 22–39.

organization for it to operate. We had to have outside help. A black man was discussed sometimes as being president. And I was discussed at one time. But we decided, that if a black man got to be president it might divide us. So we decided, well at least we'll put him in second spot, make him vice-president.

This is the way most blacks wanted it. There were some few who felt like they were able to lead. When one was found, and he felt thataway, we always found somewhere to put him in a leadership position. I didn't feel like I was a leader. I just wanted to help get things better. But they felt like I was, and they put me into it.

BUTLER: The Workers Defense League was one of our chief supporters; our relation was very close and very good. They raised a lot of money and they collected a lot of clothing, things of that kind, and shipped down to distribute to the ones who were most in need.

There was a New York committee that put on what they called National Sharecroppers Week. I was in New York I guess all of the week that had been designated and any number of others were there. Mrs. Roosevelt was at the big final meeting that we had that week, the Saturday-night meeting. That committee had hired a professional fundraiser to organize a week of fund raising. I don't know what percentage they gave him for his labor, but they did raise quite a bit of money. I guess that at the end of that week, the union treasury had more money in it at one time than it ever had before or since. Might have had as much as two or three thousand dollars.

DILWORTH: I went to New York to make a speech for Sharecroppers Week in 1946. Frank P. Graham sponsored me. I sat at the speaker's table. Every table was covered with white linen and there was somebody round every table. I couldn't see nobody, just this clear blue sky. I made my speech, and when I got through, folks was just patting. I didn't a bit know what I said. I talked about ten minutes. And whenever I come to myself so that I could see the audience out there, I said, "We are climbing Jacob's ladder, and every rung goes higher and higher. We're going to organize the South as God being our helper." And the people just hollered. This was in the Henry Hudson Hotel. I stayed there five nights, room 284. And when I come out, I had integrated the hotel. I was the first colored to stay there.

IN 1937, THE UNION, ANXIOUS TO BE A PART OF THE CIO, AFFILIATED with the United Cannery Agricultural Packinghouse and Allied Workers of America (UCAPAWA). It was an uneasy and strained relationship from the beginning. The STFU found it virtually impossible to comply with the bureaucratic guidelines of the international union, and the UCAPAWA president, Donald Henderson, was neither sensitive to the union's needs nor very astute in his assessment of the divisions that should be made among agricultural workers. Finally, in 1939, the Executive Council of the STFU voted to withdraw, but not before the union had been torn apart by internal strife and its ranks depleted.

BUTLER: It was supposed to be one union then, but like I say, it didn't work out. I thought it would be a good thing if we could do it, but when we tried it, we couldn't do it. The UCAPAWA had a set of officers that were determined to control everything, and the Southern Tenant Farmers' Union wasn't ready to be controlled, never was.

Well, I think they thought that it would be a big boost to their membership for one thing. UCAPAWA was practically a paper union. They didn't have any members to amount to anything at all, but since they were a part of the CIO, they were considered more important. It wasn't but a little while until they began trying to tell us what we had to do and how we had to collect dues and how we had to send a certain amount of dues to the UCAPAWA offices and all that sort of thing. We never could collect any dues, we never did. Oh, maybe one man would pay a dime a month, maybe a dime would roll in at the end of the year. People didn't have it. So we pulled out then, pulled out of UCAPAWA.

STITH: McKinney was a communist, but I don't think his views were so different than mine when it comes down to the lower-class man, the little man, especially the farmer. But I think his difference of opinion was where we should be as a union. Partially, he did, I know, agree with UCAPAWA about the organizing of farmers in one union, sharecroppers in another, and tenants in another.

MITCHELL: We thought, and our people thought, that the CIO was going to sweep the whole country and was going to organize all the unorganized. That's what they talked about. We wanted to be a union. We wanted to be in the mainstream of organized labor. We just felt that we must get into the CIO.

We thought and wrote in 1935 and 1936 to the AFL about the possibility of a charter as a national union. The response from Secretary Morrison was not very encouraging. I don't remember the exact words, but he considered us farmers and the AFL had fraternal relations with the Farmers' Union, the Grange and Farm Bureau, and they wouldn't be interested at that time. It was not until after the CIO experience that we even tried to get the AFL consideration.

We were naive, I guess. The ordinary trade unionist never understood the STFU. We were a mass movement, something like the civil rights movement thirty years later. We could have opened the doors in areas where there were farm people. We could have moved into the farming areas around any industrial area. We could have become a great political force and been a great voice for the CIO in rural America. That's what we thought, that's what we saw in the CIO.

BY THE BEGINNING OF THE WAR YEARS, THE MASS BASE THAT THE union had so successfully built earlier had begun to fade away. J. R. Butler left in 1942 to become a machinist. H. L. Mitchell and the vice-president, George Stith, were able to arrange labor exchange programs to provide STFU members with higher-paying jobs, usually in food processing canneries.

STITH: The union sent me into the Gould area. They had a lot of locals in here, and they had formed what was known as an area local. Mrs. Dilworth was the secretary of it. Actually, headquarters was in her house, but Pine Bluff was where we finally wound up with an office. It was heavily populated with sharecroppers and tenants, and they thought that maybe, with my experience, I could come down here and help out. It was at the time that the union membership had begun to dwindle because the members were finding other places to go. The union would pay me according to my report, whatever time I put in they would pay me expenses. As the vice-president of the union you were called on to do many different jobs, to go to many different places, even though you may not be a full-time employee. During the war, the Manpower Commission asked the American Federation of Labor if they could supply them with farm labor to work in the cannery food division and we was it.

The first time I shipped labor from Cotton Plant we couldn't get buses. So we decided that we would get a truck to take them over to Memphis, and from there arrangements were made for a train. The second load I shipped, we had three trucks left Cotton Plant going into Memphis, and the State Employment Security Division had these trucks stopped in Forrest City and they put the truck drivers in jail.

DILWORTH: I took people out to New Jersey, out to California, to Washington, D.C., and even to Atlanta to work in the canneries. Getting people together was easy. I just notified them and talked at different churches. Asked how many wanted to go and I'd get the names. I carried twenty-seven people on one ticket to California.

One day them white fellows came in the office when we was sending labor

Applying for membership in the STFU

from Pine Bluff. I don't know who they were, some kinda law. They come in and ask me, "Girl, you know what you doing? Don't you know it's against the law to move people from one area and send them off?" I said, "If my area don't produce nothing, let 'em go." That's just the way I talked to them. And they didn't do nothing to us.

WILLIAMS: I sent four of my children off with Mrs. Dilworth to New Jersey to work. First, I sent my son, John Williams, Jr. He went in 1944 and every summer thereafter for four years. He worked in a cannery and cooked tomato paste. He was 19 and was going to school at Durmont Baptist College. Out of their weekly earnings, they had to pay for their groceries and reimburse the money for the ticket that was given. The next summer, in 1945, I sent my oldest two daughters, Ruby and Sadie.

MITCHELL: WE CALLED IT THE SYSTEM; YOU GUYS CALL IT THE POWER structure. It is all the same. See, we had made an inroad with the whites and the blacks here. We had done something that none of these agrarian movements had really done. They had all floundered on this damn race thing; but we didn't. We didn't flounder on it. We held our principles.

STITH: Unfortunately, most of the people coming along now don't know anything about the Southern Tenant Farmers' Union. All the things that the union fought for, that the people on the farms have been able to get like social security and minimum wage, they just see that the government just give them that. And when you tell them this is something that we fought for for years, that we went to Congress hoboing our way or going in trucks or buses or cars, they don't believe it.

BUTLER: Most of the unions have gotten to where they're not rank and file anyway. Even the industrial unions are controlled by officials that are elected once every two years or once every four years or sometimes maybe not that often. Back in the earlier days, when people thought about joining the union, it was something like joining a church, getting together to work together for the things they wanted. It was never a mass movement, you know, but it was big enough and so much out of the ordinary that it drew the attention of the world, and so in that way I think we did a lot of good. There were probably things that we could have done if we had known more about what to do, but we were just novices, we just had to play it by ear as we went, and that was all we could do.

For notes on sources, see page 373.

FOURTEEN

In Egypt Land

JOHN BEECHER

"IN EGYPT LAND" IS TAKEN FROM JOHN Beecher's *To Live and Die in Dixie*. His *Collected Poems, 1924–1974* was recently published by Macmillan. The Ned Cobb referred to is the narrator of Theodore Rosengarten's *All God's Dangers*. It was partly through reading this poem and then meeting John Beecher that Rosengarten was first led to Ned Cobb.

I   *IT WAS ALABAMA, 1932*
but the spring came
same as it always had.
A man just couldn't help believing
this would be a good year for him
when he saw redbud and dogwood
    everywhere in bloom
and the peachtree blossoming
all by itself
up against the gray boards of the cabin.
A man had to believe
so Cliff James hitched up his pair of old
    mules
and went out and plowed up the old land
the other man's land but he plowed it
and when it was plowed it looked new
    again
the cotton and corn stalks turned under
the red clay shining with wet
under the sun.

Years ago
he thought he bought this land
borrowed the money to pay for it
from the furnish merchant in Notasulga
big white man named Mr Parker
but betwixt the interest and the bad times
    coming
Mr Parker had got the land back
and nigh on to $500 more owing to him

for interest seed fertilize and rations
with a mortgage on all the stock—
the two cows and their calves
the heifer and the pair of old mules—
Mr Parker could come drive them off
    the place any day

143

if he took a notion
and the law would back him.

Mighty few sharecroppers
black folks or white
ever got themselves stock like Cliff had
they didn't have any cows
they plowed with the landlord's mule and tools
they didn't have a thing.
Took a heap of doing without
to get your own stock and your own tools
but he'd done it
and still that hadn't made him satisfied.
The land he plowed
he wanted to be his.
Now all come of wanting his own land
he was back to where he started.
Any day
Mr Parker could run him off
drive away the mules the cows the heifer and the calves
to sell in town
take the wagon the plow tools the store-bought furniture and the shotgun
on the debt.
No
that was one thing Mr Parker never would get a hold of
not that shotgun . . .

Remembering that night last year
remembering the meeting
in the church he and his neighbors always went to
deep in the woods
and when the folks weren't singing or praying or clapping and stomping
you could hear the branch splashing over rocks
right out behind.
That meeting night
the preacher prayed a prayer
for all the sharecroppers
white and black
asking the good Lord Jesus
to look down
and see how they were suffering.
"Five cent cotton Lord
and no way Lord for a man to come out.
Fifty cents a day Lord for working in the field
just four bits Lord for a good strong hand
from dawn to dark Lord from can till can't
ain't no way Lord a man can come out.
They's got to be a way Lord show us the way . . ."
And then they sang.

"Go Down Moses" was the song they sang
"Go down Moses, way down in Egypt land
 Tell old Pharaoh to let my people go"
 and when they had sung the song
 the preacher got up and he said
"Brothers and sisters
 we got with us tonight
 a colored lady teaches school in Birmingham
 going to tell us about the Union
 what's got room for colored folks and white
 what's got room for all the folks
 that ain't got no land
 that ain't got no stock
 that ain't got no something to eat half the year
 that ain't got no shoes
 that raises all the cotton
 but can't get none to wear
 'cept old patchedy overhauls and floursack dresses.
 Brothers and sisters
 listen to this colored lady from Birmingham
 who the Lord done sent I do believe
 to show us the way . . ."

Then the colored lady from Birmingham
got up and she told them.
She told them how she was raised on a farm herself
a sharecrop farm near Demopolis
and walked six miles to a one-room school
and six miles back every day
till her people moved to Birmingham
where there was a high school for colored
and she went to it.
Then she worked in white folks' houses
and saved what she made
to go to college.
She went to Tuskegee
and when she finished
got a job teaching school in Birmingham
but she never could forget
the people she was raised with
the sharecrop farmers
and how they had to live.
No
all the time she was teaching school
she thought about them
what could she do for them
and what they could do for themselves.
Then one day
somebody told her about the Union . . .

If everybody joined the Union she said
a good strong hand would get what he was worth
a dollar (Amen sister)
instead of fifty cents a day.
At settling time the cropper could take his cotton to the gin
and get his own fair half and the cotton seed
instead of the landlord hauling it off and cheating on the weight
"All you made was four bales Jim" when it really was six
(Ain't it God's truth?)
and the Union would get everybody the right to have a garden spot
not just cotton crowded up to the house
and the Union would see the children got a schoolbus
like the white children rode in every day
and didn't have to walk twelve miles.
That was the thing
the children getting to school
(Amen)
the children learning something besides chop cotton and pick it
(Yes)
the children learning how to read and write
(Amen)
the children knowing how to figure
so the landlord wouldn't be the only one
could keep accounts
(Preach the Word sister).

Then the door banging open against the wall
and the Laws in their lace boots
the High Sheriff himself
with his deputies behind him.
Folks scrambling to get away
out the windows and door
and the Laws' fists going clunk clunk clunk
on all the men's and women's faces they could reach
and when everybody was out and running
the pistols going off behind them.
Next meeting night
the men that had them brought shotguns to church
and the High Sheriff got a charge of birdshot in his body
when Ralph Gray with just his single barrel
stopped a car full of Laws
on the road to the church
and shot it out with their 44's.
Ralph Gray died
but the people in the church
all got away alive.

II   **THE CROP WAS LAID BY.**
From now till picking time
only the hot sun worked

ripening the bolls
and men rested after the plowing and plowing
women rested
little boys rested
and little girls rested
after the chopping and chopping with their hoes.
Now the cotton was big.
Now the cotton could take care of itself from the weeds
while the August sun worked
ripening the bolls.

Cliff James couldn't remember ever making a better crop
on that old red land
he'd seen so much of
wash down the gullies toward the Tallapoosa
since he'd first put a plow to it.
Never a better crop
but it had taken the fertilize
and it had taken work
fighting the weeds
fighting the weevils . . .
Ten bales it looked like it would make
ten good bales when it was picked
a thousand dollars worth of cotton once
enough to pay out on seed and fertilize and furnish for the season
and the interest and something down
on the land
new shoes for the family to go to church in
work shirts and overalls for the man and boys
a bolt of calico for the woman and girls
and a little cash money for Christmas.

Now though
ten bales of cotton
didn't bring what three used to.
Two hundred and fifty dollars was about what his share of this year's crop
*   would bring*
at five cents a pound
not even enough to pay out on seed and fertilize and furnish for the season
let alone the interest on the land Mr Parker was asking for
and $80 more on the back debt owing to him.
Mr Parker had cut his groceries off at the commissary last month
and there had been empty bellies in Cliff James' house
with just cornbread buttermilk and greens to eat.
If he killed a calf to feed his family
Mr Parker could send him to the chain-gang
for slaughtering mortgaged stock.

Come settling time this fall
Mr Parker was going to get every last thing

every dime of the cotton money
the corn
the mules
the cattle
and the law would back him.
Cliff James wondered
why had he plowed the land in the spring
why had he worked and worked his crop
his wife and children alongside him in the field
and now pretty soon
they would all be going out again
dragging their long sacks
bending double in the hot sun
picking Mr Parker's cotton for him.

Sitting on the stoop of his cabin
with his legs hanging over the rotten board edges
Cliff James looked across his fields of thick green cotton
to the woods beyond
and a thunderhead piled high in the south
piled soft and white like cotton on the stoop
like a big day's pick
waiting for the wagon
to come haul it to the gin.
On the other side of those woods
was John McMullen's place
and over yonder just east of the woods
Ned Cobb's and beyond the rise of ground
Milo Bentley lived that was the only new man
to move into the Reeltown section that season.
Milo just drifted in from Detroit
because his work gave out up there
and a man had to feed his family
so he came back to the farm
thinking things were like they used to be
but he was finding out different.
Yes
everybody was finding out different
Cliff and John and Ned and Milo and Judson Simpson across the creek
even white croppers like Mr Sam and his brother Mr Bill
they were finding out.
It wasn't many years ago Mr Sam's children
would chunk at Cliff James' children
on their way home from school
and split little Cliff's head open with a rock once
because his daddy was getting too uppity
buying himself a farm.
Last time they had a Union meeting though at Milo Bentley's place
who should show up but Mr Sam and Mr Bill

and asked was it only for colored
or could white folks join
because something just had to be done
about the way things were.
When Cliff told them
it was for all the poor farmers
that wanted to stick together
they paid their nickel to sign up
and their two cents each for first month's dues
and they said they would try to get
more white folks in
because white men and black
were getting beat with the same stick these days.

Things looked worse than they ever had in all his time of life
Cliff James thought
but they looked better too
they looked better than they ever had in all his time of life
when a sharecropper like Ralph Gray
not drunk but cold sober
would stand off the High Sheriff with birdshot
and get himself plugged with 44's
just so the others at the meeting could get away
and after that the mob hunting for who started the Union
beating men and women up with pistol butts and bull whips
throwing them in jail and beating them up more
but still not stopping it
the Union going on
more people signing up
more and more every week
meeting in houses on the quiet
nobody giving it away
and now white folks coming in too.

Cliff James looked over his ripening cotton to the woods
and above the trees the thunderhead piled still higher in the south
white like a pile of cotton on the stoop
piling up higher and higher
coming out of the south
bringing storm . . .

III *"YOU"*
    Cliff James said
"nor the High Sheriff
nor all his deputies
is gonna git them mules."
The head deputy put the writ of attachment back in his inside pocket
then his hand went to the butt of his pistol
but he didn't pull it.

"I'm going to get the High Sheriff and help"
he said
"and come back and kill you all in a pile."

Cliff James and Ned Cobb watched the deputy whirl the car around
and speed down the rough mud road.
He took the turn skidding
and was gone.
"He'll be back in a hour" Cliff James said
"if'n he don't wreck hisseff."
"Where you fixin' to go?" Ned Cobb asked him.
"I's fixin' to stay right where I is."
"I'll go git the others then."
"No need of eve'ybody gittin' kilt" Cliff James said.
"Better gittin' kilt quick
than perishin' slow like we been a'doin' " and Ned Cobb was gone
cutting across the wet red field full of dead cotton plants
and then he was in the woods
bare now except for the few green pines
and though Cliff couldn't see him
he could see him in his mind
calling out John McMullen and telling him about it
then cutting off east to Milo Bentley's
crossing the creek on the foot-log to Judson Simpson's . . .
Cliff couldn't see him
going to Mr Sam or Mr Bill about it
no
this was something you couldn't expect white folks to get in on
even white folks in your Union.

There came John McMullen out of the woods
toting that old musket of his.
He said it went back to Civil War days
and it looked it
but John could really knock a squirrel off a limb
or get a running rabbit with it.
"Here I is," John said
and "What you doin' 'bout you folks?"
"What folks?"
"The ones belongin' to you.
You chillens and you wife."
"I disremembered 'em," Cliff James said.
"I done clean disremembered all about my chillens and my wife."
"They can stay with mine," John said.
"We ain't gonna want no womenfolks nor chillens
not here we ain't."

Cliff James watched his family going across the field
the five backs going away from him

in the wet red clay among the dead cotton plants
and soon they would be in the woods
his wife
young Cliff
the two girls
and the small boy . . .
They would just have to get along
best way they could
because a man had to do
what he had to do
and if he kept thinking about the folks belonging to him
he couldn't do it
and then he wouldn't be any good to them
or himself either.
There they went into the woods
the folks belonging to him gone
gone for good
and they not knowing it
but he knowing it
yes God
he knowing it well.

When the head deputy got back
with three more deputies for help
but not the High Sheriff
there were forty men in Cliff James' cabin
all armed.
The head deputy and the others got out of the car
and started up the slope toward the cabin.
Behind the dark windows
the men they didn't know were there
sighted their guns.
Then the deputies stopped.
"You Cliff James!" the head deputy shouted
"come on out
we want to talk with you."
No answer from inside.
"Come on out Cliff
we got something we want to talk over."
Maybe they really did have something to talk over
Cliff James thought
maybe all those men inside
wouldn't have to die for him or he for them . . .
"I's goin' out," he said.
"No you ain't," Ned Cobb said.
"Yes I is," Cliff James said
and leaning his shotgun against the wall
he opened the door just a wide enough crack
for himself to get through

but Ned Cobb crowded in behind him
and came out too
without his gun
and shut the door.
Together they walked toward the Laws.
When they were halfway Cliff James stopped
and Ned stopped with him
and Cliff called out to the Laws
"I's ready to listen white folks."

"This is what we got to say nigger!"
and the head deputy whipped out his pistol.
The first shot got Ned
and the next two got Cliff in the back
as he was dragging Ned to the cabin.
When they were in the shooting started from inside
everybody crowding up to the windows
with their old shotguns and muskets
not minding the pistol bullets from the Laws.
Of a sudden John McMullen
broke out of the door
meaning to make a run for his house
and tell his and Cliff James' folks
to get a long way away
but a bullet got him in the head
and he fell on his face
among the dead cotton plants
and his life's blood soaked into the old red land.

The room was full of powder smoke and men groaning
that had caught pistol bullets
but not Cliff James.
He lay in the corner quiet
feeling the blood run down his back and legs
but when somebody shouted
"The Laws is runnin' away!"
he got to his feet and went to the door and opened it.
Sure enough three of the Laws
were helping the fourth one into the car
but it wasn't the head deputy.
There by the door-post was John McMullen's old musket
where he'd left it when he ran out and got killed.
Cliff picked it up and saw it was still loaded.
He raised it and steadied it against the door-post
aiming it at where the head deputy would be sitting
to drive the car.
Cliff only wished
he could shoot that thing like John McMullen . . .

IV   *HE DIDN'T KNOW THERE WAS SUCH A PLACE IN ALL ALABAMA*
just for colored.
They put him in a room to himself
with a white bed and white sheets
and the black nurse put a white gown on his black body
after she washed off the dried black blood.
Then the black doctor came
and looked at the pistol bullet holes in his back
and put white bandages on
and stuck a long needle in his arm
and went away.

How long ago was it
he stayed and shot it out with the Laws?
Seemed like a long time
but come to think of it
he hid out in Mr Sam's corn crib
till the sun went down that evening
then walked and walked all the night-time
and when it started to get light he saw a cabin
with smoke coming out the chimney
but the woman wouldn't let him in to get warm
so he went on in the woods and lay down
under an old gum tree and covered himself with leaves
and when he woke it was nearly night-time again
and there were six buzzards perched in the old gum tree
watching him . . .
Then he got up and shooed the buzzards away
and walked all the second night-time
and just as it was getting light
he was here
and this was Tuskegee
where the Laws couldn't find him
but John McMullen was dead in the cotton field
and the buzzards would be at him by now
if nobody hadn't buried him
and who would there be to bury him
with everybody shot or run away or hiding?

In a couple of days it was going to be Christmas
yes Christmas
and nobody belonging to Cliff James
was going to get a thing
not so much as an orange or a candy stick
for the littlest boy.
What kind of a Christmas was that
when a man didn't even have a few nickels
to get his children some oranges and candy sticks
what kind of a Christmas and what kind of a country anyway

when you made ten bales of cotton
five thousand pounds of cotton
with your own hands
and you wife's hands
and all your children's hands
and then the Laws came to take your mules away
and drive your cows to sell in town
and your calves
and your heifer
and you couldn't even get commissary credit
for coffee molasses and sow-belly
and nobody in your house had shoes to wear
or any kind of fitting Sunday clothes
and no Christmas for nobody . . .
"Go Down Moses" was the song they sang
and when they had finished singing
it was so quiet in the church
you could hear the branch splashing over rocks
right out behind.
Then the preacher got up and he preached . . .

"And there was a man what fought to save us all
he wrapped an old quilt around him
because it was wintertime and he had two pistol bullets in his back
and he went out of his house
and he started walking across the country to Tuskegee.
He got mighty cold
and his bare feet pained him
and his back like to killed him
and he thought
here is a cabin with smoke coming out the chimley
and they will let me in to the fire
because they are just poor folks like me
and when I have got warm
I will be on my way to Tuskegee
but the woman was afeared
and barred the door again him
and he went and piled leaves over him in the woods
waiting for the night-time
and six buzzards settled in an old gum tree
watching did he still breathe . . ."

(The sheriff removed Cliff James from the hospital to the county jail on December 22. A mob gathered to lynch the prisoner on Christmas Day. For protection he was taken to jail in Montgomery. Here Cliff James died on the stone floor of his cell, December 27, 1932.)

FIFTEEN

A Place to Speak Our Minds

MARY FREDERICKSON

So you want to know about the Southern Summer School. Well, all I can say is—that group is responsible for whatever sense I have today! It made a big impression on me. It was the first time I had ever been away from home, but that didn't bother me. The school was so informal—it was like everyone was on the same level—it seemed as if the teachers wanted to learn from us. You were taught to be aware of what was going on around you, about the labor movement, and the fact that women should be active in it.

—Polly Robkin, New York City
November 2, 1974

It was a great inspiration to me to feel like women were considered capable of participating. It was something new and interesting and I guess it was to most of the girls. They had never had a chance to speak up and talk and express themselves about what they felt should and shouldn't be done in our government and in our industry. They had never had an opportunity to express themselves before, and it was great.

—Vesta Finley, Marion, N.C.
July 22, 1975

DURING THE LATE 1920S, A GROUP of women trained in the social sciences and committed to using their skills as teachers in behalf of social change, organized a workers' education program for women in the Southern region. The result— the Southern Summer School for Women Workers—represented a unique effort at female cooperation across class lines. Each summer from 1927 to World War II, the staff of the school sought to provide young workers from textile, garment, and tobacco factories with the analytic tools for understanding the social context of their lives, the opportunity to develop solidarity with each other, and the confidence for full participation in the emerging Southern labor movement.

The roots of the Southern Summer School lay in the opening decades of the twentieth century, when the Young Women's Christian Association (YWCA) and the Women's Trade Union League (WTUL) sought to channel the reform impulse of middle-class women into programs responsive to the needs of working women. The YWCA created an industrial department to reach working women on the local level, and the WTUL pioneered in the establishment of workers' education programs. Both supported the passage of protective legislation and the expansion of trade unions.

The founders of the Summer School, Louise Leonard McLaren and Lois MacDonald, hoped to bypass the limitations of a

Northern-based WTUL and a Southern YWCA whose local branches were dependent on the support of mill owners and businessmen. Lois MacDonald, an economist and native of South Carolina, had written a classic study of Southern mill villages in 1926. As a YWCA leader in the South, she had helped organize a summer program which placed college students in industrial jobs. Having worked as an operative in an Atlanta textile mill herself, MacDonald had grown especially concerned about the human costs of Southern industrial development.

Louise McLaren, the daughter of a Pennsylvania banker and a graduate of Vassar, had served as the YWCA Industrial Secretary in the coal-mining region of Wilkes-Barre, Pennsylvania. As National Industrial Secretary for the Southern region in 1920, she traveled across the South, and, like Lois MacDonald, she observed firsthand the impact of rapid industrialization on the lives of women. In 1928, she wrote:

The popular idea that the South is "different" and the failure to recognize the same large factors in industrial change which have characterized the industrial revolution elsewhere, handicaps the workers and retards the growth of the labor movement in the Southern states. Just as the existence of national barriers has often prevented workers from different countries from recognizing their common cause, so Southern sectionalism has blinded the textile workers to their need of affiliation with organized workers of the rest of the United States.*

Together the two women set out to overcome such sectional barriers through a Southern-based workers' movement in which the workers would "themselves take a hand."

As models for their plan, McLaren and MacDonald looked to the Brookwood Labor College, the Bryn Mawr Summer School, and the workers' education programs of the International Ladies Garment Workers Union (ILGWU) and the Amalgamated Clothing Workers Union (ACWU). For financial aid, they turned first to the American Federation of Labor. The AFL, however, was at its lowest ebb, devoted to craft unionism and uninterested either in organizing women workers or in promoting workers' education. Consequently, the two women were forced to create an organization which would draw on a wide range of interest groups for support.

Response to their call for assistance came from across the spectrum of women's organizations. Funds for the first residence session in 1927 came from the American Fund for Public Service, administered by Elizabeth Gurley Flynn, the radical feminist and IWW veteran. Meta

*"Some Aspects of Industry in the New South," *Journal of Electrical Workers and Operators* (1928), p. 345.

Glass, sister of conservative Virginia Senator Carter Glass, provided facilities at Sweet Briar College in Sweet Briar, Virginia (the school was later moved to Asheville, North Carolina). Students were recruited from local "Y" branches and sponsored by middle-class Southern women's "workers' education committees" which provided money for travel and tuition.

The faculty McLaren and MacDonald recruited included both graduates of New England women's colleges and the small women's colleges of the South. Most were single and all were fiercely independent. Almost all had worked previously with the YWCA and then moved on to involvement in other reform activities. The Southerners were "new women" seeking a public role for themselves in a society that provided few outlets for their aspirations. The commitment of the New Englanders paralleled in many ways that of the women who had traveled South after the Civil War to teach in the American Missionary Association (AMA) schools for the newly freed slaves. Like their predecessors, they were motivated by a sense of duty, and they looked to Southerners as those most in need of aid. For many, the South held the mystery and attraction of a foreign land.

Above all, like the AMA women before them, the women of the Summer School were teachers. Trained in the educational theories of John Dewey and the optimistic tenets of the new sociology, they perceived education as the way to bring about social change; and it was through their role as educators that they sought to bridge the gap between their own advantages and other women's needs.

In constructing their program, the faculty consciously avoided the literary and artistic emphasis of the Bryn Mawr Summer School and the vocational training of most adult education programs. Because their ultimate goal was to train grass-roots leaders and to disseminate organizing skills, the faculty planned to provide students with a practical knowledge of economics and the political system. As one board member put it:

This is no individual enterprise. It is not merely a session for those who may have the means to improve their individual and personal attainments and seek for themselves a little higher training in the arts and cultures of life. . . . The emphasis of the whole school is to be on social and not on individual growth and responsibility.*

Not content with the reformist goal of improving the lot of individuals, the founders of the Summer School sought regional collective change: a transformation of the lives of Southern working women.

*Atlanta, Georgia, *Journal of Labor,* April 5, 1929.

DURING THE SCHOOL'S FIFTEEN-YEAR EXISTENCE, OVER 300 WOMEN attended its sessions. All were between 18 and 25, with at least two years of industrial experience and six years of schooling. All were white. The school owned no property but rented facilities—schools and camps—each year in different locations near Asheville, North Carolina. Consequently, the faculty bowed reluctantly to the social mores of a segregated society. They did not take on the challenge of creating an integrated student body, but at the school they consistently stressed the identical interests of black and white labor. They also ran workers' education programs for blacks in several Southern cities.

Chief among the school's teaching methods was the use of the students' own life experiences as illustrations of historical change and social problems. Students were encouraged to compose and perform original dramas based on their own life histories. And their autobiographies and essays, together with faculty follow-up studies of their participation in local labor and community activities, provide a

rich collective portrait of the lives and thoughts of a cross section of
Southern working women.

For example, the work history of Nora MacManus, a cotton spooler
from Macon, Georgia, illustrated to the other students the
double-edged impact of protective legislation. She had first gone into
the mill as a "bobbin girl" at the age of 8. A short while later she left
work to attend school when the Georgia legislature passed a law
forbidding the employment of children under 14. At 14 she returned to
the mill as a spooler, working 11 hours a day until she was 15. Then
her hours were reduced by a new state law preventing children under
16 from working more than 8 hours a day. At each turn in her story,
the intervention of legal reform ameliorated the conditions under
which she worked, while at the same time working an economic
hardship on her family.

The life histories written by Summer School students graphically
mirrored other social and economic changes. They told of the

Scene from the play *Wealth and Work* produced by students in 1929. The machine is dividing Wealth and Working-Class Life

difficulties faced by those who worked the land, the movement of families from the farm to mill towns and urban centers, the high price paid for economic survival. Students wrote of the hazards of coal dust, textile fibers, and dangerous machinery, and of the additional burden of frequent pregnancies. Most suffered from an inadequate diet; many had been forced to cope with the ill health or early death of their parents.

The school drew to its campus women who longed for the means to change the patterns of their lives. They came for many reasons: some had been fired for union organizing or had joined a local and wanted to understand the meaning of their new commitment, but most students in the school's early years came simply out of a desire to learn. Many had left school at an early age and jumped at the chance to obtain additional education. Bessie Edens was a leader in the Elizabethton strike of 1929, and later in the same year came from Tennessee to the Summer School.

I didn't know what it was all about more'n nothing only they said it was the Southern Summer School for Women Workers of America or something to that effect. School was what I wanted, school. I didn't know what kind of school it was. But after I got there I liked it.*

Another student came to the school in 1930 upon the recommendation of a regional officer of the AFL. Elected president of her local union at the Kahn Manufacturing Company in Mobile, Alabama, in 1925, she had served as a delegate to Alabama State Federation of Labor conventions and, in 1928, was elected vice-president of the Federation. She came to the Southern Summer School because:

In assuming the duties of these offices I felt my inability, but it has always been my policy to do the best I can when called upon. With my work at the factory, my home and children, I haven't had an opportunity to read and study the problems of labor as I would love to, so when the opportunity to attend the Southern Summer School came, it seemed to be something I had been longing for.†

The school's students knew firsthand the difficulties women confronted in the labor movement. A woman from the Hanes Hosiery mill in Winston-Salem, North Carolina, reported that while the male employees in her plant were well paid and did not work over 8 hours a day, the local union excluded women from membership; they could

---

*Interview with Bessie Edens, Elizabethton, Tennessee, August 14, 1975.
†SSS Scrapbook, 1930.

get work only every other day. A student from Birmingham, Alabama, who worked as an organizer for the United Textile Workers during 1935, stressed that it was necessary "to convince the men of women's ability and sincerity." She argued that women often did not participate in unions because they had the double burden of working in the mill during the day and doing housework at night. However, she commented that support from women workers during times of conflict, on picket lines, and in relief efforts, was essential to the survival of any union.

At the school the women often discussed the special needs and concerns of women workers. The role of women as cheap surplus labor was the theme of a student essay written in 1927:

Among the working class, women have always helped to make the living. Women at the present time are employed in almost all kinds of work. Some employers would rather work women than men because they consider them more efficient and regular at work than men. Women are gaining for themselves a place in the industrial world, but should be careful to keep a high standard and not remain content to be cheap labor.*

In many ways, the school achieved its goal of providing the social space in which working women could gather to talk to one another, reflect upon their lives, and gain confidence for self-expression and communal aspiration. But its founders had greater hopes: they saw themselves as training leaders for an insurgent Southern labor movement. That movement, they believed, would be part of a larger struggle for "the creation of a genuine democracy in which those who work would own and operate the country."†

AS THE THIRTIES PROGRESSED, THE LOFTY VISION OF THE SCHOOL'S leaders seemed close to realization. In 1929, workers across the South had revolted against increasing workloads and diminishing wages in a series of wildcat strikes which focused national attention on the region and compelled industrialists to ameliorate working and living conditions in numerous Southern mill towns. After years of worsening economic depression, workers' discontent once again erupted when 200,000 Southerners joined the general textile strike of 1934. The formation of the Committee for Industrial Organization (CIO) in the following year spurred labor organization in mining, textile, and garment-making

*SSS Scrapbook, 1930.

†"Report on Conference on Workers' Education," Chattanooga, January 16–17, 1937, SSS Papers, Catherwood Library, N.Y. State School of Industrial and Labor Relations, Cornell University, Ithaca, New York.

industries; and the ACWA, the ILGWU, and the United Garment Workers launched Southern organizing drives. In 1937, the CIO established the Textile Workers Organizing Committee to spread the idea of industrial democracy throughout the South.

As a result of these developments, the number of the school's students affiliated with trade unions rose substantially, and by 1935, 80 percent represented Southern locals. Financial support from labor increased as newly formed unions across the South raised scholarship money and sent members to the school to receive training in parliamentary procedure, labor history, and economics.

While this new labor backing was essential to the school's program, it also presented difficulties. From the beginning, the disparate aims of creating a women's alliance across class lines while at the same time organizing Southern workers had led the school to look for support from groups historically at odds with one another: middle-class women's organizations and labor unions. Closer ties to the labor movement threatened to topple this fragile coalition.

As the CIO organizing drive gained strength, the school's leaders struggled to interpret labor's aims to reform-minded Southern women. As Louise McLaren explained in a speech to the Virginia Federation of Women's Clubs:

It is hoped that the club women of the South may study the facts before it is too late, and that they will get behind the workers' education movement since that is one concrete way in which they might help to prepare workers to do their share in bringing about right conditions in Southern industrial life.*

But this effort to mobilize middle-class support for labor met powerful obstacles. For example, in 1935, McLaren reported that the Roanoke, Virginia, workers' education committee chairman, a former YWCA industrial secretary, had been forced to sever her connection with the school "because of her lack of freedom to express her interest in the labor movement due to her husband's employment in a large corporation." This was, McLaren added, but one example of the school's growing difficulty in finding middle-class women who would "identify themselves with workers in the present tense situation."†

Even the sensitive and dedicated leaders of the Southern Summer School sometimes had difficulty understanding the realities faced by working-class women. During the late summer and fall of 1929, Louise McLaren corresponded with several students who had participated in

*Speech by McLaren, "Workers' Education in the South," May 3, 1929, to the Virginia Federation of Women's Clubs, SSS Papers.

†Director's Report, SSS, January 15–March 15, 1935, Frank Graham Papers, Southern Historical Collection, University of North Carolina at Chapel Hill.

A gathering of the staff at the Southern Summer School, 1929

the textile strike in Marion, North Carolina. She wrote to one student in October of that year, after the second strike in Marion in which six workers had been killed:

This morning I have a letter from Laurence Hogan telling me that you have been scabbing in the mill since the murders and of course I am shocked to hear it. I hope there is some mistake about this and that you will write me and tell me how it happened.

Minnie Fisher, a 20-year-old cotton mill worker, replied:

Louise, I am sorry you heard that I was scabbing. I will tell you how it was and you be the judge. They had a strike on Tuesday and we didn't know anything about it until it was pulled and our boys got killed at the gate and then I quit work. . . . Our leaders never had any meetings to tell us what to do so nearly all the union people went back. I haven't worked but two days and they asked me not to go back and now I am back home and . . . have got no job no money no anything and my man is gone and I can't find out where he is whether dead or alive and I am in debt that it looks like I am going to have to do some scabbing so you can imagine what kind of shape I am in. I have got a little girl that has to be clothed and fed . . . so now you have the truth from my heart what would you do if you was in my place?*

Such an exchange illustrates the elusiveness of the school's hope for female solidarity across class lines. Students armed with organizing skills and an increasing sense of self-worth had to venture back into

*McLaren to Fisher, October 16, 1929; Fisher to McLaren, October 23, 1929, SSS Papers.

communities that were often hostile both to female assertiveness and to labor organization. Moreover, while students returned to the pressures of factory work and family responsibilities, their teachers resumed academic posts at colleges and universities, taking up lives which made it difficult, if not impossible, for them to comprehend the constant hardships faced by working-class women.

Nevertheless, within the confines of the school itself, Louise McLaren, Lois MacDonald, and their colleagues did create a model for new social relationships. The school experience marked a watershed for many of the students. It provided a first exposure to the world beyond the mill village or city factory. For some, it served as an entry into the labor movement or community leadership positions. For most, it offered if not the means of collective change as its founders intended, then at least the incentive and opportunity for individual self-advancement.

AFTER 1935, THE SCHOOL ABANDONED ITS CONNECTIONS WITH women's groups and became more dependent on organized labor. However, contrary to union priorities, the school's leaders continued to insist that workers' education and the organization of women workers were crucial to the movement. And they urged students to maintain an independent stance toward all institutions, including trade unions.

As the radical thrust of the CIO drives of the Depression era gave way to pragmatism and political compromise, the socialist perspective of the school's leaders caused increasing tension. By the beginning of World War II, the group's relationship with a male-dominated labor movement had undermined their feminist goal of forging a women's alliance as well as their efforts to organize women workers. As a result of pressure from the unions, the school began admitting men in 1938.

When World War II brought a return to full employment, workers had little time to attend a residence school. As the unions gained strength and financial solvency, they began to establish their own workers' education programs. Thus, by the early forties, the role of the school, which had been hailed as "the classroom of the Southern labor movement," was no longer clear.* In 1943, after over two decades of work in the South, Louise McLaren decided to leave the school.

The Southern Summer School, however, did not disappear. Rather, under new leadership, it turned to other social issues. In 1944, the renamed Southern School for Workers began running literacy programs

---

*Jack Herling, "Southern Summer School Real Workers' College," Federated Press, Eastern Bureau, August 24, 1929.

for black workers, organizing voter registration drives, and fighting to eliminate the poll tax.* In 1950, the organization finally disbanded for lack of funding.

When Mary C. Barker of Atlanta, who had served for many years as head of the school's advisory board, looked back on the group's work over the years since 1927, she emphasized the seeds of change that the school had planted in the minds of many Southerners. Stressing the impact the school had made on the lives of Southern workers, both black and white, she wrote that, to her, the school had not died but "is very much alive today, for it has entered into the bloodstream of the evolving history of the South."†

*The Southern Summer School and Highlander Folk School both followed the pattern of work in the Southern labor movement evolving into a concentration on civil rights issues. The Highlander Folk School, unlike the Southern Summer School, played a critical role during the 1960s in movements for black equality across the South. See Frank Adams, *Unearthing Seeds of Fire: The Idea of Highlander* (Winston-Salem: Blair, 1975).

†Mary Barker to Brownie Lee Jones, October 16, 1951, Barker Papers, Emory University, Atlanta, Georgia.

SIXTEEN

My Struggle to Escape the Cotton Mill, 1930

ANONYMOUS

THE FOLLOWING ESSAY COMES from the collection of autobiographies written by Southern Summer School students in 1930.

After mother and father were married they lived on a homestead in Alabama. The house was built of logs with one large room. The cooking was done in iron pots. Some little distance from the yard to the north was built the crib, in which to keep feed of different kinds. Here were horse and corn stalls, for then we kept a cow and father had to keep a horse to plow his little farm and to pull the buggy for it was miles to where anyone lived and too far to walk.

I've heard my father say after he had made a crop and there was no work to do on the farm he would walk two miles night and morning to work for as low as 50 cents per day to make enough to buy the things we had to have that he could not raise on the farm. In this way he worked some on the railroad and learned how to build railroad track and later became a section foreman. Father made good crops and I can remember the little barn filled to overflowing with corn, while the hayloft would be full of peanuts and hay and several nice hogs could be found in a pen nearby getting ready to be butchered for the winter's supply of meat and lard.

"Hard times" forced my father to rent this little home and move elsewhere to run a farm for someone who had capital to farm on a large scale. This was the beginning of the end, for we moved from place to place until the home was finally sold. Then I was old enough to start to school; but we lived too far from a school and I was too small to go alone, so all the

Kahn Manufacturing Co., Alabama, ca. 1920

schooling I had up till I was 8 years old was a few months when my aunt taught me. All this time the family was growing larger, there being six children. The 1907 panic hit the country. We moved to a town in Alabama, to the cotton mills, and father, my sister, and I went to work. I wasn't quite 15 years old. In a short time another brother was born.

On going to work my sister and I were sent to the spinning room to learn to spin. My sister made better progress than I, but the bosses being harsh and I being timid I was half scared to death all the time and could not learn the work. This kept up about three months. My father was making $1 per day and my sister and I making 50 cents each per day. Then it was decided we had served our apprenticeship and should go on as "sides." I was given two sides of spinning and was paid 11 cents per side, making my daily pay 22 cents, and I was living in terror all the time in fear of the boss. When Father found I would no longer get 50 cents per day he told me to stay home. In the meantime my sister had been taken to the weave shop to fill "batteries," making 70 cents per day. After some red tape I was allowed to go to work in the weave shop and for nearly two years my sister and I worked for 70 cents per day. It took very little skill to keep this job going and there being no harsh bosses over me I was fairly happy here until Father began to insist that Sister and I become weavers. I hated the cotton mill and swore I would not stay in it all my life. My sister did not mind so much, tried, and became a good weaver.

After quite a struggle on my part to keep from learning to be a weaver, I gave it a thorough trial and found I could not learn weaving very easily, and being very anxious to earn more money I began to think of how I would find better-paying work. Then I was allowed to go to the spooler and warper rooms, where I worked at different times in both rooms making $1.25 per day and finally getting $9 per week.

The long hours and nervous state in which I worked had caused me to have much less strength than I would have had otherwise, and it was all I could do to keep the work up with the other worker who was required on the job and a boy to roll the bores for us. Then one day we were told that the boy could not help us anymore and I quit. My father had left the mill by this time because he had been too ready to talk to anyone he saw about conditions in the mill. With no one working in the mill but me, the company notified us to move and when I quit we were not living on company property.

The same day I quit the cotton mill I went to an overall factory to get work and succeeded. While talking with the owner of the business he told me that some of his employees made $10 per week, and I thought if there was even a remote chance of me making that much money it was a wonderful opportunity for me so I went to work the next day. I worked four days that week and made $2.40 on piece work. I had worked 11 hours in the mill but here I only worked 9 hours and conditions were so different. A very nice, kind, patient young woman was my instructor and the superintendent was never harsh spoken. This was a union factory and I advanced so well that in a short time I was making as much as I had made after working years in the cotton mill. However, the things that cotton mill life did to me have just now, after many years, begun to leave me.

SEVENTEEN

I Was in the Gastonia Strike

BERTHA HENDRIX

THIS EXCERPT FROM A SOUTHERN Summer School autobiography was written in 1938. The strike at the Loray Mill in Gastonia, North Carolina, was the largest and most famous of a series of walk-outs in textile mills across the Carolinas and Tennessee in 1929.

I had been working for the Manville-Jenkes mill in Loray, near Gastonia, for eight years—ever since I was 14. We worked 13 hours a day, and we were so stretched out that lots of times we didn't stop for anything. Sometimes we took sandwiches to work, and ate them as we worked. Sometimes we didn't even get to eat them. If we couldn't keep our work up like they wanted us to, they would curse us and threaten to fire us. Some of us made $12 a week, and some a little more.

One day some textile organizers came to Gastonia. They came to the mill gates at six o'clock, just when the daylight hands were coming out. They began to talk to the workers as they came out of the mill. Everybody stopped to listen. When the night-shift hands came up, they stopped to listen too. I was on the night shift. None of us went into work that night, for the organizers were telling us that they would help us get more money and less hours if we would stick together in a union, and stay out.

This was the first time I'd ever thought that things could be better; I thought that I would just keep working all my life for 13 hours a day, like we were. I felt that if we would stick together and strike we could win something for ourselves. But I guess we didn't have a chance—the way "the law" acted after we struck.

That night we had a meeting, and almost all of the workers came. People got up and said that unless they got

170 Mrs. Myrtle Lawrence, one of the leaders of the STFU, who attended the Southern Summer School for Women Workers

shorter hours and more money they would never go back to work. We all went home that night feeling that at last we were going to do something that would make things better for us workers. We were going to win an 8-hour day, and get more pay for ourselves.

The next morning, we were at the mill at five o'clock, to picket, but we couldn't get anywhere near the plant, because the police and the National Guard were all around the mill and kept us a block away. We formed our picket line anyway, and walked up and down a street near the mill.

Every day for a week we picketed. One day my husband, Red, went with me on the picket line. (He worked in another mill on the night shift.) Just as we started on the picket line two policemen came over and grabbed Red, put him in an automobile, and took him to jail. They beat him up with a blackjack, and broke his ring and tore his clothes. They thought he was one of the strikers, and they were arresting strikers right and left, hauling lots of them to jail every day.

In the second week of the strike, the bosses went to other towns and out in the country and brought in scabs. The police and the National Guard made us keep away from the mill, so all we could do was to watch the scabs go in and take our jobs.

We kept on with our picket line, though we didn't have much of a chance to persuade the scabs not to go in, because of the police and guards. We were treated like dogs by the law. Strikers were knocked down when they called to the scabs, or got too near the mill. Every day more and more strikers were arrested. They kept the jail-house full of workers. Strikers were put out of their houses. All over our village you could see whole families with their household belongings in the street—sometimes in the pouring down rain, and lots of them with their little children and babies.

We had a relief station where strikers could get food and groceries. Red, my husband, had been fired from his job in the other mill when his boss found out that he was trying to help us strikers, so he opened a drink stand near the relief station. One night about nine o'clock, the police came to the relief station as they usually went anywhere there were any strikers. I don't know what happened exactly, but there was a gun fight, and the chief of police was killed. Red, who was selling drinks there, was arrested along with a lot of others. Red and six others were accused of killing the policeman.

After Red was put in jail for the murder, my father and I moved to another town. I was expecting my baby soon, but I went to work in another textile plant. Except for what I read in the papers, I didn't know much about what was going on in Gastonia.

Seven months after the strike they tried Red and the six others accused of killing the chief of police. They had been kept in jail all this time. I couldn't attend much of the trial on account of the baby, but Red told me about it.

Almost everybody thinks that the workers were innocent, and many people believe that the chief was killed by one of his own policemen. However, Red and the others were convicted of the murder, and given anywhere from five to twenty years in the penitentiary. Red and the others got out on bail, and all of them left the country and stayed away for two years. Then Red came back to get me and the baby and he was caught, and sent to prison. He served three years and four months of his prison term, and got out last year.

After the trial, I moved to High Point, and got a job in a textile mill to support the baby and me. We have had a hard time of it, but I think what we went through in Gastonia was worth it all, because I think people all over the country learned about the conditions of textile workers in the South, and it helped the labor movement in the South.

EIGHTEEN
UAW Sit-down Strike: Atlanta, 1936

NEILL HERRING
AND
SUE THRASHER

THE DRIVE TO ORGANIZE THE employees of General Motors Corporation culminated in the historic Flint sit-down of early 1937, but it began in a small branch assembly plant on the outskirts of Atlanta on November 18, 1936. Organization had rooted in the Lakewood plant in 1933 in the form of an AFL federal local; these were industry-wide locals with less autonomy than other AFL unions. In common with so many of the hybrid unions that accompanied the National Recovery Act, the organization seemed doomed to impotence by its structure. As economic conditions worsened during Roosevelt's lackluster year of 1936, the forces that had spurred unionization multiplied. The speedup, determined by the demands of investors, was intensified while wage levels were unimproved. The seasonal character of the work militated against any job security, and the continued intransigence of management to any form of independent organization all contributed to the strike wave, both nationally and in Georgia.

The AFL local disappeared when its fatal insistence on craft division rendered it inoperative, but the conditions that spawned it had not. The need for organization remained, and the form presented itself in the creation of the CIO by dissident AFL unions in 1935. Centered around John L. Lewis's United Mine Workers, a variety of fledgling unions quickly spread tender organizational roots throughout the country. Atlanta's Lakewood plant joined the United Automobile Workers (UAW) as Local 34, although only a handful of union faithfuls had joined the local before November 1936; the participation of the entire work force in the strike showed that hearts, if not wallets, were in the right place. Holding out for over three months in the snowy winter of 1936–37, the mettle of the organization was well tested and gained rather than lost strength.

Why Atlanta, with no appreciable organized influence in the auto plant, should precede the industrial capitals of the North in precipitating the strike wave has been something of a mystery. Sidney Fine, in the standard work on the General Motors strikes of 1936–37, *Sit-Down,* gives credit to UAW General Executive Board member Fred Pieper for having called the workers in Atlanta out on strike. The following interviews reveal that the decision to stop work was a collective one and the influence of the national union was peripheral to both the call and the conduct of the strike.

Fine seems to think that Atlanta was traveling under the illusion that a nationwide strike was imminent, and that was the conclusive factor in their decision. While Local 34's president at that time, Charlie Gillman, acknowledges that they thought the rest of the plants would come out soon, the local conditions were the dominant factor in the move to strike. This is underscored by the wide support the strike enjoyed among the work force even though union membership was minuscule in the plant. Push coming to shove was a far more decisive factor in Atlanta then the Executive Board's strategy.

Fine's position is based on his source, the papers of Fred Pieper. His unfortunate reliance on the single account of a figure who seems to have been somewhat removed from the center of action during the Lakewood sit-down and subsequent picket is typical of the errors that have contributed to making academic history what it is today: an ideological commodity, baggaged with apologetics and bloodless inaccuracies.

But the labor movement, perhaps more than any other institution in our society, is a thing of flesh and bones, demanding a history of people, not individual leaders. This is particularly true in the initial stages of development, in that period when *solidarity* is not just a curious word but a culmination of human values galvanized into action. What these interviews offer, then, is history from the bottom up.

Charlie Gillman was president of UAW Local 34 at the time of the sit-down strike in 1936. A few years later he went to work full-time with the CIO to build a regional office and stayed with the AFL-CIO until his retirement in 1968. Mrs. Gillman is a staunch union supporter, and for almost fifty years has actively supported and conspired with her husband to build a trade union movement in the South.

The interview with the Gillmans was conducted in October 1973, at their home, by Neill Herring and Sue Thrasher.

MR. GILLMAN: I was born in Birmingham, Alabama. We lived in Columbus and Augusta. We were married in Augusta, and then we came up here—during the Depression, wasn't it, honey? Dad was a custom tailor, and mother, well, she was a housekeeper, but she would assist him in rough going.

[I] worked in the Fisher Body plant. As I remember it, it had been operating only a few months. I guess we had close to 900 people in the Fisher Body side, and about the same, maybe a few less, in Chevrolet. They were divided, you see. Fisher Body would build the bodies, and they would go over on one of these chain things through the wall to Chevrolet and they would put the motor in and finish them up.

We just got kicked around. We formed a union out there because in those days when a fellow went to work, he had no security of any kind. He didn't know if he would be working one day or the next, and as soon as the foreman had some member of his family out of work, why he would fire you and bring this family member in so he wouldn't have to keep him up. It didn't make any difference if you had a half dozen children, or a dozen, or none at all as far as they were concerned. They would just as soon fire you if you didn't work as fast as they thought you should. The people just finally got tired of it, and the lack of security, I suppose, was the thing that really organized our plant. The fact that people just got tired of being pushed around.

See, what they would do, when they changed models, they would bring the people in and work 12 to 18 hours a day, getting the new models ready. They would pay an hourly rate; I think at that time it was 45 cents an hour or something like that. Then when they had the dealers stocked up with new cars, they would put us on piece rates, and of course then we would only work two or three days a week.

I suppose we would rock along through the spring, until the spring season was over, working three days a week or usually less than that. But at any rate, we would work short hours like that until we got in debt again. And they always kept you in debt. They figured if you were in debt and owed everybody that you could owe, why then you couldn't quit, or you couldn't strike, or you couldn't do anything to better your life. So it was pretty rough out there at those times.

You remember, under Roosevelt they had the NRA days, and they were supposed to have had the right to organize in those days under that statute and under that declaration. So we didn't have any better sense than to think that they meant it, and we organized our union. We were ready then—we had built a good union about that time—and when things got so rough there, and they started kicking the people around, getting them to work faster, speeding up the line, we just quit. We pushed the button up in the trim department and shut the whole plant down. We just quit and stayed in there. Of course, we didn't go out. We appointed caretakers from among the people to see that there was no damage or any violation of fire regulations or any security as far as the plant was concerned, and we had no problem at all.

We finally got an agreement out of Roach, and Gallaher—we brought him in too, from the other side, from Chevrolet—that there would be no effort made to try to operate the plant; if we would go out of the plant, they would shut it down. So we agreed, and we went out. The union hall was right across the street from the plant, and we set up a picket line and built tent houses there on the sidewalk and all around the plant, and our pickets just practically stayed out there. We put stoves in the tents; it was in the cold weather, and we just set there, that's all.

Ours was the first plant that went on strike. Of course, we were crazy. We thought at the time, we had been advised that some of the other plants were organized, but none of them were. The national union didn't have any money. It was new, young then, and they didn't have anything, so we had to get by the best we could. It was getting pretty rough, too, after we had been out a few weeks, didn't have anything to eat, didn't have any money in the treasury or anything. So we set up what we called the food squad, the begging squad, and these fellows went out to the city market out here, and those farmers would give us bags of potatoes and onions and peas. I ate so many peas and onions I didn't want to see any more for a while after we got through. I'm telling you what's a fact, but they were good then. And we sent a couple of men throughout the automobile industry up North and chiseled some money out of them. Finally, when John Lewis moved in to run the national union, we was able to get some money out of them, and send around. We had a little bit.

Well, there wasn't anything we could do but stay down. They kept promising—Homer Martin, what a faker he was—he kept promising, "Ah, we're organizing, we're ready to go, we'll be ready, we'll join you," and they kept fooling around. They were organizing all the time, of course, but they had no semblance of an organization at all when we came down and struck the plant; we didn't have sense enough to know that. It was like one little old plant here trying to shut down General Motors. But it didn't take them long after we had started the thing down here. Most of the plants—Norwood, Ohio; Kansas City; and Buffalo—they all started and got right in the works, and very shortly we had all the plants organized. Of course the strike was over quite a while before we finished the organization in General Motors—the shops, parts departments, and all that—but it finally was done, and there is no relationship between the working conditions and the lives of the people who work for GM now and what used to prevail in these plants.

Wyndham Mortimer, although he was a communist they claimed, he was a smart one. He was the one that actually held the union together, to tell you the truth. He was the one that did the negotiating, he and Ed Hall. National contracts, and I believe that George Addes and Hall and Mortimer did more to build this union after Lewis turned it over as a national union than anybody in the organization. Mortimer was a communist, there is no doubt about it, in my opinion. But the thing is, communists in those days were useful to the labor movement if you would let them do their job of organizing and get them out. But if you left them in they would tear it up again, too.

But Mortimer was an exception. Because they used him to negotiate on the contracts, he was very seldom around in the plant. His job was primarily to negotiate the grievances, and he did a good job of it. Ed Hall, of course, was a big old blustery fellow, and he would holler and whoop; well, they would work together. Hall would pound the table and holler, and Mortimer would sit back and say let's quiet down. Then the two working together would intimidate the management and then Mortimer would get the thing done. He was a good man.

MRS. GILLMAN: I think one thing that many people tend to forget is the part that Roosevelt played in all of this, because I have always believed firmly that had we had another president other than Roosevelt, we would never have gotten as far as we have today. Because he made it possible for people in our level to do better for themselves by placing the Acts of Congress necessary to allow us to do the things that needed to be done, and of course, the person directly responsible for that was his wife, Eleanor. She was much smarter than he was. And she was the one that put these little ideas in his head. And then, of course, after he saw the value of it he went through with it, and I guess we just grew up with Roosevelt.

MR. GILLMAN: Well, you had another you've forgotten, I think, that was instrumental in a great deal of the welfare legislation, the welfare of the people at the time anyhow—Ma Perkins, Secretary of Labor Perkins. Wonderful person, holy cow, and she and Mrs. Roosevelt they did the social work, the laws. I think the two of them together were fantastic. Ah, she was something. And we had no trouble getting on WPA down here during the strike. And she set up training schools to teach welding to our fellows who were on strike here, we had them all over the place.

The strike lasted about three or four months. The thing about it is, with the conditions we had, if we didn't accomplish anything else, we established bargaining rights with the company. The first little contract we had just says that they will bargain for the members alone. And, of course, that didn't work very well. As we organized over in the other plant, why, of course we changed the contract. But if we didn't do anything else, it brought those people together, and there wasn't a single man in that whole 1,200, or whatever it was he had in the plant at that time, made any effort to go back to work that entire time. And we were able through that strike to bargain for decent wages. One of the best provisions of the contract was that we had a committee of workers that was able to go into the plant and time-watch jobs, to regulate the speed that the people were working and to take some of the work off of them.

The first year or so of our contract, the committee had to handle grievances after they got through working 8 or 9 hours a day. They would have to go in at night with the management and negotiate the grievances.

You know, so many people were just barely existing and not making enough to even eat on. They were losing some of their pride—the pride that people usually have to do better for their family, to have security, and to know that they will come in the next morning and go to work. The union tended to bring the people together and give them a little pride. That alone was worth the strike, if nothing else had been accomplished.

W. A. COWAN WENT TO WORK FOR THE GENERAL MOTORS LAKEWOOD Assembly plant (at that time, in the Fisher Body Division) in 1932, and retired in 1967. Harvey Pike began working for Fisher Body in February 1929, and left the "last day of February in 1966." Between 1946 and 1950, he worked full-time for the CIO Southern Organizing Committee. Claude Smith first worked for General Motors in Norwood, Ohio, in 1926, "built the first cushion" in the Atlanta plant, and retired in 1967. Tom Starling began working for Fisher Body in April 1928. From 1941 until his retirement in 1968, he was on leave of absence from the plant to work full time for the UAW, serving twelve years on the International Executive Board and fifteen years as international representative. Mark Waldrop came to work for Fisher Body in 1928. All five men were members of the fledgling UAW local at the time the sit-down strike occurred in November 1936, and they played key roles in the subsequent long, hard winter months of sustaining the strike and building a strong union.

The interview with W. A. Cowan, Harvey Pike, Claude Smith, Tom Starling, and Mark Waldrop was conducted by Sue Thrasher at the union hall of UAW Local 34 in September 1973, and was arranged through the courtesy of W. A. Cowan, current president of the Retirees' Local.

MR. STARLING: In August of 1929 there was a lot of dissatisfaction over working hours. What happened was we were supposedly on piece work, but you could barely make day work on piece work. We had no overtime provisions then, and you didn't get paid a premium for working long hours. Where I worked in the Fisher Body paint department they would run the line for 10 or 11 hours a day and then there would be a lot of repair work to do on the bodies to finish them up. Quite a big group of workers would have to stay then, until eleven or twelve o'clock at night, to finish up that work. They were paid 35 cents an hour for overtime. They would have to be back to work the next morning at seven o'clock, so it just went from bad to worse.

We decided then, just the employees talking among ourselves, that we were not going to work beyond 9 hours a day. I don't remember the date, but it was early August. We decided that we would go home after 9 hours at 4:30. We went to work at seven o'clock and got thirty minutes for lunch; 4:30 would be a regular day's work. The company wanted the time to run until 6:30—11 hours that was. Then they came back just before 4:30, and said they would agree to shut the line down at 5:30, just work 10 hours. We said no, we were not going to work over 9 hours, so at 4:30 we quit and went home. When we come back the next morning, the management had pulled the cards of the leaders and fired them, so the employees refused to go to work. They went in the plant, but they wouldn't go to work.

This was in August 1929. We had a meeting in the plant and decided then that we would organize and we painted some signs of different types—one of them was demanding a dollar an hour and overtime. Then we formed a parade and paraded down to the labor temple. We had some speakers and set up a semblance of an organization. Had different departments to elect a spokesman from each department.

The AFL set up a committee among the AFL people and they met with management. The second day we were out, we all went back down to the labor temple to get a report. They reported to us that night that we would have to go back to work, that they were not prepared to take us into the union. The management had agreed that everybody could return to work with the exception of thirty people who they considered leaders in the movement, and those people would be fired. So the AFL advised us to go back to work the next morning.

When they named the people on the list to be fired, I was on the list. But I had worked with my foreman in Pontiac, Michigan, so he told me not to come in and reported me out absent because of a death in the family. A few days later he told me to come in, and told me what he had told them and that he would substantiate my story. So that's the way I got back to work, and that was the end of the strike. Actually our first incident happened on November 18, 1936, when they told the employees they couldn't wear union buttons.

MR. SMITH: I'm the guy that went and got permission to close the line down. I was steward in the cushion department. My foreman told two of the boys that was wearing buttons, Fred Tyson and Fred Morgan, that if they didn't pull the buttons off they would have to go to the office and be fired. I went over on the main line to see the president, Charlie Gillman. I said, "Charlie, they are after two of my boys over in the cushion department about the buttons. What do you want me to tell them?" He said, "You tell them, by god, to wear them." I went back over there, and I reached up to push the button. The foreman walked up to the line and said, "Smith, if you push that button you're gonna lose your seniority." I said, "To hell with it." I pushed the button, and that stopped the line, the first line that was stopped, General Motors Strike, 1936–37.

After I pushed the button, my foreman said, "You're going to the office." And by that time all the people that I was steward over just ganged around me and said, he's not going anyplace.

After I got permission from Mr. Gillman to go back to tell the guys to wear the buttons, I went by and told Mr. Rawls, the vice-president of the local, what the score was, and he jumped over out of the paint department into the cushion department and jumped up on the table—he had great big old feet, and he weighed about 200 pounds. He stamped his feet about four times, and waved his hands like that and everything in there went just like you could hear a pin drop. Every line stopped; every man except one, Zinc, he kept working. Somebody slapped him up the side of the head with a metal finisher. He stopped working then.

We stayed in the plant that night, all night, and we left the next morning about nine or ten o'clock. Our wives had formed an auxiliary and brought breakfast to us. We formed two lines for their protection—they was going to keep them out—so we just went down and made a walkway for them to bring food in.

We all spent the night in there. Somebody slipped in and raised the skylight on us trying to freeze us out. But we pulled all the seat covers, cotton bats, and everything else. We made beds. [*Laughing*] I guess we did $10,000 worth of damage to the materials.

MR. STARLING: I think the point that really should be made is why did we leave the plant. Now, most of the sit-down strikers stayed in the plant. But the committee met with management and Fisher Body—that is where the strike started—and they agreed that if we would vacate the plant that they would not attempt to operate the plant or move any of the plant equipment out until the strike was finally settled. And under those circumstances, we come on the outside the next morning and formed a picket line.

They [the national office] had led us to believe that all the plants were organized, well organized, better organized than ours, and we were holding up the organization. We found out after we struck this plant that we were the only plant that could strike. They were not able to shut any of the rest of them down.

Later, and I don't remember in what order, but finally the Norwood plant went down, then the St. Louis plant went down, then the plant in Kansas City went down. So actually what happened in that strike that started in '36 [was that] the only plants that went down in '36 were plants outside of Michigan. Turned out that the Southern plants went down before any of the plants in the North were able to shut down. None of the Michigan plants went down until January of '37. That was when they had the sit-down strike in Flint.

MR. WALDROP: I was in the trim department. I would say in that department there were at least 250 men. I was putting windhose on the panel. That is that little roll that goes around the door. It was a rubber tube covered with fabric. I was working on the tables—I wasn't directly on the line. There was me and six girls working together. So, whenever I heard that the rest of them across the cushion room had set down, I went down the line telling them that the boys had set down, and for them to get out of their jobs and quit. So, as fast as I could go around and tell the boys what was happening they began to pile out, and it wasn't long until every line in the plant was shut down.

MR. COWAN: I was in final assembly for about two years, trim department, put in glass and c.v.'s—you know, that little bitty glass that you roll out to let the air come in—I was putting them in, then I got transferred to headliner. That's upholstering overhead.

I was working all the time for the union. When we got really active was when President Roosevelt came on the radio one night and said you laboring people get busy and get organized and pay a dollar a month and join the union, because these companies are paying more than that to get together just to keep y'all from having one. So we got strung out in there, and this gentleman Fred Pieper brought us four or five buttons that he had in his pocket, and we put them on. First thing you know, here comes the foreman or superintendent behind us wanting to see what it was, and then they would take off to the office. Well, the foreman came back in a little while and said, "You'll have ten minutes to pull them off or get fired." Now this happened in our department. We didn't have but about eight or ten buttons in there at most. We all got our heads together and said let's pull them off until lunchtime, and then at lunchtime, we all went out and several of us came back with pocketsful. Everybody came running to us wanting buttons. They went down the line like a fire was after them or something. So we put them all on then after lunch. They didn't run us out then; we had too big a thing going,

I reckon. And the men were getting the buttons, just grabbing them and running. Here, put this button on! Just tearing out down through there! A lot of men who hadn't even joined the union put them buttons on.

MR. WALDROP: There was no overtime provisions whatsoever at that time. The only promise you got out of overtime was that if you didn't work it, you was fired.

MR. COWAN: Before we even got a contract—excuse me, y'all correct me if I'm wrong—after we had started organizing, they raised it from 35 cents to 60 cents an hour, trying to get us to break it up then, you know. And we said, well, if it's that much just trying to organize, we're going to get more than that.

MR. STARLING: The most effective thing, I think, we were able to use was the statement that Roosevelt made. I don't remember now when it was or under what circumstances, but the statement that we always quoted in the leaflets that we put out said, "If I was a factory worker, I would join the union."

Now actually in the signed agreement we didn't get anything except recognition for our members only. We were not permitted to bargain for anyone but our members. But, I think, following the settlement of the strike we had some of the most effective collective bargaining in the plant that I think we ever had, because of the way we handled it.

The company wanted to bargain with the people individually, so they adopted what they called an open-door policy. The manager's door was always open. Any employee could come in and discuss any problems he had with them at any time. And what we did, in the departments, one employee had a problem, we all had a problem, and so we would all go down to the office to discuss our problem with them. Now that shut the whole plant down, because they had to settle the department's problem before they could get the plant to operate.

While we were on strike, fortunately, although the people were not members of the union—not very many of them—they all stayed with us. Then that gave the people a boost to see that they could be effective if they stuck together, and then when they came outside they stuck together.

Oh, we had some dissidents outside that tried to get petitions signed; they would go around and try to get employees to sign petitions to go back to work. The company was able to get some people to do that, some people in the bargaining unit, the production unit. But we kept pretty close check on them. We would catch them out with a petition and we would take the petition away from them and tell them they better not show up around here any more. And they wouldn't, they wouldn't come back.

MR. PIKE: Then we would go have a talk with those people whose name was on that petition, we'd explain to them that that was totally ineffective.

MR. STARLING: Some of them were foremen that was taking the petitions around.

The company hired a lot of policemen and put them in the plant during the strike. And they tried to operate their company union too during the strike, but they were not successful in having any meetings at all. They tried to bring the president of the company union in the plant there one day and we wouldn't let them bring him in. Sturdivant was chief of police [of the city of Atlanta] here then, and he tried to take him into the plant, but he wasn't able to get him in.

MR. PIKE: He had no jurisdiction out here; it was in the county at that time. But he started in the plant with two fifths of whiskey. See, his son was one of the policemen inside the plant hired by the company. He got his whiskey busted out in front of the plant and turned back. The county police made a case against him. [Sturdivant was forced to resign shortly thereafter.]

MR. WALDROP: You made mention a minute ago of who worked in the plant while we were out. They had received quite a quantity of materials, motors especially, before we came out. They had twenty-six cars on the siding, and they had the foremen loading those motors back in the cars and they was going to send them back north, but when they called the railroad to come and pull those cars out, somehow or another that phone call would wind up in the union office. By the time the engineer would get out here, we would have about a hundred men sitting over there on the railroad track and he would turn around and go back. That happened daily for a couple of months.

MR. COWAN: We had a few scabs. But it was hard to tell how many. They couldn't stay long.

MR. STARLING: Oh, yeah, we had a picket line all the time, twenty-four hours a day.

MR. WALDROP: They couldn't turn out any production.

MR. SMITH: I think this should be said: the womenfolk really stuck with us. They set up a soup kitchen and fed us, and we got a little help. John L. Lewis sent us a carload of coal, and we got a little help from other sources. Then finally we run out of money and didn't have nothing, and an old man that owned a furniture store loaned us money.

MR. COWAN: He got our business after that.

MR. WALDROP: We did have a few good friends in Florida; all the truck drivers were really good about bringing up fruits and vegetables and stuff like that that went good in the soup kitchen. It was my job, there were three or four more, we knocked on places downtown, went from place to place, and asked for donations, especially in wholesale groceries. And our ladies, they manned the kitchen day and night from the time the strike started.

MR. STARLING: I think there is another thing we should mention: we did have good cooperation from our creditors. We all owed money. We set up a committee to go around and talk to people on behalf of the workers that owed money for different things, automobiles and different things, and they deferred payment in most cases until after the strike was over. We had good cooperation there, and with water and light bills and things like that, and from the railroad.

The only thing that made the strike successful was the fact that people who were not members of the union supported it, and after we went back, those people joined the union, paid their dues and all. The few exceptions, why, their jobs were not too desirable for them in the plant under those circumstances, so most of them either joined the union or quit and left.

MR. SMITH: Tom King. He was a company union man, one of the officials of the company union. They sent him to Detroit. But after we went down and talked to him at his house that night and convinced him that he was on the wrong side of the fence, he brought the majority of the company union boys into the union.

Later on, before I left the plant in '41 to go on the executive board, we got strong enough that if you had a person in your department that didn't pay his dues, none of the other employees would cooperate with him, and working on a moving line you have got to have the cooperation of employees or you can't do your job. We had to collect our dues. I know there was one in my department that we had to do that to almost every month, but we would make it so hard on him he couldn't do his job. The superintendent would come along and he would just eat that foreman out because he wasn't getting the job done. That foreman would go to this individual and say, "Now listen, I know why you can't get your job done, because you haven't paid your union dues. Now, I'm not going to lose my job because you haven't paid your dues. If you don't pay your dues, I am going to fire you. If I don't fire you, I'm going to get fired myself." And he would pay his union dues.

MR. WALDROP: I suspect about the biggest trouble in the plant after we went back was unexplainable accidents. A lot of times heavy hammers would fall off the top of the job on somebody's poor head. That would be somebody we were having trouble with, guys that didn't pay their dues.

MR. STARLING: As good a friend I guess as I had in the plant afterwards was a fellow that didn't like to pay his dues. I was riding him one day, and he invited me outside after the line went down. So, we went outside, started fighting out in front of the plant there and got over on company property and the guards came over and made us leave. Then we went down across the railroad track where the parking lot is now, and we went down there and finished it off. He paid his dues up, and he was as good a friend as I guess I had in that union afterward. He never got behind in his dues again. He said that he realized that if he wanted to work in the plant he would have to pay his dues, and he said later after we got some more benefits that I did him a favor. He appreciated it.

MRS. GILLMAN: I THINK ONE THING THAT ENTERED INTO IT WAS THE concept of the whole plant being organized as a union, and not sections as it used to be under the AFL. And the idea of solidarity—that was their word, solidarity. I can remember so well the slogans that I saw: SOLIDARITY. And that was what it meant. And it meant that to all of us. Being one, as a unit, working for the same thing. Knowing that what one got, the other one would also get. And to be able to do that really is what I think won the whole thing. If we had to go in as sections, it never would have worked. John L. Lewis is, of course, responsible for that whole concept of being one union. And that is what won the strike for us.

But it was a terrible period with the Depression and everything coming in all at the same time. People today have no conception of what it was like, and if they have to go through something like that—and I'm very much afraid that they may have to—they will certainly get the idea of just exactly what the people in those days went through. When you see your child not having enough to eat, it is enough to put a fight in anybody. It certainly did in us.

MR. GILLMAN: There's one thing that's different today among people, working people, than it was then. Back in those days after we formed the union, anything that happened in the plant that was an infringement on the rights of any worker, we represented them, although some of them did not belong to the union. If it affected one person then it was a problem for the whole shop, for everybody in that plant. Whereas today, practically anybody that works for a living, even members of the union, don't want anyone to bother them. If something is done that affects Joe over here, so long as it doesn't affect Jim here, well, that is all right. That feeling has gone through the whole community, not just the labor unions. That feeling is prevalent in nine out of ten people who work for a living that you talk to. They don't want to upset the apple cart today—just don't care if there is a depression over here for this group of people, or if they close the plant down over here and go out of business and start up somewhere else. Don't bother me because I'm doing all right today.

As I say, people are getting too complacent. There is a good danger that the unions may weaken; they'll get weak too if they don't watch themselves. I think this country is in for a real fall one of these days, because the credit now in force is the greatest it has ever been by far in this country before. And if some kind of recession starts—it got started here a few months ago, when the unemployment figures jumped way up, and it is only 5 percent now. If the unemployment gets serious, this country is going to be in some position.

It was a great life. Lot of hard work, discouragement, and a lot of pleasure. And I think that the satisfaction that you get out of what has been accomplished by the union is worth everything you put into it. It's just criminal almost that the young fellows who go to work now have no appreciation of what a union has done to their job for them, because their jobs that they are on now wasn't always that kind of a job. It was built to where they had the benefits that other people worked for, which is the way it ought to be, but they ought to know about it anyhow.

NINETEEN

Those Who Were Not Afraid: Winston-Salem, 1943

BOB KORSTAD

THE LABOR MOVEMENT IN THE United States grew rapidly during World War II. Thousands of unorganized workers joined ranks with the coal, steel, auto, and electronics workers who had organized during the CIO drives of the late Depression years. Aided by the manpower shortages and the production needs of the war and the supportive actions of the National War Labor Board (NWLB), workers won paid vacations and holidays, seniority rights, and written grievance procedures as accepted clauses in standard union contracts.

The organizing drives of the late thirties had not penetrated far into the South, however. Southern workers were rarely protected by union contracts; wages were substantially below the national average; working conditions in the South's industries remained oppressive. Most Southern industries were still family owned and managed; workers lived in paternalistic, segregated company towns, in marked contrast to the expanding industrial cities of the North and Midwest. In 1940 most North Carolina workers, like others throughout the South, lacked the benefits and security secured by unionized workers in the North, despite sporadic attempts to organize workers in the textile, tobacco, and furniture industries.

In 1943, the R. J. Reynolds Tobacco Company in Winston-Salem, North Carolina, was the largest tobacco factory in the world. With the introduction of "Camels" in 1920, through a program of aggressive marketing and advertising and the use of poorly paid, nonunionized workers, Reynolds had quickly developed into one of the "big three" tobacco manufacturers in the country. The Reynolds production facility in Winston-Salem spread over many blocks and occupied scores of separate buildings. Over 10,000 workers were employed, two-thirds of whom were black, and the majority of whom were women—the largest concentration of black workers in the South.

The huge factories, like the community, were strictly segregated. Most black workers lived in the "colored" sections east and northwest of the factories. They had the hardest, dirtiest, most dangerous jobs in the prefabrication divisions, which prepared the tobacco leaf for manufacture. The foremen, whom one woman worker characterized as "no better than chain-gang overseers," were all white men. Workers started at Reynolds at 40 cents an hour, the national minimum wage, and few blacks advanced beyond an hourly wage of 50 cents.

Reynolds's control of the entire town made union organizing an almost impossible task. During the twenties and thirties the Tobacco Workers International Union (TWIU-AFL) had attempted the task by focusing on the skilled white workers. But they had failed.

Organizers from the United Cannery Agricultural Packinghouse and Allied Workers of America-CIO, many of whom had spent years working among agricultural workers and tenant farmers in the South and the Southwest, began organizing the black workers at Reynolds in 1941. In June of 1943 their efforts paid off.

AT DAWN ON JUNE 17, 1943, THE HAZE THAT COOLS THE EARLY morning hours in Winston-Salem is slowly burning away. In the valley known as "monkey bottom" on the east side, black men and women emerge from dilapidated "shotgun" houses and slowly begin their walk up 3rd, 4th, and 5th Streets to one of the seventy gates of the Reynolds factory. The ever-present smell of tobacco is in the air, a smell that ties all the city's inhabitants to the giant company.

Farther to the east, the buses of the black-owned Safe Bus Company make their rounds. At each stop, Reynolds workers get aboard, joined by hundreds of domestics who work in the white homes of Winston-Salem.

From the north and south sections of town come white Reynolds workers, some in cars and some riding the Duke Power buses. From the west—from the foothills of the Blue Ridge—come more white workers, four or five to a car. Many of these workers have been up since daybreak, tending to the livestock on their farms or putting in an hour on their tobacco crop before coming to work at Reynolds.

In western Winston-Salem, on Brookstown Road, John C. Whitaker, vice-president of the company, glances at the headlines of the

Winston-Salem *Journal:* the Allies had begun the attack on Italy with the bombing of Sicilian bases, and Churchill was planning his Balkan drive. The war was going better, but it had also caused problems for Reynolds. The lack of manpower had reduced the size of the tobacco leaf crop the previous year and was certain to do so again. New machinery was almost impossible to obtain. The shortage of labor in the Carolina Piedmont could possibly affect the "green leaf" season beginning in August. The company needed 1,500 additional workers, but many who traditionally filled these seasonal jobs had found war jobs. At the same time, the demand for cigarettes far exceeded all possible production. The armed forces alone bought about 20 percent of Reynolds's entire product. The work force seemed stable enough, though the decision in early May to increase workloads had brought reports of grumblings from some workers.

John C. Whitaker had worked for Reynolds since graduating from the University of North Carolina in 1912. He had developed the employment office in 1919 and had been a vice-president since 1937. Certainly there was no thought in his mind that by the afternoon he would be the antagonist in the most tumultuous community and labor struggle in Winston-Salem's history.

Neither did Thedosia Simpson, as she rode the bus to her job in the stemming division of Plant #65. A tall, attractive black woman, Mrs. Simpson, like Whitaker, had deep roots in old Carolina and strong feelings for family and education. But Mrs. Simpson had been forced to leave college to go to work for Reynolds to help earn money for her family.

Theodosia Simpson knew more than she cared to about the process that transformed aged tobacco leaves into cigarettes, smoking tobacco, and chewing tobacco. It began in the stemmeries, where the soft leaf used in tobacco products was cut away from the hard center stem. Until the mid-1930s this process was done by hand, but by 1943 most of the stemming at Reynolds had been mechanized. The tobacco moved continuously, the speed of the work in the stemmery geared to the needs of the manufacturing division it supplied.

The fifth and top floor of #65 contained sixty-six machines lined up in three rows. The work was hard, the rooms were hot, and tobacco dust covered everyone in the plant from head to toe by the end of the day. Theodosia Simpson remembers:

There were three people on a machine. The tobacco was brought to the machines in large boxes by men. One untied the bundle and laid it down for the spreader who spread it out. It went through the machine to the feeder of the machine. They paid the untier less money than they did the spreader, and the spreader less money than they did the feeder of the machine. So the feeder thought she was better than the other two people on the machine. I worked as a spreader.

To the foreman who walked the lines of machines hour after hour, checking the work and disciplining the women, things looked normal on June 17. He didn't know that a few black workers had been meeting for months with representatives of the United Cannery Agricultural Packing and Allied Workers of America (UCAPAWA). Together they formed the Tobacco Workers Organizing Committee (TWOC).

SIMPSON: They gave us cards and I would go back to my department and try to get these people to join. Oh my God, the resistance that we ran up against. A lot of them remembered the old AFL trying to organize. A lot of them remembered the AFL down at Brown & Williamson, where they had segregated locals, and they didn't want to belong to anything like that. But I finally got about twelve people in my department to sign cards. But they were afraid for even the person on their machine to know that they had done it.

We wore uniforms that buttoned down the front. One day I tore all the buttons off my dress and buttoned it up with union buttons and went to work like that. The foreman didn't know what to do about it. So he just asked if I would go home and change uniforms please, and he paid me for the time I was gone. Then a memo came out the next day. No pins in your clothes. No pins, no earrings, no rings but your wedding rings. They were afraid this stuff would get into the tobacco; that was the excuse they gave. After that I was able to get people to sign up, when they saw I didn't get fired for it. That's why we had a nucleus in #65.

Weeks previous to the stoppage the workload had been getting heavier and heavier. We weren't allowed to open the windows. The heat was almost unbearable. The foremen spent most of their time going from person to person arguing and hurrying them, saying, "If you can't get this work out, get your clothes and get out." Instead of cutting down on the boxes of work, if he discovered a box not tightly packed, he would roll it back to the Casing Room to be repacked. Several people had gone to the nurse sick, and she wouldn't excuse them to go home.

The lady who worked on the machine next to me, she was a widow with five kids, and she was sick that day. Oh, you could get sick up there in a minute the way you had to work. And it was so hot in there. She couldn't keep up. She didn't have too good a relationship with the other two women on the machine, so they weren't helping her. So the foreman came up and said, "There was the door that the carpenter left." She started crying and went into hysteria, because she had these children to rear, and nobody working but her. And that kind of got next to me.

So I called a couple of people I thought I could trust "down house" [down to the lavatory] and said, "When we come in here tomorrow morning let's not work until we get some understanding on how these people are going to be treated."

I don't know who overheard it, but the lady who cleaned up the toilet came to me and said, "You know what you plan to do tomorrow." I said, "Yes." "Well, Will (that was the line foreman) knows about it." So at lunchtime we got together and decided, let's do it after lunch. So when they pulled the whistle for us to go to work, all that I had talked to just sat down on the little stool that was out from the machine, and turned their backs to the machine. Well, when some of the others saw what was happening, they didn't turn on their machines. They weren't members of the union, but they didn't.

A middle-aged Negro man, James MacCardell, who was responsible for providing the unprocessed tobacco leaf for the stemming machines, stood near us. He listened as we explained to him why we were refusing to work and he put down his box of tobacco, declaring, "If you women are gonna stand up, I'm with you."

Within moments Mr. MacCardell collapsed on the floor. The few machines on the floor that were still running quickly came to a halt as the women rushed to see what was wrong. Two male floor attendants carried him outside to the nurse, but within minutes they returned to say that he was dead of a heart attack. James MacCardell had been sick all week. He had repeatedly been refused permission to go home by the nurse. He wasn't sick enough, the nurse had said, and he knew that if he left without permission he would lose his job. Angry and frustrated, the women turned on the head foreman, Mr. Strader, and demanded that their grievances be heard.

News of Mr. MacCardell's death and the work stoppage spread through the factory, as the stemmed tobacco that normally fell to the searching tables below was not moving. Elevator operators and the "floor boys" passed the word: "They're sitting down upstairs." The 200 women on the fifth floor were quickly joined in the sit-down by the 198 women on the fourth floor and the 25 on the third floor.

Word went quickly up the management ladder to the executive offices in the Reynolds building. Mr. Strader immediately called the Reynolds office with a report of the sit-down and a demand for help in settling the protest. Company officials ordered all the doors locked so that no one would be able to come in or go out.

On the fifth floor, the women continued to talk and wait for the Reynolds officials to come. They would ask for an end to the increased workload. They needed more money. What about enlarging dressing rooms? Also, they couldn't see why people should have to work when they were sick. Respect. They were going to demand that the foremen treat them with respect.

"It didn't take the company officials long to get to the shop floor," Mrs. Simpson remembers. "The main office was only two blocks away. Through the door walked John C. Whitaker, E. E. Baumgardner, head of the Employment Office, and B. C. Johnson, superintendent of the stemmeries. B. C. Johnson introduced Mr. Whitaker, who climbed up on one of the machines to address us. This was the first time we had ever laid eyes on Mr. Whitaker."

John Whitaker was of the "old school" of Southern management. He assumed that the workers would go back to work if he assured them that the company would take care of any problems. Though his paternalistic manner contrasted with the roughshod practices of most foremen, both methods aimed at achieving the same result.

SIMPSON: He gave a little speech to start. As I remember it he said: "Let me first remind you of the very important responsibility we all have to maintain production during this crucial period of the war. Neither you nor I want to have our boys overseas think badly of our effort here in Winston-Salem. I know you have some grievances, and I want you to tell me about them so that the company can study them and make changes where they are necessary. I want you to remember, however, that this is a very large company, and many different people make different demands on our time and resources. Your demands are part of that, but so are the workers over in #12, or the stockholders who furnish us with the capital to operate."

Everybody started mumbling and finally a few talked out loud.

"We can't work this hard," someone said.

"I don't make enough money to give my family a decent meal."

"We're tired of these foremen treating us like dirt."

Finally Mr. Whitaker spoke up loudly. He promised us that he would take note of all our grievances, that the company would investigate them and make changes where needed. "I know the problem of money is very real for you," he said. "Prices are going up for all of us. We have given two wage increases in the past two years. We would like to give more. Remember, we have controls imposed by the federal government that will not allow us to make increases without their permission. But we will look into the possibility of getting wage increases."

At this point I stepped forward. "Mr. Whitaker, according to the 'little steel formula'* you can give us a wage increase without filing a petition to the National War Labor Board," I said.

He was caught off guard and he stammered, "Who told you about the little steel formula?"

"Whether you know it or not, I can read and I can think. It's been in all the papers."

"I don't know anything about the little steel formula," he countered, "but I'll have the company attorneys look into it."

Suddenly Theodosia Simpson had become the spokeswoman for the group. She poured out her feelings, her experience of years in the plant, in North Carolina. She crystallized in words the events of that day—the foreman's abuse of the widow, Mr. MacCardell's death. She emphasized the strain of the increased workload, the need to pay everybody the same wage for the same work.

Other women rose in support of Mrs. Simpson. The complaints

*The little steel formula was a labor/management/government agreement that allowed for moderate wage increases to offset wartime inflation.

multiplied; the details became more precise. Most of all, the tone changed. People said what they really felt.

Mrs. Simpson finally told Mr. Whitaker that the workers would select a committee to meet with management the next morning to discuss the grievances. The women and the men (who moved the tobacco or cleaned the floors) chose Mrs. Simpson as their spokeswoman. Elected with her on the committee were Geneva McClindon, Bessie Phillips, Viola Patterson, Willie Bird, Moses Brown, and Marion Lyde. All were either in the union or supportive of the union. "It was just a matter of who was not afraid," says Mrs. Simpson.

AS THE WORKERS LEFT #65 THEY WERE MET AT THE GATES BY THE night-shift workers in #12 who wanted to know what had happened. Soon women from the stemmeries in #8 and #256 led by TWOC member Velma Hopkins hurried down Chestnut Street to see what was going on.

SIMPSON: We arranged a meeting for later that afternoon at Union Mission Holy Church, pastored by Reverend Frank O'Neal, who was a Reynolds worker and a TWOC member. He was a big, tall, good-looking guy who was the highest-paid black worker in Reynolds. He did piecework in the plug department. He had been an active member of the TWOC from the beginning, and we had used his church as a meeting place.

Mrs. Simpson wanted to have all the grievances presented to Whitaker in writing, and she wanted the workers to be prepared to argue their case adequately. The union organizers wanted to make sure the workers understood the power of presenting their grievances as a committee. The UCAPAWA officials pointed out that spreading the word about the workers' stand in #65 would help the push for increased union participation, especially since no workers had been fired for their part in the sit-down.

Neither group foresaw massive support among the Reynolds workers for the women in #65 or thought that protest from other parts of the Reynolds factory might arise. But as the women from the other stemmeries listened to the report of the #65 committee, they began thinking about their own plants. First Lola Love spoke up, then Janie Wilson, then Velma Hopkins and others. Things were just as bad where they worked. Why couldn't they sit down too?

Meanwhile, groups of women gathered on the street corners and front porches in the black neighborhoods. The mood was excited and everyone talked of one thing—what had happened in #65. No one knew all the details, but everyone knew people in the TWOC were involved. Most had heard about the TWOC but few had been willing to join. Now they heard that Theodosia Simpson had stood up to Mr. Whitaker, had even talked back to him. And they hadn't fired her.

As the meeting at the Union Mission Holy Church broke up, the participating women went searching for their co-workers. They passed the word that on Friday morning people should report to work, but no work was to be done until company officials agreed to discuss some of the grievances. Each of the predominantly black departments had one or two TWOC members who could be relied on to offer leadership and explain the tactics to the other workers. They also hoped that a number of workers who had shown interest in the organizing project, but had not come forward strongly, would join the protest.

Friday, June 18, looked much like the day before as workers converged on the giant tobacco factories. The first indication of something different came as the women from the largest stemmeries— #60 and #60 Extension—approached the doors of their plants. Instead of going right in, one by one, as they usually did, the women stopped and talked anxiously in groups. Finally a decision seemed to have been made, and everyone went on into the dressing rooms, changed clothes, and proceeded to the plant floor.

When the whistle blew, most of the machines simply remained idle. The women stood by them but didn't turn them on. Soon all the machines were quiet. The superintendent came out. A TWOC spokeswoman—a worker—stepped forward to say that they were not going back to work until the company met to discuss their grievances. She also demanded that the company allow Robert "Chick" Black to come from #64 and help them present their case.

ROBERT BLACK HAD WORKED IN THE REYNOLDS PLANTS SINCE HE WAS 6 or 7 years old. While hand stemmers were still paid piece rates, his mother had brought him and his sisters before and after school each day to help stem tobacco leaves. A tall, thin, handsome man with a strong voice, Black's work in the TWOC and his familiarity with the black workers and their problems made him a good choice to represent the workers in #60 and #60 Extension. No union organizers were allowed in the plants. "I think they called on Brother Black because they knew he was honest and he was a good talker," Mrs. Simpson said.

BLACK: About 9 A.M. that morning my foreman, Mr. Harper, came up to the machine where I was working and told me that there was someone out there to see me. So he and I walked over to the plant office and he introduced me to Mr. Whitaker, who I'd never seen before. Then he introduced me to Mr. Baumgardner, who I knew because I went through his office when they hired me, and then to the lawyer and the stenographer.

Mr. Whitaker said, "Robert, we've got a problem over there in #60 and #60 Extension. We've got 1,500 or 1,600 of your women who are sitting down at their machines refusing to go to work. They want you to come over there and ask them to go back to work."

I replied, "I think they want to ask me more than that Mr. Whitaker. I'll tell you, I'll be glad to go over there to talk with the women if you'll give me permission to go. But I'd like to go with you so that you can hear whatever complaints they have."

Mr. Whitaker said, "No, Robert. We can't let you go over there unless you just ask them to go back to work and tell them to write out their complaints and we'll listen to them. But we can't listen to any complaints until those machines are running."

"Now Mr. Whitaker, you don't want me to go over there and speak for those women, you want me to go speak for the company," I replied. "I'm not going to do that. I've got a wife working over there. Just to let you know how I feel about it, we're going to close down this plant. I think it's wrong for me to be working in #64 with my wife over in #60 trying to better her condition with all those other people. I'm going to send word up and down this five-floor factory and in thirty minutes we'll have every one of these machines at a standstill."

Mr. Whitaker said, "Robert, before you close down the plant, give us a chance to talk to the people over in the other plant."

"Mr. Whitaker, I'll be glad to go over to that plant with you, providing you let me go in and that a group of those employees come together and *we* talk. Let them put in writing their complaints, and then have me submit them to your committee with them there to discuss them."

"We can't do that. I refuse to grant you permission to go," Mr. Whitaker said.

So I just walked out.

Black's threat to close the plant was no idle boast. Like Theodosia Simpson, he was now in a position, as a worker and as a member of TWOC, to be an effective leader among the black workers.

BLACK: This is what put me in that position. I had been begging people to go to their foreman and demand more money. They would quiet me by slipping me a 3 or 4 cent raise. Each week they would give you your pay envelope turned upside down so the worker behind you couldn't see what you made. Chances were nine out of ten you got paid more than him for doing the same work. Down through the years I kept hounding the foreman for a wage increase and he would give it to me. I would show my envelope to the other guys who operated the machines and say, "Man, why don't you get that man to give you more money!" Therefore they felt that I was trying to help them to get better pay. They had confidence in me. I was confident that if I went back out there and asked them to close it down, they would do it. We just had that kind of relationship.

I went over to Maso Fields, who operated one of the machines. Everyone was loading their machines but peeking to see what was going on. I explained what was going on and said, "Maso, ask the men to cut off their machines." He just held his hand straight up and all four machines cut off. Then I went to the elevator operator and asked him to take word up to the floors above, to Grover Philpin in the casing and cutting department, to ask everyone to stop work in support of the women who were sitting down in the stemmeries.

The foreman called me back into the office. Mr. Whitaker was still there, only now he had my employment record in his hand.

"Robert, this is your record. You have ten years of exemplary service, with only three days absence in all that time. You are one of the highest paid colored workers in all the company. You should be proud of that record, and you should do everything you can to help the company continue its production. We've got a war going on. You don't want those soldiers overseas to find out that you people are refusing to produce cigarettes for them."

"Mr. Whitaker, now you're trying every trick in the book. I am not going to ask those women to go back to work unless you come and listen to their grievances. These men here have turned off their machines, and I'm gonna ask them to go get dressed and then remain on the company premises until closing time, so you can't accuse us of refusing to work. We're just refusing to work under present conditions."

WHILE THE NEGOTIATIONS CONTINUED, WORKERS FROM #65 GATHERED outside the factory. Mrs. Simpson and the committee talked about the meeting the night before, their specific list of grievances, and their plans to meet with Mr. Whitaker. The committee reminded the workers that everyone had agreed to return to work. The workers went upstairs to their respective floors while the committee waited.

But Mr. Whitaker, occupied with the protests developing in the other stemmeries, never came. The committee met instead with B. C. Johnson and Mr. Baumgardner, who by this time had little interest in the few hundred workers in #65. They promised that the company would immediately reduce the workload and seek permission from the NWLB to grant a wage increase.

The UCAPAWA officials were in a quandary. As of eleven o'clock, they had only limited information on the extent of the work stoppages. There was still no thought that actions would become widespread. It was a great opportunity, but it had to be handled carefully.

SIMPSON: At 11 A.M. we took a few new TWOC members to the union office to talk with Frank Hargrove and William DeBerry [two organizers from UCAPAWA, the former white, the latter black]. The more people you could get to the union office so that DeBerry and Hargrove could talk to them, the better they would understand just what we were up against. Hargrove talked about the strength and power a union could have. He felt the most important thing to come out of the protests was more support among workers for the union.

Hargrove also didn't want the company to get the idea that the union was keeping the workers out. He wanted to keep it as much of a workers thing as a union thing at that particular time, which wasn't hard because they [UCAPAWA] had known nothing about the plans for the sit-downs.

This thing hit DeBerry. When the committee went to talk to him he couldn't hardly believe it. He'd been in here all the time, meeting with us and trying to encourage the organization.

Reverend Owen Whitfield, Harry Koger, and DeBerry had gone over this city, into the churches, and the people just didn't budge. So it shocked DeBerry that something had happened like this.

By early afternoon hundreds of black workers were on the streets around the factories. #60 and #60 Extension were closed down. Departments in three other plants had joined the sit-down.

As an organizing committee of UCAPAWA, the TWOC was in a difficult position. As a CIO union it strongly supported the "no-strike pledge" for the duration of the war. Therefore it was important to arrange a settlement so that work could be resumed. Frank Hargrove's published position in the Winston-Salem *Journal* as head of the organizing drive said that the TWOC was not "officially" involved; that the work stoppages were a "spontaneous act on the employees' part without discussion with the union"; and that the workers should return to work, but not "under previously existing working conditions," which he described as "unbearable." Hargrove wanted to see employee committees organized to meet with management and "iron out their grievances with the company."

By early evening the TWOC leaders had made their way to a house in the heart of the black community where a meeting had been arranged. They found the streets around the meeting place packed. Thousands of black workers wanted to hear about the happenings of the day, to find out if it was true that all those women had refused to work.

As thousands of people walked slowly up the street, the TWOC members began to realize the developing strength among the Reynolds employees and knew they had to organize themselves quickly to provide the leadership for this growing mass of workers.

SIMPSON: We didn't know whether the company would hire thugs to start something. Our people being hot under the collar and a little bit angry, the company could very easily have sent people in and started a mass riot.

If a goon had gotten into this meeting he may have hurt somebody or have been beaten.

The point would have been that it would have been a disturbance. If we had had any sort of disturbance, everything would have gone down the drain.

We got up on top of cars and I had to scream. We finally got hold of a megaphone. I told them they had nothing to be afraid of. Because we had stood together, the company couldn't do anything to us. I told them if they stood together, they could make the company listen to them.

During the meeting people would come up to us and submit their names and the names of other people in their departments that hadn't yet joined the strike. People were volunteering. They said, "We want to become part of it too. We want to be the representatives of our people."

ON JUNE 19, 1943, A COMMITTEE OF BLACK WORKERS MET WITH Reynolds management to discuss the strike issues. The company released a statement that admitted that certain grievances existed but refused to recognize the union or a workers' committee. The workers' committee rejected the company's proposal.

The TWOC called a mass meeting for Sunday evening on the grounds of the Woodland Avenue School, where they would read the company's proposal and ask the workers to continue the strike. That Saturday afternoon a small group of white workers who had been meeting with UCAPAWA organizers issued a statement in support of the black workers and asked to meet with management to discuss their grievances.

Sunday morning for the black community in any Southern town revolves around the church. Gathering outside before Sunday school, Reynolds workers continued to talk about the strike and the meeting planned for that night. TWOC leaders active as church members urged support for the union. In all but a few churches the ministers addressed the issues of the strike. Citing the long history of oppression of black people, the poor working conditions and low pay of tobacco workers, and the conditions of racial segregation, they urged Reynolds workers to join and support the union.

SIMPSON: It was a nice sunshiny day. The Woodland Avenue School grounds provided a natural gathering place for the nine to ten thousand people who were there. People were out in the streets, on sidewalks, in parked cars, standing on top of their cars. People were in trees. They were everywhere; everywhere they could find a spot. There were even a few hundred white workers.

At 3 P.M. Reverend R. M. Pitts, pastor of the Shiloh Baptist Church, began the meeting with the invocation. He was a dramatic man of substantial stature, and he was loved and respected by his congregation and the whole black community. He was also an outspoken advocate of the struggle against segregation. As the mass of people echoed his final Amen the fervor of the crowd began to build. Then Theodosia Simpson led the singing of the Negro spiritual "Do Lord, Remember Me."

SIMPSON: We didn't try to reach out and get big words, or paint any pretty pictures. We just talked to them like we were sitting in the house talking to each other.

We had to get the points over. I told them again about that day in #65. "The lesson," I said, "was that you have to stick together and stand up to the company."

Frank Hargrove outlined the policies of the TWOC, and Conrad Espe, international vice-president of UCAPAWA, brought greetings from the union's president, Donald Henderson.

TWOC organizer William DeBerry continued. He was the best known of the organizers. He had worked closely with workers, meeting with church groups, leafleting at the factory gates, and going door to door in the black community.

SIMPSON: The thing that really hit the heart of the workers was when DeBerry told about his experiences as an organizer among sharecroppers in the South; how he had been shot at, had to hide in the bushes to escape arrest. The dramatics of that experience really hit home with the workers. We felt these guys can really take it. We had a lot of respect for DeBerry.

BLACK: As I climbed up onto the platform someone told me that Mr. Whitaker and those had stopped in a car on 12th Street. To begin I gave him a greeting from the platform and asked him to come on over and hear what we had to say. My reputation as a big talker was now on the line as I addressed those thousands of workers, but it gave me a chance to pour out all the bitterness against the company. All I had to do was to open my mouth and the words just rolled out.

I brought it down to one thing: to win we've got to stick together. If we lose the fight its not going to be because someone grew weak.

When the vote was taken on the company's proposal, the workers registered a massive shout of defiance: "No!" They would stay out until Reynolds recognized their workers committee.

BLACK: THE COMPANY HAD THE PLANT GATES OPEN [ON MONDAY], BUT WE instructed the workers to follow their leadership. If the company had not signed an agreement they were not to go inside. They came with their aprons, their overalls, and their lunches. The streets were full of people. The foremen said, "You'll come on in." The people said, "No, sir." We went around to the gates and told them an agreement had not been signed, not to go to work. The people went on back home."

R. W. Goodrick, a member of the U.S. Conciliation Service, had come to Winston-Salem on Sunday night at the request of UCAPAWA officials. Cigarettes were almost as necessary a part of war production as bullets, so the government was anxious to see a quick solution to the strike at Reynolds. When it was obvious that the workers would not return, Goodrick contacted Conrad Espe at the TWOC office. Espe outlined the situation and suggested that Goodrick arrange a meeting with the workers' committee and Reynolds management.

It soon became clear to TWOC leaders and Reynolds officials that a settlement on wages and grievances would take more than a couple of meetings. The grievances were too numerous and too complex for the company to respond to without investigation. Poor company record keeping and uncertainty of War Labor Board involvement complicated the wage issue. The committee decided to ask the company for written and binding assurances that no disciplinary action would be taken against workers, and that the company would continue to bargain (on company time) with the workers' committee. In exchange for those assurances the committee would ask everyone to go back to work.

The company agreed. A statement was drawn up and signed by Mr. Black. Mr. Whitaker promised to sign a copy and send it to the union hall later in the evening.

TENSIONS IN WINSTON-SALEM WERE HIGH THAT MONDAY EVENING.
The night was hot. Workers had been outside all day. There were strikes at Brown & Williamson Tobacco Company and the Mengel Company. Black workers at Hanes Knitting Company had also stopped work on Monday morning.

BLACK: The people realized something they had never thought of before: we hold the strength in our hands to stop this company. They had allowed that company to ride over them roughshod all those years, with their heads bowed. When they realized they could stop that big giant, they got bitter. If we [TWOC] had not handled the situation the way we did, the whole thing could have turned into violence.

At 6 P.M. that Monday evening the TWOC held another mass meeting at the Woodland Avenue School. People were enthusiastic after their "day off." The TWOC reported on the agreement with the company to recognize the committee for the purpose of discussing wages and grievances. They explained that Mr. Whitaker had not yet signed the agreement and that until it was signed, workers had no protection. The workers agreed to return to work upon receipt of a signed agreement, but not until then.

The signed statement was never delivered.

BLACK: That Tuesday morning people were marching, marching. The streets were just full of people. One of the militant workers came to my house. We had an executive board meeting and I hadn't gotten to bed till four. He said the people were going in the factories. I said, "Oh, no! We've got to keep them out of there." A neighbor of mine had a Ford with a rumble seat. So I got in the back of the car and we went around to the plants where we had designated leaders who had accepted leadership. We asked them to keep the people outdoors. The foremen's argument was, "Come inside, pull off your clothes, and then we'll talk." The workers went back to the factory expecting

Trade-union leadership at R. J. Reynolds Tobacco Co., 1946–47. Velma Hopkins is third from left, second row; Robert Black is fourth from left, first row

that the agreement had been signed. So I told them, "The Reynolds Tobacco Company has pulled a sneak."

They called us back to the Reynolds building that morning. I said, "Mr. Whitaker, you're going to have to make up your mind. These people want to go fishing. Are you going to sign the document?"

"The lawyers tell me it's not binding," Mr. Whitaker replied.

I told him, "We want something to protect those workers. We're going to have something, a written statement with your signature on it. I'll take the responsibility with the elected workers committee of guaranteeing you that once we get this thing behind us, more than 95 percent of our members will be in the plants ready to work, but not until."

And so finally Mr. Whitaker signed.

We held a mass meeting that night, and the workers voted "unanimously" to return to work. Folks said they wasn't ready to go back to work. It was June. It was hot. They wanted to stay out a month. But they went back— together.

THE MOMENTUM OF THESE SIX DAYS CONTINUED. AN NLRB ELECTION was won in December of 1943 and a contract was signed the following April. By November of 1944 thousands of blacks had registered to vote in city elections and helped elect a pro-Roosevelt congressman.

But in the years right after World War II, national business and government leaders sought to restrain the turbulent labor struggles of the preceding decade. With the aid of conservatives in the AFL and CIO, attacks were made on those union forces that called for continued mass organizing efforts and increased participation by working people in the political and social institutions of the country.

Reynolds bitterly fought every attempt by its workers to build democratic organizations in the factories and in the community. Traditional Southern racial animosities in the community were heightened to turn white workers against the predominantly black union; union leaders were framed by the local authorities; automation was used to lay off union members. Finally a prolonged "red-baiting" campaign attempted to divide the union leadership from the workers. In the midst of these attacks, intensified by the national cold-war atmosphere, the union narrowly lost an NLRB certification vote in 1950.

Despite the defeat, the struggle at Reynolds and in Winston-Salem significantly altered the lives of black workers. Wages, benefits, and working conditions improved in the factories. Black activism in the city resulted in public housing, improved medical facilities and social services, and the election in 1947 of the first black alderman to take office in the South in the twentieth century.

Many of the goals of the union were realized during this period; others were won during the civil rights activism of the 1960s; and still others remain to be accomplished by the present generation of workers.

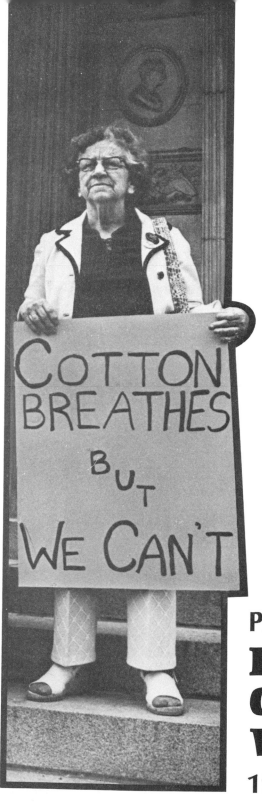

PART THREE
Here Come a Wind
1945–1980

THE 1930S BROUGHT UNION VICTORIES IN PLACES ONCE THOUGHT impregnable. The great strikes that swept the United States in 1945 and 1946, led by John L. Lewis's angry coal miners, proved labor was now sufficiently organized to challenge the biggest corporations in America—and the government, if need be.

As it moved into the fifties, the labor movement also broadened its focus from class struggle to racial justice. The basic grievances they shared made the alliance a natural step: both movements demanded that management respect the individual as a person, with dignity, and recognize the collective right of workers to have a say in the affairs affecting their lives. The successes of the civil rights movement became a source of optimism for supporters of workers. The enemies of black America—men like Strom Thurmond and Sam Ervin—were also behind antiunion legislation, while labor correctly understood that enfranchised and employed black workers were their best hope to crack the South. Indeed, victories at Oneita and recently at several J. P. Stevens plants grew directly out of the interest in unions shared by blacks working in the textile mills. In Charleston, South Carolina, black hospital workers brought both the activists and the methods of the civil rights movement into their union drive.

The struggle between labor and management focuses most often on money, but other issues—health, job security, human rights—come right behind. The movement to create safe and clean working conditions directly contradicts management's desire for absolute control over the workplace. The militance of workers' concern for their own lives and health led to the establishment of the Occupational Safety and Health Administration, which provided workers with a powerful tool, though hobbled by the same bureaucratic machinery that plagues other federal agencies. Left to their own devices, few corporations spend the extra money necessary to make the workplace safe, but independent organizations like the Carolina Brown Lung Association are forcing the textile industry to confront the fact that cotton dust kills thousands of men and women working in the mills.

But the cold war and the anticommunism of the fifties also put all unions on the defensive, allowing corporations to erode labor's strength in the factories, in Congress, and in public opinion. The first management offensive resulted in the Taft-Hartley Act in 1947, which severely limited the rights of workers spelled out in the thirteen-year-old Wagner Act. Businessmen learned to use the law in sophisticated new ways to control workers and keep out unions. Greenville, South Carolina—home of eighteen J. P. Stevens plants, Michelin Tire, Daniel International (builder of textile factories and nuclear plants), and several national antilabor leaders—is the showpiece of the Southern antiunion forces.

Labor clearly must challenge the corporate stranglehold on communities such as Greenville, but just how to do so is not so obvious. Everywhere organizers face increasingly sophisticated and determined management tacticians who strive to bind workers and communities even further. Management still has the ability to control many towns with simple economic blackmail: the threat to take its jobs and money elsewhere. Unions are beginning to fight back, as illustrated by the United Auto Workers' successful fifteen-year campaign to organize a plant that ran from Detroit to Hartwell, Georgia, to escape the union. At the same time, unions are forming new and powerful coalitions, as the United Mine Workers did at Brookside. And while the bosses use labor law to fight unions, reformers like Selina Burch use the conservative-inspired Landrum-Griffin Act to make their own organizations more democratic and more representative of all workers.

The civil rights and women's movements, corporate investments in high technology, organizations such as the Brown Lung Association— all these create new twists that keep the need for organizing always alive and dynamic, as labor and management continually adjust their strategies. Though textiles no longer have the hegemony over the region they exploited so well fifty years ago, the struggle between the textile unions and the textile elite still sets the pace for labor-management relations throughout the South. As corporations look South to break strong unions elsewhere, the struggle here increasingly determines the fate of worker organizations throughout the nation.

TWENTY

On the Line at Oneita

CAROLYN ASHBAUGH
AND
DAN MCCURRY

JONES AVENUE IN ANDREWS, SOUTH Carolina, is as unpretentious as its name. On the sandy soil along the blacktop strip are settled the homes and gardens of black families—not so long off the farm or out of the piney forest—who came to Andrews looking for steady pay. Employment in this coastal plain town of 3,000 usually means Oneita Knitting Mills, a "runaway shop" from Utica, New York, which moved to Andrews in the early 1950s.

Owned by the Devereaux family of New York City, Oneita Mills was locally supervised by plant manager Frank Urtz and a company director, Andrews banker A. H. Parsons. Their large brick homes were a far cry from the houses on Jones Avenue. In fact, Frank Urtz didn't even live in Andrews. He commuted the twenty miles from the larger coastal city, Georgetown. Meanwhile, Oneita's payroll helped Andrews grow, and Parsons' white-columned bank regularly made home, car, and furniture loans to the Oneita pieceworkers.

Before the early 1960s, those workers were all white—except for two black janitors. They enjoyed the relative protection of a union contract which the International Ladies Garment Workers had maintained since it followed the underwear company south from Utica. But in 1963 all that began to change. In that year, the company decided to break the union.

Herbert White, one of the two black janitors, went out on strike with the other ILGWU members in a vain attempt to win a new contract. Plant manager Frank Urtz had told White that he couldn't join the union because his face was black. But White joined anyway. After six long, bitter months, he and most of the other workers went back into the plant without a contract and without a union.

After the strike, several ILGWU leaders received office jobs from Oneita; the former president of the local became the personnel manager. Needless to say, many workers were disillusioned about unions. Richard Cook, Herbert White, Dorothy Glisson, Effie Shurling, Rena Edy, and a few others remained firmly committed to unionization, but they had to wait. They knew that Urtz relied on "pets and spies" to maintain control and spread suspicion through the plant.

Then, in 1964, the Civil Rights Act forced Oneita to hire black workers. Although Andrews had not experienced an active civil rights movement, black people watched the events in Montgomery, Selma, Birmingham, and across the South on television. They took pride in their blackness and in their leaders. When jobs opened up at Oneita, they gladly moved in, leaving jobs as maids, waitresses, or farming wives for a steady income in the single-story, aluminum-sided sheds of Oneita Mills. At the same time, the South's expanding economy lured away the white semiskilled workers with better-paying jobs in other shops.

By 1971, Oneita had opened a second, smaller plant twenty miles away in Lane, and its total work force of 920 had shifted to 75 percent black and 85 percent women. The Textile Workers Union of America* saw Oneita as an ideal place to organize. The racial mix was a clear plus; and the company was a relatively small, family business that could not shift its production or hold out with the limitless power of a diversified giant like J. P. Stevens. And from Andrews, they could begin to organize the 20,000 textile workers within a thirty-mile radius of the town.

In June 1971, the TWUA sent in its first organizer, Philip Pope, who, with family friends and oldtimers like Richard Cook and Herbert White, began signing people up.

On November 19, 1971, the union won the election for bargaining rights. The workers laughed the day before the election when Frank Urtz made a half-hour speech to his "family" telling them how good he'd been to them. That Thanksgiving week, they got their first company turkey.

Negotiations began in February 1972, but with little result. In effect, Oneita refused to discuss provisions for dues checkoff or arbitration of

*In 1976, the TWUA and the Amalgamated Clothing Workers of America merged to form the Amalgamated Clothing and Textile Workers of America (ACTWU).

Oneita prounion meeting

grievances. On January 15, 1973, nearly ten years after the ill-fated ILGWU strike of 1963, Oneita workers walked off their jobs in protest against the company's bad-faith bargaining.

The workers held fast, black and white together, and carried their struggle into the community and into a national boycott of Oneita underwear. Finally, in July 1973, the company agreed to recognize the TWUA and negotiate a contract with grievance procedures, pension and seniority rights, and dues checkoff.

It had been a costly strike for the union and the community. Women stood on the picket line and yelled "scab" while their sisters went to work. Neighbors no longer talked as one replaced the other in the mill. But the battle also united the strikers and established a firm base for building the union.

The wounds of a community divided, the ugliness of the company, the enthusiasm for the union, the excitement of becoming friends with blacks or whites for the first time, the sweetness of victory, the lessons of united action—all were fresh in the minds of those we interviewed in 1973; the commitment was still there when Carolyn Ashbaugh returned in 1975.

CARMELA MC CUTCHEN: What was it like in there? I'll tell you, working conditions at Oneita were like the nineteenth century. There was no seniority, no protection at all from layoffs, no pensions, no safety protection, no medical benefits. If you got a needle in your finger, they'd tell you to go back to work.

CAROLYN JERNIGAN: Whenever you'd go into that place, it was rush, rush, rush until you get out of there. Sometimes I get so nervous and tensed up that when I get out of there, I'm just not worth a cuss to live with when I get home. You'd be so tired and irritable, especially on hot days when there is no air conditioning.

LAURA ANN POPE: There was no seniority. Nothing! If Urtz [the plant manager] decided he don't like you and you don't do what he say—I'm not speaking about the job, I'm speaking about his dirty work—he will bust you down and hire somebody out of the street. He wanted stool pigeons, he wanted Peeping Toms. It didn't matter if it was false or true, just you bring the report to him.

Philip Pope, the first organizer, came in June 1971. I was on graveyard shift, so I was asleep. He knocked on the door, and finally he woke me up. He wanted my son Pete. They worked together at Georgetown Steel. He said, "I'll tell you what I'm trying to do. I'm a home boy around here. I have a job with the International. I have a letter here to organize the Oneita Knitting Mills." I said, "Yippee. I work there." He says, "What!" "That's right," I said, "I was hoping somebody would come along to help straighten this joint out. You don't know how happy I am." He went to the car and brought back a stack of blue cards. He said, "I know if you are Peter's mother, you're going to work, you're going to help me."

I didn't sleep any more that day. About 10:30 I started getting dressed to go to work. Started signing those blue cards. My son came home; he got in his car; Philip and I got in mine. We begin knocking on doors. We took Jones Avenue first. Then we stretch out all over town. Then we went on for days. That's how I began.

I was getting so many cards signed that they had an idea I was doing it on the job, which I was. I'd call the employees the night before and say I'm going by you to check on your machine and say a few words to you. And I'm going to put a blue card in your pocket or your hand or somewhere. It's going to be in a piece of paper towel. Then I'm going to the rest room and when I come back through, you have it signed and in your pocket or in your hand. And I'd go through, "Hi, fella, how's your machine working today?" with my hands in my pocket. I'd say, "Boy, you better go ahead and try to make production," and I'd put that card in his hand so quick it would make your head swim; go on into the bathroom. And I'd maybe drop off twenty cards on my way going and pick up twenty coming back. And I would eat my lunch before break. I could sign blue cards in the mill on break time.

After we won the election, they played this trick on me: they took my set of machines from me. He couldn't just fire me, because I had a contract to use on him and he knew it, so I stayed in the mill. He knew I could do it [take him before the NLRB]. So he took my machine away from me, put me back in training, thought this would belittle me.

One night, I went to work. The mechanic told me, "I'm sorry, you've got to run the swing-top." I said, "I'm sorry, I'm not going to run it." I went and sat on a stool and said, "Good, I'll sit here until seven o'clock in the morning." So I sat there about thirty minutes, and then the supervisor came through. He says, "Laura Ann, what you doing sitting on that stool? Don't you have anything to do?" "That's the way it looks. Sitting down, making easy money." He said, "Why you don't go run your set of machines?" I said, "My set of machines was given to another girl." When he sent me back, I checked the cloth, turned it on, started working. I cleaned off everything. Then I got out my pad and went by each machine and counted every end. Each machine is supposed to have 144 ends to make production. And he's given me 102 ends.

Supervisor checked things out for me; before I left, he said, "You won't have any trouble tomorrow night." The next night he treated me like pie.

And everybody started clamming up, those pets, those pimps, those supervisors. They started watching me when I go to the bathroom. They wanted to get something on me. They didn't want me to stay too long; they didn't want me to hold a conversation with other employees as I passed, and I would do it every time.

SCOTT HOYMAN, SOUTHERN REGIONAL DIRECTOR, TWUA: When you go up against a company this size, a relatively small, family-owned company, one of the hard things is that personalities become very important. Frank Urtz, the plant manager, and Bill Smith, their lawyer, are the two people whom I would charge with responsibility for such a long strike. I think they led the top people in the company to believe that, first, the people wouldn't come out. And secondly, when the people did come out, that they wouldn't stay out. And if either of those things had been true, the company's strategy would have been correct. But they were wrong.

Urtz was a smart man. He used these things that we may think are silly, like the analogy of the family. Well, that happens to be a pretty doggone effective tactic. It worked for an awful lot of people for quite a long while. You know, Southern whites transfer family concepts to owners and managers. There's a code of personal relationships and responsibilities, in the old-style textile communities, between a worker and a man that lives in the white house on the hill and runs the plant. And so, the family analogy is sort of an attempt to project that image. "The father may spank you, but he will also feed you."

You know, whether you like it or not, bargaining between a company and a union is exactly like diplomacy. It has all the suspicions, attitudes, vehicles, and devices as relations between two countries. Usually, you have informal channels. But one of the frustrating things was that Oneita purposely did not present us with any informal channels. Bill Smith is an old adversary of mine. I spent off and on four years dealing with him for another plant. He wanted all the threads going through his fingers. We tried to talk to this banker, Mr. Parsons, who was on the board of directors of Oneita. He was also the Democratic county chairman, and we were interested whether that would help. But it didn't.

Smith would only offer us what I would call a highly restrictive contract. He imitates the Blakeney formula,* which in essence insisted on a contract proposal which is very unsatisfactory to us, and the union is left with three choices: refusing the proposal and striking; accepting the proposal after long negotiations and finding ourselves unable to make the union work to furnish satisfaction to the members; and third, we have the choice of a stalemate, to continue bargaining. And that could go on for years.

So we had a big decision to make. We counted noses and made the estimates and talked to the negotiating committee about what they thought we could do. We had an excellent committee. They were tough—whites and blacks. So that was how we made the decision to strike.

We ran the strike in terms of union structure with a negotiating committee that was fairly large. I guess it had ten or twelve people because we were

*Named for J. P. Stevens's antiunion counsel Whiteford Blakeney.

representing two plants. Then we had picket captains. They were very, very important people. You know, the Bible talks about people who were leaders of tens and those who were leaders of a hundred, and then leaders of a thousand and so on. Well, our picket captains were leaders, basically, of twenty, and they had a book and they would take attendance and it was a very important activity. We had that in both locations [Andrews and Lane]. It turned out to be a good structure. And we had a commissary.

Financial liability would be considerable. I would think we paid out between $300,000 and $400,000 from the international union treasury. This is only in terms of direct financial assistance. I'm not talking about staff salaries; I'm not talking about time. This was a major effort by the Textile Workers Union.

TED BENTON, TWUA STRIKE COORDINATOR, NOW RETIRED: Just before the strike started, another representative and I went down to the local sheriff and introduced ourselves and we told him we wanted to conduct a peaceful strike here. We noticed on the first morning we were overwhelmed with police—over twenty cars. I was trying to keep them from escorting the people in and instructed our pickets to walk between the cars. They had a right to go in, but [the police] didn't have a right to escort them in such a manner as they was doing. And the sheriff threatened to lock me up. And I said if he was going to lock me up for carrying on legal picketing such as we were doing, then he'd just have to lock me up. He turned and walked away then, and he didn't lock me up. But during the strike, they did escort people in.

We never got hit with an injunction, which is one of the most surprising things to me. Usually they hit you the first few days to limit your pickets and destroy their effectiveness. I do feel that if it hadn't been for this sheriff, that injunction would have hit us, and the company tried every way they could to get an injunction. Of course, he read the riot act on us and told us he could bring it down on us any time he wanted to, only if there was not too much violence out there, he would not have an injunction.

CAROLYN JERNIGAN: The one thing that made the strike a success was that you gotta pull together. One or two people can't do it. That's one thing that I've found out. Frank Urtz told me himself that we didn't have enough guts to walk out of that mill and go out on strike. But we did and we made a win. It don't make no difference what color you is—black or white—you gotta stick together. You find out one thing, that you got a lot of friends outside, and a lot of people who will stick together.

CLYDE BUSH, TWUA ORGANIZER: The black and white unity in this strike was very important. You can't take anything for granted anymore. Back in the late 1960s, whenever you went into one plant the first thing that you looked to was how many blacks are there working in here. And if there were forty blacks you could count on forty votes. Today, you can't count on that. Management some way has got to them. They're going in and hiring the best-liked, the best black they have in the plant, and they're making a damned supervisor out of him, and he's the one carrying the load.

We had to work very hard on the picket line. We would tell black workers as they would scab into the plant what management thought of them. The blacks on the picket line would say, "Remember the good old days when you had to walk into the back of the restaurant? You wasn't a human being, couldn't come in the front door. Remember the days when you went in and asked for mayonnaise on your hamburger and the restaurant operator put mustard on it and told you to take it? Like it or leave it? Remember the day the plant manager Urtz wouldn't speak to you because your face was black?" By using these tactics on the picket line, we were able to steal the tactics from management and they couldn't come back and use them.

TED BENTON: We had them where it hurts. It's not a J. P. Stevens or a Burlington. We had the bleachery strong, and we had the knitting department strong. They couldn't operate without them. When the strike first started we had about 70 percent of the people out. They had a number of scabs in there, but they couldn't get out any production. They couldn't keep up the quality. We had the skilled workers with us; the ones they had in the plant were mostly flunkies. Buyers were saying, "If you can't send me good stuff, don't send me anything at all." That really hurt them. The boycott helped, too, but it's very hard to carry on a boycott when you don't have a brand name. They made stuff for K-Mart, but they put a K-Mart label on it. You'd go in a K-Mart store and you couldn't tell what was made by Oneita. I think the strike was won on the picket line, as are most strikes. I kept telling the people, "We have all these forces at work for you, but the strike is going to be won right here on the picket line."

SCOTT HOYMANN: The international union put more energy into this boycott and strike, I think, than any other activity since the Henderson, North Carolina, strike of 1958 to '60. It involved a number of very hard decisions. You always have to have priorities and make choices, and this strike was a priority. We postponed other things so they wouldn't get in the way. Another important decision—and this had to do with the character of your representative on the scene—was the style of the strike. We ran it as a very peaceful strike, although there were some complaints about that. We had black union people coming from Charleston and from Georgetown who said that this ain't the way to run the railroad. And we had a couple of confrontations over this.

At a mass meeting, I made the offer that if the folks wanted to vote for some other union to take over the strike and the other union would pick up the bill and furnish responsible direction to the strike, the Textile Workers Union would respect that decision. And nobody jumped up, and so I guess that we retained direction of the strike, and we also kept paying the bills. But that issue, that challenge, or however you want to phrase it, that question which arose as to who should determine this kind of strategy and make these kinds of decisions was over that precise question: Were we going to try to preserve a very peaceful atmosphere? And we felt that we didn't have any choices. I'll tell you one effect that it had. It really confronted the company with an unusual problem. You know, usually the company keeps talking about the violence and the disorder and the dynamiting and the homes being shot into, and judges respond to that. But even the sheriff said that there wasn't any base for talking like that.

So despite some complaints, mostly from people far away, that style turned out very well for us. We were also concerned about whether the company would be able to get significant black leadership in the community to take a stand against the strike, or encourage people to scab. The black community pretty well stayed on our side. But in the white community, it was harder—and still is.

JOYCE LAMBERT: Now my husband, he won't let me ride a scab to work. My neighbor right next door worked in the knitting department. Well, I don't hold a grudge. But he said, if she was able to find a ride while I was on strike, she can find her a ride while you're working. She's never asked me to ride again, and I'm glad. I really don't know what I would tell her.

But another girl that was out with us, she was secretary of the Sunday school at the Pentecostal Holiness Church, and they gave her a hard time. Because somewhere in the Bible it says—I believe in Romans—it says something about "to strike" and we looked it up in the dictionary, and it means to strike with your hands, to hit back. Some of these people, they think it's sin to strike; they tried to have her thrown out of the Pentecostal Holiness Church. She really went through holy terror. She had a hard time but she said she prayed her way out of it.

In July 1973, the Oneita workers won a contract giving them arbitration, a good grievance procedure, a pension, dues checkoff, and job bidding. They had a contract to defend them from arbitrary power.

In the year and a half following the strike, the union won forty-one out of forty-three grievances filed; the strike convinced the Oneita Knitting Company to deal with its employees with more respect. By the end of the strike, the company had brought in someone over Frank Urtz. In March 1975 he was removed completely.

DOROTHY GLISSON: What affected me, really, before we had a contract we didn't have the job bidding. If they wanted to give a good job or an easy job to someone, they would usually pick who they wanted. Their special ones. So after the contract—I've been here going on twenty-three years—I got to bid for a job in the mill. About six of us bid for this job which would take me off the sewing machine, off production, which I'd been on for twenty-two years; And it was doing rework; it wasn't all that much better, but it seemed like it was somewhat easier. Took the strain off me, wasn't quite as harassed. So I bid for the job. But they still, I think, had a little prejudice, because out of the ones that bid it they give it to another lady that didn't have as much seniority as I had. That kind of got me hot, because I figured that's what I wanted a union for, so I filed a grievance about that, on the basis of seniority.

When they checked on the six that had bid for the job, they classed us. They had a merit system giving us points. This other woman was number one, and I was number two, and the other one that was in the corner was number three. We was in there with Mr. Martin; I said, "I want to ask you a question. Why if I'm number two on the paper, why is number three over there in the corner doing the job?" He said, "I don't know, but I'll see." So in just a few days they posted the job again, and I bid it, and I got it.

That's the main thing; the people that's running the mill can't run it just exactly as they please. The union bargains, and we have something to help us out. We have grievances, we have seniority, we have job bidding. We have many other things in the contract, but those are the three that really affected me, and if it hadn't been for that I know I wouldn't have gotten the job.

CHARLENE JUNE: One really stirred up something. We had nine girls who filed a grievance on a quality-control job. They had the job up for bid; nine girls bid on the job, and the girl with the lowest seniority and who was a scab got the job.

The eight girls got together and they filed a grievance. They went through all of the steps and they didn't get any satisfaction. The company said that they went by "adaptability," "suitability"—anything unreasonable, that's what they went by. "How the lady's legs looked?" They didn't say that, but that's what it meant. Finally they took it to arbitration, and we won. A union person got the job, and all of her back pay dating back to the day that they put the scab on her job.

GEORGE JUSTICE, LOCAL TWUA REPRESENTATIVE: We solve a lot of complaints for nonmembers. The mechanics came over as a group and asked for a meeting with me. None of them belonged to the union. They said, "We don't feel the company is paying us right; we're entitled to more money. If the union can do anything, we're all going to join." We met with the company and some of them soon got over 50 cents an hour increase. They all went to top pay and now they wouldn't even talk to us about joining the union; they want the sewing machine operators and the people that are on lower rates to foot the bill for them. With dues at $1.75 a week, the wage increase that they have gotten this year for just one hour would pay their dues.

We're not getting very far with the older people who've been there twenty years and who didn't come out on strike. But we pick up one or two a month. And, you know, the ones we've picked up surprisingly have become more active than many who went out with us. They sign up and in turn will pick up another one who worked during the strike, and they'll pick up another one or two.

Take Danny Lambert. He was bitterly opposed to the union and fought us tooth and nail and caused several fracases at the gate and was really vocal against the union. He joined in August this past year, and since then he's signed up six or seven of the other people who were very vocal against the union. You can count on Danny to carry the union message in the plant. In fact, he told the manager right after he joined that all these years he'd been there and all the company did was lie to him and he'd better get on the side that would do something for him.

The union couldn't stop the layoffs and reduced hours caused by the recent recession. In early 1975, many Oneita workers were on only twenty-one hours a week—seven hours on three days. TWUA attempted to get a week-on, week-off schedule so employees could collect unemployment the week they were off and maximize their incomes. The company refused, knowing that many would find other jobs before they were called back.

The recession also slowed plans for further organization in the

Andrews area, because layoffs were very heavy at many plants. And the rapid turnover now in Oneita's mills coupled with the open-shop law in South Carolina makes building a strong union difficult, if not impossible.

Still, the Oneita victory was tremendously important for all Southern workers. It showed that a union could organize textiles in the South and that black and white workers could and would stick together—at least in union business, if not in social relations outside the plant. It was the victory needed to take on J. P. Stevens, the nation's second largest textile corporation.

TWENTY-ONE
A True Poem: You Just Can't Fire a Man Like That!

JOANIE WHITEBIRD

MY GRANDFATHER
worked as a gauger
for humble oil
for thirty-five years,
he walked the long fields
from derrick to derrick
adjusting pressure valves
and counting
the big gummy barrelsful
that came
belching out of the earth

he taught his children
how to "change the wells"
and went bird hunting
for weeks at a time
my mother
tells the story
about the night young bobby
changed the wells
and she and terrell and russell
went tearing down to fix it
before pumps and black gum
went spewing into the air

the day the new foreman
from dallas tried to fire him
grandpa had been working
in the fields twenty years
he had never
made a mistake in his books
for twenty years
his rolling script
(which wrote love letters
on the side
for the amorous, but illiterate,
young men of Little Rock)
sent in perfect ledgers

but the new foreman
didn't like it
that grandpa had such a perfect record
and so much leisure time, too
so he said
"bledsoe,
the other men
don't like it
that you get paid
for eight hours a day

and spend every afternoon
in the pool hall
with the company car parked outside"
so grandpa told him
any d--- fool
could do the job in four
and to prove it,
took him out to the fields
walked the foreman's legs off
and did it in three
and the foreman said
"well,
don't leave the company car
in front of the pool hall,
go home and get your own"
but grandpa wouldn't do that either
wasted gas, he said

so the foreman fired him,
grandpa laughed
and went on
to the same fields
he'd worked for twenty years
and nobody dared take over
his route
because you just didn't
mess with
old man bledsoe

when he didn't get his paycheck
in two weeks
he got in the car
and drove to houston
where the district manager
read over the careful report
the foreman had written
calling grandpa "obstreperous"

the district manager
looked at grandpa's records
he looked at the foreman's report
he looked back at grandpa
who was shouting
"the d--- fool fired me!"
and then he transferred the foreman
back to dallas
and told him
"you just can't fire a man like that"

the foreman's wife was mad
the foreman was confused
but grandpa thought he had seen
Justice Administered
and went down to the pool hall
in the company car
to celebrate
and the kids changed the wells

TWENTY-TWO
Runaways
DON STILLMAN

EVEN NOW, YEARS LATER, ALMOST no one in the sleepy north Georgia town of Hartwell likes to talk much about it. But the folks who fought Monroe Auto Equipment Company remember the events quite clearly. For their efforts linger like the early morning mists that frequently envelop this rolling, red clay farmland.

July 24, 1964, was steamy hot— a fitting day to end a long and tough election campaign. On that Thursday, workers at Monroe would finally vote on whether or not to have the United Auto Workers union represent them.

Monroe was determined to keep the union out at all costs. It had moved this part of its operations to Georgia from Michigan specifically to avoid the UAW—and to widen profit margins by running to an area where it could pay workers only $1.35 an hour instead of $3-plus. But the union struggle had followed them South.

As National Labor Relations Board representative Scott Watson began to tally the votes, the frowns etched across stone-faced Monroe execs gave way to grins. Their campaign of violence, intimidation, fear, and reprisal had given them a three-to-one victory over the UAW.

Even John Tate, the attorney who masterminded Monroe's antiunion battle, broke into a rare smile as plant manager Charlie Gordon quietly passed the word to hand out the half-pints and beer to the workers on the second shift.

By 12:50 A.M., when the union's 466–147 defeat was formally

217

announced, refreshments had provided the momentum for a planned march to the courthouse square. About 200 people gathered in front of the Hart County Courthouse, milling around and blocking U.S. Route 29, the main road then between Atlanta and Charlotte, North Carolina. Surly, not jubilant; the crowd became a mob.

Shortly after 1 A.M., a chunky, crew-cut boss strung up a lifelike dummy on a tree on the left side of the courthouse. Grinning, he yelled to the crowd, "C'mon boys, let's string up Walter Reuther here and show these communists what'll happen if they ever set foot in Hart County again." The mob cheered as a sign was draped around the limp neck: "Notice to all. Here hangs UAW. Caught trying to steal jobs from Monroe employees."

Pistol shots cracked across the square and the dummy recoiled once, then again—six times finally and little dribbles of sawdust and cotton batting fell from the holes. More beer was passed around and more shots were fired before the crowd began to drift away. As the man with the crew cut climbed back into his pickup, he yelled to the stragglers, "Let's go find us some real ones, boys, what d'ya say?"

UNION ORGANIZERS LOU ECHOLS AND RALPH CRAWFORD WERE NO strangers to violence. A year earlier, when they tried to leaflet the Monroe plant, they had been attacked after the company shut down operations early, and the workers came out, ran off the organizers, and burned their handbills.

A second effort to handbill the plant included UAW Vice-President Pat Greathouse, Nick Zonarich, and other top officials of the AFL–CIO's Industrial Union Department. About 150 Monroe foremen and employees armed with crowbars and billy clubs ran the group off while local police looked on. One of the mob, now a UAW supporter, recalls, "There were a lot of licks passed." Greathouse, wearing a UAW T-shirt, was attacked. The organizers found their car tires slashed. The mob surrounding the car forced the unionists to send a tow truck across state lines from South Carolina the next day.

Even though no one would rent a room to them, Echols and the other organizers kept coming back to Hartwell. "We'd stay in a little ol' motel in Royston; that's where Ty Cobb was born," Echols remembers. "Monroe would send fellas who'd park their cars right in front of our room and shine their high beams on us all night and sling rocks against the side of the place hoping to run us off."

They didn't succeed.

Eventually, enough workers at the Hartwell plant signed UAW cards, and the July 24 election was ordered by the NLRB. Threatened with the very element that initially caused them to move out of Michigan—

the union and the higher wages and benefits it would bring—Monroe pulled out all the stops. Court records and interviews reveal the massive campaign of intimidation the company engaged in to fight the UAW. In addition to the violence, Monroe launched a propaganda campaign that in a more refined form has become the chief weapon of union-busting runaway shops across the South. Its centerpiece is the multipronged effort to convince workers that the plant would be forced to close and move elsewhere if it was unionized. In effect, according to the company, choosing the union does not mean job security—it means unemployment.

Inside the factory Monroe hung huge banners covered with pictures of their Hillsdale, Michigan, plant that had closed. Across the photo was a big X and the line: "IT CAN HAPPEN HERE." The local newspaper carried articles from the *Congressional Record* "proving" that then UAW President Walter Reuther was a communist and that the union gave donations to the NAACP, the Jewish Labor Committee, the Americans for Democratic Action, and the Leadership Conference on Civil Rights. Local radio stations day after day echoed the theme, as did many of the preachers in the predominantly fundamentalist area. A vote for the union was a vote against God, Jesus Christ, the Holy Ghost, and everything sacred.

Monroe practiced its own brand of brotherly love within the plant, complete with widespread harassment and reprisals against workers who publicly indicated they believed a union contract might bring better working conditions and decent wages. Those favoring the union were frequently moved to the toughest, dirtiest jobs in the plant at lower pay. Against such a vicious (and illegal) campaign, it seemed an outside shot that the Monroe workers would choose the union.

LOU ECHOLS WASN'T EAGER TO STAND AROUND AND CHAT ONCE THE votes were tallied July 24. He wondered why the National Labor Relations Board let the company set up the election so the ballots would be counted late at night.

"A lot of folks was feelin' real strong about things because of the way the company had used the churches and the radio and all to make 'em think we was all communists who were going to steal their jobs," he recalls. "Some of them was good people, but they'd been confused and misled. I knew when we heard the liquor was being passed out and they was getting ready to hang Walter Reuther at the courthouse that it was time to get on our way."

Oddly, it was another act of violence that may have saved them. Several days before, nightriders shotgunned a black civil rights worker traveling north on Highway 29. FBI agents visited the Monroe plant

The "funeral" ceremony near the UAW effigy in Hartwell

immediately prior to the elections seeking links between the slaying and the high-pitched mood the company's hate campaign had engendered. While none were found, the presence of FBI agents helped Echols and Crawford make arrangements for protection that night. "We took on off out of there fast," Echols recalls. "We'd left two men back in Royston and I'd told them if we weren't back by 1:30 A.M. to call the police and tell them there'd been a wreck on the highway between Royston and Hartwell. I told them to also report a fire there too so we'd maybe have a hope.

"Two cars pulled out after us and chased us about halfway, until state troopers we arranged through the federals and Governor [Carl] Sanders blocked them off," Echols says. "When we got to Royston, we found they'd beat up on the men we'd left there and run 'em off. I never felt so good as when we got out of there. If they just wanted to whip us, it wouldn't have been so bad. I've been whipped a few times before, but that wasn't what they had planned that night, no sir."

The next day, the plant shut down at noon and about 500 people gathered in the courthouse square for a mock funeral. As women, children, and workers looked on, Carey Thrasher, J. L. Herring, and James Boleman placed the effigy in a coffin from a local funeral home. Broughton Sanders, the Hart County coroner, who also worked as a foreman at Monroe, took the microphone and informed the crowd that he as coroner had examined the body and found it to be legally dead.

The funeral hymn "Just One Rose" was sung and a wreath of pine and bitterweed placed on the coffin. The Monroe foremen covered it with sand and placed a grave marker atop the site:

Less [sic] we forget

Here Lies UAW

Born in Greed

Died in Defeat
July 23, 1964
Hartwell, Georgia

IN DETROIT, TOP UAW OFFICIALS REALIZED THAT IF MONROE'S
strategy of running away to an area where it could pay workers half
what it did in the North was successful, other companies would begin
to do the same thing. Under the leadership of Vice-President Pat
Greathouse, the UAW and the IUD decided that although company
goons had pronounced the union dead—or murdered, as it were—in
Hartwell, it would have to, like Lazarus, rise again in health.

When lawyers Morgan Stanford, Joe Rauh, Steve Schlossberg, Dan
Pollitt, and others documented the numerous violations of the National
Labor Relations Act Monroe had committed, the election results were
eventually set aside and a second election ordered. Unsure of its
support, the UAW informed workers they would have to get cards
signed on their own. Within three weeks, more than half the workers
signed cards asking that the UAW represent them.

"I guess we realized we'd done got taken," says Eury Nannie, who
has worked for Monroe for twenty years. "For some folks this was
their first job ever. They was farmers and kept on farming while they
worked at the plant—this was the first time they'd ever seen a
paycheck in their lives and they didn't want to do anything to lose it.
But while the company put a scare in people, that didn't make 'em
like the company much either. They saw the way people got
mistreated and all. We're country, but that don't mean we ain't
smart."

The second time around, in 1966, teams of UAW supporters—
coalitions of blacks and whites, men and women—set about to debunk
the company's threats to close down and move away if the union got
in. Their efforts paid off, as the UAW won the representation election
342–264. This time there was no hanging and no mock funeral.
Workers expected to be enjoying the benefits of a union contract
shortly—a contract that would give them job protection, a grievance
procedure, seniority rights, decent pensions, health insurance, and
maybe even a wage increase that would get them back in the range of
what Monroe workers in Michigan had been paid for doing the same
work.

But the battle had only begun with the election victory. For the next twelve years, Monroe Auto Equipment ignored its employees' desires by successfully evading the orders of the National Labor Relations Board and a variety of courts. The Labor Act, originally hailed as the Magna Carta for American workers, effectively protected the company from the workers by allowing them to stall to death efforts toward a contract. Like J. P. Stevens, Monroe used the law to make crime pay.

The company's outrageous tactics began the day after the second election. On election day, both the UAW and Monroe had certified that all ballots were counted. The cardboard box was torn up and the union declared the winner. But the next day, Monroe presented the ballot box, pasted back together with a ballot hanging out of it, and filed a protest claiming all ballots had not been counted.

The NLRB regional director found Monroe's claims ludicrous and overruled them without a hearing. After months of maneuvering, the UAW was finally certified as the bargaining agent for the Hartwell employees, but still Monroe continued to file a variety of appeals. Even after an NLRB trial examiner found Monroe guilty in 1967 of refusing to bargain as required by the Labor Act, it continued its strategy of delay, appealing and losing in both the Fifth Circuit and the U.S. Supreme Court. Some eight years had elapsed and Monroe had yet to bargain with the UAW. At the cost of some lawyers' fees and little else, the company saved millions of dollars by evading a union contract over the eight-year period.

When a new suit by Monroe against the UAW wound up in the Fifth Circuit, the judges, having seen this case for the third time, strongly rebuked Monroe for refusing to obey the law. They assessed double costs and attorneys' fees because the legal maneuvering by Monroe was so clearly just a delaying tactic to avoid the law and previous court rulings.

Finally, in 1973, Monroe attorney John Tate agreed to begin bargaining. Not surprisingly, the company's version of bargaining was to meet at a Ramada Inn conference room, listen to union proposals, and respond with one word: "No."

Among the proposals rejected were those as basic and simple as a union dues checkoff, any sickness or accident benefits, pensions, seniority protection, grievance procedure, health insurance, and cost-of-living protection. "We'd ask this guy Tate why the company could provide those things for the remaining workers in Michigan who had all of them," says Claude Pereira, who led the bargaining team. "What was good enough for those up North wasn't good enough for us."

Negotiations continued every six weeks or so and were often delayed because Tate, chief negotiator for Monroe, had been retained by Willie Farah to aid the clothing manufacturer in combating the

Amalgamated Clothing Workers unionizing efforts. As bargaining continued without results, frustrations grew among union supporters. "Those of us who grew up in the South were taught if you stole a penny, the federal government would spend a million to track you down and see justice done," organizer Lou Echols says. "People can't understand how Monroe could evade the law year after year after year. They lose faith in our system."

Echols saw the company's strategy as saving management millions, while at the same time confusing employees, who were tired of hearing about legal actions. Uncertain that it could effectively prosecute a strike, the union turned to a boycott of Monroe products. But Monroe's shock absorbers, the product made in Georgia, are sold under twenty or more brand names, making an effective consumer boycott quite difficult.

In November 1975, a Texan named David Cox arrived in Hartwell and began to solicit union cards on behalf of an organization called the Allied Industrial Union of Auto Workers Independent. The group, with no constitution, no bylaws, and no collective bargaining agreements, had never been recognized anywhere. Equipped with a complete mailing list, which observers believe was supplied by the company, Cox succeeded in getting enough cards to petition for an election. The campaign that followed proved to be, in many ways, a repeat of those of ten and twelve years before—full of company threats and intimidation.

John Tate, by this time a master campaigner against labor unions (now in wide demand for such services throughout the South), recycled old ads about how the company would have to shut down if it went union, just like the Hillsdale, Michigan, facility. With the relatively high labor turnover since the UAW first won ten years before, the old threats were as good as new for many Monroe workers, particularly in view of the massive downturn in the economy and in the auto industry in particular. Although David Cox's phony union received only eleven votes after he had been revealed as a former labor relations official for a Texas supermarket chain, the UAW was defeated.

For the moment, it appeared that the union was back where it was the day they buried the UAW in the courthouse square. But the massive violations of federal labor law caused the NLRB to throw out the vote and order Monroe to begin bargaining immediately with the union.

TODAY, LOU ECHOLS OCCASIONALLY PASSES THROUGH HARTWELL, BUT he doesn't have to spend much time there talking union. After fourteen years of struggle, the UAW finally won a contract with Monroe Auto Equipment.

"I think management realized that every time they knocked us down we'd get up and come back, again and again," Echols says. "Some unions might have gotten frustrated and written off Hartwell as too tough a nut to crack. But not the UAW."

The new contract raised wages an average of 97 cents an hour. Prior to the union agreement, workers had averaged only 12-cent increases between 1966 and 1977. Just as important, the UAW negotiated a host of improvements in working conditions. Seniority, job bidding, and a grievance procedure all were included in the first contract.

"After we reached agreement, I said a prayer of thanks," says Marion Crawford, 34, an electrician with ten years seniority. "The grievance procedure is the top accomplishment. Employees haven't had any place to go with problems in the past. It's probably the most important thing for blacks: for years we wouldn't even open our mouths in the plant."

The agreement, which came only after Monroe had been purchased by Tenneco, Inc. (which was recently embroiled in a battle to prevent union representation of steel workers in Newport News, Virginia) was a sweet one for Crawford. Fourteen years earlier, a student at a segregated high school, he had watched the mock funeral in the courthouse square.

"When you see something like that, it puts a scare into you for a long time, especially being black in Georgia at that time. But this shows that you have to have the courage to fight, no matter how long it takes."

Since the union victory, the atmosphere in Hartwell has shifted some. The new UAW headquarers is just down the street from the still-wary Chamber of Commerce, but it is also near a pharmacy that gives members of UAW Local 1427 a 10 percent discount on prescription drugs. In the last election, eleven local politicians came out to the local union hall to seek the UAW's endorsement. The local has sponsored a Little League team and has involved itself in community projects. Like most new locals, it has had its share of growing pains, but there is no question that the union has made a real difference not only in the plant but in the community at large.

But there are still questions unanswered. When Lou Echols does take a break from his new organizing campaigns at other nonunion plants in Georgia, he occasionally stops at the Local 1427 hall. As he looks out the front window onto the courthouse square where they hanged Walter Reuther in effigy in 1963, he asks himself why a company like Monroe can succeed so long in denying workers the rights federal law tells them they have.

THE MONROE STORY HIGHLIGHTS THE CURRENT NEEDS OF WORKERS, their labor unions, the South as a region, and the country as a whole, including a renewed effort toward a massive overhaul of federal labor law to keep it from being the companies' chief tool to repress workers; expanded union organizing strategies to deal with the increasing number of runaway shops; new legislation placing restrictions on the ability of corporations to close and/or relocate plants without accountability to workers and communities affected; and an effort toward strengthening the international labor movement to deal with multinational corporations.

In 1978 the labor movement put labor law reforms in Congress at the top of its Washington agenda. The AFL-CIO established a special task force of lobbyists and public relations experts who worked solely on the issues. But, despite widespread public support and an overwhelming positive vote in the House of Representatives, the long-overdue reforms did not become law. A minority of senators, with strong corporate-right backing, filibustered to block Senate passage.

Pushing legislation, particularly labor legislation, through Congress today is extremely difficult, and as we head into the 1980s, Congress displays a disturbing inability to develop and enact legislative solutions to the country's problems. Yet the magnitude of abuses of worker rights by corporations demands a revitalized labor effort on behalf of labor law reform. The final results of such an effort inevitably will reflect tradeoffs and compromises, but some ambitious changes can be sought:

1. The Labor Act must be streamlined, and loopholes that allow employers to delay for years must be limited. While employers are entitled to due process protections, the current protections they enjoy virtually nullify the purpose of the Labor Act. To eliminate the worst loophole, the decisions of administrative law judges should be enforceable immediately.

2. Workers dismissed for union activity should be allowed to bring private lawsuits for triple damages against employers who fire them. Discharges are frequently a key element in intimidating workers who support unionization; the present remedy is only reinstatement and back pay.

3. The union should have access to the work force—just as the employer does—to present its arguments. Time after time, companies hold "captive audience" meetings on company time in which workers hear of the "dire consequences" of a union victory (plant might shut down, workers might be laid off). Union organizers deserve a chance to make their arguments with equal access to workers—on company property and on company time, if necessary.

4. Companies that repeatedly commit unfair labor practices should

be denied government contracts. The Walsh-Healy Act provides similar penalties against employers who violate minimum wage laws.

5. Employers should be required to bargain with workers for a union contract on the basis of authorization cards showing that 70 percent support the union as their representative. Such a procedure used to be legal in the United States and still exists in Canada.

6. The NLRB should seek court injunctions ordering dismissed workers to be reinstated while the board is investigating and processing charges filed on their behalf. Many of the 2,000 unfair labor practice complaints issued against employers in fiscal 1973 involved such dismissals. Yet the NLRB sought federal court orders restraining the unlawful conduct of these companies only five times, while it sought similar injunctions against unions hundreds of times.

7. Provisions limiting secondary boycotts and hot-cargo restrictions should be repealed. For example, if the UAW and the Amalgamated Clothing and Textile Workers could have boycotted J. C. Penney's for handling Monroe shock absorbers, the Hartwell fight might have been significantly shortened. Similarly, if the so-called hot-cargo limitations of the law didn't exist, UAW workers in Ford assembly plants in Detroit could have supported Southern organizing efforts by refusing to handle Monroe shock absorbers. Workers in other countries, such as Great Britain, have the right to refuse to handle nonunion or struck goods.

8. All state right-to-work laws—and section 14-B of the Taft-Hartley Act, which made the laws possible—should be repealed. Compulsory open-shop laws still give workers, particularly in the South, the "right" to work for less.

Although reform of labor law is crucial, other legislation would greatly aid efforts to organize, particularly in the South. Most important are efforts to control runaway shops like Monroe. Major companies, such as General Motors, have made significant corporate decisions at the highest levels to open new plants in the South and attempt to keep those plants nonunion, threatening the very existence of the labor movement today. The best remedy is organization, but what else must be done?

One major need is for legislation providing workers with new rights and imposing new restrictions on corporations in cases of plant closures and relocations. Very simply, plant relocations affect too many people to be left to corporate executives who seldom live in the areas devastated by their decisions. Most other Western industrial countries recognize this fact and put some controls on runaway plants.

Another important potential check on the runaway shop is the control of local grants and various tax concessions to new industry.

Frequently, as in the case of Hart County and the Monroe plant there, a local unit of government offers to build the new plant and lease it back to the company. Railroad spurs, access roads, and sewage treatment may also be provided by the taxpayers. The community residents who have the "opportunity" to work at wages 25 to 40 percent lower than those paid elsewhere thus also get to subsidize the company that profits from their labor. Major restrictions should be placed on such public giveaways, aimed at limiting the degree to which workers and community residents pay for corporate profitmaking on the part of rogue employers such as Monroe.

Federalization of many key social benefits, such as unemployment compensation, welfare, and workers' compensation, would prevent some states from operating at substandard levels. Current practice, particularly prevalent in many Southern states, provides an added incentive for corporations to relocate in the South, but it also makes possible economic blackmail, with corporations like General Motors stopping construction of a new facility in Michigan until the the state legislature refused passage of improvements in workers' compensation.

Given the current conservative mood of the country, many of the legislative goals Southern workers and their Northern counterparts are fighting for may not be achieved in the near future. And workers have known for years that corporate interests and their many friends in and out of government often subvert and reorient even well-intended legislation.

For that reason, the fight for justice must not be limited to legislative arenas. The labor movement must quickly expand its international scope. In this era of multinationals, companies have little difficulty finding low-wage areas outside the United States. Even without widespread unionism, the South already faces the problem of runaway shops. Monroe Auto Equipment still produces most of its products in nonunion plants here, but in June 1979 it imported a major shipment of assembled shock absorbers from Onner de Brazil, S.A., and MAP Auto Pecas, S.A.—two Brazilian companies it recently purchased. Monroe also bought interests in plants in Mexico and Venezuela and acquired a wholly owned subsidiary in Argentina.

Efforts must be made to achieve multinational cooperation and solidarity between labor unions, which might seek coordinated bargaining, common contract expiration dates, and information exchanges. The UAW, for example, has been instrumental in the efforts to raise wages and improve working conditions both in Europe and Japan through the International Metalworkers Federation.

Most important, as population and plants shift South, labor unions must organize or their power will be severely eroded. Southern organizing cannot be regarded as a futile luxury. The very future of the labor movement is at stake. New kinds of coalitions must be created between unions and others with community power—the churches, environmental groups, local media outlets, civil rights activists, and elected officials—if the Southern organizing challenge is to be met.

Like the UAW's fight at Monroe, it must be viewed as a long-term struggle—one that may take years and years and still not be over. Corporations, with their tremendous power, will continue to use violence, threats, intimidation, race, sex, politics, and everything else at their disposal to break the union movement in the South.

But they will not succeed.

TWENTY-THREE

It's Good to Be Home in Greenville

CLIFF SLOAN AND BOB HALL

"WE'VE BEEN TAKING ON THE WHOLE damned city," says a textile worker active in the unionizing drive at Greenville's J. P. Stevens mills. "The newspapers, the TV, the businesses, the churches, the schools—we have to take them all on."

The *New York Times* called Greenville, South Carolina, one of the "most relentlessly anti-union cities in the nation." It is a reputation that many in the Greenville business community are proud of, a reputation they have self-consciously built and intend to maintain. Less than 8 percent of the workers employed in the county belong to a union; and those who try to increase that rate or lessen the $2,830 wage gap between industrial workers here and the rest of the country find themselves very much in the minority.

"People come to Greenville to get away from unions," says an executive from a major textile company. "They say, 'I want to live again, I don't want to be harassed all the time.' "

Greenville has changed over the years—drastically, some would say —but it remains a place where executives feel they can get away from union demands and government regulators. "It's Good to Be Home in Greenville," boasts the city's Chamber of Commerce. In an era of runaway shops, conservative politics, and resurgent religion, it is also a place whose national significance far exceeds the size of its population—62,000 in the city, 278,000 in Greenville

County. Consider the following who make their home in Greenville:

Michelin Tire Corporation, the French-based multinational firm and
pioneer of the radial tire, chose Greenville and neighboring Anderson
and Spartanburg counties to locate its first plants in America because
the area's work force was both familiar with factory work and hostile
to labor organizing. The United Rubber Workers, fearful that the
presence of nonunion plants in the United States will weaken its
bargaining position with the Big Four tire makers, has tried to organize
Michelin's new workers—with little success. Michelin, which is
completely unionized in France, plans to build more plants in the
South, adding to its present $350 million investment and work force of
over 2,500.

Robert T. Thompson, of Greenville, is chairman of the U.S. Chamber
of Commerce's labor relations committee, senior partner in one of the
country's top antiunion law firms, and chief strategist behind the
massive lobbying campaign and filibuster that scuttled the Labor Law
Reform Act of 1978. "I've been sort of a technical advisor to Chamber
lobbyists," Thompson says dryly. Defeating the bill, which would have
strengthened the National Labor Relations Act, became Thompson's
number one obsession in 1978. His law firm—Thompson, Mann &
Hutson—contributed over one hundred amendments to weaken the
bill; the firm's clients include a score of the biggest companies and
trade associations in the country, including Deering-Milliken, GE,
Campbell Soup, and the American Textile Manufacturers Institute. "I
happen to think that defeating this thing is in the best interest of the
companies I represent," Thompson concludes.

Daniel International Corporation is the third-largest industrial
contractor in the nation. After World War II, founder Charles E. Daniel
"sensed the tidal strength of the [Southern industrial development]
movement and became its captain through his ability to offer sites,
survey information, and good, fast, low-cost, and complete plant
construction."* Before his death in 1964, his company had built over
400 plants in the South—250 in South Carolina alone—for companies
like Celanese, J. P. Stevens, and Dan River Mills. His nephew, Buck
Mickel, follows in his footsteps, especially in his opposition to union
labor. In 1977, Daniel International merged into the large,
California-based Fluor Corporation, a move both firms believe will give
them a stronger position in the burgeoning nonunion construction field,
particularly in Daniel's current specialty—building nuclear and fossil-
fuel power plants for utilities.

Clement Furman Haynsworth, Jr., segregationist judge, comes from
one of Greenville's oldest families. His great-grandfather, the Reverend

---

*From Kenneth and Blanche Marsh, *The New South: Greenville, South Carolina*
(Columbia: R. L. Bryan, 1965), p. 100.

Richard Furman, founded Furman University while serving as the president of the Southern Baptist Convention 152 years ago. Richard Nixon appointed Haynsworth to the U.S. Supreme Court, but the Senate eventually rejected his nomination. While chief justice of the U.S. Fourth Circuit Court of Appeals, Haynsworth frequently wrote decisions upholding segregationist practices, which the U.S. Supreme Court regularly overturned on appeal. His nomination was part of a package of favors which Strom Thurmond won from Nixon in exchange for campaigning for him in the South in 1968 against George Wallace. The deal, worked out in an Atlanta hotel room meeting between Nixon and the South Carolina senator, resulted in protective tariffs for the textile industry, relaxation of the federal role in school desegregation, and the insertion of twenty-odd friends and associates of Thurmond into key administration posts. According to writer Neal Peirce, "rarely in American history has a political debt been so handsomely, consistently paid off."

J. P. Stevens & Company, the nation's second-largest textile company, is the city's largest industrial employer. Eighteen of its eighty-five plants are in the Greenville area, and its manufacturing, personnel, and purchasing headquarters are located in the Daniel Building, Greenville's largest. The New York–based textile firm more than doubled its size in 1946 by merging with a network of Southern mill owners centered in Greenville. The target of a national union organizing campaign, the company moved its annual stockholders' meeting from New York to Greenville's Textile Hall in March 1978 to avoid a recurrence of embarrassing demonstrations that met its owners in 1977. Stevens is so incensed by the continuous barrage of public attacks from New York politicians, labor leaders, editorial writers, and even Wall Street insiders, that it has threatened to abandon the Stevens Tower in midtown Manhattan, no doubt to consolidate its troops in Greenville.

Roger Milliken, head of Deering-Milliken, the nation's largest privately held textile company, lives in Spartanburg but is a major influence in Greenville (where his Judson Mill employs 1,100), the rest of South Carolina, and the country. Besides sponsoring the Ronald Reagan editorials on WMUU, he contributes heavily to a wide variety of ultraconservative causes, including the John Birch Society and the National Right to Work Committee. He gives his executives free subscriptions to Bill Buckley's *National Review*. He gave Richard Nixon $84,000 in 1972, some of it secretly, and was a key figure in what Jack Anderson called "a direct link between a campaign payoff to President Nixon and his efforts to restrict textile imports." In labor circles, Milliken is known for "the Darlington case," a thirteen-year battle which followed Milliken's decision to close his Darlington mill after the textile workers union won an election in 1956. Even after the courts finally decided Milliken should compensate the employees for being fired illegally, Deering-Milliken attorneys kept the case on appeal for several more years, preventing any of the 550 affected workers from receiving a dime.

NESTLED IN THE ROLLING FOOTHILLS OF THE PIEDMONT, GREENVILLE was originally a second-home community for wealthy Charlestonians seeking refuge from the heat of South Carolina's Low Country. By the late 1880s, the town became the center for a new kind of plantation: the mill village. At first spurned by the Low Country cotton planters, industrialization soon impressed many of the post–Civil War elite as the only means for "resurgence." Greenville, with the waterfalls of its Reedy River and its proximity to the impoverished white farmers in the hills, became the natural hub of the movement. New South advocates like Benjamin F. Perry urged local businessmen to "educate the masses, industrialize, work hard, and seek Northern capital to develop Southern resources." Perry, who had argued against secession with men like Dr. James Furman, was not exactly a popular figure among the wealthy whites. But his new advice seemed to possess more merit.

In 1873, Vardry McBee and three Bostonians newly arrived in Greenville began the Vardry Mill, powered by the falls of the Reedy River. It was the town's first textile factory. The next year, Colonel H. P. Hammett opened the Piedmont Manufacturing Company on the Saluda River, following the lead of his father-in-law, William Bates, a Rhode Island native who had started Greenville County's first cotton mill a half century earlier on the banks of the Enoree River. And in 1881, Captain Ellison Adger Smyth, grandson of a Charleston banker, joined with F. J. Pelzer to organize the Pelzer Mill.

To attract and hold workers from the surrounding countryside, the mill owners had to provide housing. Newly created mill villages like Piedmont and Pelzer flourished, inviting other capitalists to open their own versions in or around Greenville. Whole towns, with company-owned houses, stores, and churches, sprang up almost overnight. By 1882, Greenville County employed more "hands" (1,250 workers, including children) in cotton mills than any other South Carolina county; the South's total textile employment of 19,400 in 1880 and 44,800 in 1890, while gaining rapidly, was still dwarfed by New England's 217,700 textile workers in 1880 and 259,500 in 1890.*

*Georgia and North Carolina had more textile workers than South Carolina in these decades. The region as a whole depended on child labor: 24 percent of Southern cotton mill hands were boys under 16 or girls under 15 in 1890, in contrast to only 7 percent in New England. By World War I, South Carolina's mill employment surpassed Georgia's, ranking third behind Massachusetts and North Carolina.

At this early point, labor organizing challenged the hegemony of mill owners. In October 1886, while conducting a strike at cotton mills in Augusta, Georgia, the Knights of Labor came to the Greenville area. According to textile executive and amateur historian Malcolm Cross, the workers' enthusiasm produced "a frantic correspondence among South Carolina textile leaders about the Knights and what to do about them." The solution, then as now, seemed to hinge on firing the leaders and vigorously repressing the momentum for union organizing. When the Knights helped employees at the Pelzer and Piedmont mills, Cross says, "Captain Smyth and Colonel Hammett responded quickly and effectively, sought out and discharged the troublemakers and brought to a halt the abortive attempt to organize their workers."

The industry's policy of racial segregation also took shape in these early days. Captain Smyth, generally recognized as the "Dean of Southern Cotton Manufacturers," organized rifle clubs with the single purpose of defending white rule from scalawags and carpetbaggers and keeping blacks in their place. When Wade Hampton won the governor's office in 1876 with the help of roving bands of "Red Shirts" like Captain Smyth's men, Reconstruction ended; new rules rigidly segregating the races soon circumscribed every part of society.

From then on, mill owners could always point to the "white only" status of textile factories as visible evidence of their loyalty to their workers. Racism, in a state that was still 51 percent black in 1920, thus became the linchpin in a new form of Southern paternalism whose finer accoutrements included everything from free Christmas turkeys to garden plots, company-sponsored sports teams to scholarship funds.

Between the 1890s and World War I, Greenville experienced its "textile gold rush years." Mills and mill villages sprang up throughout the Piedmont, especially in Anderson, Greenville, and Spartanburg counties. Greenville's population jumped from 1,518 in 1860 to 8,607 in 1890 to 23,127 in 1920; meanwhile, employment in the county's

Greenville area mill owners, 1905

cotton mills rose from 1,800 in 1890 to 8,500 in 1920. Owners added more looms and spindles to old factories and opened new ones, borrowing capital from machinery manufacturers, the commission houses which sold the finished goods, the local banks which mill owners established, and from each other. Stores, hospitals, utilities, newspapers, schools, churches—all were organized and either owned outright by the mill men or tied to their fortunes through marriage and an elaborate network of middlemen (lawyers, realtors, financiers, contractors) and interlocking boards of directors. For example, James Orr, Jr., who married Colonel H. P. Hammett's daughter, is described by a biographer as

president of the Piedmont Manufacturing Company, Piedmont, S.C. He was organizer of the Orr Cotton Mills of Anderson, S.C., vice president of the American Company, the Mills Manufacturing Company, the Greenville *News,* the Paris Mountain Hotel Company, and the Greenville Gas and Electric Company. He was a director of the First National Bank of Greenville, the American National Bank, and the People's Bank of Greenville, also of the Easley Manufacturing Company and the Cox Manufacturing Company. He also served as trustee of the South Carolina Medical College of Charleston, of Converse College in Spartanburg, and Clemson Agricultural College of Clemson.*

Such inbreeding and intricate interweaving of interests has long characterized the Piedmont, and has made Greenville the aristocratic center of upper South Carolina, as Charleston is for the Low Country. Captain Smyth's daughter married A. F. McKissick, who was president of Ninety-Six (the name of another mill town) Cotton Mills and later owner of Alice Manufacturing Company. Their grandsons, A. Foster and Ellison, still play an active role in Greenville textiles and banking. Similarly, the Stone, Earle, Haynsworth, and Furman families—all among the most powerful in Greenville today—are interconnected through common ancestry as well as current business interests.

The actual consolidation of several mills under one corporation—rather than through interrelated but independent stock owners—did not occur until Lewis W. Parker merged a group of sixteen mills into the Parker Mills Company in 1907. He organized the corporation to rescue mill owners who had suffered large losses in the financial panics of the early 1900s. But in 1914 his own company went into receivership when the bottom fell out of his investments in the cotton market.

The trend, however, had been established; larger and larger

*From William P. Jacobs, *The Pioneers* (Clinton, South Carolina: Jacobs & Co. Press, 1935).

companies formed or expanded by buying Southern mills. Commission houses such as Milliken & Company, J. P. Stevens, Josiah Bailey, and Iselin-Jefferson (later Dan River) moved into direct ownership. By the end of World War I, when the market for textile products soared, these Northern interests joined Southern mill owners in capitalizing a host of factories. In 1920, Greenville County had twenty-two mills with 750,000 spindles, making it the largest textile center in the state, with neighboring Spartanburg County a close second. Only Gaston County, North Carolina, had more spindles in the South.

By 1930, with Northern investment flowing faster and faster into the region, the South finally surpassed New England in the number of spindles and looms in production. Newer equipment, cheaper labor, lower taxes, combined with the introduction of scientific management techniques (the speedup and stretch-out), helped profits in Southern textiles leap past those in the North. But the industry's commitment to maintaining the paternalistic control of the earlier generation of mill owners remained unchanged. When workers in Greenville County joined the national textile strike of 1934 (the country's largest mass strike), their meetings were infiltrated by company spies, they were harassed by company "deputies," and chased off picket lines by the National Guard. On September 6, 1934, six strikers in nearby Honea Path were killed and thirty injured in a shootout between company men and strikers. Shootings also occurred in Judson Mills and other area plants. The National Guard, on orders of the South Carolina governor, patrolled the mill villages until the strike was finally crushed in late September.*

BY WORLD WAR II, GREENVILLE HAD FIRMLY ESTABLISHED ITSELF AS the "Textile Capital of the World." And with a mixture of brute force and graceful paternalism, its leaders had taught both blacks and whites how to stay in their places. The well-disciplined work force and probusiness climate of the area attracted other employers in the postwar economic boom. The size of Greenville (58,000) and the area's textile employment (21,000) grew little after 1950, but a plethora of nontextile plants opened on the outer edges of the city, especially along the thirty-mile Interstate 85 corridor to Spartanburg.

*Greenville was not immune to other labor protests throughout these years. In 1915, the IWW shocked the entire region by marching through downtown Greenville with a red flag. The wave of textile strikes in 1929 also rippled through the town's mills, though not with the violent consequences of a Gastonia or Elizabethton. Several walkouts in Greenville brought concessions from the mill owners in their use of the stretch-out and speedup (making fewer people do more work).

The value added by manufacturing factories in Greenville County jumped sevenfold between 1947 and 1976, the population rose from 158,000 to 278,000, and the number of nonmanufacturing jobs (trade, finance, utilities, government, services) climbed from 15,800 to 51,800. In the sixteen-year period from 1960 to 1976, over $650 million in new industrial investment entered Greenville County, with much of that in the nontextile field. The number of jobs in these industries—chemicals, electrical equipment, rubber, apparel, even aerospace—doubled from 15,000 to 30,000 during those years; and the contribution the textile mills made to the total value of products made in the county declined from more than one-half in 1960 to less than one-third in 1975 ($571 million out of $1.85 billion).

Other changes in the postwar era further complicated the plantation-style rule of the old mill men. The automobile helped render the mill-owned village obsolete; workers could be recruited from outside the county, and those in the mill houses possessed a new mobility. The new employers that arrived offered higher wages, pulling skilled loom fixers and others out of the mills and raising the expectations of other workers. Legislation to improve the pitiful educational levels of South Carolinians, while consistently opposed by the textile interests, gradually made headway. In 1960, the South Carolina attorney general, with the agreement of the mill owners, finally declared unconstitutional the state law effectively barring blacks from work in textile factories. But it took the civil rights movement and Civil Rights Act of 1964 to open the gates. Black employment in South Carolina mills rose from under 5 percent in the early sixties to 17 percent in 1968 to 30 percent in 1976. Federal regulation of many other areas formerly considered the sole prerogative of management also stepped up in the sixties and seventies. No longer could a handful of men make decisions the way they had for a century.

"It used to be that a man could make a decision, put on his hat, and that would be the decision of the board of directors," recalls a descendant of one of Greenville's most prominent textile families. "It's an awful nice way of doing business and we miss it now."

"So many Yankees have come in," rues a construction company executive, "the courthouse crowd just doesn't have the power anymore."

But some men recognized that there were ways to adapt to the changes. Alester Furman, Jr., like his father before him, is one of these. At 80, he has lived long enough to hear others call him a man of great vision—and, indeed, he has led two generations of Greenville's elite in making the transition from mill-owned schools, churches, homes, hospitals, and clubs to independent, but friendly, enterprises.

Furman tells a story about a 1946 train ride he took with Robert

Stevens, then chairman of the board of directors of J. P. Stevens. Stevens was touring the South, putting the final touches on the merger plan that would bring the modern J. P. Stevens into existence.

As they passed a mill village, Furman turned to Stevens. "Bob," he asked, "when are you going to sell your houses?"

The very thought horrified Stevens. "Never, I'll never do that," he said emphatically. "We'd lose control of our workers."

Furman smiled and shook his head. "We'll manage," he told Stevens confidently.

Indeed they have, though in ways much less obvious, though no less effective.

ONE OF THE PRINCIPAL TACTICS IN MAINTAINING CONTROL WHILE expanding the circle of power involves letting in only your friends. For Greenville's elite, this strategy has meant blocking the entrance of companies into the area that are not aggressively antiunion.

"There's a long history of local interests, textile interests, encouraging or discouraging new industry," recalls E. D. Sloan, Jr., a Greenville road construction magnate. "The mills that were here controlled the water commission. . . . The water commission would say, 'I'm sorry, we don't have enough water.' It was the prerogative of the good ol' boys in the courtroom."

Many in Greenville remember a time in the thirties, for example, when the Manhattan Clothing Shop tried to open a plant in Greenville. Manhattan had a "closed shop" contract and likely would have opened a unionized plant. The good ol' boys in the courtroom quickly mobilized to keep it out altogether.

Recently, the most highly publicized example of screening a prospective business followed Philip Morris's 1977 announcement that it had bought an option on land near Greenville as a possible site for a $100 million plant that would employ an estimated 2,500 workers. Several bankers were anxious to have Philip Morris, with its huge payroll and purchasing power, come into the area. But some of the biggest names in Greenville business, and in South Carolina politics, made known their opposition to Philip Morris on the basis of its contract with the Tobacco Workers Union in its North Carolina plants. The heavy guns came out blasting.

"It would be like inviting the devil into the dining room," says Sloan. "I told one of those bankers, 'Let's run those bastards off; somebody else will come.' "

"It was going to be a large plant," antiunion lawyer Robert Thompson recalls. "My objection was that they were coming here and not giving employees a free choice. The industrial climate of South

Carolina is based on nonunionization. If Philip Morris were here with unionized workers and families, this would no longer be a nonunion community."

"No way that plant should ever have come here," Buck Mickel declares. Mickel is generally considered the single most powerful man in Greenville. His uncle, Charles Daniel, founder of Daniel Construction Company, is still revered as the patron saint of Greenville's business community. "Philip Morris would have brought in a union," Mickel says in explaining his opposition to its proposed move. "It's a corporation that takes and never gives. I know, I've worked for them."

Most textile companies shun publicity, but Bob Coleman, chairman of Riegel Textile, admits he is "very opposed to organized labor"; and another Riegel executive went on record during the Philip Morris debate expressing "concern . . . about Philip Morris's union status. It's very difficult to believe they're going to have the will to preserve our open-shop environment."*

Even Michelin Tire, a newcomer to Greenville, publicly said it had "reservations" about the new tobacco factory. Ironically, when Michelin first located in Greenville in 1974, it encountered the same kind of scrutiny and resistance. Local businessmen were afraid its higher pay scale and better package of benefits would disrupt the prevailing rates for Greenville workers. They also feared Michelin would not strenuously oppose organizing by the United Rubber Workers Union. Its new plants would be susceptible to unionization, mill owner Eugene Stone III complained to the newspaper in 1973. And that would be "just like a cancer; once they get a foothold, it tends to spread."

Michelin has since established itself as a strong advocate of antiunionism. It took the unusual step of naming as plant manager not an experienced production supervisor, but an expert in "personnel management." It regularly sends representatives to the antiunion courses offered by the Chamber of Commerce and area schools. And it has established personal ties to Greenville's old-line elite; the Michelin family has become close friends of the Furmans.

---

*The Chamber of Commerce ultimately wrote the company a lukewarm letter saying it would be welcome; but most observers consider the gesture only a formality to obscure behind-the-scenes maneuvering. Some even believe that Senator Strom Thurmond and Governor James Edwards contacted the tobacco firm and discouraged the move. Both men deny the charges, but one prominent businessman's doubts reflect a widespread attitude: "You take the fact that Roger Milliken and some of those other guys who were opposed to Philip Morris are some of the biggest Republican contributors in the state, and it's not hard seeing Thurmond and Edwards getting involved on their behalf."

Orienting new businesses like Michelin to the Greenville way of doing things is one of the roles of the local Chamber of Commerce. With a full-time staff of twenty-four professionals and an annual budget of $650,000, the Chamber operates an extensive program of lobbying, management training, and public education. It is most sophisticated and best organized at what it considers most important: the effort to keep unions out. Plenty of people, it seems, remain unpersuaded about the dangers of unions. A Lou Harris poll of South Carolinians in 1971 found that most citizens thought the lack of labor organization hurt their standard of living. In answer to the question, "Industry is just running away from labor unions by moving South—we should unionize here too," 44 percent agreed and only 30 percent disagreed.

While unions like ACTWU eagerly organize a newly responsive work force, the Chamber has its own programs to preserve the status quo. A Communications Action Program is "directed toward the general public stressing its stake in maintaining a climate free from union organization and collective bargaining." A Communication Network Task Force monitors "labor activity in its formative stages." A Business-Industrial Relations Committee serves as troubleshooter to combat "third-party intervention" (the Chamber's term for union representatives). Significantly, the Committee's guiding light is GE vice-president Stephen Dolny, another indication of how "diversification" has actually provided the Greenville business community with some of its most aggressive antiunion leaders.

The Chamber's Leadership Greenville program most clearly reflects the changing methods of control exercised by the Greenville business community. As the old-line leaders died or moved out of the limelight, others in Greenville, and at the Chamber in particular, feared "a crisis of leadership." Leadership Greenville is designed to meet this crisis by training forty to fifty young professionals a year in a variety of subjects: "labor . . . leadership . . . economy . . . education . . . media . . . the arts." The goal is "developing a core of informed, committed, and qualified individuals," a core of individuals who will share the Chamber's perspective in their leadership of Greenville.

TRAINING THIS CORE OF LEADERSHIP HAS PROVEN CRUCIAL TO fulfilling the primary goal in the business control of Greenville: the prevention of independent sources of opposition or criticism to corporate policies. When Alester Furman, Jr., and other established leaders relaxed their personal control of key institutions in the community and guided the transition to "independent" enterprises, they needed to make sure these new entities were headed by friendly, promanagement people. Independent-minded newspapers, churches, universities, professional and civic associations,* and social service agencies could play a vital role in challenging the status quo and creating an atmosphere conducive to critical thinking and dynamic interchange. Significantly, such free-spirited institutions are not allowed to thrive in Greenville.

Greenville's two newspapers—the *News* and the *Piedmont*—are both owned by Multimedia, and both consistently run promanagement editorials.† A top textile executive calls Jim McKinney, editor of the *News* editorial page, "a good ol' boy you can count on." McKinney himself proudly tells visitors that his friends are among the top businessmen in Greenville and his brother-in-law is a former Burlington Industries executive.

Neither paper seems very interested in investigative reporting, or in asking Greenville's leaders any embarrassing questions. "The basic policy is 'keep your eyes closed,' " says one of the papers' reporters. "It's not an explicit policy, but it's implicit." Even a reporter from the *Daily News Record,* the textile industry's trade newspaper, calls the papers' coverage "miserable." J. Kelly Sisk, chairman of the board of Multimedia, has a different opinion: "We recognize that the textile industry is extremely important. . . . In the newspaper business, you have to think about people—advertisers, merchants, stores where newspapers are bought and sold. It's our purpose to give good, solid coverage of the textile industry. That's our avowed purpose. . . . We're respected for it."

Sisk's curious sense of his newspapers' constituency—advertisers, merchants, and store owners—reveals much about the independence of the *News* and the *Piedmont.* So does Multimedia's extensive

---

*The failure of the professional community to achieve independence from the business interests it often represents is best illustrated by Greenville doctors. Not a single one is willing to diagnose a case of byssinosis, or brown lung, the disease mill workers may get from breathing cotton dust. Medically certified diagnoses are required before a mill worker can collect disability compensation payments from the state. Consequently, the Carolina Brown Lung Association says it has been forced to take disabled Greenville workers to other parts of the state for fair medical treatment—though they still run into resistance from many doctors. The head of the South Carolina Lung Association's task force to instruct doctors how to diagnose byssinosis is a consultant for a textile firm, M. Lowenstein & Company, and for Liberty Mutual, the textile industry's largest insurer and chief opponent to paying brown lung claims.

†One editorial in the Sunday, July 13, 1976, *News-Piedmont* condemned the consumer boycott of J. P. Stevens undertaken by the Amalgamated Clothing and Textile Workers Union (ACTWU) as "evil . . . deplorable . . . tyrannical." Two days later, an editorial in the *Piedmont* claimed that if ACTWU's attempt to organize Stevens workers in Greenville succeeds, "individual workers' rights would be trampled in a mindless union. . . . We hope Stevens workers, who for so many years have played such an important part in this community's smooth development, will not fall for the false siren song of union rocks and shoals waiting as sharks to snare unwary travelers."

involvement in running its personnel through the Leadership Greenville seminars; and so do the numerous corporate interlocks between Sisk, other Multimedia executives, and the Greenville business establishment. The cordial relationship Multimedia's local television station, WFBC, maintains with the city's elite is perhaps best illustrated by the fact that the station recently had two women broadcasters change their surnames to two of the most important in the city— Furman and Daniel. "It was no coincidence." says WFBC news director John Poston. "Furman and Daniel are familiar and easy names in Greenville."

GREENVILLE'S ELITE HAVE MADE A HABIT OF KEEPING THE CITY IN THE dark—and then claiming credit when a ray of sunshine breaks through. From the creation of public schools—originally opposed because they would take the children out of the mills—to the technical colleges, all social advances are projected as gifts from the benevolent owners concerned for the welfare of their beloved workers. The same self-serving distortions allow business leaders to claim credit for opening mills to black workers and for providing higher-paying nontextile jobs with national corporations which have located in Greenville—even though both changes were vigorously resisted for years. Adopting these changes as their own is one of the ways Greenville's corporate power structure maintains its control: rather than fight to the death on an issue, it absorbs the inevitable into its own framework and thus keeps the upper hand. Graceful, but thorough, control.

There are still a few realities that Greenville's rulers have not faced, much less accepted as consequences of their backward policies and hegemonic control. Most significantly, Greenville suffers from chronic poverty. People who work hard remain poor. Two hundred families made more than $50,000 in 1970. For fully one-third of Greenville's families, their year's income failed to top $6,000. "Poverty is not a real big problem," says Dr. Larry McCalla, chairman of the county council, from his spacious home in a secluded suburban neighborhood. "There's no place you could pick out as a real deep poverty situation."

State Senator Charles Garrett also doesn't think the problem is all that bad. His attitude is perhaps best expressed by a sign in his office in Dan River Mills: "Stamp Out Poverty—Get Rich Quick."

Men like McCalla and Garrett are likely to tell you that poverty is on the decline in Greenville, that wages are going up. They'll cite statistics to back that up—the estimate that, by 1980, four times as many local families will have annual incomes exceeding $50,000. But they might not mention estimates that, in 1980, a third of Greenville's families will still be getting by on less than $10,000 a year. Or that South Carolina ranks forty-sixth in per capita personal income ($5,126 compared to the national figure of $6,441 in 1976).

Nor are the annual-income figures the only evidence of serious and unmet social needs in Greenville. In 1970, for example, Greenville had the third-highest murder rate in the country. As far as public education, the Greenville County Planning Commission put it succinctly: "Outlays per pupil in Greenville County are approximately the same as those in the state of South Carolina as a whole, even though income per capita in the county is 15 percent greater." The illiteracy rate in the state is the second highest in America, yet teacher pay and per-pupil school expenditures are the second lowest. In the early 1970s, the South Carolina Education Association grew so disturbed by these inadequacies that it threatened to impose sanctions if the legislature did not grant a sizable increase in teachers' pay. Until a $500 increase was granted in 1973, the average teacher earned $1,400 below the Southeastern average.

These continuing needs—the poverty, the crime, the schools—have not moved Greenville's leaders to tax its corporations or its wealthy citizens more heavily. A study in 1970 revealed that the state could collect $165 million more a year in property taxes and $31 million more in personal income taxes without exceeding the national average tax rates. The same study showed that South Carolina reaps $36 million *more* from its sales taxes (which fall most heavily on the poor) than the national average. But Greenville and South Carolina continue to make those least able to pay support the costs of government services. After all, low taxes are one of the preconditions for a healthy business climate. Even the so-called leading progressives accept this assumption without question. "Our schools are better than some people might think," says Max Heller, who served as the city's reform-minded mayor from January 1971 to January 1979. "If our taxes were higher, we would have less development."

Ironically, Heller takes his liberal credentials as "a man who serves the people's interests" to his new post as head of South Carolina's industrial development office. Part of his job involves continuing— albeit under state sponsorship—the paternalistic tradition of convincing workers/voters that *their* best interests are served by granting more concessions to industry. But the facts suggest that the principle of "business first, the people's welfare second" has had an overall stifling effect on the social conditions of Greenville and South Carolina. Because Greenville is the most industrialized part of the state, its low corporate and property taxes have left South Carolina poor and helped lead the state to the bottom of the stack in many areas: South Carolina ranks forty-third among the states in percentage of families with income less than $3,000; forty-second in number of hospital beds per one thousand persons; forty-eighth in average student-teacher ratio; forty-ninth in the percentage of the work force unionized; forty-seventh in average industrial wage; and forty-seventh in per capita welfare assistance payments.

As long as the interests of Greenville's corporate elite take precedence over the interests of the majority of its citizens, such backwardness can be expected to continue. A reversal of those interests—especially through the organization of Greenville's workers—poses a direct threat to men like attorney Robert Thompson, builder Buck Mickel, realtor Alester Furman, and textile man Robert Coleman. The circle of power is not large enough to let the unions in—not without a fight anyway.

"You can develop an industrial community, as we have, where there's no place for a union," says Robert Thompson, almost as an article of faith. "You can live forever without them."

For notes on sources, see pages 373–74.

TWENTY-FOUR

Charleston Hospital Workers' Strike, 1969

STEVE HOFFIUS

DURING SPRING IN CHARLESTON, South Carolina, the newspapers run banner headlines about the flowers. Not just because they fill the city with long-awaited colors and smells, but because every year they attract swarms of tourists. Businesses in town depend on this influx of people, which provides them with so many sales that one merchant describes it as "our second Christmas."

In the spring of 1969, the flowers bloomed as brightly as ever, but the tourists stayed away. Even local residents refused to leave their homes to shop. Retail business, which had been expected to boom, dropped by 10 percent. Instead of the expected tour buses and khaki-shorted visitors, the streets were filled with tanklike troop carriers, with 500 National Guardsmen equipped with fitted bayonets, with long lines of demonstrators being carted off to jail. Snipings were not infrequent. Firebombings were widespread. A curfew at times lasted from 9 P.M. to 5 A.M.

On March 20, 1969, hundreds of licensed practical nurses and nonprofessional hospital workers at the local Medical College of South Carolina (now the Medical University) went out on strike. A week later, many of the employees at nearby Charleston County Hospital joined them on strike. The nonprofessionals included nurses' aides, orderlies, and members of the dietary and maintenance staffs. All of them were black, and nearly all were women. They began the most important labor battle in the city's history. It was also Charleston's biggest civil rights struggle, and that combination of labor and civil rights—"union power plus soul power," said one magazine—captured the attention of the nation.

Walter Reuther publicly presented the hospital workers with a check for $25,000 and marched side by side with Coretta Scott King, Ralph Abernathy, and Andrew Young. King said to the strikers, "If my husband was alive, he'd be with you now, joining in your struggle." George Meany announced a contribution of another $25,000. Forty thousand hospital workers in New York pledged to send a dollar a week to the Charleston strike fund.

Twenty members of the U.S. House of Representatives asked President Nixon to intercede on behalf of the hospital workers. Seventeen senators urged him to send federal mediators, and eventually he dispatched a team of observers. In the middle of the strike, presidential deputy counsel Harry Dent, one of the architects of Nixon's "Southern strategy," called hospital President William McCord at 6:45 one morning and insisted that he settle the strike at once. Investigators from the Department of Health, Education and Welfare threatened the school with the withdrawal of millions of dollars of promised federal funds. Dock workers suggested that they would shut down the Port of Charleston if the strike continued.

When representatives of the hospital workers accepted the administration's "Memorandum of Agreement," they were trumpeted as the victors. An article by A.H. Raskin in the *New York Times Magazine* claimed that the strike "welded organized labor and civil rights groups into an indomitable alliance" that "won a full victory." *Business Week* was less pleased with the results, but reported that the strike forged "a successful union-Negro alliance in which a fight for economic betterment is fused with a fight for racial dignity."

The four-month-long strike and the resulting administration-worker agreement stood as a model to workers—especially to hospital workers and other public employees—throughout both the South and the nation. It suggested that no institution, in any state, was immune to the power of organized workers, and it identified the union representing the hospital workers, Local 1199 of the National Union of Hospital and Nursing Home Employees, as a powerful national organization, a union capable of taking on the challenge of organizing many of the largely unrepresented public service employees, and doing so in new and innovative ways.

Ten years later, many of the results of the strike can still be seen. Working conditions of all state employees in South Carolina were improved in important ways. A far more progressive tone was established in local dealings between the races than ever existed before. However, the strike also led to bitterness and resentment, because the gains were, in the end, limited. While the workers won virtually every specific demand they made, especially those for wage increases and a grievance procedure, they did not win their major demand, recognition of 1199 as their union. Because the Medical College was run by the state of South Carolina, the hospital administration maintained that they were legally unable to recognize the union, and they stood firm. At the time, the workers and their union representatives felt they could accept an agreement that did not include union recognition—they felt they had no choice—and could push in the future toward that greater goal. But without recognition, the workers felt impotent. They had just completed an exhausting battle and had been judged by many observers to be the victors. They were ready to rest awhile. As they rested, though, their unity and organization fell apart.

The workers' basic anger is still directed, as it was before and during the strike, at their employer, the Medical University. Yet by meeting so many of their other demands, the institution took away many of the workers' opportunities to organize in the future. Anger toward the hospital was bound to be frustrated, and so the workers have directed much of their resentment at the only other targets available: at each other, and at their union. Events of the strike that had been accepted without complaint have in the past ten years been analyzed and dissected in great detail. The workers have settled on one major complaint: they feel they were not sufficiently involved in the strike planning. They, after all, were the ones on the line, the ones whose jobs were threatened, who were marching, who were jailed. And it was their home, Charleston. The union representatives, they knew, would leave; the workers would not.

The daily planning and strategy sessions were conducted by four representatives, one from each major group involved in the strike: Henry Nicholas represented the national union, Andrew Young represented the Southern Christian Leadership Conference (SCLC), Bill Saunders represented the local community, and Isaiah Bennett stood for the workers. Not one was a hospital worker. Though nearly all the workers were women, not one of the four main planners was. The workers were to have been consulted regularly for suggestions on the strike's directions, but today few of the workers can remember these meetings. For the most part, they remember small groups of workers— usually just Mary Moultrie and Rosetta Simmons, from the Medical College and the Charleston County Hospital respectively—being consulted about strategy, and they remember mass rallies. They remember little worker involvement in the daily planning of the strike. At the time, few had objected. "This was our first time out on strike," remembers striker Naomi White, "so everybody was inexperienced. These people that were sent down here were the pros of a strike and a union, so who were we to question how things should be run?"

Today, a great many Charleston workers question how the strike was run.

But the strike was much more than a Charleston affair. "We realized quickly," says Moe Foner, one of the national union leaders then and now, "that if we kept it a Charleston thing, it would have taken forever. We'd be there still. We made it into a national issue, and to do that we brought in SCLC, we attracted national media. Toes were bound to be stepped on, but we did everything we could to avoid it. We had daily meetings with the workers, with *all* the workers, sometimes a couple of meetings a day."

In retrospect, the workers certainly won the battle, but the war belonged to the state and the Medical College. Mary Moultrie, president of the Charleston local during the strike, now says, "I don't see where any of it was really a victory, other than the wage increase. In terms of working conditions and everything, everything is basically the same. We're right back down where we started, and the workers right now, they're having a pretty bad time. If we had gotten union recognition and had adequate representation over there, had somebody who would be able to bargain with management, it probably would have worked. But the Memorandum of Agreement wasn't worth the paper it was written on."

THE ORIGINAL IDEA FOR A UNION CAME SLOWLY. FIRST, CHARLESTON hospital workers simply realized that they needed to work together. In December 1967, more than a year before the walkout, a group of five nonprofessional workers were fired in a dispute with a charge nurse over access to standard reports on the patients they would care for. Eventually the Department of Health, Education and Welfare was asked to investigate, and upon the department's recommendation, the workers were finally reinstated. Mary Moultrie remembers that hospital workers had certainly been fired in the past,

but it had never happened with that many people before. There had been what they call being insubordinate—one person might refuse to do something or talk back to a head nurse or any white nurse, and he or she would be fired right on the spot, but to my knowledge that's the first time it ever happened to the group like that and we were really concerned. So people started talking about it and then other things came up and we decided that we needed to organize ourselves. At that time we didn't have a union in mind to affiliate with or anything like that. We just knew that we had to do something.

At first we didn't know how the administration and staff would accept what we were doing. We didn't want to be picked off one by one. So we sort of kept it a secret. We'd go round and whisper to people and we'd catch people during breaktime and on lunch hour. We kept it out of the ears of the whites.

They turned to two people for assistance. Bill Saunders, a local community organizer, published a bulletin of news important to blacks in the area, called the *Lowcountry Newsletter.* He gave the first community-wide attention to the problems of the hospital workers. And they met with Isaiah Bennett, an official with a local tobacco workers union and one of the few people in the city with experience negotiating workers' grievances. Bennett offered the use of his union's hall, and eventually worked full-time organizing the hospital workers.

"We started having weekly meetings," says Moultrie. "What we would do, when people would show up for a meeting we'd say that you should bring the best friend that you have, somebody that you can trust. They would bring one person with them to the next meeting, and we kept doing that until we had about 550 out of 600-and-something nonprofessional workers between the Medical College Hospital and Charleston County Hospital." They discussed the incident of the group firing, but they also talked of their own personal grievances. "It was amazing," remembers Bennett, "how many people had problems similar to those who had been fired."

Some of the complaints dealt with money. Moultrie, for instance, moved back to Charleston in 1966 after five years of work as a practical nurse in Goldwater Memorial Hospital in New York. The move south, of course, meant lower pay, but also a lower job, as local hospital officials refused to recognize the training she had received in New York. Unable to afford the cost of the required eleven months of school, she took the lower position of nurse's aide, making, she says, "about a dollar or a dollar five an hour, less than poverty wages. It was basically the same for the other nonprofessional workers." Less than five years before the strike, some hospital workers had been paid as little as 38 cents an hour.

As much as the financial issues, however, the nonprofessional employees complained of a lack of respect on the job. "People never called you by your name," remembers one employee. "They'd just yell, 'Hey, you!' "

"It was mainly wages and working conditions," says Moultrie, and "a lot with the discriminatory practices toward us as blacks and nonprofessional workers. The RNs and practical nurses, who were predominantly white, gave the orders, and we just carried them out. And one thing that really upset me was that nursing students would give orders too, although they would come on a unit that they were not familiar with. We knew more about what was going on on the unit, we had to tell them what was happening on a unit. But they shouted out the orders."

After meeting among themselves for more than a year, the group attempted to meet with the administration of the hospital. The meeting was refused, and a cartoon was posted on employee bulletin boards representing a voracious union boss taking the workers' money. "After the cartoon came out," says Moultrie, "we got even more members— you know, people really got angry about it." The group asked repeatedly for meetings with the president, or with others in the administration who could deal with their grievances. But no one accepted, and the hospital workers didn't know where to turn. A union, any union, seemed like their only option.

"We talked with Isaiah Bennett about becoming a part of the tobacco workers union," says Moultrie. "He suggested we talk with a union that dealt with hospital workers." They asked Local 1199 of the National Union of Hospital and Nursing Home Employees to investigate their situation. The union did, and took on the Charleston workers, chartering them in October 1968 as 1199B. "The next thing we knew," shrugs Moultrie, "1199 was in Charleston."

Mary Moultrie and Rosetta Simmons were appointed chairmen of the Medical College and the County Hospital workers, respectively. Each woman worked with Isaiah Bennett and with Henry Nicholas, a national union representative who moved to Charleston for the duration of the strike. As events in town escalated, Moultrie— representative of the much larger institution—was elected president of the union.

THE SIMPLE DECISION TO TALK WITH 1199 SUGGESTS THE DESPERATION felt by the hospital workers. In South Carolina, as in so much of the South, groups do not ally themselves with unions unmindful of the many problems that that decision will produce. As much as they may be helped by the union assistance, they are also burdened by tremendous political and social stigma. South Carolina has the second-worst rate of unionization in the country, only slightly better than that of North Carolina, and the most familiar example of organizing efforts in the state concerns the frustrated textile workers of the Upcountry.

In addition, hospital workers in general are largely unorganized. For years, hospital administrators have sought to connect the twin images of organized workers and abandoned patients. Despite the fact that most hospital employees' contracts contain more levels of negotiation than other contracts before a strike can be called, the administrators' efforts have been largely successful in minimizing support for union efforts. And the hospital workers at the Medical College of South Carolina were officially state employees. Virtually no state employees in the country had gained union recognition until the mid-sixties. Those in Charleston were not expected to be among the first.

When 1199 agreed to take on the challenge in Charleston, then, they stepped into a storm of problems. It was not, however, a situation with which the organization was unfamiliar. The union first entered the field of hospital worker organizing in the late 1950s when it began signing up employees at Montefiore Hospital in New York. Hospital porters there were then being paid $36 for a 44-hour week. After a number of bitter strikes, by the time of the Charleston strike, the union had become representative for more than 36,000 hospital employees in the metropolitan New York area.

Shortly after union organizers first arrived in Charleston, they stepped up the efforts to meet with hospital administrators and discuss problems. They were refused. About 200 workers demonstrated outside the hospital in December 1968, protesting the working conditions, "starvation wages," and "discrimination." The administration responded by increasing the security measures at the hospital. The workers picketed, they met with the Charleston delegates to the state legislature, and they asked HEW to investigate wages, working conditions, and discriminatory practices at the hospital. Finally, the president of the Medical College, Dr. William McCord, agreed to meet with some of the workers. Instead of calming the workers' frustrations, though, the meeting heightened them.

Mary Moultrie remembers:

We tried to put off going out on strike. I think everybody was kind of afraid of it and we weren't just going to walk out. We needed something to actually push us out. That was the meeting we had requested with Dr. McCord. When we went in, it was supposed to be seven people from our group and we thought that we were going to sit down with McCord. But when we got to the meeting, he had about twenty other people who were not members of our group, who were antiunion. It wasn't the type of meeting that I had asked for, and I flatly refused to meet. Word got around of what McCord had done, and people just started leaving their working areas and coming downstairs to the meeting place.

So I had all my people downstairs in front of McCord's office, and we decided that we'd just take his office over. We went in and had a prayer meeting and we sang and we just had a good time. He was hiding in the back room and he called the cops. That was the first time I had met Chief [John] Conroy and he came and talked with us and wanted to know who was the leader. He told me, "You either send your people back to work or you go to jail." I had never been to jail before so I was kind of scared. We went back to our units and nobody said anything about what had happened until it was just about time to get off. Then they told the twelve of us who had gone down to the meeting we had been fired. We left and then two days later we went out on strike.

The hospital workers presented two major demands: recognition of 1199 as their representative (and establishment of the dues checkoff that would make that practical) and reinstatement of the twelve fired workers. Through union recognition they expected other gains such as pay increases, establishment of a grievance procedure and a credit union, an end to discriminatory practices, and more respect directed toward nonprofessional workers by the professionals. The hospital administration refused to consider either of the two main issues. The workers, claimed administration representatives, had deserted their patients. It had been the workers, not the administration, who had shown up at the meeting with more people than expected, ending all chances for a fruitful exchange. The office takeover had been the final straw. The administration representatives said they had no choice but to fire the workers.

For some time, the hospital officials simply refused to consider seriously the workers' demands. President William McCord captured much of the tone of the administration in a phrase quoted in *Business Week:* "I am not about to turn a $25 million complex over to a bunch of people who don't have a grammar school education."

Of course, the hospital workers, many of whom had high school diplomas, had no interest in taking over the Medical College. They just wanted better jobs. But the administration had been unwilling even to meet with an organized group of the workers, and the hospital workers alone could not have taken on such a locally powerful institution. They needed help. The national union leaders from 1199 provided that help.

BECAUSE OF THEIR FORMIDABLE OPPOSITION, UNION OFFICIALS decided quickly that the Charleston struggle had to be fought on many different levels. First, the workers had to be united, and they had to have near-unanimous support from the Charleston black community. To help gain this, each worker attended church one Sunday in her uniform and announced to her congregation the issues of the strike and the need for the community's support. When the workers finally walked out, the Medical College was unable to find many scab replacements. The community stood by the workers.

To involve the community further, the union invited the Southern Christian Leadership Conference to take part. For the local black community, the presence of SCLC's leadership, especially Ralph Abernathy and Andrew Young, provided a tremendous boost to morale, and in part legitimized the strike for those who had previously been uncertain. In the same way, when Coretta Scott King, who was the honorary chairperson of 1199's national organizing campaign, arrived in Charleston, she led the largest march of the entire strike. SCLC representatives coordinated the often daily marches and oversaw the picketing, which led to hundreds of arrests and the accompanying focus of national media attention. They organized the local high school students to support the strike, and called for a boycott of schools which at one point saw 30 percent of the student body absent. Other SCLC officials organized a boycott of all Charleston stores. "Buy Only Food and Medicine," announced one flyer that covered the streets. "Support our Soul Power with your Green Power!!!"

In Charleston, the strike seemed to be everywhere. The workers picketed at the hospital and at many of the downtown stores. They were at the Old Slave Mart Museum (one marcher carried a sign reading, "In Memory of the Old Slave Tradition, Consult Dr. McCord"), and at the homes of the hospital officials, of U.S. Representative Mendel Rivers, and of U.S. Senator Ernest Hollings. Demonstrators once took over the Charleston County Council chambers. During a four-day period more than 350 demonstrators were arrested. They filled the local jails, until at times the local police officials had to establish extra, impromptu facilities.

Some of the workers took the word of the strike around the country, rallying support. Mary Moultrie became a powerful, eloquent public speaker and met with labor groups and civil rights organizations. At one AFL-CIO meeting, she conferred with Golda Meier and Hubert Humphrey. At the same time, the union used its own labor network to develop outside support. For weeks, the Charleston strike was the major labor issue in the country and received the support of unionists from every state, from nearly every field.

All of that, of course, cost a great deal of money. Hundreds of thousands of dollars raised by 1199 paid for the organizing efforts, the generation of support around the country, publicity, and assistance to the hundreds of workers who left their jobs. For four months the union was able to pay each striker $15 a week and money for rent and food expenses when they were needed.

The 1969 strike marked one of the first times that a labor battle had been fought on so many levels. It worked. Local businesspeople complained to hospital officials about their slump in sales and Charleston's negative image in the national media. Local bankers were threatened with the loss of large depositors. A growing list of unions and other organizations pledged support for the hospital workers, and at least one could have had a chilling effect on the city: the International Longshoremen's Association voted to support the strike, and suggested at its national meeting that the group might attempt to shut down the busy Port of Charleston. The city was torn apart by the strike. A pair of Catholic priests were jailed, and a photo of them behind bars was widely distributed. Even antilabor forces in the state were embarrassed by the administration's crude handling of the strike, and they too pushed for negotiations.

Critical pressure ultimately came from one unexpected source: the Department of Health, Education and Welfare. National union official Moe Foner had been calling everyone he knew from his many years of organizing experience to gather countrywide support. At one point he spoke with James Farmer, the civil rights activist who was then assistant secretary of HEW. "I called him from this bar," Foner remembers, "and had to shout over the jukebox. I said, 'What are you doing about this Charleston hospital situation?' and he said, 'You mean about the contract and the violations?' I said, 'What contract? What violations?' "

The hospital, Foner discovered, had been found guilty of thirty-seven violations of civil rights guidelines since the previous September. President William McCord had been ordered to submit an affirmative action plan for the school or lose all federal funds, which at that point amounted to $12 million. When this fact was revealed, McCord admitted that without the federal funds the Medical College might have to close its doors. Much of South Carolina was in an uproar. Harry Dent called McCord from Washington, D.C., and pushed him even further toward a settlement of the strike. Finally, and secretly, the Medical College administrators changed their most basic position: they agreed to meet with the workers to discuss their demands.

From that point on, things moved quickly. HEW Secretary Robert Finch tried to soften the sound of the department's threat. He was encouraged by John Ehrlichman, President Nixon's counselor, who, when told of the department's efforts to settle the strike, said, "You know . . . the blacks aren't where our votes are." Still, Medical College representatives told gatherings of their nurses and doctors that they were about to settle the strike and would rehire the twelve workers who had been fired. A settlement was expected shortly. Suddenly, administration sources inexplicably denied to local media the earlier reports of a settlement. One week later, they claimed that a number of the hospital's nurses had threatened to quit if the workers were rehired. When they found out this was no ruse, Foner said, "We ended up sneaking Andy Young into the hospital to talk with the nurses, and they decided they wouldn't quit after all."

All this time, secret worker-administration meetings were taking place. Finally an agreement was made. The hospital accepted virtually every specific demand the workers had made: rehiring the twelve, $1.60 minimum wage and regular raises, a grievance procedure, and a credit union through which union dues could be instituted. They did not, and would not, agree to union recognition. As they had throughout the strike, they pointed to a statement released by the state attorney general confirming that no state institution, such as the Medical College, had the right to recognize a union. "There is no law actually specifying this," he admitted. "At the same time, there is no authority delegated, and in the absence of this authority the agencies of the state have no power to bargain with unions."

Many workers and their supporters and lawyers hoped for the

chance to fight that claim in court. It was, after all, merely the statement of the state's lawyer, and was in no way binding. They were particularly hopeful after the Charlotte *Observer* revealed that the state had already signed contracts with several railroad unions. But, says Mary Moultrie, "the national 1199 people said that it would take too long and cost too much money. They're probably right, that it would have been awhile and a lot of money, but by not challenging that, we lost our most important issue. And what's a lot of time? We weren't planning to leave. We had to go back to our jobs."

The union, says Foner, felt they had no choice. "A court case would have taken years. Smart lawyers could contest it at every stage. It wouldn't have brought satisfaction." They were adamant, and the union was adamant.

Without the obstacle of a suit, the workers and administrators quickly reached agreement, and on June 27, negotiators announced the terms to the ecstatic workers who had gathered at the local headquarters. In the excitement and frantic pace of the time, no one happened to take a vote: agreement was approved by assumption. Moultrie, the local president, was in New York. "Had I been there," she now says, "I never would have agreed." Today, the workers at the Medical University find plenty to criticize in the agreement and the way it was reached.

"I'm going to tell you about a union," says striker Gloria Frazier:

If you don't work with your people, you don't have anything. You are the people! You've got to have the people! And if you don't have the people, I don't care what you call it, you don't have anything. You should never get into the place of thinking that you are so superior that somebody has to look up to you. Someone put you there, and someone can bring you down.

The leaders of the strike—the national leaders and the local leaders both—forgot: the workers in that hospital is your body. You have a head. But the workers in the hospital is your body. And if you cut that body off, that head cannot function. It's going to die. And that's what happened to the union. Because they would not listen to their body.

The workers returned to the hospital with a mixture of pride—they had won, they were told—and apprehension. They knew they were powerless in future dealings with the administration. Hospital worker Catherine Washington says, "People promise you things and they sound good, and you vote for it hoping that they will keep their word. But you find out in the end, it doesn't work like that."

Washington claims that when the workers returned to the hospital, "You really had to watch each step that you made, and you really had to watch your mouth because the least little thing and you'd be back on the streets. They were bitter and really hostile, I think administration and the strikers both, because I know personally when I thought of the number of days I'd been out in that sun and all the things I'd went through, to come back and not even come back with the full union— you went out to have things to be better, and you come back with the same pressure and even worse pressure—brought some hostility down."

The first lesson of the strike is one of the most basic ones to any union battle: if the workers involved do not win their union, if their union is not recognized by management, they can win no more than a partial victory.

The workers maintained an office, and they tried to put the dues checkoff into effect through the credit union. They had no success. "We kept asking for meetings to discuss how that could be done and they kept putting us off," says Bennett. "So people started paying dues themselves, but that didn't last too long either."

National union representatives maintain that they had a staff person in Charleston over five months after the strike, and pulled out only when local workers insisted on more local control. Many workers disagree. "Nobody from 1199 stayed in Charleston for five months," says Mary Moultrie. "One person would stay for a few days and then later someone else would come for three or four weeks. No one for a longer period of time than that. For a long time, about ten of us were staffing the office and trying to keep the workers together. But I was working three shifts, and I didn't have the time. No one did. And for a lot of people, being out on strike was a scary time. Once they got in, I guess they felt that if they got really involved again, it would come back to a strike again. They sort of shied away."

Today, the effects of the strike are evident. Nonprofessional workers at the hospital are part of a statewide employee pay scale, assured salaries of at least 10 cents above minimum wage, and guaranteed periodic raises. A grievance procedure has been instituted, and when, after many years of employee criticism, the administration perceived that it was inadequate, they changed it. The hospital has begun an affirmative action program that has allowed for the hiring of a great many blacks and women into positions that were formerly filled only by white males. William McCord is no longer president, having submitted his resignation. Bill Saunders, once an organizer for the hospital workers, and in 1980 a candidate for the state senate in South Carolina, points to improvements in both the black and white communities of Charleston. "For blacks," he says, "it made us proud. It convinced us that we have power when we organize ourselves together and convinced many of us of our real worth for the first time. And the white community too was convinced that these people who

Prounion march in Charleston

they'd ignored were somebody. They respect the workers more for what they did. And now they are sure to negotiate before they reach the same point of polarization that they did in 1969."

IN JULY 1969, THE CHARLESTON WORKERS WERE PRAISED THROUGH-out the country for accomplishing something few groups of workers had ever done. They had beaten an intransigent administration in one of the most fiercely antiunion states in the nation. But as important to them as the hospital struggle had been, the workers had other lives to live, other responsibilities. Many dealt with their frustrations with each other and with the national union leadership simply by dropping out. Within four months, says Mary Moultrie, the unity of the workers was clearly fading. Those still committed to the union kept an office open for about four years, often with their own money, but they were merely holding on.

If the first lesson of the Charleston strike is that no full victory can be won without union recognition, the second lesson is equally basic: the struggle is never over. Of course the workers needed to rest a moment after their battle. Of course they feared that further involvement with the union would mean more painful experiences. All of that is certainly understandable. But the workers' gains had to be maintained and bolstered with the same firm determination that they exhibited during the strike. At the root of their demands to the Medical College were questions not just of pay but of power. After almost four months of the strike, they won more pay and other benefits. That was only part of what they felt they needed. But to gain the power they sought, they needed recognition as a group, as a union. That demanded a struggle as fierce—though longer and less volatile—as the strike had been.

The third lesson is the one that the workers live with now more than anything else: tensions between the workers and their supporters, disagreements that are never fully resolved or explained, will always return. As many workers saw it, they were the darlings of the media for four months, they brought both 1199 and SCLC much-needed publicity, and then their support organizations abandoned them and turned their attention elsewhere, according to their own agendas. Events in Charleston encouraged hospital workers throughout the country to petition 1199 for representation. Union representatives maintain that much of their work in Charleston was completed, that the workers had to lead their own struggle from then on. The workers agree, but feel they needed more direction before being left alone. They needed more experience. They needed a larger leadership base.

SCLC had been floundering ever since the death of Martin Luther King, Jr. The Charleston strike provided the SCLC staff with an event to propel them again into the spotlight. They assigned staff person James Orange to Charleston to build a local chapter, but the hospital was only one of a number of issues he faced. Besides, he had no more idea than the workers of how they could deal with the administration without recognition, of how they could maintain their support without checkoff apparatus.

Certainly the hospital workers won major job improvements from the strike and made important changes in Charleston and in South Carolina. But they did not win what they most wanted. They realized this slowly and with much bitterness, and it made what they did accomplish seem weaker, more tentative. They won a grievance procedure, for instance, but the workers recognized quickly that they rarely if ever won. They received a hearing, but not a fair hearing. Now many of the hospital administrators agree, and they have changed the grievance system. Yet without a union to back them up, to hold them together and give their words strength, the workers could only complain, and hope that the administrators would one day choose to correct the problem.

The Charleston hospital strike of 1969 has no clean ending. Few strikes do. The workers won important gains. Today, though, when they look back, they see that they did not win a victory.

TWENTY-FIVE

Contract at Brookside, 1974

A PERSPECTIVE BY TOM BETHELL, WITH INTERVIEWS BY BOB HALL

HARLAN COUNTY, KENTUCKY, IN the summer of 1973. The Brookside mine supplies coal to Duke Power Company's plants several hundred miles away in the Carolinas. Six months ago, the leadership of the United Mine Workers of America changed hands. Tony Boyle is on his way to jail, soon to be convicted of ordering the murder of his opponent in the union's 1969 election, and Arnold Miller has won election to the presidency of the union on a platform promising sweeping reform. He has promised, among other things, to dust off the union's grand old slogan— "Organize the Unorganized!"—and carry it proudly to the portals of every scab mine in America.

Harlan County is full of such mines, Brookside being one of the bigger ones. In the collapse of the coal industry after the boom years of World War II, a long depression had swept across the Kentucky coalfields, and in a flood of joblessness and mine closures and tumbling prices, the United Mine Workers had lost its grip on the mines. Some men said the union was gone forever. When, in the midst of a depression, a mine goes down and a picket line goes up across the road; when the operator puts the word out that jobs are available; when, in that county, ten men are out of work for every man working; when those ten men have families to feed and no prospect of another job in sight—when all that happens, you do not do much organizing of the unorganized, not without inspired leadership and a lot of help from your friends.

259

The leadership of the 1960s in the UMWA was not inspired, and the friends were not there—not in government, not in the press, and only very thinly scattered through the rest of the labor movement. Within the union there was restlessness, men here and there willing to take a chance to salvage what they and their fathers had spilled so much blood to win. The leaders of the union told them, on the one hand, to go out on a limb—"Boys, you gonna lose your medical cards unless you sign them operators"—and then, when they were all the way out at the end, the leaders lopped off the limb, refusing to commit the International's resources to the fight.

But now, in 1973, everything had changed.

Coal, the long-forgotten fuel, was in demand again, and in a few months would command the highest prices in history, thanks to the Arab oil embargo and the machinations of the oil industry. Old mines were expanding, new mines were opening. The new leadership of the UMWA had promises to keep. Miners at Brookside, chafing under the notably hard-nosed management of Duke's subsidiary, Eastover Mining, sent word to Washington that they wanted to join the UMWA, but Duke would not sign a contract with them. A month passed and their picket lines could not keep the scabs out. The men needed support.

The union was in no position to deny them. But it was not, in fact, fully prepared to help them. The transfer of power from Boyle to Miller had been bitter and chaotic. Reform leaders with no previous administrative experience were already stuck fast in the molasses of bureaucracies old and new, discovering with horror that it was hard enough to get the mail answered and the dues processed, let alone launch new programs for an uncertain constituency.

Miller's 1972 mandate had been by no means unanimous (45 percent of the vote had gone for Boyle) and he shared the leadership of the union with an executive board divided against itself. The UMWA's outward image of shiny reform masked a troubled interior—whole departments, such as safety and organizing, were in turmoil; policies, to the extent they existed at all, were subject to change without notice. And at Brookside, Eastover Mining, backed up by the Harlan County Coal Operators' Association, had fought the UMWA, generally successfully, for half a century.

But these things had changed; the coal operators could no longer settle the strike with sheriff's deputies and machine guns, could not count on the governor of Kentucky to send in the National Guard, could not effectively intimidate the reporters and television crews. The UMWA could and did pour in millions of dollars to sustain the strikers. But far and away the most important, Duke Power was vulnerable in its home territory, subjected to a barrage of propaganda in the newspapers of North and South Carolina about mine conditions that gave the lie to Duke's carefully nurtured image as "your friendly

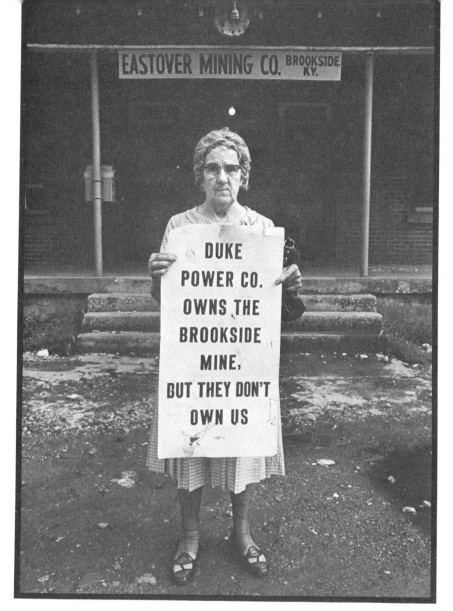

Harlan County, 1974

neighborhood power company," whose linemen were so busy rescuing kittens from trees that you hardly even noticed when your rates went up. Proposed rate increases came in for new publicity, thanks to the UMWA; citizens' groups joined forces to oppose them. Duke found itself fighting an unfamiliar kind of war on too many fronts at once.

The lines deepened and hardened in Harlan County; there were bitterness and violence to spare. Duke Power could keep its plants running with coal from other mines, but gradually the company realized that the UMWA was not going to let go of its ankle. As long as the strike continued, there would be citizens' commissions holding hearings, reporters asking awkward questions, embarrassments on the evening news, full-page ads over the breakfast table, and bad times in front of the commissioners deciding rate increase applications.

When finally the violence brought the inevitable result—the death of a striking miner, Lawrence Jones, shot to death by a mine foreman— Duke had been defeated. The company had already been forced to the bargaining table, and a contract with the UMWA was still being resisted but was in fact inevitable. The murder was too much; there was too much blood on the coal and the UMWA had been too successful in getting that fact across.

THE BROOKSIDE STRIKE, COMING ON THE HEELS OF THE INSURGENT "Miners for Democracy" campaign, enjoyed more press coverage than perhaps any strike of its size in history. This was no accident. Planning events to attract favorable publicity was itself part of a sophisticated union strategy that brought national pressure against an insignificant electric utility in the Carolinas. The Duke Power Company had thought getting into the mining business would be a good investment for the second largest private consumer of coal in America. Its subsidiary, the Eastover Mining Company, had signed a sweetheart contract with the Southern Labor Union (SLU) a few days after purchasing the Brookside mine in 1970. Everything seemed to be going smoothly for the company—until mid-1973 when the Brookside miners voted 113 to 55 to throw out the Southern Labor Union and bring in the UMW, setting in motion the innovative strategy that ultimately brought the country's sixth-largest utility to its knees. These excerpts of interviews conducted by Bob Hall outline that journey to victory.

DARRELL DEATON, VICE PRESIDENT OF THE BROOKSIDE UMW LOCAL: We went out because we wanted a better future, you might say. Coal looked like it was going to be good for the next fifteen or twenty years, and we wanted a good future. Mostly for security reasons. The UMW is a good organization for a coal miner. For the health and safety program, for better working conditions. And job security is what I really was after. Without a union, a company can move you around. They can put you on any shift they want to. Or any job. Or lay you off.

And then, too, I been raised in the union, in my family. My dad retired at Brookside—this same mine, under different owners—as a United Mine Worker. I was always what you'd say a prounion man. Then we worked under the Southern Labor Union for about three years. But we had no future working through them. It was what you call a company union, a yellow-dog union. So we voted them out.

We had a couple meetings with the company after we won the election. They looked encouraging, so we kept working even without a contract. Well, it became pretty obvious what they was doing. They had no intention of signing the UMW contract. It wasn't anything to do with specific issues, really. In my opinion, the company just didn't like the idea of the union having any say in how to run the mine. To a certain extent, the union can dictate a whole lot to them, as far as where you can place a man and such as that. They wanted it all under their control.

JAMES "GOAT" THOMAS, UMW ORGANIZER: Brookside was my first campaign; it was a real experience, you know. It brought me in contact with lots of different types of people and things which I never did understand before. You could read about it, but you really couldn't believe that people lived that way in Appalachia, and I went down there and seen and it's still kind of hard to believe. The coal camps, they've been nonexistent around this part of the country for thirty-five years. Company house, company stores, things like that, you just don't realize it's still happening. That Brookside mine was very, very bad. It had bad top, and no safety at all in the mine. There was no ventilation. It was the younger ones who wanted change. The older ones had been there in '64 when the UMW pretty well abandoned them. They had gone out on strike, but the union only gave them $25 a week for relief, and the district office kept part of that. Harlan County had been 90 percent UMW in the 1950s, but after that there was a lot of mistrust toward the leadership. That was one thing the new UMW had to combat. When the union sent organizers in, half the miners were out on strike and half were in scabbing and it wasn't working. So the first job for Houston Elmore and Tom Pysell, the organizers, was to get that stopped. Things started moving, and the pensioners, they saw how the union was keeping up the families, and they got on board. It became a real revival sort of thing. You know, "The United Mine Workers is back."

BERNIE ARONSON, UMW PUBLICITY DIRECTOR AND TOP STRATEGIST FOR THE DUKE POWER CAMPAIGN: It became clear that if we were confined to Harlan that we were at a real disadvantage given how insignificant the production of that mine was to Duke's overall needs (only 4 to 5 percent) and given how militantly antiunion the coal operators in the county were. It was the bastion of independent coal operators. More than a third of the non-UMW coal mined each year comes from eastern Kentucky. And the antiunion forces had plenty of resources: money, political officials, in some cases the police, the courts. So that began us looking at Duke Power Company and trying to figure out where they were vulnerable.

We started by going to Charlotte, North Carolina, where Duke was headquartered. We set up picket lines there and began to get publicity in North Carolina. Then in researching the company, we found they had a 17 percent rate increase pending before the North Carolina Utilities Commission, so I did up thousands of bumper stickers saying "Stop Duke Power's 17% Rate Increase" and took out full-page ads in the Charlotte *Observer* and other papers which talked about two points: one, the conditions miners worked under, emphasizing the medical, safety, and housing conditions and showing what they were actually fighting for, so that even in a state like North Carolina, which was not friendly to labor, the issues would be understood; it wouldn't be seen simply as a union trying to gain more power, but as individual people, coal miners, working people, trying to do something for their families, trying to better themselves. The second point we made was to suggest to people in

North Carolina that they too were being victimized by Duke Power in terms of the pending rate fight.

We also began contacting and speaking to groups around the state. We went to Duke University, which was largely supported from money earned by stock in the Duke Power Company; miners spoke to students there, and they in turn started pressuring the university officials and trustees. Groups that were fighting the rate increase, the Institute for Southern Studies and North Carolina PIRG, began to see us as an ally and offered their support. We ran more ads tying up what was happening in Brookside with the rate increase, with coupons urging citizens who wanted to learn more about fighting the rate increase to join Carolina Action, a citizens' organization in Durham initially formed around the rate fight. When the case was held in the Utilities Commission, Carolina Action won the right to have a series of hearings around the state, and from those names they were able to organize huge public meetings against Duke Power.

We expanded the fight to Wall Street, because as a utility, Duke was continually trying to raise more capital. Disrupting their ability to sell stocks and bonds was serious business to them. We had miners go to Wall Street and pass out leaflets at the New York Stock Exchange. We used full-page ads in the *Wall Street Journal* to warn any potential investors against Duke Power. We went to their annual meetings of stockholders with miners and consumers and made the Brookside strike the issue to be dealt with. We urged various institutions to boycott the stock and got commitments from sixty-six union pension funds that they would not buy any Duke bonds or stocks. We found out that the seventh-largest stockholder of Duke was the Ohio Public Employees Retirement Fund, and we made a presentation of our case to them. We went there and found the Duke Power people in the hall with their slide projector to present their case. But the directors of the fund in fact voted not

to buy any more of Duke's stock. We kept that kind of pressure up, and the stories kept appearing in the business and general media about Duke's "problems."

It was described by *Forbes* recently that that year was the worst year of Duke president Carl Horn's life. What we had done was make an obscure strike in an obscure coal mine that probably none of Duke's directors knew much about into the most pressing issue that confronted them. We forced them to move from their original position—which was that Eastover ran its own affairs and they couldn't interfere—to taking the personal initiative to end the strike. So all these tactics were a way of giving our home base in Harlan leverage and making Duke Power feel it. When the negotiations were going on at the last day, the Harlan County Coal Operators still wanted to fight it out, to not settle, but it was Duke Power that give the word that they had to settle. The real decisions were made outside the county and we had the job of making them be accountable for what was going on locally.

The campaign outside was an extension of the miners' base in Harlan, where the traditional organizing work continued: keeping the picket lines up, dealing with the courts and the law, keeping the mine closed, keeping spirits up, doing community work. Then, coupled with that, we had the Duke Power rate fight campaign. Neither substituted or diluted from one another. The campaign translated the miners' power into something that the company could feel. It also helped to keep morale up in Harlan at the same time that it generated national publicity. They would come to Charlotte and meet with people and see people they didn't even know saying, "We're with you." They saw their press; they got a sense of their own power, that Duke Power couldn't sit back, but was vulnerable.

DARRELL DEATON: I would say the publicity played the biggest part in winning the contract. It kept the men kind of interested. It built morale up, made them want to do things they probably wouldn't have done. Normally, people in small towns and in counties can't get away with too much like you can in these cities, like a lot of demonstrations and things that wouldn't be tolerated in a place like this. But this thing got so much publicity that it turned the tables, you might say. Instead of all the pressure being on us, the company had to watch out what it did. We had a lot of press coverage and television people coming through all the time. The company was put on the defensive, and anything it did could be blown up.

Some of the press got a little out of hand, I think. All the references to the 1930s and Bloody Harlan, and saying things were coming back like then. But it never really got that bad. Back in the thirties, it was just a do or die thing. They weren't making nothing, starving to death. They didn't have no choice. They had to do it. We did have a choice, as far as wages and benefits. Most of us chose to come back here. This is a fine place to live. Of course, I might be a little partial. I was born and raised within a hundred yards of where I live now. I've been all over. I've been to Korea and Japan. I worked in a shipyard in Norfolk just before I came back here. I've worked in Detroit and Dayton and Cincinnati. But I wouldn't give up here for nothing I've seen nowhere.

GOAT THOMAS: Harlan is like the hub, with all the towns in the hollers out from it. You've got like 5,500 pensioners in the county. They have a really strong union spirit, probably more so than anyplace in the country. It was giving them something to do to spread the word, and they did it. It was a really countywide type of organizing. We had a very strong base, and it was with the old and young, the women as well as the men—which was very important.

When Byrd Hogg, the Harlan County judge, put out an injunction to limit the number of pickets per entrance to three men, the women got together and they just went up there and put up their own picket lines. They weren't covered by the injunction against the mine workers, you see. Well, they carried clubs and sticks up there, and when the scabs came through, why they beat the hell out of a couple of them. And that turned the tide. The men had done what they could. It's a hard thing when you're on a picket line and the law's there, to know how far you can go without bringing too much trouble on yourselves. Well, those women, they just didn't give a damn. They just took it over and that fired the men up. I never seen anything like it. That stopped the Eastover people. The second time they tried to bring scabs in was February 1974, and the women came out in full force. They trapped twelve scabs who had gotten through in the mine and wouldn't let them out. They chased them back in the mine. And the pensioners were there, too, helping keep the mine shut down.

BESSIE LOU CORNETT, TREASURER OF THE BROOKSIDE WOMEN'S CLUB: We kind of organized ourselves and got to talking to each other about how these scabs were crossing the picket line. The first weeks of the strike, the miners—you know, our husbands, sons, our fathers—were able to stop the scabs, but then Duke Power got an injunction limiting the miners to three pickets on an entrance. So, with two entrances at Brookside, that was six miners, and as many as seventy-five scabs were crossing every day. Six miners couldn't do that much. They were taking shifts, and the scabs were spitting on them and cussing them and calling them names, and they would come home and they'd be talking about taking their shotguns down to the picket line, how they were going to stop the scabs and that was the only way to do it.

We wanted to be able to help the men stop the scabs and get a contract without all that violence. And so what we did was we talked to each other. We had a march and said, "Why don't we just go down to the picket line ourselves. We can stop the scabs. The court don't have an injunction against us." So that's what we did.

We didn't stop them by asking them not to cross the line. We whipped them with switches and with whatever we had. At one point we laid on the picket line. That was when there was so many state police there that the state police were ready to escort the scabs through. We had tried all tactics, but we didn't want to get arrested. So we thought if we were peaceful—by laying down, instead of whipping them as usual—then we wouldn't get arrested. But as it turned out, several women were arrested—my sister, my mother, and a couple of other women. But the scabs were stopped. They turned on back because the police could see they were going to have to arrest everybody there if they let the scabs in. So what they figured they'd do is they'd take a few key people to jail and the rest of us would leave. But we didn't. We stayed and stopped them.

DARRELL DEATON: The women was a real important factor. Women can get away with more than men—as far as the law is concerned. Course they got manhandled a little bit, but they came out real well. We had real good women

Darrell Deaton and Arnold Miller, president of UMW, in Harlan County

on the picket line. They was brave women. They weren't necessarily mean women. They was pushing their luck a whole lot. They done a real good job. It could have possibly saved some violence. Every time you get men confronting each other, there's a danger that somebody'll get hurt. There was a lot of guns carried during that period, too. Of course, there was men there to back up the women. Men would be all up and down the road or railroad track. But the women took it on themselves to keep down the violence.

It did get hot when we picketed at Highsplint, Eastover's other mine there in Harlan. That's where the scabs from Brookside was working. Tempers did get pretty hot there. That's when Lawrence Jones got shot. One of the bosses from Brookside who knew Lawrence, he lived near him, he shot him down. And he died. That brought things to a climax. Things were building then, and I think Arnold Miller and Carl Horn were already meeting, but that got them down to business. That's when Duke signed the contract.

BERNIE ARONSON: The shooting was in a way proof that our strategy was right. Miners have been killed in organizing drives for forty years in Harlan County, but this time it was different. Had not there been a year of organizing, of publicity and pressure tactics, of bringing the strike to North and South Carolina, had not that all happened, the death of Lawrence Jones would have been just one more miner killed, and nobody would have heard of it. But Duke felt it was one more level of pressure that they would feel directly. They were told by the UMW that we would bring Lawrence Jones's casket to their doorstep in Charlotte. And bring the miners with it, and hold a national ceremony there. It would be another escalation of pressure on them. We had just had a march with 4,000 miners in Harlan after declaring a week's memorial that closed down *all* the union mines in the nation. We finally had the President's top labor negotiator at the negotiating sessions, for this obscure coal mine, and here he was twisting the arm of Duke Power to settle.

No single event turned Duke Power. They saw constant escalation, a series of events, from pickets to intervenors at their rate increase requests, then interference in their stock sales, then increasingly bad publicity and a damage to their image and demands on their time to answer more and more of the charges, then the pickets moving on their other mines, then there were lawsuits threatened from stockholders. They knew they had to step in and settle it.

It was a very important, historic victory. It helped the people at Brookside and really changed everybody who was involved in it. It showed that there can be a real, effective, working, and productive alliance between groups which are not traditionally viewed as allies—consumers, students, church groups, and labor, in this case all worked together. It helped give life to an organization in North Carolina—Carolina Action—which is still going, and helped other organizing for people there in the Carolinas. It had the immediate effect in the rate increase case of forcing Duke Power to restructure its rates in such a way that the large corporate users got the burden of the increase. And it helped the union's credibility throughout the mine fields, although we couldn't turn that into election victories easily.

We actually believed that once the Brookside mine fell, that all the other mines in Harlan County would just capitulate and wave the white flag, but like some other domino theories, this one didn't seem to be true. In fact, in some

ways, the victory had the opposite effect. It stiffened the resolve of the coal operators. They recognized that the union was going to stick it out, and they had to develop their own sophisticated techniues. They formed an organization called Keep Informed Neighbors, and they started using our tactics—taking out ads and using public relations techniques against us. So in addition to the standard practice of buying off people and intimidation, they got tougher. We lost some important mines in Harlan County as a result.

I think we learned how difficult organizing is. We have won more victories in the last three years than this union won in the last thirty years. We've won over thirty-five mines. But organizing is very, very hard. And the NLRA [National Labor Relations Act] and the way it is enforced makes it easier for companies to beat unions than the other way around. I think these nontraditional techniques overall will be increasingly used because the companies are larger. They're able to withstand the economic effects of a strike.

With Duke Power, the rate case fight and the investment strategy were partly dictated by the nature of that company. And I think that will be increasingly necessary: to identify the kind of company that the labor movement faces, determine its weaknesses where it can be pressured, where consumers and support efforts can make a difference, and go after those areas.

In developing these strategies, I think there are a number of lessons we learned from Brookside that are helpful. One thing to remember is that it's very important to humanize a strike to people. People don't respond simply to terms like wages, pensions, and cost of living, they respond to people. So if you're trying to run a boycott or whatever, it's important to put your people out front—not the New York officials, but the rank-and-file people themselves, the people you want others to identify with, to get to know and appreciate and want to join. Pictures of people, quotes, get them on TV and the like. It's too easy for people to hate the union as an institution, but when you see Joe or Mary Jones and get to know their story, then people can respond to them individually.

Secondly, you should take your case to the public and learn how to attract the press, how to develop picket lines and demonstrations that can be media events, how to use the press in the same way that a politician does to get your message across. Sending a press release is not enough. We would always have the miners dress in their mine caps and knee pads because that caught the press's attention.

Third, you have to adapt to the peculiar characteristics of the company you're dealing with, the way they feel pressure. It may be how they raise money for their expansion, or who their suppliers are, or their public image, or their management's sensitivity to community pressure, or a consumer boycott.

Fourth, the union should be involved in fighting for other issues that are not directly related perhaps to bringing in membership. For example, with the textile workers, it would be very important for the union to organize around the issue of brown lung, to do something concrete for textile workers. If they saw the union as the only organ or institution that was caring about protecting their lungs or seeking legislation to keep dust down, or getting them compensation, then they would understand concretely what the union was about, rather than simply having it continue to be a situation where the union came in and said, we're going to win you a contract. They would respond better if they had already seen what the union could do. We need to publicize the fact that unions are not a narrow type of institution. In fact, unions are doing many things like tax reform and getting benefits for the unemployed and civil rights and lobbying for senior citizens. All these things labor is doing, but it's not getting the message across very well.

TWENTY-SIX
The Rebel in Me

SEAN DEVEREUX

IN 1945 SELINA BURCH WAS A 17-year-old switchboard operator in Dublin, Georgia, when she joined the Communications Workers of America (CWA). In a town with only one movie theater, going to a union meeting was a social event, a place to meet the young men who worked in the Western Electric plant. Instead of as an antagonist, she viewed her employer as a benevolent parent— "Mother" Bell. Her first strike in 1947 was "like being out of school on vacation."

By the mid-1950s, Selina had run against the male leadership for the presidency of her local in order to get it "into a position where we would not have to take any crap again." And she had gone through another strike where she was personally harassed by Bell Telephone and accused of committing an unfair labor practice.

Selina Burch became a top official in CWA, an administrative assistant to one of the union's twelve district vice-presidents. She regularly pushes Southern Bell to the wall in negotiating sessions, demonstrating the skills that have brought her respect from employers, politicians, and other union members. She has learned a great deal about power in the years since she first asked callers, "Number, please." As a woman, a worker, and a union leader, she learned how power worked, how to get it, and how to use it for her members—and against her enemies.

As she tells new members, the union is like a choir, dependent on no one voice, but deriving its effect from a harmonic, collective force. She believes deeply in her union but also recognizes that her voice, representing the desires of the women and black members who support her, "has shaken up CWA from top to bottom."

Teaching workers and settling their grievances has been her work; electoral politics, her hobby and avocation. She has, in fact, gained considerable fame as an expert coordinator of phone-bank campaigning. After all, who knows better how to talk to a voter over the telephone than a telephone operator? She knows that a tightly organized union is a ready army to offer a candidate, and a politician's friendship can be a tool for accomplishing personal and organizational goals.

Her most recent "friend" is Jimmy Carter, who sought her help in the Georgia and Florida primaries and, early on, asked her to be a Carter delegate at the Democratic convention. She accepted largely because she saw that, at the Democratic mini-convention in 1974, "Jimmy Carter just stood out head and shoulders above everyone else when it came to insisting that women's rights be written into the Democrats' program."

In the following interview, Selina Burch tells the story of her education as a labor leader and woman trade unionist; how, as she says, "the rebel in me came out."

I grew up in Dublin, Georgia. My father was a farmer and my mother was a homemaker. My mother died when I was 13, and I moved in with my grandmother and four old-maid aunts—three of them were schoolteachers. There was no labor background in my family at all.

I began work for Southern Bell on August 7, 1945, as an operator. I had graduated from Dublin High School and had worked in a coffee shop for about a year—there's no labor market in Dublin, Georgia. After a year, I applied for a job with the telephone company. The chief operator had gone to school with my father, so I was put ahead of all the other applications.

At that time, remember, there was a manual board where you said, "Number please." There was no automatic dialing in Dublin. If you've ever walked into a telephone company, you've seen all those cords being put up. It became a fascinating thing to me to see if I could put up all the cords, and then move over to another position, because I was very adept at handling telephone calls. There was one other girl in Dublin who could keep up with me, but only one. This was a challenge to me, to see how fast I could work the switchboard.

In 1946, some people from Macon came to Dublin and signed us up to a union. If you were a female, you paid 75 cents a month to belong to a union, and if you were a male, you paid a dollar. I was an operator and was working eight to five every day, the best shift because of my family's friendship with the chief operator. Suddenly, I was assigned to that horrible tour of one to ten. Someone had come along and taken my privileges away. I was young and carefree, though, 17, 18, and it really didn't make any difference to me, that part of it.

Also, right away in 1946, we obtained our first wage increase. At that time, I was making $15 a week as an operator and I got a $10 increase. It had a great impact on me that somebody had almost doubled my salary, but I did not understand at that time what it was all about. I had no idea what unionization meant. Pay, it meant more pay. But as for any other privileges, all it meant was that I went to the bottom of the list, because I was the junior person there.

I remember the first union meeting I ever went to. Over in Macon. It was during a strike, and we wanted to see what we were striking for, but we didn't find out. I'm not real sure that anyone in Macon knew.

The strike didn't bother me because even though my family were schoolteachers, we had a car. There was only one movie in Dublin, so driving to Macon was something for us to do. I could borrow a quarter to buy a little gas. The Western Electric guys were out on strike also. Everybody would get together at meetings and we'd laugh and talk about the strike, whatever it was about.

Dublin was a pretty small place. We were a close-knit group. I guess that we were friends more because we worked together all day than because we were members of the union. When we returned to work in '47, I remember that we gave the two who had not come out on strike a pretty hard way to travel. I resented them.

It was like being out of school on vacation. In fact, the day we were supposed to return to work, I had a big date that night, what I considered at that time a big date. I called the chief operator and said that I couldn't possibly come to work because I had such a sore throat.

We were so young and naive that we did not even think of picking up the telephone and making calls. You see, with only a manual board there, if we had been militant and had known what we were doing, we could have driven Mother Bell nuts. But we did not want to inconvenience her in any way. We thought we were a big inconvenience just being out on the street. It was part of this Southern upbringing: we respect authority at all costs. And with Dublin so small, I didn't think of "the company" as huge, nationwide Bell Telephone Company. I thought of the company only as the people I worked with. My grandmother broke her hip during this time, and the chief operator called me at home—my grandmother's home where I was still living—to assure me that she would make sure that any calls from our number went through, even though they were having trouble keeping up on the switchboard because of the strike.

I WAS MARRIED IN 1948. MY HUSBAND WAS IN THE NAVY, STATIONED in Charleston, South Carolina, and I transferred there, still an operator. Charleston did not have a manual board; everything was automatic. It was a much larger office. It took time to get acquainted. I had never lived in a town that size before.

The union was much stronger because the local was right there in Charleston. You personally knew the local officers because they worked with you. The local president and vice-president worked in the building with us. The secretary-treasurer of the local was a woman. This was the first time I had seen the union operate. What I remember is seeing meetings being held with management on grievances. With this closeness and knowing the people involved, you would hear the news as soon as the grievance meeting was over; who had won and who'd lost. I got a much better sense of what a union could do for its people.

After we had lived in Charleston for several years, I began to have marital problems. My husband was no longer in the Navy. Through this time, I began to turn more and more to the union for some way to occupy my time. I began to handbill for the local. In 1952, on a dare, I ran for local secretary-treasurer against five opponents and won. All of my opponents were women, because at that time in Charleston, you have to remember, the woman could only be secretary-treasurer. They let the males have the president and vice-president—you know, be the spokesperson.

Anyway, I won on the first ballot. I had never even been to shop steward school, so I knew nothing about the technical parts of the contract—how to handle a grievance or any of that. I did know that we were not as well organized as we should have been. From the start, I enjoyed the battle of wits across the table from the company. I was always pushing to see how much I could win.

I was divorced by this time and giving all of my time to the union. I was very dedicated to seeing that we became the best local in South Carolina—having the most political contributions, the best-settled grievances, being more active in the community. I saw what you could do if you just made up your damn mind to do it.

It's a thousand wonders that I didn't get fired, that the people who followed me, that we all didn't get fired. We would do stupid things like going into the company cafeteria and setting all the vacant chairs up on a table so, unless you had a union card, we wouldn't let you sit at our table. I wasn't angry with the nonunion people, just determined that they would join. We laughed it off in the cafeteria, but we still wouldn't let them sit there. The company threatened to fire us all, but we told them that if supervisors could save seats for their boyfriends, we could save a chair for any friend of ours. Except [*laughing*] we were saving twenty chairs.

We came from a 55 percent local into a 92 percent, tightly organized local in short of nothing.

By this time I had been promoted to an "instructor," teaching new people who came to work as operators. The job meant more money and it got me away from the board. But more than that, it gave me a direct advantage in organizing for the union. Two new people showed up every other Monday morning and, of course, they were eager to learn because they wanted to stay. If they didn't join, they didn't learn.

I didn't come right out and say, "Look, I'm not going to teach you to be an operator if you don't join the union." But I would tell them about the union and tell them that I was an officer and what benefits there were. They'd have to take every break and lunch hour with me. New students always want to get along with whoever is teaching them. To them, I was the authority. So they joined the union.

There was only one girl that ever reported me to the company for my tactics. She told the chief operator that I had threatened her. I laughed and said, "Yeah, I carry a gun and a knife with me at all times. You believe that don't you?" That ended that. The girl did not last.

I had learned one important thing about working for somebody: be better than everyone else. The company left me alone because of my ability to operate a switchboard, my ability to teach, and my ability to get people to follow me. They had no gripes about my work. It has always been my belief that the best steward, or the best local officer, is the person who doesn't have the grievances himself. That person can become a leader without having to submit to anything from the company. Because of my ability to work and my ability to lead, I didn't have to ask the company for anything.

I remember that we were having trouble finding a place for the CWA to meet, except in the Tobacco Workers' Hall, which was down by the railroad tracks in pretty dangerous territory. Through working with the Community Chest, collecting for the company, I met the man who ran the Jewish Community Center in Charleston. They offered us their hall, free of charge. It was funny, because later, during the '55 strike, after I was gone, the Jewish Community Center became the CWA strike headquarters. They put pressure on the Center, saying they would cut off their Community Chest funds, but the guy at the Jewish Center just reminded them that CWA had collected a lot of that money. So the union kept on meeting at the Center.

I GUESS THE REBEL IN ME REALLY BEGAN TO COME OUT SOMEWHERE between 1952 and '54 when I saw that, or felt that, I was doing all the work and a male was getting all the credit. In the fall of 1954 I decided that I would run for local president.

There were no women local presidents in South Carolina, nor in Georgia then. The men in the local came to me and told me that I could remain secretary-treasurer of the local as long as I wanted. They promised always to vote for me for secretary-treasurer, but they said they would never vote for a woman for president.

I said, "I can count also, and I know that there are more women than men in this local, so just come along to the election." I won the thing hands down.

In this district, which then covered nine states, there were three females on the CWA staff. Sometime earlier that year, the guy who was in charge of the nine Southeastern states, Bill Smallwood (he later became the international secretary-treasurer of the union) came to a state meeting in Columbia, South Carolina. I was the one presenting the local reports. I did not know it at the time, but later on I found out that when he heard me that night, he said to one of his people, "That's my next staff person."

In the early part of '55, when I had been local president for a few months, one of the three females on CWA staff married some guy and left the union. I had built a well-organized local. We had contributed money to PAC [the CIO political action committee] over and above union dues. Our local had a good record of settling grievances. So, I was offered the staff job.

I had never really thought about being on CWA staff. I was just trying to get the Charleston local into a position where we would not ever have to take any crap again, that we would be so well known in the community and so respected that no one would dare say anything to us.

I told the people at CWA headquarters in Atlanta that I didn't know if a staff job was what I wanted to do for the rest of my life and that I would go home and think about it. You see how naive I was: people were dying for that job, people had worked a long, long time for a staff job, and here I was, asking to think about it. I thought it over: I enjoyed teaching, and teaching in Alabama, Mississippi, and Louisiana was going to be my assignment. In about a week I called them and said I would accept. I was 27, the youngest person ever on the CWA staff.

On March 14, 1955, CWA struck the company. I hadn't even moved into my office in Jackson, Mississippi. I always laugh and say that CWA threw me into the fish pond to see if I would sink or swim. I was sent to New Orleans to administer the CWA defense fund. When I arrived, I had with me a check for $25,000. All the strike funds were being set up in personal accounts, so the company would not find out how much we had and how much we were spending.

The strike went on for seventy-two days. In that time, I paid out $699,000 in the state of Louisiana for bread and beans and house payments and car payments. We did not give any money to strikers, but we would not let them lose a house or a car. We had ten million little problems with the defense fund, like, maybe a local buying something that was not authorized under the defense fund rules of the international union. We'd have to refuse them and spend a great deal of time explaining why to the local.

I was living in a hotel, not getting much sleep at all. It is terribly hot in New Orleans in March, April, and May. I felt very grimy and dirty all the time. And it was still a male-versus-female thing. They assumed that women were more adept at doing the clerical work and taking all the garbage from the locals, so that is what I was doing.

But, also, I figured I'd come a long way from saying "Number, please" in Dublin, Georgia, just three years before. Working in the strike was exciting to me. I learned that women could get by with more than the males. We could stir the scabs up and police would threaten us, but there was no violence. CWA had it set up where the women would picket from six A.M. to six P.M. and the men would take up the signs at six P.M. to six A.M.

I decided that we needed some lively things to get the spirits of the strikers built up. We made up songs, like, "Oh, when the scabs come crawling out. . . . Oh, Lord, I don't want to be in that number, when the scabs come crawling out," and "Old Ma Bell, she ain't what she used to be . . . a couple of months ago." We would sing with the police surrounding us. We told the police that we would not get involved with them in violence. One night we had a parade, 10,000 people in the parade. You could see the scabs peering out the windows. The street had been empty when they went to work. They must have been petrified looking out at 10,000 people. But, after the strike, we had only four people fired out of 5,000 members of the New Orleans local. That was because of these kids getting their emotions placed in pranks and singing instead of in violence.

The CWA workers in New Orleans were just looking for someone to lead them, and once we got the morale up and the spirits up, there was no problem. You'll find that people will strike over a principle sooner and longer than they will over money. We wanted maternity leave in the contract and we wanted the right to arbitrate any suspension and the right of any union member not to have to cross a *bona fide* picket line. Seventy-two days later we got those things.

There was bitterness left on both sides. After this '55 strike, we had the biggest set of arbitration hearings that have ever been held between a company and a union in the history of the labor movement. Two hundred and forty-eight people were fired from Southern Bell alone. I think there were some forty fired in Louisiana. There were four arbitrators after the strike and all four were put on a blacklist by Bell Telephone and not a one of them was ever used in any arbitration hearings again, anywhere in the Bell System. It wasn't like the '47 thing, when I was back in Dublin. There was a real split after the '55 strike. The company and CWA were no longer one big happy family.

I felt the bitterness personally. I watched the company's reaction to the strike. The company would send down supervisors every night to watch us, you know, and say nasty things to us. Their emotions were very high; they didn't even like our singing and joking around. They didn't think our people would last that long. The company had these movie cameras going. They had spotlights on me everywhere I would move in the crowd. They must have reels of movies of me. Of all the staff people in the nine Southeastern states, I was the only one accused of an unfair labor practice. The company charged me with not carrying a picket sign correctly, swinging it too fast, turning on my heel too fast. Nothing came of it, though, with the labor board.

CWA asked me to stay in Louisiana after the strike. We had a number of locals in Louisiana that thought they could do without a national union; they were fighting national and district headquarters all the time—Monroe, Shreveport, Lake Charles. The district vice-president carved out those locals and said, "Here you are, Selina." I had the central, northern, and southwestern part of the state. It was a big assignment. I had a title, "North Louisiana Director," and I was going to set the woods on fire.

When I first agreed to come on staff, I'll never forget, I was taken into a room by the assistant district director. He was kind of a reserved guy and didn't really know how to approach what he wanted to say. Finally, I caught his eye and I asked him right out, "Are you trying to tell me about the birds and the bees?" And he says, "Yes." And I said, "I know all about the birds and the bees."

He said to me, "But you, with your youth, you are going to be confronted with so many situations." And I said, "No, I won't. I know exactly how to handle it."

All the locals in the state had male presidents. No matter how well I did, they were always going to think, some of them, that a male could have done it better. He thought that I would be put in difficult situations, that I wouldn't know exactly how to handle them. But I did.

I believe the old saying, "You don't get your honey where you make your money." I had one basic thing that I required of a local president. The first time I met a local president, he had one of two options: he could take me home for dinner, or he could bring his wife and family and we'd go out to dinner. I did not have a family of my own, but I knew something about families. If you wanted a local president to really do a job, he had to have an understanding wife and a trusting wife. I built this type of relationship for myself and for the union. There was a great love and a great closeness between me and the wives of local presidents. I still get graduation invitations from children all over Louisiana.

I HAD LEARNED EARLY ENOUGH THAT THE ONE THING THAT MADE mother talk was money, and whoever controlled the purse strings would have the biggest influence with the company. In Louisiana, the Public Service Commission sets the pay telephone rates and—what's more important—the intrastate long distance rates. I decided that CWA should put an effort into electing friendly Public Service Commissioners. There were three commissioners, one on our side and one who voted most often for the company. The third man was from near New Orleans and he was not an enemy, but he was not what we considered a friend to CWA, either. After we had made a difference in the election of that commissioner, CWA came to have great influence with the commission.

Well, it came about that the company was seeking a $20 million rate increase. Until that time, Public Service hearings where telephone rates were being considered were attended only by company officials. I got notice to all local presidents and officers in my territory, and we started going to Baton Rouge to attend every commission hearing. This got the local officers close to the commissioners and it made the company realize that we were to be reckoned with.

So the commission voted: instead of a $20 million increase, the company got a $10 million decrease. The pay station reverted back to a nickel. The vice president in charge of Southern Bell in Louisiana was shipped back to Atlanta.

The company brought in a guy named Homer Bartee from Kentucky to be vice-president. He came with a pretty bad reputation for being hard on the union. Of course, he was going to set the woods on fire, too. Right away, he refused to sit down with us and deal with our grievances.

CWA is neutral in most rate increase fights. But in Louisiana at this time, 200 union members had been laid off, because of the rate decrease. I decided to take a risk: the union was all for the increase, but I wouldn't give a CWA endorsement until the company came and asked me for it.

Bartee held an executive session and said that he'd never ask the goddamn

CWA Convention, Cleveland, Ohio, 1956; Selina Burch is on the far right

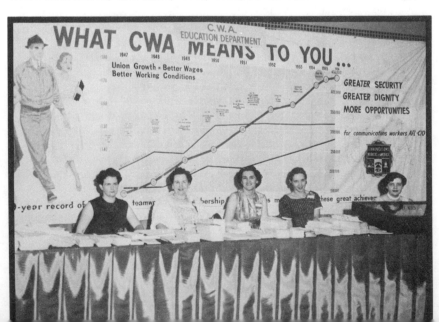

Communications Workers of America for a thing. "Fine," I told his people. "I hope him all the luck in the world with his rate increase."

We sat through another rate hearing. The company was denied their intrastate long distance rate increase again. They decided that they would appeal to the Supreme Court.

Now Bartee wanted to know what I could do to help him. I told him I didn't know, but we got permission to file a brief in the Supreme Court in support of the increase. The Court upheld the commission, but the CWA brief was the only one mentioned in the opinion when it came down. After that, there came to be a very good relationship between Bartee and myself.

So when emotions died down and I was able to sit down and talk with the company, CWA accomplished new things that could not have been accomplished without building that kind of relationship. I was learning that it all tied together—your relationship with the company and your relationship with the locals—but I had no idea in the beginning how it would work out. I was playing it one step at a time—praying.

My big problem was with the North Louisiana locals. Monroe was the worst. You have to remember that from Alexandria north is the Bible Belt. In the early 1960s all through that north section, everybody was calling everybody else a communist. Chet Huntley, David Brinkley, and Walter Cronkite were all suddenly communists. There was an organization in North Louisiana—a John Birch sort of group—that was taking up money for General Walker and trying to have *Life* and *Look* magazines banned as communist. You couldn't talk reason with people about integration at that time.

Down in New Orleans, I had involved CWA in several school board elections where integration was a problem. Some of the New Orleans school board members who were liberal were being accused of being communists. I picked several contests where it meant something to the community and ran a CWA phone bank for the liberal candidate. I did it more for the children of CWA members than for any other reason. So the Monroe local knew where I stood. I had had a rough time at one of their meetings where I talked their members out of donating a thousand dollars to this crazy organization. To them, every liberal-thinking person was a communist.

One of the loudmouths in that local was a cable splicer who had been suspended for falsifying work reports. The local officers asked him if he wanted CWA to process a grievance in his behalf. He told them, hell, no, that he was going to work, union be damned.

Then, the company fired him. Now, he's without a job at all, and the guy wants the union to help him. So the local tried to process the grievance, but they allowed the time limit to expire. Everybody in management all over the state was laughing up their sleeve. Even this crazy John Birch organization was trying to get involved in the thing. The local officers were all excited and didn't know what to do. They were calling me by now.

I called the personnel guy for Southern Bell at Monroe and asked him to tear up the envelope that had the postmark on it and accept the grievance. He wouldn't do it. He was having too big a time embarrassing the local.

So, I called Bartee and asked him if he would take me to lunch. At that stage of the game, I had decided that I wanted this cable splicer reinstated with no loss of service. I didn't just want the grievance reinstated, because if the union had arbitrated the grievance we could not have won it. The guy was guilty as sin. While Bartee and I were eating lunch, I told him what I wanted.

"Well, hell, no damn problem. Is that all you want?" he asked me.

I told him, "Before you give me a fast answer, Bartee, remember everybody in your company in Louisiana is laughing up their sleeve over this."

He said, "I don't give a damn. I'm the vice-president of the company and I tell you that the man will go back to work next Monday morning."

The company personnel man was very embarrassed by all this. He tried to fandango with me, trying to get me to accept something else, anything else in the whole state. Bartee had already told him to put the union man back to work, see, and it made the personnel executive look bad. I just said, "I haven't asked *you* for anything. If that cable splicer's not going back to work on Monday, just tell Homer Gray Bartee to call me."

The man went back to work. That one thing brought the Monroe local back together, and brought them back into the international. I didn't have any more trouble with them after that. In fact, at that time, the president of CWA said that if we had the type of relationship with the Public Service Commission in other states that we had in Louisiana, we would be very fortunate and not have to work so hard. I was riding high then. I was showing the world that I knew a thing or two.

I DID A LOT OF TEACHING. ORGANIZING AND TEACHING COME BEFORE politics. You've got to have members supporting you before you can start involving the union in politics. I was forever going around from one little town to the other, spending the day with the local president, making sure that he knew the members in his town, that he knew their problems, that everybody had a job steward. I had to be sure in my own mind that their job stewards were the caliber of people that would be leading them and not someone that was using the union to better himself first, just looking for the prestige, because there is a lot of prestige in being a job steward.

Politics was something else beyond organizing, but it all ties together. You had to give the members something that they could be proud of and wanted to hang on to. You see, for most of the members there's only one thing the union does: handle their grievances. That's the most visible thing. It was hard at first to get union members involved in the Public Service Commission election because that is not an exciting race. I had to work with the kids day and night, showing them what could be accomplished if the union was active in this election. Once they saw that their working conditions and their livelihoods were better, much better, than they had been before CWA developed a relationship with the commission, the members became proud and worked very hard at politics.

When I went to Louisiana, the locals that were put under me never contributed to COPE [the AFL-CIO's national political arm, the Committee for Political Education]. By law, any money contributed to COPE is over and above union dues and must be hand-collected. Every year after I was assigned to Louisiana, I got a plaque at the International Convention because every one of my locals was 100 percent.

But, see, COPE can only do so much. You can have a state AFL-CIO leader like Victor Bussie in Louisiana who's very active, but unless you have the contacts yourself, you can't bring pressure to bear to help *your* people in CWA.

Another thing: I realized at that time that CWA had something special to offer a candidate in any election. Many of our people were professionals at one thing—they spent eight hours a day talking to people over the telephone. An operator gets so adept at listening, when she talks to a voter for a few minutes, she can almost tell you how that person is going to vote.

I was looking for a way in which CWA could get the most mileage from its own membership. The phone bank was made to order. A union leader needs to place his people where the candidate can see them. And the union members need to feel a part of the campaign. Having me collect money from members and get my picture in the paper handing a check to the candidate doesn't do either of those things. COPE originally set up the phone bank system, but let me tell you in my opinion what's wrong with the COPE thing. They have it set up where union members call only union members. In my honest opinion, you don't get the kind of benefit for your union that you get working directly for the campaign. The members don't feel nearly as close to the campaign. I've tried to tell that to COPE.

When CWA ran a phone bank in Louisiana, we first got a list of every registered voter in the precinct, along with his address and telephone number. You just go down, calling everyone on the list. An operator doesn't identify herself as a union member. She just says, "I'm a volunteer working for the election of so and so . . ."

In 1960, Hale Boggs saw a CWA phone-bank in operation. He became fascinated with it. He had never seen anything like it. We started experimenting in that election: we would leave one precinct alone and we would call down the list in the next precinct. The results were astonishing.

Anyway, in 1960, CWA ran a phone-bank operation for Boggs and John Kennedy in Louisiana. Boggs was Whip of the House then. CWA always had a big shindig in Washington when the congressmen were sworn in. Before 1960, Boggs had never been to a CWA function in his life. After we worked with him at home in Louisiana in 1960, he came and he and Lindy [Mrs. Boggs] stayed late until they could see Joe Beirne [then president of CWA] to tell him about how great the Communications Workers of America were. Beirne called me from Washington the next morning to thank me. Boggs and Beirne became very dear friends after that.

I was very active in the Women's Movement for Kennedy, speaking for him at many AFL-CIO programs. Through that campaigning, and working for Boggs, I got to know many community leaders in New Orleans, people who probably had hangups where labor leaders were concerned, but by working together in a campaign, you get to them personally and erase any bad ideas they may have about "labor people."

Working for Boggs did not have the direct bearing that working in a Public Service Commission election would have. But the company did have great respect for Boggs. You have to remember, the company also understands power and where the power is. Anyone who becomes Whip is in a very powerful position. Boggs generally lined up with labor on bills we wanted passed. I think that some of the company officials, men I worked with, were envious of my friendship with Hale and Lindy, but they could have gone out and worked for him just the same as we did.

I learned many, many years ago that a union could sit and negotiate a contract and have the best contract that anybody could ever have, but one stroke of a pen could take everything away from you. If you did not have some say in political races, if you did not elect the right people, this could happen to you overnight. Congress could pass a law tomorrow, outlawing all unions; the President could sign it. Where would you be then?

I CAME TO ATLANTA IN 1963 ON A TEMPORARY ASSIGNMENT—ALL OF my jobs have been "temporary"—to relieve a guy who was arguing executive-level grievances with the company. After three months had gone by, at the end of each month they'd ask me to stay another month—the vice-president offered me a promotion if I would leave Louisiana and come to the Atlanta office permanently. They started tugging on my heartstrings, telling me how much the members needed me settling their grievances in Atlanta. All

Selina Burch speaking for John Kennedy, 1960

this garbage about how the women in the union would now have a spokesperson at headquarters, how it was the first time that a woman had been given the "privilege" of settling grievances at that high a level. What they really wanted was somebody who would work 16 hours a day on all the grievances that had piled up. They were so far behind when I came to Atlanta. I was spending every night in a hotel room, just reading through the backlog of grievances. From March through December, I handled, at the executive level, 510 grievances.

You always have to remember that if you are a woman, it's twice as hard. They want you to work, but only at the job they've got laid out for you to do. If you go beyond that, and get into something on your own, then you are "aggressive." You start hearing, "You're a throat cutter," "You've changed," "You're not what you used to be."

I decided: well, then, if I'm an aggressive bitch, I'm an aggressive bitch. I didn't care. I was aggressive on the side of the members and that's what I was there for. As far as most members are concerned, the union does one thing: fight for their grievances. I honestly feel that any member who has been discharged or suspended or denied a promotion deserves his day in court all the way up through the grievance procedure. That's the only avenue he or she has. I feel strongly that you go as hard as you can when you are handling grievances.

In June of 1967, a CWA area director named R. B. Porch was elected vice-president of District 3. That's when my life took a backward step. I had strongly supported Porch's opponent.

My first assignment under Porch was to talk with the blacks who worked for Southern Bell in our district and bring them into the union. That was fine with me. But for all his trying to portray himself as a freethinking person, Porch never really wanted me to work too hard at organizing blacks.

You have to understand, before 1965, blacks worked as janitors and elevator operators. When Southern Bell started hiring blacks as switchboard operators, the phones in the CWA office were ringing off the wall. Members of the union were demanding that we stop it, hollering that if niggers came to work, they were going to walk off their jobs.

My answer was always the same: you have the right to walk off your job, but the union will not protect you if you do. Then, when blacks began to show up at union meetings and voting in elections, my *home* phone began ringing all night. Members calling to shout "nigger lover" into the phone and hang up. It would have been hard enough if I had been getting any support from the union vice-president and his people, but I wasn't. It got to where the first thing I would look for when I came home in the evening would be two double martinis.

Porch had very little vision, and his assistant, L. L. Bolick, had less. Porch wanted to be a big shot, he wanted me to build a name for him, but he and Bolick had the idea that you can do union work without ever leaving the office and mixing with the members. They forgot that any power we had *came* from the members. You have to involve the membership in anything you do—not just votes and money, either.

Porch and Bolick would not allow me to go out and teach in the locals, because they thought that once I had been teaching in a local, that local would belong to me. Union work is not 8:45 A.M. to 5:45 P.M. work. That's all I heard about, though. "Why did you come in at 9:15, Ms. Burch?" "Where have you been all afternoon, Ms. Burch?" "Why have you not turned in a vacation slip, Ms. Burch?"

I had always been my own woman. In Louisiana when I saw something that needed to be done for the union, I went ahead and did it, never mind if it was 8:45 in the morning or midnight. Now, every time I did something, they struck me down for it. Bolick started slipping memos about my attitude into my personnel file—the secretaries were my friends and they would tell me what was going on. I was threatened with discharge by both Porch and Bolick.

It got worse and worse. By 1969, I was drinking more than was good for me. My health was falling apart. In early 1970, I was in the hospital in Atlanta for a month. These men had no compassion. The whole time I was in the hospital, my secretary was the only one in the district office who called me.

Maybe it's my craziness, but I felt I should stay and fight them. I could have quit and gotten another job, but I had a lot of benefits built up in CWA, retirement and fringe benefits. And I'm not made that way that I could just walk off from it. I felt strongly that one day the members would understand how these guys were and change things.

In the meantime, Lindy and Hale Boggs had told Andrew Young about me. In 1971, Young was running for Congress and asked me to run a phone bank for his campaign. The district office had nothing to do with my work in that election. I worked for Young's campaign because I liked Young. He is an intelligent man. I worked for him very quietly, though. I had to sneak off time to do it. I wasn't about to bother to sit down and explain to Porch and Bolick how my working for Young could benefit the union. They wouldn't have cared anyway, unless there was some way they would have gotten credit for it, after all the work was done. It would not have helped me any that Young was black. Anyway, Young won and that was that.

Then, in '73, [then Atlanta Mayor] Sam Massell had taken the checkoff away from AFSCME. There was a garbage strike. Most of the union members out on strike were black. While Massell was trying to break the strike, Vice-mayor Maynard Jackson had walked the picket line with the sanitation workers. So, when Jackson announced that he was going to run against Massell, CWA sent a guy down from Washington to meet him and see if CWA wanted to support him.

Porch had decided that I knew how to give a good party. He asked me if I would prepare a cocktail party for Maynard Jackson and the CWA man from Washington. The party was going fine, and after a while Jackson got started talking about his campaign. I had just come into the room, carrying a tray or something or other and I heard him say, "If there is any expert on political campaigning in the world, then she is standing here with us."

I was thinking, "Oh, God, don't say me. I'm in enough trouble already."

Of course, that's who he requested. The union was more than happy to have me work for Jackson's election. He had promised to give AFSCME back the checkoff and he did.

When Jackson won, he appointed me to the Civil Service Board. That's when the fly hit the ointment. The first and third Thursday of every month, I had to be at board meetings. Bolick didn't like my being out of the office. He wanted me where he could watch over me, where I wouldn't make any more friends. He went to Porch and they decided I was spending too much time with the board. Two days a month! No thought for the good it was doing CWA, my being there where everybody in the world could see CWA represented on the most politically important board in the city. Bolick wrote me a formal letter demanding that I spell out what the duties of a Civil Service Board member were. I told him he could call City Hall. Then, I wrote my own letter: I charged CWA with sex discrimination.

A group of women I had known over the years in the union had gotten together at a CWA convention in Miami and formed a Women's Movement in CWA. They elected me the chairperson. They didn't know about my personal problems in Atlanta. All they knew was that I was a woman with their same point of view who didn't mind telling the men in the union to go to hell when it was necessary. It put the union in a bind that I was head of the women's group.

Before any of this could be settled, it came time for elections. That's the only time Porch paid any attention to the locals, and then only to the officers. Usually, a regional vice-president stays in office for as long as he wishes. Porch, though, had made one *big* mistake. A year or so before all this, he decided that I should take over the leadership school that CWA runs at the University of Georgia. He didn't give a damn about the school and left me to run it however I wanted. The district office was only allowing 45 people into the program from ninety-five locals. I opened it up to as many members as the classroom would hold, about 135. Most of the members who came to the school were young, and they were tired of hearing about COPE and organizing, community services, and so on and so forth. They had heard all that. They were looking for something lively, something that meant something to them. I wanted to give them that but, at the same time, give them some reason to want to work for the union. I moved things around so that the school was teaching psychology, sex discrimination, race relations, things like that in addition to the usual.

I expected that some good would come out of that teaching, but I had no idea it would turn out the way it did. I was just trying to involve the members.

CWA members looked upon Porch as *the* politician—back-slapping, "Goddamn, how-ya-doing, greatest guy since Seven-Up" kind of politician. Unbeatable. There was a guy who was the area director of Georgia and Florida, Allen Willis, a very down-to-earth kind of fellow. People who had been in CWA for a long time didn't think that a guy like Willis could touch Porch in an election.

Well, Willis won. The way it happened was funny. I bought $44 worth of buttons and streamers and led a little parade around the convention floor, hoping for, hell, ten more votes. That's how close it was, right down to the wire. The people who voted for Willis at the national convention, those delegates, many of them were the people from the black locals and the kids who had gone to the leadership school. The women and the blacks made the difference, and a friend of mine in Washington told me the other day that CWA is still shaken all the way to the top by that election.

Now, I am Willis's administrative assistant. Bolick reports to me. It kills him just to have to come in to ask me for a favor, or for advice. I guess I could make him punch a time clock every morning, but I'm just not like that anymore.

Porch and Bolick thought I was screwed up, a nut. But crazy or not, I never did forget that little telephone operator out there who is oversupervised to begin with and here the company goes and runs in a speed-up program on her. We just had a meeting today: the company is trying to bring in paid directory assistance in Florida. That'll mean laying off information operators. If I don't do something about that, I'm nothing. I've got no use. I may have gone after power, but I never forgot where it was coming from.

Porch forgot and he's out. For now. But I hear he's traveling around, talking to people about the next election.

IN 1976, SELINA BURCH WAS RESTING ON HIGH GROUND. PORCH, defeated by Willis in the election and charged with misappropriation of union funds, pleaded guilty to a lesser charge, and Willis suspended him from any duties in the District 3 office. Soon, however, Burch and Willis found that they had only scotched various snakes.

Porch was undeniably a master politician. "A spellbinder," Burch's lawyer would concede at the height of her troubles. Now, CWA President Glenn Watts came to Porch's aid. Always before in the union, a former vice-president just deposed by the electorate had been reassigned to another district. This time Watts overruled Willis and ordered that Porch be allowed to remain in the Atlanta office. The CWA executive board named Bolick as an administrative assistant in the District 3 office.

In June 1977, Willis beat Porch again for the leadership of District 3, and Porch's people challenged the vote. For the first time in the history of CWA, the union backed away from a decision and placed the disputed election before the U.S. Department of Labor, even though the CWA constitution provided for the circumstance of a questioned election result, and other district elections just as closely contested were not taken outside the union for settlement by the federal government. The Department of Labor ordered the election rerun and, six months later, Porch won narrowly. Willis's supporters, the District 3 progressives, claimed that Watts's kid-glove treatment of Porch after his guilty plea and loss of the 1974 election allowed him to strengthen his position in an unfair way, while restricting Willis's effectiveness. Watts claimed neutrality.

On January 20, 1978, Burch was summoned to Porch's office. "He told me to clean out my desk, go home, and wait for further orders," she recalls. Two district secretaries, Willis supporters, had been summarily fired within two weeks of the victory. Willis and his assistant, Michael Handley, were shuttled into the same limbo as Burch. Porch lacked the power, under the CWA constitution, to discharge an administrative assistant, or a former district officer. The three were kept on the CWA payroll but had neither work to do nor a place to do it.

From January 20 until the middle of May, Burch sat idle at home. On May 17, Watts telephoned her. She was ordered, without explanation or apology, to report to CWA headquarters in Washington, D.C., by 9 A.M., May 22, 1978. Burch explained to Watts that she had no desire to leave Atlanta, her home and workplace for fifteen years. She asked if she had any choice in the matter. Watts replied that her choices were to report to work in Washington within five days or be fired. At the same time, Willis was exiled to the CWA regional office in St. Louis, while Handley was sent to Cleveland.

Burch did as she was told. She also hired herself a lawyer. Joseph A. "Chip" Yablonski knew a great deal about unions and their internal workings. In the eight years before he took Burch's case, the lawyer had lived very immediately with the question of personal freedom within organized labor. His father, Joseph Sr., "Jock" Yablonski, had been a progressive and, for that reason, dissident, voice within the United Mine Workers. In the fall of 1969, Jock Yablonski had challenged Tony Boyle for the presidency of the UMWA. Yablonski nearly won and, when he lost, had asked that the federal courts consider the conduct of the election. Only weeks after the election, while his lawyers were preparing a lawsuit that accused Boyle and his followers with violations of the Landrum-Griffin Act, Jock Yablonski, his wife, and his daughter were found shot to death in their Clarksville, Pennsylvania, home. The crime, ultimately, was laid at the feet of Tony Boyle. In a ten-year marathon of investigations and trials, nine people, five of them UMWA members, including Boyle and the president of UMWA District 19, were convicted of first degree murder. Chip Yablonski was an active member of the prosecution team that finally ran to earth those who had killed his father, mother, and sister.

The CWA manhandling of Burch seemed an echo—less harsh, perhaps, but distinct—of the Yablonski story. Chip Yablonski, formerly general counsel for the UMWA under Arnold Miller, Boyle's replacement, is now in private practice in Washington. When Burch first went to him, he seemed sympathetic, but told her that he had too much business at that moment to take her case.

"I knew the history of the family. Chip had been raised in the labor movement and was the best lawyer in D.C. for the job." Burch asked again. Yablonski agreed to represent her.

In August, advised by Yablonski, Burch appealed her removal from Atlanta to the CWA Executive Board. The board—Watts and eleven regional vice-presidents, Porch among them—denied her grievance. On September 1, 1978, Yablonski filed a lawsuit alleging that Watts and the union had violated the Landrum-Griffin Act by punishing Burch for political activity within the union. The suit asked that she be reinstated in Atlanta in a position comparable to the one she had held under Willis. She also asked for money damages.

The union defense claimed that Burch had been transferred because she was a malcontent, a troublemaker in District 3. Watts maintained that Burch was the cause of constant upheaval in the Atlanta office that had been hurting the union. The union's attorneys—the Atlanta firm of Adair, Goldthwaite & Daniel—cited Burch's 1976 *Southern Exposure* interview as an example of her malcontentment.

In the preparations for the trial, the defendant's attorneys worked to shift the focus from their client onto details of Burch's personal life. The questioning at times became vicious and seemed more an attempt to wear her down than to elicit information for use at trial.

The time was an ordeal for Burch. She felt betrayed by the union that she had served for thirty-four years. She was separated from friends and fellow workers in the South and cut off from the only work she cared about. The union would require her presence at a day-long deposition, then dock her that day's pay.

Yablonski believes that she was borne up by the fight itself, but Burch says that her endurance derived from Yablonski's support.

But behind Burch, too, were the rank and file of CWA. To counter Porch's accusations, Yablonski argued that during the time of her struggle with Porch in District 3, Burch had chaired the bargaining committee that negotiated a new union contract with Southern Bell, had represented union members' grievances in arbitration ("There's nobody better at grievances than Selina," Yablonski maintains), and had continued undertakings—negotiation of a collective bargaining agreement, arbitration advocacy, and labor education—that were the primary business of a union. So clearly Burch was getting the job done in Atlanta despite the district office infighting. Any loss of efficiency was the price a union paid for democracy.

"CWA's lawyers tried to dig up anything and everything bad to say about Selina," says Yablonski. "What they couldn't come up with was one live rank-and-file witness who would say that she had ever hurt the union. Their own witnesses were forced to admit her value to the union. And I could have put on scores of rank and filers who would have testified for her." Union members, union officials, men and women, whites and blacks that she had struggled to recruit into CWA and had stood behind and beside in years past now stood up for her.

"It made me feel very proud," she says of the trial. "Adair would get finished with one of his witnesses and Chip would ask the witness, 'How many times have you ever called on Selina Burch for help with a contract, or with arbitration, and so on?'

"The CWA witness would say, 'Fifty times, no, seventy-five times.'

"Chip would ask, 'Did she ever fail you?'

"The CWA witness would have to say no every time."

Yablonski views Watts as a thoughtful intellectual caught between two gifted, instinctive politicians, Porch and Burch. In his actions in 1978, Watts felt he had to end the turmoil in District 3, long a public embarrassment to his leadership. Word went out in the union that he intended to "burn some asses" in Atlanta. Burch, a woman in the man's world of union politics, a spokesperson for women and blacks, was the more vulnerable target. Determined to assert himself as a strong leader, he uprooted Burch and sent letters out to every local, broadcasting his solution to the District 3 problem. "In the history of the union, no one has ever been reassigned with so much fanfare," says Yablonski.

But Watts made two serious miscalculations. First, as Yablonski contended at trial, his trust in Porch was widely misplaced. "Porch just went in there and used a meat ax and Watts either willingly or reluctantly consented to it all." Watts's second error, of course, was to think that it would be easier to pick on Burch than to deal justly with Porch.

BEYOND THE PERSONALITIES, BEYOND THE IMPORTANT ISSUES OF THE ongoing Porch-versus-Willis struggle, were several larger questions.

"The whole case was built around the question of whether or not people, union members and staff people, have rights in the union," says Burch. "We wanted to prove that we did have a bill of rights in the union. That we had the right to conduct our internal politics, to support the candidate of our choice."

Yablonski agrees. The Landrum-Griffin Act is more than another dry page of legislation; it is a bill of rights for union members. Jock Yablonski had invoked the Landrum-Griffin Act against the UMWA. It was the rights protected by Landrum-Griffin that Chip's father had been shaking in Tony Boyle's face when Boyle ordered him killed. Boyle had run a thug-enforced dictatorship, and it was not coincidental that the element of his union that brought about his downfall called themselves Miners for Democracy. Jock Yablonski's Landrum-Griffin action—along with Boyle's conviction for the Yablonski murders—eventually toppled Boyle and brought in Arnold Miller, a Yablonski supporter, as reform president of UMWA.

Burch, too, prevailed. On September 14, 1979, a Washington, D.C., jury returned a verdict for the plaintiff, finding Watts himself and his union liable for violations of the Landrum-Griffin Act. The federal district judge then gave attorneys for both sides an opportunity to agree to a remedy before the court would impose a remedy of its own. Based on discussions between Burch's and the union's attorneys, Judge June L. Green issued a final order consented to by both parties which provided that, within ten days, Burch was to be permanently reassigned to Atlanta, with all costs of moving paid by CWA, with duties similar or related to those she had had before she had been brought to Washington. Her salary was to be the same. The union was permanently enjoined from interfering with her political activities, and the court would retain jurisdiction over the matter for seven years and could intervene at any time without the necessity of filing and arguing another lawsuit. The question of money damages was dealt with in a sealed verdict. The CWA lawyers weren't taking a chance on the jury compensating Burch for her year of suffering.

Yablonski believes that there were a number of lessons in the outcome of the case. "We made the point that there is something to be gained by hard work for the rank and file, that all of Selina's years of good service had not gone for nothing.

"I think that Selina's success in the action will be a beacon to women in organized labor: you might get pushed around but if you fight hard enough, you'll ultimately win. Selina fought harder than the other two, both men, who received the same treatment in District 3. Women need to know that they *can* win, although they may have to fight harder than a man would. And women need to be more involved at the policymaking levels of the union."

Watts ordered Willis and Handley returned to their home region. Again, as he had done when the three were split up and scattered, he announced their return home in a letter to the entire union membership. The evening after the verdict, Burch went to see Watts.

"I told him, 'Let's forget the last eighteen tragic months of my life and let me be creative for the union again.'

"He said, 'I agree with that.' "

Yablonski says, "There are not many people in labor—in real life— who are that big. Remember, I had said an awful lot of nasty things about Watts during the lawsuit. He proved to be a hell of a man."

When it was all done, Burch gave Yablonski a small crystal eagle. She can't explain why very well, something to do with his strength and leadership, not attributes of the bird so much but something that, when she talks about it, seems to have to do with her notion of America. That's all she can say. A way she would have it be, a system that can enforce fair play and put down bullies.

TWENTY-SEVEN

Puttin' Down Ol' Massa: Laurel, Mississippi, 1979

DAVID MOBERG

THE MAKESHIFT TENT, WITH ITS fluttering, bright plastic pennants around the door, offered little refuge from the sodden heat of Mississippi in August. But it was the only shelter in the open field beyond the new cyclone fence surrounding the home of Miss Goldy chickens, the trademark chickens of Sanderson Farms. A dozen women gathered in its shade. Their best strategy was simply to sit still and hope for a breeze. But Myra Seals kept leaping up whenever she saw a car, a truck, or a passing stranger. "Where are you going? What are you doing in there?" she shouted with imperious anger. "Scab! I don't want to catch you in there!" She was on guard, protecting her strike, now nearly half a year old.

Six months is a long time to be on strike, with benefits that started at $30 a week now trailing off to $15. But the strikers were no strangers to lean times: when they were working, they were making $2.95 to $3.15 an hour on the disassembly line where chickens are killed, cleaned, cut up, and packaged—slightly more than the federal minimum wage of $2.90 an hour. (Mississippi, in line with much of its labor legislation, has no state minimum wage.) Oddly enough, however, the women gathered on the picket line had not gone out on strike for more money, although they would like better pay. Rather, they risked their jobs because they finally decided that working under Joe Frank Sanderson, Jr.—"Little Joe," grandson of the founder of the firm —was no longer tolerable.

"It's better since when I first came in 'cause we got a union," said Pressie Clayton, 60, an eight-year veteran, "but everywhere else is so much better than this. That's what I don't like. For break they weren't giving us what they promised. They promised ten minutes twice a day and gave us four or five minutes and sometimes only once a day. We want more. We want sick leave. Now you just take your own time. And we want to go to the bathroom when you have to." The rule at Sanderson Farms was only three toilet breaks a week outside of normal breaks. It was not only irritating and demeaning, a symbol of the hard regimen within the factory, but a potential health problem. There were the inevitable horror stories, some recalled with a darkly comic edge (the woman with diarrhea who shit in her pants), others more clearly painful (such as the pregnant woman who was denied a toilet break despite her pleading and then had a miscarriage the following day).

The work was hard and had been getting harder: hanging up 140 live chickens on the line each minute (up recently from 100 a minute); cutting a major incision in 60 chickens a minute; "venting" (making a cut and pulling out the chicken's guts) 20 to 24 a minute; completely cutting up 5 whole chickens a minute.

The arbitrary and strict rules, the low pay, the safety hazards, the hard work, and the casual violation by management of their feeble contract weren't all that angered the workers at Sanderson Farms. "We really feel it's a question of human dignity," Gloria Jordan, 46, vice-president of the local union, said. "They didn't have no manner of talking to you like human beings. They order you in a loud tone of voice. They don't ask you. They don't care if you're hurt."

"All they're concerned about it seems is those chickens and not employees," Alice Musgrove, 41, mother of seven and a six-year employee at Sanderson Farms, said. "One of my children called to tell me one day that another of my children was sick. They didn't tell me right away about the call. When I said I was going home, because I had lost one child when I was working on another job, the foreman was saying I shouldn't be so concerned about my own blood. They tell me, 'What's more important, your child or your job?' "

LAUREL IS THE COUNTY SEAT OF AN UNUSUAL PIECE OF THE SOUTH that dramatically contrasts some of the most progressive and most reactionary sides of the region's history. During the Civil War, Jones County broke away from the Confederacy and declared itself the Free State of Jones, its sovereignty defended by a guerrilla army under the leadership of Newt Knight. Later, the county had the only substantial socialist vote in the state and even elected local socialists to office, according to Ken Lawrence, a veteran organizer and labor historian. It was also the site of the first CIO organizing victory in Mississippi, at the local Masonite plant.

At the same time, it is in the heart of Ku Klux Klan country. In the late 1940s the Klan was a leading agent of the drive to break the CIO in Jones County. After a celebrated trial in 1948, a black man, Willie McGee, was executed for rape, despite the efforts of his attorney, Bella Abzug. Newt Knight's grandson, the descendant of Knight's relationship with a black woman, was tried on a charge of miscegenation. "It is obvious that they were waging war against that tradition," Lawrence says.

More recently, Jones County, one of the more unionized counties in the state in the past, has been the scene of militant strikes and organizing efforts among poultry workers and the Gulf Coast pulpwood workers. In 1967 a bitter wildcat strike at the 2,300-worker Masonite plant dragged on for seven months. Hundreds of workers were fired for fighting against work-rule changes by the new management that undercut the workers' considerable shop floor power. Serious racial tensions accompanied the strike, Jim Youngdahl, then attorney for the union, recalls, as the Klan tried to take over the strike and as many blacks crossed the picket line. Management's success in breaking that strike dealt a serious blow to unionism in the area.

During the sixties, the civil rights movement didn't affect Laurel as deeply as many other towns in the state, local activists now say, but the specter of violence against civil rights workers was glaringly evident. Laurel was home to some Klansmen, including the notorious Sam Bowers, accused of killing the three civil rights workers Andrew Goodman, Michael Schwerner, and James Chaney in 1964. Local people also recall vividly the later killing of NAACP leader Vernon Dahmer. "Nobody forgets that," organizer Kim Pittman says. "They shot him up and burned his house. You don't have to do that more than once every twenty-five years to frighten people." One of the men arrested in connection with the Dahmer murder (and later acquitted of the charges) was Charles Noble. Today he is a supervisor at the Sanderson Farms plant in Laurel. Nearly all of the foremen and supervisors there are white men. Nearly all of the workers are black women.

"You start talking to them about a white man and they're just scared," Gloria Jordan says of many of her fellow workers. "They often say, 'Girl, you better be careful when you talk to that white man or you'll be burned out tonight!' Having Charles Noble, a Klansman, in there affects a lot of people."

So the two traditions of Jones County and of the South come up against each other at Sanderson Farms, even if few workers there would respond to a call to "remember Newt Knight!" But William Magee, 39, now president of the local, was urged to start a union by his father-in-law, who was a union man at Masonite, the original CIO stronghold. Virtually nobody at the Sanderson Farms plant in 1972 had ever belonged to a union, but they were upset with the arbitrary authority of management. A minister made contact with a union— nobody seems to remember how it happened to be the International Chemical Workers—but the workers organized themselves, with inadvertent assists from the owners.

Joe Frank Sanderson, Sr., fought the union vigerously but lost. Just before the balloting, Magee recalls, Sanderson called all of the workers to a meeting. In a commonplace antiunion tactic in the South, he had a table covered with groceries. Standing before them in his white three-piece suit, he explained how one could buy all of these groceries with a year's union dues. When he finished, the workers dutifully applauded, but their real sentiments were different. "Man," one of them whispered to Magee, "maybe if we get a union in here I can get one of them three-piece suits."

D.R. SANDERSON FOUNDED SANDERSON FARMS AS A POULTRY growing and processing business in 1951 after a career as a salesman and a retail feed dealer. Gradually the business expanded to include hatcheries, poultry farms, a feed mill, and three plants capable of processing 180,000 chickens a day. As of 1977 its assets had grown to $8 million, its annual sales were $50 million, and its payroll numbered 1,200, making it one of the biggest poultry companies in Mississippi, which ranks fifth among the fifty states in broiler production. The family owns 80 percent of the stock.

In an industry with a reputation for low wages and bad working conditions, estimates of the extent of unionization run from only 30 percent (a United Food and Commercial Workers Union representative) to a "majority" (the Mississippi Poultry Association), still higher than many Southern industries. Sanderson Farms wages are typical for nonunion plants: around $3.10, or just above minimum wage. Union plants average around $3.75 to $4 an hour for the same work, according to James Paris of the Food and Commercial Workers.

The union contract at Sanderson Farms started weak and stayed that way. There never was a well-developed grievance procedure. The international union did little to build the local.

The union came close to striking during the last contract negotiations, but they backed off partly because they feared they lacked the strength. Meanwhile, many workers drifted away from the union. The local won some grievances in arbitration, but others had to be dropped because it couldn't afford to fight them. By the fall of 1978 the union membership had dropped to 44 out of approximately 375 workers in the plant. The remaining union activists became

Picket line in Laurel, Mississippi

convinced that Sanderson was systematically firing union people in an effort to eliminate the union altogether. Part of the union's problem stemmed from the high turnover: Sanderson had to hire 213 new people in 1978 to maintain his work force.

Recently, the international union—a roughly 85,000-member AFL-CIO affiliate based in Akron, Ohio—has shown signs of increased vigor and openness to leftist politics. In an attempt to strengthen the union's work in the South, special international representatives and new black organizers were sent in and older, white officials were shifted aside. Membership in the Laurel local climbed to around 200 shortly before the contract was due to expire on February 26, 1979.

Little Joe had already offered the union a raise of 50 cents an hour for extending the contract eighteen months. It wasn't a purely altruistic offer, since the minimum wage was scheduled to increase 45 cents by January 1981 in any case. Besides, as the strikers now insist adamantly, they were most concerned about the contract language, rules, and working conditions. Hubert Mills, then the international representative, urged the local to accept Sanderson's offer.

The local instead presented a long list of contract changes that would give them more power, starting with a revision of the management-rights clause, which reserved exclusive power to management over virtually everything. They wanted a change in the absenteeism policy: workers only six minutes late for work had been counted as absent as far as discipline was concerned. Three absences within sixty days were grounds for firing. Anyone who refused overtime was counted as absent for the whole day. They wanted relief for toilet breaks as needed, fifteen-minute rest breaks guaranteed twice a day, company-paid insurance, and more vacation. (Now workers get one week after a year's work, two weeks maximum, but frequently they were told they couldn't take vacations because there were no relief workers.)

They wanted a strong seniority system. "Seniority don't mean nothing in there now," Jordan said. People are easily transferred or stuck with undesirable jobs regardless of seniority. Anyone off sick, without pay, had to start back with jobs from the "extra board" rather than in her old assignment.

They wanted a safer plant—guards in place on the saws, knives sharpened, freedom to go to the doctor when injured. They wanted to be able to negotiate the line speed, which Sanderson now can raise at will. The list went on and on, and they hadn't even spelled out pension and wage demands yet.

The union and company negotiators met three times before the deadline. The local even offered to extend the contract. But the company offered no response or counterproposal, claiming that the demands were so numerous and overwhelming that they didn't know where to start. "We had a union here for six years and we were never accused of anything like this," Sanderson, Jr., told me. "We really don't know what's going on." There was agreement to change the notorious rule allowing only three trips to the bathroom a week, but little else. The union's strike vote was overwhelmingly approved.

Then, the day before the contract expired, Little Joe pulled out his big guns. He called each shift into a meeting and ominously threatened that all strikers would be replaced immediately, starting with the better-paying "upgrade" jobs. Then he asked anyone who had questions to come into his office individually. The threat seemed to have cowed many of the second-shift workers, judging from the numbers who later crossed the picket line. But on the first shift, Magee stood up and asked Sanderson why people couldn't ask their questions in the group so everyone could hear the answers. Sanderson blew up, told Magee to sit down and shut up, and threatened to throw him in jail. Soon afterward, police were seen in the building.

"That was the most important speech he made," Magee said later. "The people said if he threatens to put the president in jail, then we better go out."

The next day, three union leaders led out the day-shift strikers. The union estimates that roughly eighty workers refused to strike. Since then six strikers have returned, and Sanderson Farms has hired enough —many of them reportedly white—to run one shift. Negotiations continued but broke off in June. In May the National Labor Relations Board issued a complaint charging the company with bargaining in bad faith. More appeals and other delaying tactics can be expected as the company follows the advice of its law firm—Kullmann, Lang, Inman and Bee, one of the oldest, most established union-busters in the South. The company was also assessed a penalty for violating the child labor laws by hiring a 13-year-old strikebreaker.

In the spring of 1979 a petition was circulated to decertify the union. Circumstantial evidence suggests that the company was actively involved. Since there was already a charge of unfair labor practices, the vote can't proceed, but the company recently announced that it was no longer recognizing the union as a bargaining agent and gave its strike-breaking employees a raise of 20 cents an hour.

TO GAIN GREATER LEVERAGE AGAINST SANDERSON FARMS, THE International Chemical Workers (ICW) tried to organize the one Sanderson Farms plant without a union in Hazelhurst, Mississippi. (The plant in Louisiana has a Food and Commercial Workers local.) Robert Chinn, president of a Jackson ICW local and a civil rights movement veteran, was sent in to organize, and soon a small committee had union authorization cards signed by 130 of the 199 workers. But the onslaught from the company and its consultants was overwhelming. Workers were deluged in the plant with antiunion leaflets. If the union came in, they read, "You could lose some of your present benefits, your pay could be cut, your job could be eliminated, you could end up with *less* than you presently have. . . . Don't take a chance—vote to keep what you already have. Keep the union out of the plant." There was another leaflet about four plants in Mississippi—*"all four* had unions—*all four* are now *closed.* . . . Vote for *real job security.* Vote *NO!"* The specter of strikes—such as the one in Laurel—was raised repeatedly: "The plain truth is that while Chemical Workers Union members suffer on picket lines, often losing their homes, cars, and other possessions, the union bosses live high on the members' dues and fees money." In another leaflet, the union's way was described as "your way to work blocked by pickets—picket line violence, hate, and intimidation. . . . Part of your paycheck to be spent as the union sees fit. . . . Loss of freedom as an individual to handle your own affairs." And in a final reminder, a black worker speaks out on one leaflet titled "Don't Make a Mistake": "I'm voting *no* union for my family and myself. . . . I'm voting *no* dues, *no* strikes, *no* fines, *no* violence, *NO* UNION!"

The union organizing committee emphasized its commitment to needs expressed in a worker survey: wages, insurance, machine repair, control of overtime, more vacations. But the company determined that the workers' weak point was fear of a strike, and they hammered away on the theme. Management showed antiunion films and held propaganda meetings, excluding union committee members whenever possible. There were individual talks with employees. There was a promise of a raise of 50 cents an hour (which turned out to be only 20 cents). And there were the lightly veiled threats, such as the message rubber-stamped on the final paycheck before the balloting: "A Strike Will Stop This Check." The union lost 101 to 85, the third defeat at Hazelhurst.

WHY, WORKING UNDER SUCH CONDITIONS, DO WORKERS REJECT A union or cross a picket line? Chinn blames "harassment and the lack of knowledge about unionism" for the defeat. Many of the workers were poor country people who had never had another factory job. They were both grateful for what they had and scared of something that seemed unknown. "I think a lot of the people are old and just don't know anything about a union," organizing committee member Charlene Tanner said. "A lot of them grandmas just don't want to listen to what you have to say if you're young." But in Laurel many of the strikebreakers are the younger workers, new to the job and desperate for some money to support their babies.

Beulah Ramsey, 48, another Hazelhurst union backer with twenty years' experience in the factory, blamed ignorance and inexperience: "They're satisfied 'cause it's more money than they've ever made. They don't know what a union is. Some can't even read or write. And some of 'em just love Little Joe. They'd just be clapping for Master Joe." The old deference of blacks to whites, of serfs to lords, and of women to men has not passed from the Mississippi scene, despite the victories of the civil rights movement. Many of the workers at the Sanderson Farms plants come from tiny towns and isolated rural homes, not even from larger towns like Laurel, with a population of around 23,000. Workers compare the New South industrial plants to the Old South plantations. "Little Joe always used the term, 'These are my people,' " Jordan said. "That's a plantation phrase. He sincerely believes that."

"There are still a lot of people who believe the white man is supreme," says George Freeman, the international union director of community relations who has worked with the local since last fall. "They say, 'I can't cross Master Joe. He been good to me. He gave me a job.' But the day comes when they can't produce and they'll be gone."

The plantation tradition shows up in the way the warp of sexuality weaves in with the woof of coercion to form a blanket of social control. Many of the mainly white male supervisors and foremen make sexual advances toward the younger women or those seen as more vulnerable, fostering loyalties to management and attempts to cater to the supervisors, workers charge. Many times, various women said, foremen would put their arms around them, caress them, or play up to them sexually as a way of countering resentment of discipline or of persuading workers to accept orders. "It's a big thing for some people in the plant for a white man to put his hands on them," Jordan said. "They hug and pet on them and rub on them—and then they forget the grievance."

Strikers repeatedly explained the behavior of the scabs as a result of deference, ignorance, and fear—of economic hardship, but also of the

violence that has flared in the area. "There are people in there who believe whatever the boss tells them," Alice Musgrove complained as she sat on the picket line. "If he says the union is keeping them from getting a raise, they believe him."

"Most people down here are kinda scared of unions," Magee explained. "They feel if you start organizing the man will fire you. Now people if they got a job feel it's the only one they can get. Most of the strikebreakers say they've got a car note, a color TV note. They also say you can't make Joe move. They felt like they had to work, and they couldn't work anywhere else."

Lack of education and lack of experience beyond their community also make many workers, especially women on their first job, extremely unconfident. "Most of those people are illiterate," Jordan said of the people crossing the picket line. "They don't know how to read and understand. You explain it all to them and they seem to get nervous, frightened, shaking like a leaf on a tree. It comes from not being able to understand, to read."

Not all of the strikebreakers are hostile to the union, but some don't understand the importance of solidarity. "What they was doing was right and I knew it," Verlina Forthner, 21, a striker who returned to the job, said about the union. "But the company kept hiring and I was afraid I'd lose my job. I thought the union demands was fair. I hope they win and get what they want. I think unions are okay, but I don't see any sense in having a union in Mississippi because of the right-to-work law."

ALTHOUGH THE UNION IS CHARGING SANDERSON FARMS WITH UNFAIR labor practices in the Hazelhurst election, it has temporarily lost that means of pressuring management. With the Laurel plant still operating as of the summer of 1979, the immediate hopes were that many of the strikebreakers were kids who would go back to school in the fall and cause new labor supply problems for Little Joe. They have also launched, with the support of the AFL-CIO, a national boycott of Miss Goldy brand chickens. And they have joined in sporadically with a makeshift local coalition of civil rights activists.

There hasn't been strong support from the black community, which has a long tradition of disunity and political bickering. Only a few ministers have publicly backed the strikers, leading to some bitterness. "My preacher said he ain't got no time," Grace Stevens, 37, said, "and I haven't been to services since. If the preachers had asked people to stay out of the plant, I believe they would have."

Critics of the labor leadership, such as Ken Lawrence, claim that the union efforts are really halfhearted: "I think it's partly because the majority of union members in the state are black and that poses a threat to the old guard of union leadership, which is white." Although some white union leaders, such as AFL-CIO state president Claude Ramsey, have supported the civil rights movement since the 1960s, many young black union activists and progressive politicians share Lawrence's sentiment, chiding the labor movement for timidity and lack of aggressive plans for organizing and for political influence. Many of these heirs of the civil rights traditions see such a revived labor movement as a leading mechanism for black progress. Some leaders, however, notably Charles Evers, the mayor of Fayette who sprang to prominence after the assassination of his brother Medgar, are antiunion.

Union leaders tend to blame antiunion consultants and the failure of labor law reform for many of their difficulties, but unions have managed nonetheless to establish themselves in all sections of Mississippi. In every major town the biggest industry is organized, presumably a solid point of departure for tackling the tough small shops.

The battle against Sanderson Farms will probably take more than victories in the courts and before the National Labor Relations Board—and even more than determination by the strikers—if the union is to win. It will take pressure from the community, from progressive forces around the state, and from the broader labor movement and its supporters. Already the strikers see their actions linked to others' lives. Alice Musgrove says, "Those places will say if Joe can get away working people the way he does, then why can't we?"

There is much to be overcome not only in the opposition from on high but also in the culture of those held down below. But struggles such as those at Laurel and Hazelhurst, the penetration of unions into the life of communities throughout the state, and the conviction of many blacks that their progress now lies with the labor movement all suggest that the future for the labor movement in Mississippi may not be as bleak as it now looks.

Ella Sheehan, 25, mother of two, a worker at Sanderson Farms for five years, has no regrets about her decision to strike—despite the hardship—and no hesitations about the value of a union: "I made up my mind," she said. "I'm not going back in without a contract. It would be like slavery. I feel a lot different being out here from being up there treated like a dog. It makes me want to fight harder, even for my kids, because they'll have to work. It makes me feel good to have gone out on strike."

POSTSCRIPT, 1980: FIFTEEN MONTHS LATER, SANDERSON FARMS WAS still processing chickens, 65,000 per day instead of the usual 85,000 according to the company, on one shift instead of two. But the strikers were also gaining much-needed support, through the Committee for Justice in Mississippi, which counts the Southern Christian Leadership Conference, the United Auto Workers, and the National Organization for Women among more than 150 endorsers. On May 17, 1980, 1,500 people with ICW president Frank Martino and SCLC president Joseph Lowery in the lead marched 5.6 miles through Laurel, chanting "We can't take it no more."

TWENTY-EIGHT

Cotton: The Fiber You Can Trust

EARL DOTTER

THROUGHOUT THE MISSISSIPPI Delta in late October, a sense of tranquility settles over the landscape. An endless white carpet stretches out across the fields, thickening nearest to the levees of the meandering Mississippi River. Cotton is everywhere, ready to be harvested.

It is easy to imagine legions of black slave families gathering in the crop over a century ago. They are gone now, and their sharecropping tenant farmer offspring are almost gone as well. In 1948, a cotton grower in Bolivar County, Mississippi, used 105 sharecropper families to plant and harvest 2,500 acres of cotton. By 1978, fifteen tractor and cottonpicking machine drivers and six laborers did the same work. The mixed blessing of minimum wage laws and advances in mechanization in the early sixties had all but eradicated the sharecropper system with its thousands of laborers needed for the harvest. Joblessness in the Delta forced families to seek work in the cities and led many into the civil rights movement. "Hands that pick cotton can now pick our public officials," read a voter registration poster of the time.

Ironically, nearly all of the few remaining handpickers work on black-owned land. The black farmer generally cultivates a smaller parcel and finds it more difficult to invest in costly mechanical pickers. Growers with large landholdings also still occasionally employ schoolage children to harvest the cotton missed by the machine as it turns at the end of a row. The use of child labor was and still is encouraged in Mississippi because no compulsory public education law has ever been enacted there. With the competition from the machines the meager wages paid in years past have now been reduced to a pittance. It takes an adult with years of experience from sunrise to sunset to pick two hundred pounds of cotton, for which he or she receives approximately eight dollars.

"Cotton: the fiber you can trust, the fiber of choice, of versatility, of profit." These words come easily from growers, brokers, and stockholders in the Cotton Belt, but as we see in these faces from the Bolivar harvest in 1978, the benefits don't come quite so easily to everybody who lives and works in the Delta.

TWENTY-NINE

Cotton Dust Kills, and It's Killing Me

MIMI CONWAY

WHEN A HAND TRUCK FILLED WITH yarn smashed Jesse Hawkins's rib, his employer, J. P. Stevens and Company, didn't even send him to the doctor. The 55-year-old black man had to go on his own. Hawkins's personal physician, Dr. R. E. Frazier, was also designated by J. P. Stevens to examine any of its Roanoke Rapids workers hurt on the job.

Dr. Frazier told Hawkins to wear a ladies' girdle and wrote him a medical slip saying he could do a full day's work. Hawkins, who was spitting up blood, went to the local hospital for an x-ray. The results were sent to Dr. Frazier, who told Hawkins, "Jesse, I'm glad you didn't have a broken rib. Go back to work. Tough it out as best you can."

Hawkins, who was still coughing up blood and getting no satisfaction from either his doctor or the company, stopped by the local office of the Amalgamated Clothing and Textile Workers Union. The union made an appointment for Hawkins at Duke University Medical Center, where doctors found Jesse Hawkins had a broken upper rib and a blood cancer that weakens the bones. "At J. P. Stevens, they put people back to work that is sick and they know that they're sick," Hawkins said. "If you can't do nothing but sit around, they let you sit around to keep from paying compensation. And all Dr. Frazier was interested in was that big sign they have outside the mill saying 'three million man-hours with no lost-time accident.' "

In terms of cost to the company, accidents such as Hawkins's represent minuscule outlays of cash compared with the costs of occupational disease. Both J. P. Stevens and its workers' compensation carrier, Liberty Mutual Insurance Company, know the bald statistics: the average occupational disease case is 50 percent more expensive than the average accident case.

Jessie Hawkins filed a claim against Stevens and Liberty Mutual to get workers' compensation for the rib he broke. And he is filing another claim as well, for Jesse Hawkins had only 59 percent of his breathing capacity. Hawkins has the classic symptoms of byssinosis, or brown lung, a disease caused by excessive exposure to cotton dust, a crippling respiratory illness that has permanently and totally disabled 35,000 former textile workers. In addition, 150,000—or 19 percent— of the 800,000 textile workers in this country have some degree of byssinosis. Of these, so far only 167 brown lung victims have received workers' compensation benefits.

While he was still able, Jesse Hawkins could be found most Wednesday afternoons at the weekly meetings of the Roanoke Rapids chapter of the Carolina Brown Lung Association. In the year before his death in 1978, Jesse Hawkins had joined forces with other disabled mill workers in the CBLA's fight since 1975 to clean up the mills and win compensation for workers disabled with brown lung.

The organization, which originally was made up mostly of retired workers, was the primary educator and organizer of textile workers in the area of their own occupational health. Today, the CBLA membership in a dozen chapters in the Carolinas includes active and partially disabled mill workers. In some locations, such as Roanoke Rapids, they are members as well of the Amalgamated Clothing and Textile Workers Union, which is also working for occupational safety and health in the mills.

Erwin, North Carolina, the "denim capital of the world," is, like Roanoke Rapids, the site of a CBLA chapter. Nearly everyone in Erwin has worked in the giant red-brick Burlington mill that spews America's favorite cloth round the clock. But the largest single maker of denim also produces a lot of brown lung victims. By Burlington Industries' own count, 141 workers in this mill had the classic symptoms of byssinosis in 1971. In a company-wide survey that year, Burlington found that 460 workers in nineteen Burlington-owned mills had symptoms of the disease.

Unlike J. P. Stevens, which is the target of a nationwide consumer boycott because of its antiunion, antiworker policies and practices, Burlington Industries leads the textile industry not only in profits but in reputation. Burlington is particularly proud of its medical surveillance program instituted in December 1970, after Dr. Harold ("Bud") Imbus came to Burlington to head its medical department. No other textile company has come close to Burlington in studying byssinosis among its workers.

Burlington built its public image as a fighter against byssinosis largely on its 1971 study of 10,133 employees exposed to cotton dust. The Burlington study established that 18 percent of the 1,266 workers in the preparation departments, the dustiest mill areas, had "classic byssinosis symptoms." The study also showed that 4.5 percent of all the workers tested had byssinosis. A 1976 Burlington study, according to Dr. Imbus, showed that out of a sample of 12,519 employees, 1.09 percent had byssinosis. Dr. Imbus explained the reduction: "A number of employees have been compensated, a number have left, and a number who had the symptoms have been transferred." He also accounted for the drop by saying, "The number who have the symptoms has gone down, quite simply because of a lowering of the dust levels."

Some of the Burlington employees examined by Dr. Imbus in his 1971 study think the issue is not that simple. One is Linnie Mae Bass.

On April 26, 1977, the second anniversary of the CBLA, Bass, president of the Erwin CBLA chapter, and a delegation of fifty CBLA members traveled to Washington, D.C., to testify at public hearings held by the Department of Labor's Occupational Safety and Health Administration (OSHA) on the proposed cotton dust standard.

As the phalanx of old and disabled mill workers began their slow procession to the witness table, cameras whirred and ranged over the lined faces, the two wheelchairs, the denim overalls, the respirator, the two oxygen tanks. And still cameras snapped at the buttons each member of the delegation wore: a large brown one reading "Cotton Dust Kills" and a smaller yellow one which said "And It's Killing Me."

The delegation from the Roanoke Rapids chapter had brought with them a photograph of one of the chapter's officers, Louis Harrell, a disabled J. P. Stevens worker. The picture showed a big, angry man with clumps and tangles of cotton covering his cap and shirt. They also brought with them a tape recording of the faint voice of their brother, who was too ill to testify in person. The recorder clicked on:

My name is Louis Harrell. The last thirteen years I have been having trouble breathing. I seem to be getting worse and worse. I can't lay down and rest without oxygen in the night. My doctor told me not to go back in there under any circumstances.

They let you quit. They don't try to find you a job, and that shouldn't be that way. They should be bound by some kind of law that if a man works on one job for thirty years, he should get to work for so many hours. There isn't any way in the world that I could start somewhere else and work my way up.

I think the law or the government or somebody should make a law that if a man has to transfer out of a place because he is sick, he should be given at least pay on a regular basis until he either gets better or retires. He shouldn't be penalized as much as he has to suffer for being sick from the dust thing.

The recorder shut off.

When it was her turn to speak, Linnie Mae Bass cleared her throat and said:

The denim that made blue jeans for you has made brown lung for us. I worked for Burlington Industries for twenty years in the spooling and warping department until I was forced to retire because I couldn't get my breath. I had to come out of the mills seventeen years earlier than I should have. Right now my breathing is only 28 percent normal.

Mill workers are scared. They are scared of losing their jobs. They are even scared to admit that they are sick, because I was myself until I knew.

We never knew about our rights to compensation for an occupational disease. Definitely the companies have never told us about this disease. You cannot trust the company to do their own education of the people. They cannot be trusted to do their own medical tests. Even Dr. Imbus, Burlington's famous company doctor, cannot be trusted. It has been the Brown Lung Association and not the company that has been educating the people about this disease.

As she talked, Bass was oblivious to her photogenic attraction to the cotton industry, but Jerry Armour, a photographer for the National Cotton Council of America, dressed in a synthetic blue jean suit lined in red, white, and blue, snapped her picture again and again.

Asked why he had been flown from the Cotton Council's Tennessee headquarters to take pictures of the CBLA members, Armour answered, "To show what we're up against." He added, "We're using stills, color slides, and 16-millimeter film. We're going to put together a presentation and show it at the Cotton Growers Association, various board of directors meetings, the National Cotton Council, of course, and to textile manufacturers. We'll probably show it to people like Burlington Industries."

I interviewed Dr. Imbus at Burlington's headquarters in Greensboro, North Carolina. Sitting in was Burlington's Manager of Community Relations, Dick Byrd, who was taking notes on me taking notes on Dr. Imbus.

Dr. Imbus referred to a sheaf of papers as he told me that the Erwin chapter of the CBLA had not been truthful in their testimony at the cotton dust hearings. I asked what he was reading from. He told me that material had been prepared "in house" relating to the public statements of disabled Burlington workers. When I requested a copy, Imbus told me that Burlington was not yet ready to release the information publicly.

A few months later, Dr. Imbus submitted to OSHA a rebuttal of the testimony of disabled Burlington workers on behalf of the American Textile Manufacturers Institute, Inc. According to Imbus, the testimony of the Erwin chapter of the CBLA "contains distortions, half-truths, and outright falsehoods." Imbus came down hard on Linnie Mae Bass: "It is clear that the individual was advised of the results of every single examination and evaluation that was made regarding her breathing problems."

Few reporters were present in the makeshift courtroom in the small North Carolina town of Lillington on the sizzling July 1977 morning when Linnie Mae Bass had her workers' compensation hearing for brown lung.

The hearing was held during the one week of annual vacation that the Erwin mill is closed, and the courtroom was filled with mill workers, many of them disabled with breathing problems. Bass's fellow CBLA members had traveled from Roanoke Rapids and Greensboro to attend the hearing.

Dr. Imbus, subpoenaed by Bass's lawyer, took the stand. Before the lawyer for Liberty Mutual, Burlington's compensation carrier, moved to strike it from the record, Dr. Imbus verified his signature on a 1971 document stating that Bass had irreversible byssinosis.

"Did you tell Mrs. Bass she had byssinosis?" her attorney, Charles Hassell, Jr., asked the doctor.

"No," replied Dr. Imbus.

"Why not?"

"I did not tell *anyone* they had byssinosis. I have assiduously avoided making a diagnosis of byssinosis for anyone. I have relied on outside consultants to make the diagnosis."

"Did you tell Mrs. Bass the results of her test?" her attorney asked.

"I told her that her breathing was abnormally low. To me that is making the results of her test available. I did not give her the detailed results."

Hassell asked again why the company doctor, a recognized byssinosis expert, did not tell Mrs. Bass she had byssinosis when he first learned it in 1971. Imbus, flustered, answered: "Because that word was not known then, nor was brown lung."

"What exactly did you tell her?" the lawyer persisted.

"I said, your breathing capacity was not what we would expect of a person of your height and weight. She was unable to move the air in and out of her lungs. I told her there was some question of the dust." Then Imbus testified that Bass's breathing capacity in 1971 was "51 percent of predicted normal."

The mill workers in the courtroom, many of them coughing and wheezing, did not take their eyes off Dr. Imbus as he ticked off the results of Bass's breathing tests in successive years: 48 percent in 1973; 44 percent in 1974; and in 1975, the year she had to leave the mill totally disabled, 41 percent.

One person not looking at Dr. Imbus was Linnie Mae Bass, who sat with her hand cupping her eyes, shaking her head as she listened to the Burlington doctor confirm under oath what she had contended all along.

OTHER ERWIN MILL WORKERS TESTED AND FOUND TO HAVE "CLASSIC symptoms" of byssinosis in 1971 are making charges against the mill, and they have documentation for what they say. Talbert Faircloth, one of these workers, received no compensation when he was forced to retire because of his breathing disability. Burlington did not even do the necessary paperwork that would have made compensation possible.

Dora Faircloth spoke publicly about her husband's case at a North Carolina Insurance Commission hearing on the insurance industry's requested 28.4 percent rate hike on workers' compensation:

About a year after Talbert came out of the mill [in 1971], the plant nurse and the personnel man came out to our house and wanted him to sign a bunch of papers. They said that there might be some money in it for him. They came to the house four times, but they never told him what it was for.

I thought this was fishy, so [in 1973] I wrote to the Industrial Commission to see if Talbert might be eligible for workers' compensation. They said that in order to get compensation, the mill would have had to turn in a Form 19 report on Talbert. The Industrial Commission said that they didn't have any record of a report ever being turned in. Back when Talbert had to leave the mill, we never knew nothing about this Form 19.

Dora Faircloth told the Insurance Commission that her husband learned this past summer that Burlington did not file the Form 19 until September 17, 1976, five years after Faircloth left the mill. The document was signed by the Erwin plant's personnel manager directly above the bold print at the bottom of the form reading: LAW REQUIRES REPORT TO BE FILED WITHIN FIVE DAYS AFTER KNOWLEDGE OF ACCIDENT."

Dora Faircloth, irate, asked North Carolina Insurance Commissioner John Ingram, "Did Burlington ever file a report on these [other] 140 people? We think that they didn't. They were covering up [in 1971] and they are covering up now. That is how they cover up brown lung and that is how they keep down their insurance rates by breaking the law."

This time Burlington was more guarded in its response to the charges leveled against it. Of Dora Faircloth's statement, the company said, "We can neither confirm nor deny the accuracy of these claims."

A few days after Dora Faircloth spoke publicly on her husband's case, she was at his side in court as Liberty Mutual and Burlington Industries continued their battle against Talbert's compensation. "I guess they are stalling and stalling until he dies so they won't have to pay him a penny," she said. As it happened, Dora Faircloth, who had also worked in the mill, died before her husband's final hearing. Talbert, still in mourning, relied on the moral support of fellow members of the CBLA when he presented the evidence which won his case.

Until cases like Talbert Faircloth's came to light, according to CBLA, the mill companies routinely shunted disabled workers with brown lung to social security, where disability only—and the liability of the employer—is considered in determining that disability payments should be made. A recent Department of Labor policy study confirmed this. It found that only 2 percent of workers disabled with an occupational disease were receiving payment from the workers' compension system that had been created to serve that purpose automatically. Fully 43 percent of these workers, people like Talbert Faircloth, had to depend on social security disability payments.

The same study reported that today over 2.8 million disabled workers and 2 million dependents draw social security disability insurance. In 1978 alone, benefit payments were $13 billion. Significantly, this cost is paid by the American taxpayer, not the textile manufacturer or the mill companies' workers' compensation carrier.

The odds against a byssinosis victim or any other worker with an occupational disease winning a compensation award are enormous. According to the Department of Labor, of the 1.8 million disability payments awarded through the compensation system, only 30,000 were for occupational diseases. In fact, the Department of Labor found, less than 3 percent of all workers' compensation disability awards are for occupational diseases. Yet 100,000 Americans die annually as a result of occupational disease, according to the National Institute of Occupational Safety and Health (NIOSH). In addition, 846,000 Americans were permanently and totally disabled as a result of occupational disease in 1978 alone, and an additional 1,534,000 workers were partially disabled that year, also as a result of workplace disease.

THE CRISIS TODAY IN UNCOMPENSATED AND UNDERCOMPENSATED occupational diseases is as severe as the situation at the turn of the century when an unconscionable proliferation of the maimed bodies and sundered limbs of American workers caused a national scandal that prompted passage of state workers' compensation laws. S. B. Black, a past president of Liberty Mutual Insurance Company, recalled the reform spirit of the early twentieth century in an interview he gave in 1950: "I think the philosophy back of workmen's compensation laws was that injury was almost a normal by-product of work, and that

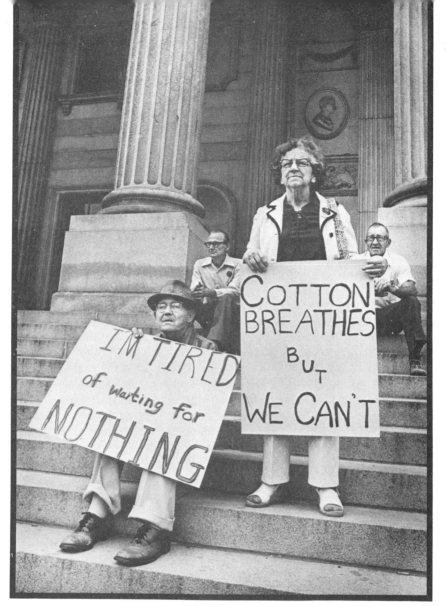

Protest on the Columbia, South Carolina, Capitol steps

perhaps there wasn't very much that could be done about it. Therefore, industry should assume a fair share of the loss that the injured employee sustains.''

Liberty Mutual Insurance Company, today the nation's largest workers' compensation carrier and the carrier for 70 percent of the textile industry, grew out of the 1912 Massachusetts law which made workers' compensation insurance mandatory. The first stockholders of the company were the leading Massachusetts industrialists of the day, many of them cotton textile manufacturers. The industrialists had another motive besides a humane response to the immense toll taken on the life and limb of American workers: they needed to protect their pockets from costly liability suits. The workers' compensation system offered an orderly no-fault method of compensating injured workers through state industrial commissions.

In return, the workers' compensation laws took away the worker's right to sue the employer outside the state-administered system, thereby eliminating the possibility of enormously expensive liability suits. From the beginning, workers' compensation was linked to wages earned. Today in North Carolina, in cases of total disability, disabled workers can collect only 66.6 percent of their weekly wages, not to exceed $80 a week. And textile mill workers are the lowest-paid industrial workers in America—by $75 a week less than the average factory worker.

Because the worker's compensation law limits the worker's right to sue an employer, many states protect the worker's right to sue third parties. Omry Glenn of Columbia, South Carolina, a member of the CBLA and a diagnosed byssinosis victim, was the first brown lung victim to do so. In his million-dollar suit, Glenn sued the manufacturer of the mill machinery and ventilation system for "negligence, recklessness, and willfulness" for designing equipment in such a way that it would "create dust and/or chemicals" causing Glenn to become "permanently disabled." Glenn's attorney, Ronald Motley, said, "If the insurance carrier undertook to advise the company on safety, we're going to sue them, too." Glenn and Motley were forced to drop the suit when the court ruled against them on a preliminary point, but the CBLA quickly initiated other suits against insurance carriers and medical directors.

Dr. Arthur Larson—a professor of law at Duke University, a leading authority on workers' compensation, and an Undersecretary of Labor to the Eisenhower administration—has written, "By failing to keep compensation benefits up to the standards and needs of the times, great pressure has built up for supplementing compensation benefits in other ways." Discussing the nationwide trend toward suing insurance carriers, Dr. Larson noted (in his treatise on workers' compensation) that "what really set off alarm bells" was the 1961 case in which the Illinois Supreme Court "upheld a judgment of $1,569,400 against a carrier based on a negligent performance of a gratuitous safety inspection. Perhaps the sheer size of the judgment added to the shock." Larson also pointed out that the case stands as "a clear decision without dissent that a compensation carrier can be made liable as a third party in tort for negligence in safety inspection. After this case, suits against insurance carriers appeared in jurisdiction after jurisdiction."

Of course, the insurance industry is not taking this lying down. In countermoves, state legislatures—New Hampshire's, for example— have amended portions of the workers' compensation law so that insurance companies are exempt from liability as third parties. As Dr. Larson noted wryly in an interview, "When it comes to legislature, insurance companies are no slouches." In North Carolina, the insurance industry lobby, the largest and most effective in the state, spent $40,865 in 1977 on legislation to reduce Insurance Commissioner John Ingram's power.

LIBERTY MUTUAL'S VULNERABILITY TO THIRD-PARTY SUITS STEMS FROM its participation in the 1971 Burlington byssinosis survey. The insurance company's role came to light in testimony given at the cotton dust hearings by Dr. Moon W. Suh, senior operations research analyst for Burlington Industries. Dr. Suh testified that Liberty Mutual conducted the sampling of cotton dust levels in nineteen Burlington mills that "constituted the data base" for the study. Russell Van Houten, Liberty Mutual's director of field services, confirmed that the company had conducted extensive cotton dust testing "at least as far back as 1968."

Liberty Mutual offered its services as safety inspector in testing cotton dust levels to other companies as well. About five years ago, Liberty Mutual did the "raw cotton dust testing" in Cone's twenty-two plants producing cotton fabric. Dr. Theodore H. Hatfield, J. P. Stevens's first medical director, appointed in 1976, said that "Liberty Mutual was instrumental in encouraging the company to bring me here." Hatfield said that Stevens had "twenty-seven or twenty-eight plants that have significant exposure to cotton dust."

And Samuel Griggs, who heads Stevens's dust sampling program out of its Environmental Services Laboratory in Piedmont, South Carolina, said: "Before we were not encouraged and not required to do tests. We used to depend almost entirely on Liberty Mutual. We'd call them up and ask, 'How do we get out of trouble?' I mean, if we thought we had a problem as far as cotton dust goes. We'd tell Liberty Mutual, 'We'd like for you to come in,' and they'd come in and survey the plant. They'd do an overall survey." Griggs stopped talking suddenly, then said, "This doesn't connect with labor, does it? We're not supposed to talk about labor."

If occupational health and labor relations are not linked in the mind of Stevens's environmental safety personnel, top-level Stevens management does make the connection. Even as Samuel Griggs talked, Joseph Jelks, Stevens vice-president in charge of industrial relations, was winging to Boston for a high-level meeting with Liberty Mutual. Jelks is on Liberty Mutual's advisory board for South Carolina. Half the members of Liberty Mutual's North Carolina and South Carolina advisory boards are top textile executives.

Before his company was sued in a $15 million class-action suit in October 1979, Liberty Mutual president Melvin B. Bradshaw did not seem aware that his company was vulnerable to third-party suits resulting from possible negligence in serving as a safety inspector in the mills. Bradshaw said: "Our vulnerability is covered by law. It is totally unthinkable that the carrier that is asked to uncover hazards is then sued for it." In a telephone interview in the spring of 1977, when asked if Liberty Mutual felt any obligation to inform endangered Burlington workers that it had found dusty conditions in Burlington mills, Bradshaw seemed impervious to the suggestion: "I don't believe it is our prerogative to give employees this information. We do this work strictly as a consultant to the company. I'm sure we told Burlington." He added: "If they are working in the mills, they must know it's dangerous. To what extent it's dangerous, I don't know."

In his class-action suit against Liberty Mutual and Burlington Industries as well as Dr. Harold Imbus, plaintiff David Burdette, who had worked in Burlington's F. W. Poe plant in Greenville, South Carolina, charges that Burlington defrauded employees of workers' compensation benefits when they became too sick to work. The suit also alleges that Burlington knew that its employees would eventually be disabled as a result of "the dangerous and excessive levels of cotton dust" that Liberty Mutual found as part of its regular safety inspections prior to 1970.

A number of congressional hearings have been held to examine the question of whether the present workers' compensation system is adequate to deal with byssinosis claims in the Carolinas. One who thinks it is not is Ernest Hollings, U.S. senator from South Carolina, where the state motto is "While I Breathe, I Hope." Hollings introduced a brown lung measure in the Senate; U.S. Representative Phillip Burton had introduced a byssinosis bill in the House in February 1977.

The Hollings bill had its inception at a meeting of the South Carolina chapters of the CBLA with the South Carolina congressional delegation in April 1977, immediately after they testified at the cotton dust hearings. Senator Strom Thurmond told his constituents with brown lung: "You all speak out now! We *want* to hear from you people!" The CBLA needed no prompting.

The delegation told the senators and congressmen that J. H. ("Hub") Spires, the first president of the association, had been buried the day before, his lungs so riddled with disease that his doctors could not risk a necessary operation. Lonnie Moore, then president of the Spartanburg chapter, got right to the point:

We want the mills to clean up or ship out. One of the two. If they had wanted to put in cleaner equipment, they would have done it by now. I've been in there for forty-six years, and they still haven't cleaned it up.

Now I've got a hurting all across my body. I just hurt all over. My last day in there, at Mount Vernon Mills, I got so sick I couldn't stand up. The company wouldn't even let me call an ambulance. The overseer wouldn't even call my wife for me. When I got on the phone to ask her to carry me to the hospital, my wife thought I was a child, my voice was so faint. When I got to the hospital, the doctor told me, "Your lung is full of fiber. Get out of that mill or make your funeral arrangements."

Looking at each of the politicians, Lonnie said, "Now *you* need our help just like we need your help. And we're telling you, we need some help *now*." Before the senators and congressmen could respond, the room was filled with shouts of "Amen!" "Amen, brother!" "Tell it like it is, Lonnie!"

Senator Hollings rose to his feet. "In old-time politics, you could always sneak into the mills and get the votes. I'd always come out coughing. And I had to carry a special campaign suit that wouldn't pick up lint. I've always wondered how you all did it. Maybe we should look at that black lung legislation and make a special bill like that for you. There may be some problems, but, one way or another, I'm going to introduce a bill to deal with compensation benefits and this OSHA question."

Interviewed after the meeting with the CBLA delegation, Senator Hollings said: "I can't say I didn't realize they had breathing problems before. I can't say I didn't know about conditions in the mills. But I'm tired of the indecisiveness. Something has to done for these people. If you work for fifty-three years in a cotton mill and end up on welfare, something's wrong."

I asked Hollings, the former governor of South Carolina, about the current drive for unionization of textile mills in the South. "There's no labor movement afoot in my state. But it seems to me that if these people don't get remedial action on this [brown lung issue], that would be reason to organize and have a union."

The next day, the North Carolina chapters of the CBLA went to the Capitol to visit their congressmen. Jesse Helms, U.S. senator and a leader of the conservative wing of the Republican party, addressed the group:

I think I can speak for the delegation in regard to Senator Hollings' bill. I want to say that we will carefully scrutinize it, and we will see how it can best be handled, whether by state or federal legislation.

You did the right thing coming up here. There are a lot of doors to money up here. Now don't be discouraged if one of these avenues doesn't work. There are lots of avenues. We will take whatever action is deemed proper to take, whether on the state or federal level. We will work to try to get relief for these people who have worked for so many years and have excessive medical expenses.

It's ironic the way priorities work in this country—that people like you who have built our country, who have never asked for a handout, are forced to spend a lot of time getting around technicalities to get compensation.

On his way out of the meeting, Senator Helms was stopped by a Charlotte, North Carolina, television reporter. Yes, he had time for an interview for the evening news. He stood before the camera and put an arm around Lucy Taylor, the first chairperson of the Carolina Brown Lung Association. "In all candor," Helms began, "extreme care must be exercised in connection with any brown lung legislation. I must say that this is fraught with complexity. But the bottom line is that we've got to arrive at some help for these people."

Helms kept Lucy Taylor in his embrace when it was her turn to speak. Lucy said, "The people have suffered for so long. Now I think we will get some help, which I think is wonderful. We've known them for a long time, and they have promised to help."

The moment was recorded. The camera turned off. Helms walked away. The CBLA officer was left standing there, her exhaustion beginning to show. The newscaster noticed and said sympathetically, "You must be tired."

Lucy nodded in assent, put her hand on her chest and said, "Talk, talk, talk."

IN THE 1960S, AREND BOUHUYS, A DUTCH PHYSICIAN AND PROFESSOR of epidemiology at Yale University Medical School, visited the South on a U.S. government grant to determine whether U.S. cotton mill workers, like cotton processors in the rest of the world, suffer from byssinosis when exposed to excessive amounts of cotton dust. Although byssinosis has been discussed in medical literature since 1705, the U.S. textile industry had successfully blocked research on the disease in this country by refusing access to the mills. Then Dr. Bouhuys found that a federal penitentiary in Atlanta, Georgia, had a cotton mill. Bouhuys tested the prison workers and found that 29 percent of them had byssinosis. He published his study in 1967; the following year, the U.S. government recognized the disease.

Despite the medical findings, the U.S. textile industry still denied the existence of byssinosis. The July 10, 1969, issue of the industry's *Textile Reporter* said that byssinosis was "a thing thought up by venal doctors who attended last year's International Labor Organization meetings in Africa where inferior races are bound to be afflicted by new diseases more superior people defeated years ago."

In 1970 the U.S. Department of Labor said that an estimated 100,000 U.S. workers had the disease. And in 1972, OSHA zeroed in on cotton dust as one of five hazardous workplace substances in its "Target Health Hazard Program." The same year, the then head of OSHA, George Guenther, made a proposal in a confidential memo in answer to then President Nixon's appeal for "responsiveness" on the part of government agencies to his reelection campaign. Guenther recommended that "no highly controversial standard [i.e. cotton dust] will be proposed through November 1972 as part of the program to promote the advantages of four more years of properly managed OSHA for use in the campaign." This OSHA scandal was uncovered in material subpoenaed during the Watergate hearings.

Very slowly, and in response to pressure, the textile industry has been forced to alter its stance on byssinosis. In November 1975 at a byssinosis hearing held at Wake Forest University in Winston-Salem, North Carolina, Dr. Harold Imbus, who at the time was Burlington's lobbyist at the North Carolina legislature as well as the medical director of the world's largest textile company, addressed the issue. He said, "I do think we presently have, even with our imperfect knowledge, a reasonable basis to provide compensation for victims of byssinosis." Dr. Imbus added: "However, the system is one of delicate balance. Too much resistance from employers will result in injustices, undercompensation. This then results in forces to correct this situation . . . and the end results then become more a matter of test of strength and political considerations with little consideration to the rights of employee or employer and perhaps with disastrous results."

One of the first members of the CBLA was Louis Harrell, who had worked in one of the dustiest areas of Stevens's Roanoke Rapids plant. "You know," Harrell told me in June 1976,

back before we heard what was wrong with us, people thought they just had asthma or something. That's what they said about my uncle. He worked in the card room all his life. And he had spells where he couldn't lay down for a week at a time on account of it was so hard for him to get his breath. He got a spell one day, though, and he felt so bad he wanted to lay down. They rested him down on the spinner, and that's where he died. They didn't know nothing about byssinosis in them days.

The first time I ever did hear it named was last year when the Carolina Brown Lung Association set up that health clinic. They tested me and found out I had a 63 percent breathing capacity. And that's tops for me. I've been tested at the Duke University Medical Center at only 60 percent.

As he talked, Harrell had a coughing attack followed by a frighteningly difficult time regaining his breath. "My chest feels like it's gonna bust. And you know how your arm feels when they take your blood pressure? Well, mine feels exactly like that. You know, there are people up in the mill that still thinks brown lung is a made-up thing," Harrell said. "There are people in there with it in almost as bad a shape as I am who think I'm putting on so I won't have to work."

Harrell, who began working in the mill when he was 13½, continued working for J. P. Stevens despite his breathing disability. "What I'm trying to do," he explained, "is hold off retiring till the union can get a pension plan out of Stevens. You know they're trying to work on that in these contract negotiations. But I don't think I can make it."

Shortly after I first spoke with him in 1976, Louis Harrell was carried out of the mill. He spent much of his long-awaited retirement battling J. P. Stevens and Liberty Mutual to win compensation for brown lung. He spent a lot of time, too, in and out of hospitals. Outside the room in the Halifax Memorial Hospital the sign read: OXYGEN IN USE. Inside, Louis Harrell was alone, staring out the window, weak and sick.

Louis, his voice barely a whisper, said,

You know that last day I was ever in the mill . . . I wasn't feeling too good. I was still having trouble getting my breath. Most of the times before, I could make it all right at work by sneaking out and getting some air or just getting near an air conditioner for a few minutes. That last day, I just couldn't make it at all. They had to carry me out.

After I left the mill, I went down to get my social security. They examined me down there. They run me through a pulmonary machine, the same like what we had at the brown lung clinic. They found enough wrong with me to say I was unable to work, and they gave me my social security compensation. They never did say nothing about my brown lung. They told me I had heart trouble, which I knew, but they didn't say what my doctor did, that it was from the strain because of my lungs.

I can't get to first base with my workers' compensation. It's so slow. I told you the doctor already told me I had brown lung, but the way they've got it rigged up here in North Carolina, one of these ten doctors the state says is brown lung experts have to tell you you've got it before the mill's insurance company will give you your money.

Guess who gets to pick which doctor you go to? The insurance company that's fighting you, that's who. You have to wait and wait until *they* decide to fix you up with an appointment.

Louis Harrell pulled himself up in his hospital bed and said, "That Liberty Mutual that [J. P. Stevens] got, they've stalled me and stalled me. They finally gave me an appointment with a doctor a hundred miles away. After I had already left home that morning to go over, they called my house. Do you know what they wanted to say? They'd canceled my appointment. Can you beat that?"

Harrell had a heart attack on the steps of the Duke University

Medical Center, where he'd gone to keep his rescheduled appointment. "So I never did get my lungs tested that time. Now Liberty Mutual is saying they'll get me another appointment when I'm well enough to go again." But his health deteriorated rapidly. One year and one day after he was officially retired, Louis had yet another breathing attack. That one was fatal.

At his funeral, the Roanoke Rapids chapter of the CBLA filed past the casket of their fallen brother. After the service, the funeral cortege wended through the streets of the town where the Harrell family had woven and spun, lived and died, since before the turn of the century. Family, friends, and members of the Carolina Brown Lung Association mournfully followed Louis Harrell's body on its last trip past the mills.

As he was being buried, in Washington the Department of Labor was announcing the promulgation of a cotton dust standard that allowed the textile industry an additional four years to reduce the levels of cotton dust in the mills. The Amalgamated Clothing and Textile Workers Union filed suit in the U.S. Court of Appeals in Washington, asserting that the new standard would fail to protect the health of workers. The American Textile Manufacturers Institute went to federal appeals court in Richmond, Virginia, in an attempt to block the new regulation, saying that it was highly inflationary and technologically impossible to meet in some parts of the mills.

In Raleigh other chapters of the Carolina Brown Lung Association met with reporters to express their dismay with the standard which they felt was too weak and which, in any case, they told the press, was too late for mill workers like Louis Harrell.

THIRTY

OSHA: Dynamite for Workers

CHIP HUGHES AND LEN STANLEY

NEXT TIME YOU OPEN A BAG OF Fritos or a pack of cigarettes, think about Marvin Gaddy. Marvin has worked in Olin Corporation's Film Division for over twenty years making cellophane wrapping for just about any product you can imagine. He can't see as well as he used to and still gets nightmares every once in a while. He's watched the lives of many men change after they came off his floor. For one man it got so bad he may have taken his own life. Others were luckier and got out with only minor nerve problems to remind them of what it was like up there.

Marvin works in the chemical building at Olin's Film Division near Brevard, North Carolina, on the edge of the Pisgah National Forest. Built in 1951, the Film Division produces viscose which is extruded, solidified, and dried to form cellophane. The second floor houses the xanthation process. Twelve massive barettes are kept in constant rotation, each mixing together seven to eight hundred pounds of ripened alkali cellulose (raw wood pulp and 16 percent caustic acid). Marvin used to add carbon disulfide (CS_2) to the rotating vats, which helped to quicken the process of breaking down the raw wood pulp into a liquid cellophane-like mixture. Nobody ever told Marvin and his fellow workers that the CS_2 could harm them. But they finally found out. Only then it was too late.

"A lot of people would leave," says Marvin.

The younger ones would come in there, work a few days, and then they'd invariably get a big whiff of CS_2. People would act real unusual, get headaches and think they were getting the flu. After a few overdoses, the nightmares would start coming on them. We'd go in and tell the company, "Dammit, you'd better do something about this CS_2 stuff." They'd tell us to get the hell out—"We don't need you. If you don't enjoy your job, then go home." Course we didn't have a union back then. And we didn't have Jimmy Reese rummaging through their trashcans and filing all those grievances and complaints.

James Reese is a maintenance man at the Olin plant and chairman of the union safety committee for Local 1971 of the United Paperworkers International Union (UPIU). He explains:

The thing about us mountain people is that we never had to depend on someone else for our livelihood. If a man didn't like it where he was working, he could get his gun and go out in the woods and get him something to eat.

Some people don't fear losing their jobs no way. They just like to fight, and this is what comes out of their tradition. They don't act like mill people, who are always being dependent on the bossman for jobs and food and houses and schools. People around here rely on themselves more. They're more willing to take chances and stand up.

Olin workers had to stand up and fight for more than thirty years before they got the union in. The battle left a trail of beaten-up organizers, fired union sympathizers, and heartbreaking, one-vote Labor Board election defeats. Finally, in 1971, the union won a contract which included a safety committee to monitor working conditions and the in-plant environment. For the past five years, James Reese has used the committee to help his fellow workers investigate numerous toxic substances: asbestos, carbon disulfide, formaldehyde, tetrahydrofuran, flax dust, noise, radiation, methyl bromide.

Now this OSHA thing that I'm into, I volunteered for this because it was mine from the word go. I had learned the OSHA standards even before we got our union organized, till I almost had them memorized. It represented a kind of challenge to me because I've seen some of the conditions up there and I've been hurt on the job myself. I'm not sure what set me off. I think it's just the fact that I'm a kind of militant type of character and this way, for once, I had something that they had to listen to. I finally had a law to back me up.

Congress passed the Williams-Steiger Occupational Safety and Health Act of 1970 in response to escalating on-the-job injury rates and intense pressure from national unions. The act created the OSHA Administration within the U.S. Labor Department, with the responsibility for inspecting the workplace for hazards and imposing penalties of up to $10,000 when unsafe conditions are uncovered. In addition, the act gives bold rights to affected workers to assist them in cleaning up their plants. It is these workers' rights which are the most important aspect of the law, because unions and employees cannot depend on the chronically understaffed and underfinanced OSHA Administration to initiate enforcement. Workers can now file a complaint requesting an unannounced inspection, accompany the OSHA inspector during his inspection, demand an investigation of potentially harmful substances, and even challenge the amount of time given a company to clean up recognized hazards.

For James Reese and the other members of Local 1971, OSHA has become more than another law or bureaucratic agency. It is a tool they can use to take matters into their own hands, a weapon they can hold to the company's head to force them to clean up unhealthy conditions.

I can just talk about getting an inspector in here and the company safety man will about go to shaking, trying to get things straightened out. Of course, it wasn't always that way around here. Back in September of '72, I heard from people that the company was gonna be doing these noise tests, so I went up there with them to see what was going on. This guy got on me pretty hot. He says, "You get out of here, you got no business in here." I says back, "I represent all the people in this union as their safety man." He kicked me out of there, but I filed a grievance on it. In the first two steps of the grievance procedure the company says that the contract does not allow that an employee can leave his work station at any time.

So then I got all fired up. I threatened to file charges with the federal government through OSHA on it. Well, that scared them, so they sent it up to the highest corporate levels. Pretty soon a letter comes back from the higher-ups saying that we can watch any of their tests and also get all the records of what they find. This was just great.

I don't know whether they realized it or not, but I was making a lot of records. That's what I was really after 'cause records have a way of kinda flying back in your face. And that's what I was doing, getting it down on paper to show what their real attitude is toward safety and health—in spite of those big awards they got plastered all over the cafeteria walls and their reputation as a safe company.

ALTHOUGH THE HAZARDS OF CARBON DISULFIDE EXPOSURE WERE recognized as early as 1851 in France, little has been written about the chemical in the United States. Both liquid and vapor are highly irritating to the skin, eyes, nose, and air passages. This local irritation, however, is overshadowed by the serious long-term effects on the body after the chemical has been absorbed through the skin and lungs. High concentrations rapidly affect the brain, causing loss of consciousness and even death. Lower concentrations may cause headaches and giddiness or lung and stomach irritation.

Prolonged repeated exposures to relatively low levels of CS_2 affect several parts of the body. Brain damage results in mental abnormalities such as depression, euphoria, agitation, hallucinations, and nightmares. Nerve injury can cause blindness when the optic nerve is involved or weakness of the arms and legs when peripheral nerves are inflamed.

In 1943, Dr. Alice Hamilton, a pioneer in occupational health in the United States, described the symptoms of CS_2 poisoning in her classic book *Exploring the Dangerous Trades.* After studying workers in the newly blossoming viscose rayon industry, she remarked that the men "knew that a distressing change had come over them, one they could not control. It spoiled life for them, it ruined their homes, it broke up friendships, it antagonized foremen and fellow workers, it made day and night miserable."

The reactions were the same three decades later. Working around the barettes is definitely the nastiest job on the second floor at Olin's chemical building. Nobody likes to do it, but it is essential to making cellophane. After an 800-pound batch of cellulose (wood pulp) is mixed up with the CS_2 for an hour and a half in the barettes, the syrup-like mixture drops down a floor to be aged. Following this mixing process, a vacuum sucks off most of the CS_2 fumes.

As Marvin Gaddy remembers:

Sometimes when we'd open those barettes, you get enough fumes to just about knock you out. We'd then take our scrapers and scrape out all that was stuck and there'd still be a lot of CS_2 in it.

The company had given us testing machines to measure the fumes, but they would only go up to 50 parts per million (ppm). The OSHA standard was at 20 ppm. I'd know that it'd be a lot higher, but there was no way to prove it. Everytime I'd file a grievance on the CS_2, I'd just mark it "50 ppm+." No telling how high it went. I filed over twenty grievances on it. Nothing happened.

One night I was scraping out a barette and a maintenance man was cleaning out a tank that pumps the CS_2. So he takes a gallon or so that was in there and dumps it in a garbage can right near me. And there wasn't enough water in the trash can to cover over all the CS_2 fumes. So the fumes is coming out real strong. I was very irritated and went on home. I didn't go to work the next day, 'cause I thought I'd taken the flu. My family doctor just said, "Go see the company doctor." So Dr. Ryan put me on observation for three months.

They kept me off my job for sixteen months after this thing. Management and the safety department said I couldn't go back to work. Now I'm on another floor; I can't go back there because of my eyes, really because of the CS_2. I've been trying for years to prove that my problems come from CS_2, but they've been fighting me. My eyes used to be 20/20. While I was working in there I began wearing glasses, but it got worse. One doctor told me the nerves in my eye started drawing the eyeball over to the side and getting it all out of focus.

I went to a Dr. Trantham down in Greenville. He said it was the most unusual case he'd ever seen. He said that if it's a cataract I got, then hold off for three years and the other eye will develop the exact same way the first one did. Well, I've been waiting around for five years now and nothing else happened to the other one."

I went to Dr. Sunderhaus up in Asheville. He's an eye doctor. I said, "Insurance should take care of all these doctor bills!" He said, "No, no. We'll do this up as an industrial injury for workers' compensation." Now I guess the company found out who he was and started sending everybody that had these problems to Sunderhaus. He wrote a letter to the Industrial Commission saying that CS_2 had nothing to do with my eye problems. On April 7, 1976, they turned down my claim. I got nothing and it made me mad.

Gaddy's case is far from unusual, and by no means the most mysterious. Bobby Roberts was in his late twenties and only worked with the CS_2 for about a week. He was also with the voluntary fire department down in Etowah. On the Friday night after his first week at Olin, they called him out on a big fire. "He just never showed up. They went to his house. They found him lying there dead with his gear half on him. No doctors ever said what caused it. He died just before they started the NIOSH study."

THE NATIONAL INSTITUTE FOR OCCUPATIONAL SAFETY AND HEALTH (NIOSH) was set up by Congress in 1970 as the research arm for the OSHA Administration. At an employee's request, NIOSH inspectors will determine whether any toxic substance found in the workplace is causing harmful effects. Unfortunately, NIOSH does not have enforcement powers.

James Reese had heard about NIOSH investigations at a union training session in Richmond. He'd also been hearing about more strange happenings up on the second floor from Marvin Gaddy and others. So he filed an official request with NIOSH for a health hazard evaluation survey for the CS_2.

John Snipes of the Erwin, North Carolina, Brown Lung Association, has his breathing capacity tested at a brown-lung screening clinic

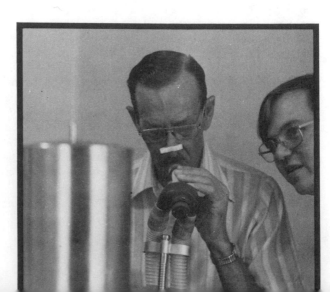

"This just scared the britches off of 'em," Reese remembered. "They are just afraid that somewhere down the line something is gonna get proved on them, and they'll have to spend a lot of money cleaning it up. There's no laws for testing chemicals put in the workplace, like the Food and Drug Administration or EPA. They put things into practice too quick. They should've checked this stuff in the beginning."

On July 27, 1973, Jerome Flesch, a NIOSH industrial hygienist, came to Olin's Pisgah Forest plant to investigate the CS_2. Flesch and his NIOSH team went to the second floor and observed the leaky gaskets and pipes and the air vacuums that clogged every once in a while.

They also tested to see how much carbon disulfide was in the air when the big barettes were opened for scraping. Like Marvin Gaddy's CS_2 tester, the dials on the NIOSH equipment went up as high as they could—except on their machine the limit read 288 ppm. The OSHA standard for carbon disulfide is 20 ppm.

According to Emil A. Paluch, a Polish research scientist: "From the toxicological point of view a concentration of about 300 ppm of carbon disulphide is the amount which exceeds almost everybody's tolerance in a comparatively short period of time and can produce serious pathological changes within a few days."

The scientists from NIOSH could only mark their test results "288 ppm+."

Three months later, NIOSH sent down a physician, James B. Lucas, to do a follow-up medical survey on neurological problems with the workers on the second floor. He reported back that twenty-nine men were interviewed, most of whom complained about recurring nightmares, abdominal pains, headaches, dizziness, and insomnia. He summed up his findings on nerve problems with a short statement: "A number of bizarre neurological findings were noted." Among his findings were the following:

— A 34-year-old man worked 14½ years in the chemical building prior to his transfer. He has a several-year history of numbness, pains, and tingling involving the right side of his face. A neurological consultant for the company diagnosed him with "a typical facial neuralgia."
— A 44-year-old man with 22 years exposure. He has been on leave from work for two years with a vague arthritis-like ailment.
— A 46-year-old man with 22 years exposure notes numbness in both his legs, which he attributes to spinal problems and pinched nerves.
— A 37-year-old man with 16 years exposure had the onset of a convulsive disorder two years ago beginning with a three-day period of status epilepticus. His doctor told him his seizure was due to "a swelled blood vessel in the temporal area." An extensive report by a neurological

consultant hired by the company indicates no such finding to explain the onset of his epilepsy. He is currently depressed by his downgraded position (janitor). His neurological exam was normal.

"That last guy you read about, that was Jimmy Massey," explained Bert McColl, who suffers himself from a rare form of hipbone decay that makes walking difficult.

Massey got this stuff worse than anybody. They called it epileptic fits for a long time so they wouldn't have to pay no workers' compensation to him. First time it happened, he was just sitting there eating supper with his wife and kids. Then he started having a fit. So the company said, "If it just happened at home, then it couldn't have anything to do with his work." Later on, they found all the tumors.

There was another guy—Herbert Higgins. He was 38 too, in the same shape, started doing the same things. Only they didn't find the tumors in his brain till after he died. Nobody ever laid it to CS_2 though. That was before these studies.

Jimmy Massey is still barely living over near Canton. They give him a few more months before the cancer will eat up his brain. His wife just had a baby recently. The family started runnin' out of money with all the medical bills they had to pay, so the company put Jimmy back to work again. They put him on the janitor crew, going around the plant picking up trash. He'd wander round and round not even knowing what he's supposed to do. He'd sit around by the time clock without even knowing when he should punch out.

George Sanders worked with us on the second floor, too. He used to empty all these trashcans full of CS_2. Boy, did he get a lot of fumes! I worked around him the week before he died and you could definitely tell that he was in a strain. He was awful bad depressed. He wouldn't say nothing to no one. His wife was pregnant at the time. He died of a shotgun wound one Saturday night. Everybody said it was just an accident.

At the end of April 1974, NIOSH finally released its health hazard evaluation report for the CS_2. The evidence showed that acute exposures to carbon disulfide had been occurring episodically and these exposures provoked the symptoms in the Olin workers. However, the report stated, "There does not appear to be sufficient medical evidence at this time to warrant a conclusion that chronic exposure is occurring in a sufficient degree to provoke illness. Without question, several atypical and unexplained illnesses were encountered during the study. Time may eventually resolve these diagnostic problems."

The report recommended that the chemical operators be rotated on a weekly basis to reduce their exposure time. Other workers should be assigned to the area to increase the maintenance of the barettes and help insure compliance with all safety precautions. Respirators were also recommended, as well as a training program to inform employees

Mill Village, Greensboro, South Carolina

about the hazardous properties of working with carbon disulphide. The report concluded with a very disturbing statement: "It is difficult to postulate that such diverse and asymmetric neurological problems are due to common exposure to toxic substances or due to some unusual personal susceptibility. Local problems of this type are probably related to chance distribution."

MARVIN GADDY: That's all wrong. We can definitely show you why at least twelve out of these twenty-four people have had all these weird problems. They all worked with the CS_2. The stuff goes about working on the weakest nerves that you got. Now, my nerves and Bert's are different. He can't walk or move around the way he used to; I can't see too good.

BERT MC COLL: I started going to nerve doctors down at Emory in Atlanta. They said I should never go back to work. But with social security and insurance, they say you gotta be 100 percent disabled before they'll do anything. I left Emory in February of this year. I begged 'em to let me put in three months time to help in paying the doctor bills before I come back. They tell me that my bones are decaying all around the hips. They won't say for sure that it's cancer, but it could be. Otherwise they're just decayed and gone.

AFTER THE NIOSH STUDY WAS RELEASED, SOME SMALL CHANGES occurred around the Olin plant. At least there were some written records showing what the carbon disulfide had done. The company had to post the report in the plant, and some people started reading it and getting their own ideas. Workers started calling James Reese after hours and telling him about health and safety problems that were happening in their departments—fumes, chemicals, machines without guards, trucks without brakes.

Some of the chemical mixers came to Reese one day with a label that they'd taken off a bag. They said they'd just started using this dusty stuff called Cyclo-Fil, but the labels on the bag had worried them: "Caution—Contains Asbestos Fibers—Avoid Creating Dust—Breathing Asbestos Dust May Cause Serious Bodily Harm." Reese immediately called up the safety department, which said there was no asbestos in the plant. "That stuff is called Cyclo-Fil," the safety man calmly reassured Reese, but Reese persisted and Olin agreed to send the material off to be tested by an impartial party.

Two months later, the report finally came back from the Georgia Tech research scientists. The next day they ordered that all Cyclo-Fil be taken out of the plant.

JAMES REESE: Olin uses beta rays to measure the thickness or thinness of the cellophane as it is being processed. These "Accuray" scans used to be regulated by the Atomic Energy Commission, but now they're regulated by the North Carolina Department of Human Resources. One time, some people told me that they'd seen a state inspector in the plant looking over all the company's radioactive equipment. This made me mad 'cause they'd agreed to inform me whenever they had an inspector come in here. I got into a real darn hassle with Governor Holshouser and others over this. I wrote all kinds of letters trying to get a copy of his report. They didn't give it to me till I wrote the governor. I wanted to get it out of them, even if I had to write to the President of the United States.

This is all part of it. They thought that they were being real smart. But in my scrounging in the trashcans, I knew the man had already come in here and found all those violations. I had the report before I wrote to anybody.

They are so dumb. That's all I can figure. Do you think that I'd let this kind of stuff go in the trashcan? I'd run it through the shredder, just like Nixon did. Course if there's ever anything that I want to know about this company, I know where all the trashcans are.

People have been turning up things, all these untested chemicals, like this Kepone thing in Virginia. They had to even bury the plant and the St. James River got ruined. I think it's coming to the stage where industry is gonna have to first prove its point. It's not gonna work the way it's been working. Cause people, when they start to see what's really happenin', then they'll take things into their own hands and start closing these places down.

The more pressure that's put on them, the more publicity that can get generated, you start to get results from pushing on 'em, from finding out stuff about Kepone and vinyl chloride and asbestos. It's gonna start building, and people aren't gonna stand for it no more.

TRADITIONALLY, MANY COMPANIES HAVE AVOIDED SAFETY AND health problems in bargaining contracts or arbitrating grievances on the grounds that these areas are "of mutual concern" to both unions and management. Other companies contend that safety and health are areas of "management prerogative only." Joint union-company safety committees have been set up as a "consultative device" for giving suggestions to management. Consequently, the committees haven't been given any decision-making power for implementing their "suggestions."

For most employees in the South, occupational safety and health means little more than wearing masks and ear plugs. Corporate safety programs have mainly been built on the premise that the workers are to blame for the injuries or illnesses they receive from the workplace. As in the Olin situation, the existence of occupational diseases has historically been denied.

With the passage of the OSHA Act in 1970, companies across the country are finding that they can't get away with paying lip service or petty cash for better working conditions. Workers, like the Paperworkers in Local 1971, are learning that they have rights now, too—to question, to be curious, to complain, and to demand better treatment.

J. P. Stevens Mill, Piedmont, South Carolina

As the American chemical feast continues, the safety and health committee is emerging as a new structure for industrial self-protection. We can expect that the OSHA Administration will continue to limp along without adequate funds or personnel to carry out the laws they're supposed to be enforcing. Consequently, as James Reese has learned, the only way to get laws for self-protection carried out is by vigilantly enforcing the laws yourself. The companies learned this long ago. They are well protected and they know how to use the laws.

JAMES REESE: Olin brought Fletcher Roberts in here as the new "Director for Safety and Loss Prevention" right after we started filing all those OSHA complaints. He's supposed to prevent them from losing money. In fact, he used to be the one who inspected all these companies around here for OSHA. I went to school with him, he used to date my younger sister. I'm his friend when I can use it to my advantage and that's the same way he works it. We know what we're doing to each other.

I know that OSHA and the companies are working together—this don't upset me—my purposes still get served. This company knows, after all the hell-raising that we've done, that we're not gonna sit still for some halfway deal.

We kept giving Olin such a hard time, and I was calling in outside people quite a bit. I wasn't making too many points, but at least things were getting uncovered. Fletcher Roberts has been put in here to soft-soap me and stop all us people because somewhere it's appearing on record in the corporate levels. Somewhere up there in Stamford, Connecticut, somebody don't like it. 'Cause they figure sooner or later the law of averages is gonna catch up with them and some of this information is gonna get out to the public.

They worry some about having to spend money for cleaning up, but losing their reputation is what really makes 'em squirm.''

MARVIN GADDY IS STILL GOING TO WORK IN OLIN'S CHEMICAL
building every day, although he's not up on the second floor anymore. They won't let him go back. Now he's got an easier job—no fumes, no scraping, no fear.

I may have to leave my department, though. Especially on the graveyard shift, I feel what I'm doing, but I just don't see it. Like this morning, I had to pull up aside the road on the way home from work. My eyes started watering and blurring . . . I couldn't see. . . .

All that we've told you is the facts. I've got only four more years to retirement and all I care about is helping somebody else now. What I've said here, I've told all the doctors, all the lawyers, all the company men. But they can't hurt me now.

When you got a company that's got the kind of money that Olin's got and they go and tell their lawyers to fight on this and we'll feed you—that's the way the world is run. There's some people that get caught and some that don't. . . . Now Nixon, course he got caught.

THIRTY-ONE
A New Twist for Textiles

CHIP HUGHES

THE LAST DECADE HAS SEEN A NEW era begin for the Southern textile industry. Haunted for years by its low profitability and poor public image, at last, industry executives are determined to put on a new face. For the first time in over a century of operation, Southern textiles may develop into a modern, capital-intensive industry. But the pace of the process and the extent of its success are complicated by a morass of labor stirrings, capital shortages, entrepreneurial caution, and governmental interference.

The change taking place is a momentous one, comparable perhaps to that caused when the textile industry crossed the ocean from England to New England, and again when it left New England (and the workers who had begun to demand higher wages) and headed South a century ago. This new period, however, is not marked by a geographic move, but by simultaneous forces demanding changes of all aspects of the industry, and by the determined responses of textile executives. To understand the new directions, one must take account of the economic and social realities that form the industry's background.

The textile industry has been, and remains, the dominating force of the Southern economy. Its $16–18 billion of sales annually is 30 to 50 percent larger than the volume of Southern agriculture. In five Southern states it employs over 25 percent of the labor force, despite growing automation. The majority of U.S. textile mills are located in an arc across the South, extending from northeastern North Carolina, through the Piedmont to the textile "capital" of Greenville, South Carolina (60 percent of the textile work force is said to live within a hundred miles of that city), down to Georgia and into the black belt of Alabama.

When textile owners began operations, many located their mills in small towns or wilderness areas. They made their towns dependent on the mill economy. Often the mill was the only employer, rented all the homes, and owned the stores and shops. The company alone made up the local power structure; without it, the town would not exist.

Low-income whites traditionally filled the Southern textile work force, with whole families frequently employed at a single mill. Women have always been a major portion of the work force, and even in 1974, 47 percent of textile workers were women, compared to 29 percent in all manufacturing industries.

No industry avoided unionization as successfully as textiles, primarily by settling in the South. Twenty years ago the industry included 252,000 union members. Nationally, there are now 141,000 members among the 800,000 workers. Less than 10 percent of the Southern workers are unionized.

In 1950, textile workers earned $1.13 per hour, while the industrial average was $1.09. By 1955, however, the textile average wage had slipped a penny below the national average. In 1975 the average textile wage was only 61 percent of the national average, $1.30 less.

Production and marketing continue to be archaic and unpredictable, and profitability is always uncertain. When one company hits on a hot-selling consumer item, others jump into the marketplace, crank out a similar product, and inevitably glut the market, sending the industry into another tailspin. These cycles of oversupply occur every three or four years.

Well-connected Northern investors historically shunned Southern textiles. Its cycles have been too irregular, its profit margin too small, its selling operations too haphazard. An investment in textiles has always been a gamble, and investors avoided it for more lucrative industries.

Given the little amount of capital required to begin a new mill, the competitive nature of the industry, and the government's ban on mergers, no companies dominated the field. The industry's two giants, Burlington Industries and J. P. Stevens, together hold less than 10 percent of the textile market, while the rest is scattered amid 4,000 small firms, almost three-fourths of which are still family owned.

Without money from investors, textile companies could not afford the few high-priced pieces of automation that had been developed. And with a steady supply of cheap labor they had no need to.

For years these were the unchallengeable givens of the Southern textile industry. Now their firmness is crumbling, and with their fall, a new era is beginning.

In the last few years, for instance, the industry has witnessed a significant shift in the composition of its work force. Mills no longer operate as white-only reserves; low-income blacks now account for more than 20 percent of the textile work force. They brought with them independent attitudes and strong feelings of support for the union. For an industry that has intimidated workers and fought unions with more success than any in the country, this can only signal trouble.

At the same time, the federal government recently established restrictive federal pollution, safety, and health regulations. And though the government has rarely pushed for compliance, new organizations of retired and active textile workers have arisen, demanding that companies abide by the laws and clean their plants of such health dangers as excessive cotton dust in the air.

In response to these worker-related problems, the textile industry would like nothing more than simply to eliminate their workers through automation. Until recently, textile companies were unable to afford automation, for they stayed small compared to most major American corporations. For the past seven years, the federal government has even banned mergers, encouraging companies to remain small. Now that ban has been lifted, and the large companies will soon begin to buy up smaller ones, to gain the capital necessary to automate even more.

In looking ahead to the 1980s, industry analysts made a number of startling predictions:

One-third of the companies in the industry, as well as 7,000 of the industries' mills, will permanently shut down.

The top fifteen textile manufacturers, which today account for 25 percent of domestic production, will be putting out as much as 40 percent of total textile production by 1990.

Capital expenditures in the 1980s will increase to about $22.5 billion, almost three times what the industry spent during the 1970s.

In spite of the new trade agreements, imports in textiles will continue to increase 7 to 10 percent annually, while domestic production grows at only 2 to 3 percent. From 1970 to 1978, imports in textiles increased 82 percent, while domestic textile production grew only 29 percent.

Most of the capital spending will be used for plant modernization and automation, which, in the process, will eliminate about one-third of the industry's 800,000-person work force.

NO PART OF THE INDUSTRY IS IN MORE FLUX THAN THE WORK FORCE. For many years, blacks had been used as an effective threat in keeping mill workers' wages at low levels. Whenever there was discontent among the white mill hands, the owners could play on the whites' racial fears with the threat that blacks would take over their jobs.

But as the late 1960s brought about a new round of industrialization for the South, many longtime textile workers chose to leave the mills on their own. Electronics, metal fabrication, heavy equipment, and chemical manufacturers moved into the region, often fleeing the North's unions and higher wages. These new industries took white workers out of their traditional mill jobs and moved them into higher-paying job categories, forcing owners to look toward a group that it had systematically excluded—poor Southern blacks.

Many plants that were once all white now include work forces that are more than half black. Throughout the industry, 20 percent of the workers are black. These workers, offspring of the civil rights movement, are unlike their paternalized white predecessors. Employers complain of "discipline" problems, increased costs of employee training programs, and a higher turnover. They do not blindly follow all the rules their bosses establish—and above all, are sympathetic toward unions.

Already, young black textile workers have played leading roles in union victories at the Oneita Mills in Andrews, South Carolina, and at J. P. Stevens's seven-mill complex in Roanoke Rapids, North Carolina. Employers responded to this activity with threats, rumors, and accusations. They equated the advent of unionism with a black takeover of the workplace. During the organizing campaign at the J. P. Stevens plants, the supervisors circulated pictures of the San Francisco "zebra" murder victims and the black suspects in the case. The pictures were captioned, "Would you want this to happen here?"

ALTHOUGH ORGANIZING EFFORTS HAVE BEEN MADE SINCE THE 1880S, only 17 percent of the textile work force is unionized. For the Textile Workers Union of America (AFL-CIO), every day was another struggle to stay alive.

During the 1950s, the Northern-based union lost most of its membership base when the textile industry increased its flight to the low-wage, nonunion South. Many of the union's Northern locals were eliminated, depleting its financial resources and making the cost of new organizing too expensive. Impoverished, the TWUA was forced to depend on the Industrial Union Department, the organizing arm of the national AFL-CIO, which under the leadership of George Meany and I. W. Abel has been less than enthusiastic in carrying out its mandate to "organize the unorganized."

Organizing in textiles has always been a dangerous business, yielding mainly Pyrrhic victories and numbing defeats. Since 1963, efforts have been concentrated on the industry's second-largest chain, J. P. Stevens. With the exception of a few union election victories, the drive has been largely unsuccessful. In Roanoke Rapids, Stevens executives responded to the union victory with a vicious antiunion campaign: union supporters have been fired en masse, organizers have had their phones tapped, and supervisors have tried to spread rumors of black takeovers, higher crime rates, and interracial marriages.

Despite fines and reprimands by the NLRB for unfair labor practices, Stevens continues to believe it's cheaper to fire union supporters than to give in to their demands, a strategy that has effectively squelched most organizing efforts. With each new organizing drive, the company steps up its antiunion efforts, filling other workers with fear, while the union's main adherents have been effectively eliminated. Months or years later, the slow wheels of the NLRB may turn, fining textile companies and possibly reinstating the fired union supporters. But the damage has been done, and the NLRB can only give too little, too late.

Still, the union has been a continual aggravation for the industry. And since winning negotiation rights at Stevens's Roanoke Rapids plants in August 1974, the union has posed the threat of staging a major comeback.

In the aftermath of the surprising victory at Roanoke Rapids, the aging leadership of the fledgling TWUA realized that they needed more money and resources in order to make good on their promises to organize and support the workers at J. P. Stevens's eighty-five textile plants. With this in mind, TWUA president Sol Stetin initiated merger talks with the much larger Amalgamated Clothing Workers Union, which during the CIO days had helped to start the TWUA. The merger talks, a rarity in the turf-conscious AFL-CIO, climaxed with a merged convention in June 1977 and the birth of ACTWU, the Amalgamated Clothing and Textile Workers Union.

As a result of the merger, the Amalgamated inherited the largely unsuccessful legacy of the Stevens campaign, as well as the difficult challenge of organizing in the Southern textile industry. To meet these dual challenges, ACTWU initiated two nationwide campaigns: labor law reform in the legislative arena, and the J. P. Stevens boycott to build national support for Southern textile organizing. ACTWU was drawing on two of the union's proven strengths: a strong union-label/boycott department, which had chalked up an impressive victory against Willie Farah in 1974 to back up Amalgamated's organizing campaign among Chicano women in El Paso, Texas; and a strong legal/legislative department whose lawyers had set numerous precedents for labor organizing in front of the National Labor Relations Board (NLRB).

Unfortunately, the union was not prepared for the specific demands of the J. P. Stevens campaign. Because TWUA had been caught by surprise after the 1974 Roanoke Rapids victory, the union had lost the momentum of the breakthrough election when it went to the bargaining table in Roanoke Rapids or began organizing campaigns at other Stevens plants. As the merger talks progressed with ACWU, TWUA officials and leaders of the Industrial Union Department (IUD) pushed for more organizing support from the national AFL-CIO, finally assembling a beefed-up organizing staff for the Stevens campaign, which covered most of Stevens's Southern plants.

The renewed Stevens organizing campaign swung into action during early 1977 with a commitment to stay at the plant gates until a company-wide contract with Stevens was achieved. The campaign staff, many of whom had previous organizing experience in Southern communities and the civil rights movement, scorned the union's previous organizing methods, which focused on signing blue union certification cards and calling for NLRB elections. In the past, this approach had spawned flighty, euphoric union excitement in the early stages, a company antiunion propaganda barrage down the home stretch before the election, and then a smashing union defeat at the NLRB ballot box.

The new campaign organizers hoped to overcome this cycle of defeat by utilizing traditional community organizing techniques on specific workplace issues and grievances, and slowly building union strength *before* going for an NLRB certification election. To supplement this new in-plant organizing approach, the union began to pay attention to another key component in labor-management textile battles: the local community.

As the labor law reform fight heated up in Congress, the union decided not to ask for any more elections in Stevens plants until the labor law reform bill passed, since ACTWU contended that Stevens's continuing labor law violations made a fair election impossible. This decision came at the same time as union organizers were moving full steam ahead to build union majorities in Stevens's Southern plants. This conflict created tremendous internal strife within the union between leadership in New York and organizers and workers in the South.

With the defeat of labor law reform and a standoff in the boycott, the union has recommitted itself to the slow and difficult task of organizing in Stevens's Southern plants, as evidenced by a victory at Stevens's High Point plant in October 1979. Although this may not be the most glamorous strategy, or the most politically expedient, or

produce the most immediate results, it is the only way to beat Stevens and keep alive the hope of a better day for Southern textile workers through unionization.

FOR MANY YEARS, THE TEXTILE INDUSTRY HID BEHIND LOW PROFITS TO excuse its inability to clean up either the working conditions in the mills or the pollution they produce. With its new plans for automation, the textile managers hope to eliminate many of the dangerous and unhealthy working conditions by ridding themselves of the workers entirely.

But most textile workers still labor amid numerous toxic substances, deafening noise levels, unsafe machinery, and deadly, disabling cotton dust. According to figures from the U.S. Department of Labor, as many as 100,000 textile workers now suffer from the chronic lung disease byssinosis, caused by excessive exposure to cotton dust. Medical researchers have also estimated that as much as 25 percent of the textile work force has been deafened by the noisy looms.

During 1975 the Carolina Brown Lung Association formed expressly to fight for better conditions for mill hands, as well as for just compensation for those whose health has already been destroyed by cotton dust. In North and South Carolina, the CBLA is pressuring the Occupational Safety and Health Administration to carry out a vigorous enforcement policy against mills that violate the OSHA cotton dust standard. Thus far, the governmental agencies have been unwilling to move against the powerful textile interests.

The textile industry has always been particularly hostile to the development of indigenous community organizations. While gathering financial support from sympathetic churches, foundations, and governmental agencies, the CBLA built a base of organizational support among thousands of textile workers in small mill towns who had been forced to leave their jobs because they could no longer breathe well enough to keep up production. None of them knew about brown lung disease.

The textile industry has responded to these initiatives with a torrent of rhetoric attacking the "imposition of unreasonable government regulations." F. Sadler Love, secretary of the American Textile Manufacturers Institute, claims that the proposed government regulations on noise, cotton dust, and waste-water quality would cost the industry $3.5 billion over a five-year period. According to Love, "This would amount to more than all the profits of all the textile companies in all the states of the union and would result in soaring textile prices to the consumer, no wage increases for employees, no dividends for stockholders, and no modernization of plants or machinery."

To overcome the industry's conspiracy of silence about brown lung, the CBLA sponsored one-day screening clinics with medical equipment and doctors in the mill towns. Afterward, hundreds of textile workers began to file for workers' compensation. In its first four years of work, the CBLA filed almost a thousand compensation cases and won over $3 million in benefits for disabled textile workers from the state industrial commissions.

Even more important have been its programs and work on behalf of active workers, who are still exposed to the dangers of cotton dust in the mill. In conjunction with ACTWU, CBLA members are pressuring the U.S. Department of Labor to institute new regulations on cotton dust exposure through continuing legal actions, hearings, and public demonstrations. After seven years of administrative procedure, OSHA finally announced a cotton dust standard in June 1978, after the textile industry had gotten Jimmy Carter to intervene on their behalf.

Recently, the controversial cotton dust regulation was upheld in federal appeals court after both sides filed suit contending that it was either too strict or too weak. The outcome awaits the Supreme Court's interpretation of the cost/benefit impact of federal regulation—whether the benefits in terms of lives saved outweigh the costs of cleaning up an industrial health hazard.

The CBLA's more important long-range accomplishment may be in showing that textile workers are not fundamentally antiorganization, as many historians have contended. Defeat in textile organizing is usually blamed on the antiunionism of the workers and not on the ineptness or insensitivity of the union. The experience of the CBLA shows that when local textile workers are encouraged to take positions of leadership, the mill company finds it a lot more difficult to portray the organization as "a group of outsiders," or to split off the organization from the people it represents. In many cases, the union defeated itself either by not making a long-term commitment to the workers in a textile community or by not encouraging or developing local workers to take leadership positions.

SINCE JIMMY CARTER WAS ELECTED PRESIDENT, THE TEXTILE INDUSTRY has increased the tilt in its political lobbying operations toward the Oval Office, in order to shore up and retain the special treatment the industry receives from the federal government. In three important national policy battles, the textile industry played a key role in "getting to Carter in time" to prevent the enactment of legislation which would seriously impinge on their operations: the battle for labor law reform (J. P. Stevens bill), the GATT agreement (foreign imports fight), and the cotton dust standard from OSHA. The American Textile Manufacturers Institute (ATMI), the industry's major lobbying group, shifted its entire operation to Washington, D.C. During 1978, ATMI closed its headquarters in Charlotte, North Carolina, where it had resided for over fifty years.

The year 1978 also saw the development of the textile congressional caucus, one of the largest and most powerful of the new special interest political groupings, led by Senator Ernest Hollings and Senator Strom Thurmond. The textile caucus, one of the leading opponents of labor law reform, also served as the key go-between and negotiator for bargaining on the trade agreements with the industry and the White House. In taking one of his most proindustry stances, Senator Hollings, on behalf of the textile caucus, threatened to block any international trade agreements from gaining congressional approval unless the textile industry's demands for protection from foreign imports were met. In an unusual alliance with ACTWU, the textile industry won their protection, and Hollings and the textile caucus chalked up one of their first victories.

More recently, Senator Hollings and the textile caucus have threatened to sabotage President Carter's plan to grant "most favored nation" trade status for the People's Republic of China, warning that unless there are adequate import safeguards, the Chinese could "inundate" the United States with cheaply produced textiles.

According to the industry, because the low-wage imports flood into the United States without adequate tariffs, our domestic textiles are underpriced and outsold even here at home. In addition, textile industries in other advanced countries beat out our domestic industry in jockeying for export markets because of special incentives that their home governments give to stimulate exports.

The industry presents the issue to the public and its employees in a simple fashion: cheap foreign imports from sweatshops in Taiwan or the People's Republic of China take away American workers' jobs. In actuality, this oversimplification is a mask used to shift the blame for domestic textile job losses onto Third World textile producers, while covering up significant production shifts here on the home front. In the United States, the "shakeout" within the industry is proceeding tenuously and quietly: unprofitable product lines and outmoded production processes are being eliminated; the larger producers consolidate their operations while buying out the smaller, successful operators; the smaller, marginal producers are run out of business. All this in the name of efficiency.

From the industry's point of view, the flood of imports, not consolidation, causes unemployment cutbacks. Ironically, the answer to the trade imbalance problem—too many imports and too few exports —is for the industry to increase its overseas investments to reach foreign markets, and to beef up its domestic capital spending to modernize its plants and automate further. Unfortunately, both of these

CAPITAL SPENDING ON THE RISE

	Capital expenditures (in million $)				Number of employees				Long-term debt (in million $)			
	1966	1970	1974	1978	1966	1970	1974	1978	1966	1970	1974	1978
Burlington Indust.	159.37	123.10	142.50	215.96	69,000	86,000	81,000	66,000	298.6	398.3	422	448.20
Cone Mills	12.30	11.05	15.00	12.50	14,100	14,000	14,100	12,500	21.37	29.58	30	28.30
Dan River Mills	13.95	8.33	30.90	21.30	19,000	20,000	19,000	16,000	39.33	68.28	78	85.90
Lowenstein & Sons	28.10	19.46	22.69	13.30	16,000	17,550	16,000	15,800	52.21	47.03	119	94.50
Spring Mills	38.51	14.94	19.06	33.90	18,000	18,000	19,000	17,000	0	32.88	95	59.10
J.P. Stevens Co.	47.04	28.14	47.51	60.99	43,527	49,000	46,000	43,400	114	141.95	187	275.50
West-Pt.–Pepperell	18.06	11.78	23.52	50.10	18,900	21,271	20,000	24,000	1.05	2.71	46	126.70

This table illustrates trends toward increased spending on new equipment. Both capital spending and long-term debt have risen as companies scramble to modernize. Figures on the number of employees are beginning to reflect the impact of the industry's accelerating plans.

TEXTILE INDUSTRY LEADERS OF 1978   (listed by size)

	Net sales (million $)	Net income (million $)	Income as % of sales	Assets	% paid as dividends	Labor costs as % of sales	% stock owned by insiders	No. of institutions owning stock by insiders	Top executive and total direct compensation	Comments
Burlington Indust.	2,421	70	3.5	1,017	56%	30%	—	134 / 50%	W. A. Klopman $388,882	32 plants abroad; consumer goods, 36%
J. P. Stevens Co.	1,651	36	2.2	657	38%	31%	1.6%	68 / 16%	J. D. Finely $368,048	'74 record yr., target of labor boycott
West Pt.–Pepperell	885	32	3.7	345	37%	30%	—	62 / 30%	J. L. Lanier $244,999	Home products 40%; #4 in denims: hg profit
Lowenstein & Sons	604	12	2.1	237	7%	30%	50%	12 / 10%	R. Bendheim (n.a.)	Big printing, finishing; inside owners
Spring Mills	684	21	3.1	292	30%	27%	66%	17 / 10%	P. G. Scotese $371,800	Newly divers. Seabrook food & nursing homes
Dan River Mills	530	13	2.4	197	31%	32%	3%	18 / 11%	R. S. Small $291,149	Hardest hit wt recess; 9 wk. UTW strike
Cone Mills	617	36	5.8	211	26%	27%	26%	23 / 8%	L. S. Morris $421,450	Booming denim profits

With the lead of Burlington and Stevens, the industry has embarked on its journey toward oligopolization, yielding fewer competitors of greatly increased size and diversity. In the stock ownership column, the shift from family control to ownership by outside financial interests is apparent, particularly for the larger companies. Executive salaries contrast sharply with the average textile worker's salary ($8,340), in 1977, which now lags about $2,000 behind the government's estimate of income needed to maintain an adequate standard of living for a family of four.

supposed solutions will take away more and more jobs from the textile workers here in the United States.

While the industry continues to rave about unfair trade advantages, textile labor costs in the United States have continued to slide below the wage levels of most of the European textile manufacturers. Presently, U.S. textile wages are about half of the level paid in Belgium, which has the world's highest textile wages. European producers have gained a competitive advantage by vigorously investing in new technology and updating their capital equipment, unlike their counterparts in the United States.

DISSATISFIED (AND EVEN MILITANT) BLACK WORKERS; A POTENTIALLY aggressive union; worker and government pressure about pollution, safety, and health regulations—these forces have worried Southern textile mill owners recently. Now they have found a simple way to overcome them: replace the workers with machines. During the 1960s the industry saw a boom in the development of textile technology, particularly in Czechoslovakia and eastern Europe. New machinery was developed that will revamp nearly every step in the textile production process, combining several operations, increasing machine speeds, and decreasing the need for labor.

Burlington Industries has already begun its automation. According to Horace Jones, the company's former chairman, operating floor space was reduced by 13 percent during 1975, and the number of Burlington employees was slashed by 17,000 from its peak of 88,000 in October 1973. Despite these cutbacks, the company has maintained its annual productive capacity of approximately $2.5 billion, and spent over $100 million on new equipment during 1975. In the next year, the company's capital spending reached $175 million, almost all of which went toward modernizing plants and equipment. According to Luther

Hodges, Jr., then chairman of North Carolina National Bank, these trends may spread throughout the industry: "Burlington has rehired fewer workers than it was forced to lay off when the recession began. Other companies are following the same pattern, and it could be a long, long time before the Southern textile industry employs the number of people it did before the recession." Bureau of Labor Statistics figures show that employment in the Southern textile industry dropped by 107,200 jobs during 1975 alone, and more cutbacks are expected.

Even more jobs will be lost and automation increased in the wake of a recent government action ending its 1968 ban on mergers within the textile industry. Textile analysts have said that a major reason for the merger ban was the government's desire to protect the South's large unskilled labor pool. For years the industry provided low-wage employment for this large bloc of the South's work force, offering them some employment but discouraging them from developing other skills. The government apparently feared that if the industry giants were given free reign to carry out mergers and increase monopolization, then the process of replacing low-skilled workers with machines would also be quickened, and the South would be left with a much larger pool of unemployed, low-skilled labor than before. It passed the merger ban and the industry remained bloated with small, highly competitive and unprofitable companies. With the end of the merger ban, this will soon change. Burlington, J. P. Stevens, and the other large companies can be expected to grow. Many of the smaller ones will be swallowed up. Companies will merge, operations will consoldiate, and thousands of jobs will be eliminated.

Essentially, the forces at work within the Southern textile industry make up twin movements: the work force is becoming less docile and more willing to complain when treated poorly by the industry. The executives have responded with actions that provide more reason for complaint. It is still too early to see exactly where and how the industry will move. Even with mergers, the industry may not find the capital sufficient to automate to the extent that the new technology makes possible. The workers may take for themselves the power necessary to halt both the approaching automation and the continuing slump in their wages compared to those in other industries. Industry executives may find new tactics that will succeed in placating the new, militant textile workers, or those workers may trigger an organizing movement within the mills. Whatever the final results, one thing is clear: it's a new day for the Southern textile industry.

THIRTY-TWO

Labor on the Move: The Future

MARC S. MILLER

IN 1763 THE FREE BLACK CHIMNEY sweepers of Charleston, South Carolina, organized and demanded increased back pay. The Charleston *Gazette,* angered at the "insolent" behavior of the sweepers, warned, "Such activities are evils that require some attention to suppress."

For over two centuries, the interests of workers and bosses have diverged as consistently as those of slave and master. Over the years, the struggle has taken many forms, from the polite give-and-take of the early Piedmont mill villages to the violent explosions in the Appalachian coalfields.

The struggle broke to the surface most dramatically in the 1930s when economic depression plus a measure of protection from the federal government brought unprecedented and largely unexpected sudden strength to the labor movement, a process which continued through the prosperity of World War II. The victories of those years—by miners, textile workers, auto workers, sharecroppers, tobacco workers— still stand as symbols of the promise the future could hold. But although immediate breakthroughs still occur in isolated cases, the reality of the 1970s and 80s and the scenario for the foreseeable future will likely be more mundane. For workers—both the vulnerable unorganized and those protected by unions—the conditions that provoked the upheavals of the 1930s no longer exist. More than ever, organizing calls for commitment to a slow, dedicated struggle, with rewards not expected tomorrow or even next year. Labor's enemy is more powerful, more entrenched, more organized than ever before.

THE END OF WORLD WAR II INAUGURATED AN ECONOMIC PROCESS that has, with recent acceleration, decisively changed the world of American workers, North and South. Using profits of the wartime boom, the many small, independent textile mills—once the foundation of the South's economy—gave way through mergers and purchase to create today's textile giants: Burlington, J. P. Stevens, Dan River, Deering-Milliken, West Point–Pepperell. In this trend, Southern textiles followed the pattern set in other basic industries in the North and in Europe in the late nineteenth and early twentieth centuries. While the level of concentration and the size of the companies does not rival that of a $55 billion auto manufacturer, the largest textile companies now have sales on the order of $2 billion annually and still dominate the region's industries.

Mergers centralized control and concentrated power for the mill owners, but also allowed the corporations to draw on larger pools of capital created from their own assets and from increased ties to major banks. Textiles, traditionally considered a labor-intensive industry with a relatively low amount of mechanization, now has the financial resources to transform itself and become—like the steel, automotive, rubber, and petroleum industries—capital intensive. Should workers in the mill threaten to organize and thereby raise the costs of labor, management can bring in new "labor-saving" machinery—unnecessary or too expensive when labor is cheap and plentiful—to lessen the collective power of those workers.

Developments within the textile industry are only a part of the changing Southern factory landscape. Paralleling the birth of the textile giants in the postwar years was the much more gradual appearance of other harbingers of the "New South." Just as New England textile companies, lured by the success of their Southern competitors, once moved South to escape organized labor, so today do other major industries migrate—generally those industries in which labor unions are strongest and investment costs for machinery highest. For example, during the past five years, despite corporate denials of any antiunion intentions, General Motors opened or planned a dozen new factories in its "Southern strategy" to escape the United Auto Workers, and thousands of union jobs have disappeared due, union officials believe, to the runaway tactics of Westinghouse.

Ironically, old-line Southern industrialists had once fought to keep these new industries away, fearing a threat to textiles' monopoly on an underpaid work force. Northern companies, it was said, would arrive with Northern wages and benefits—and with a management carrying dangerous Northern attitudes. In fact, the companies lured to the New South have actually proven to be among the staunchest enemies of unions, as the entry of ultraconservative Coors to the South epitomizes. While the typical 1930 management policy had been characterized by a now obviously primitive combination of paternalism and brute force, the New South companies, such as GE, Westinghouse, and GM, wage the battle with subtler tactics. Already accustomed to paying wage levels set in Northern union factories, they take the lead in raising the stakes, willingly "granting" to workers many of the financial and fringe benefits unions promise—without relinquishing the control over workers that a union presence ultimately demands. Owen Electric Steel Company at Cayce, South Carolina, succeeded in expelling the International Brotherhood of Electrical Workers partly by planting shrubbery, serving better food in the canteen, holding small group meetings, and encouraging supervisors to be more sensitive to workers' desire for respect.

Textiles is still *the* industry in the South (indeed, the only one in many small towns), but it is no longer the only industry across the South, and it no longer determines single-handedly the patterns of labor-management relations. Even while upholding the textile industry's fervant antiunionism, the new runaways force the old guard to match higher wage levels solely to hold onto workers. While the South continues to lag behind the rest of the nation in its degree of unionization, wages have risen slightly from 83 percent of the national average in 1950 to 86 percent in 1977.

The New South's lure of higher wages further shackles unions by undermining the possibility of developing local men and women to lead any drive for worker collective action. Organizers who follow traditional rules established in Northern struggles, focusing on what the boss *takes away,* face a stone wall from workers who only see that they *gained* several dollars per hour and a benevolent master when they left the mills for a nonunion job at a Miller brewing plant. Naturally, the most aggressive men and women, those who would form the core of any factory rebellion, escape the mill into these jobs, following the time-honored capitalist path of individual advancement. In Northern cities, highly paid, highly skilled workers provide strength to existing unions; in the South, these workers take advantage of the relatively expanding Southern economy to promote their own schemes to move around, move up, and—they hope—move out of the working class to become entrepreneurs on their own. Not by chance, the pattern duplicates colonial exploitation of underdeveloped countries, where likely working-class leaders often reinforce their ruler's power rather than challenge it.

For the recent migrant factories, evading the union in Southern plants not only helps control labor in those plants but also ultimately

Allied Chemical Plant, Hopewell, Virginia

weakens the union everywhere and adds leverage in company fights to
counter union demands nationwide. As part of a 1976 campaign in
Charleston, South Carolina, the United Electrical Workers Union
calculated that transferring turbine manufacture to the South would
cost each GE and Westinghouse worker up to a total of $40,000 in
pay over ten years, due to declining wage levels as the union lost
bargaining power.*

As publicity forces image-conscious corporations to escape the

*Figures were projected for the 1968–1978 period.

stereotype of brutal exploiter, companies rely less on—but don't abandon—the traditional iron fist. But relinquishing blatant force does not indicate weakness; rather, it reflects new strength rooted in economic concentration and modern techniques for controlling the work force, or at least the workplace. The tools available to management have become far more sophisticated. Union organizers were once thrown out of towns by a combination of vigilante violence and courthouse harassment; corporations can now accomplish the same end by manipulating legislation supposedly written to protect workers. State and federal courts struck down laws declaring unions to be subversive conspiracies or requiring organizers to post exorbitant bonds, but—with delay equivalent to defeat for many union drives— violating the National Labor Relations Act and stalling through the courts can be as effective as tar and feathers. J. P. Stevens, for example, escaped serious punishment from the government in spite of being convicted of 110 violations of the NLRA between 1963 and 1978.

Threats to pull a company out of town if a union is voted in, while technically illegal, can be effectively slipped through, especially since the courts and the laws fail to protect workers when their employer defies only the spirit of the law. Nor is the threat to close a factory without a concrete basis; multinationals have far less commitment to their host communities than did the earlier, locally owned small mills. In 1966, RCA opened a plant in Memphis with much fanfare by the company and local politicians; it paid workers $2.25 an hour, 30 cents more than the prevailing wage, *and* allowed a union to represent the workers. Four years later, RCA closed the factory and shifted production and equipment to Taiwan, where labor costs are even lower and government power more audaciously promanagement than in the South.

Only when a major union—with money to chase an employer through the courts or to dig in for years of tedious organizing—enters the picture can workers even think of challenging a rich, multinational corporation. Challenges take years, and most workers cannot afford to wait for the seemingly endless legal process to be completed, with no guarantee of eventual victory. For unorganized workers, the present labor laws remain worse than useless. Right-to-work laws, enacted under the 1947 Taft-Hartley Act, exist in eleven Southern states as a major block to stable unions. In the case of runaways, few laws exist in the United States—as they do in most European countries—to force corporations to be more socially responsible. Instead of fighting runaways, communities engage in endless warfare with each other to determine who can give away the most to attract new employers. A proposed National Employment Priorities Act would require employers to notify workers and communities before a move; it would also provide federal assistance to workers and communities suffering because of runaways, and punish corporations unable to justify their move. It's unfortunate that the bill will not become law in the foreseeable future.

The net cast over labor and town is tightened by the ability of the corporate elite to maneuver in city halls, in statehouses, in Congress, and in the courts at all levels. Partly as a response to antitrust legislation and partly in recognition of *their* own class interests, American companies first pooled their resources in the late nineteenth century; as the industrial base broadens, they continue to do so today on many levels, clinching their economic and ideological hold in a community simply by cooperating with each other. The local chamber of commerce usually coordinates this network, which extends through countless educational, civic, economic, and social channels. For example, in Greenville, South Carolina, the old textile elite has been neatly interwoven with the new elite represented by Michelin. Selected by the AFL-CIO's Industrial Union Department as an organizing target in 1961, today the Greenville area is instead a showpiece of the union-free New South.

On a wider level, corporations join together in antiunion associations, armed with high finances and sophisticated methods. In alliance with the New Right, big business recently defeated all congressional attempts to reform the antiquated federal labor laws, despite organized labor's massive, unified lobbying effort. In a dramatic demonstration of business's own ability to organize in defense of its interests, the United States Chamber of Commerce, the Business Roundtable, the National Association of Manufacturers (NAM), and the National Right to Work Committee (among others) formed the coalition that defeated the Labor Law Reform Bill.

Established in 1895, the NAM has been a leader in the fight against unions since 1903, and now has 12,000 member companies; its National Industrial Council ("The Strike Force for Business") collects dues from 260 member associations representing both regional and industrial groupings. Even more conservative than the more "respectable" NAM (although with a great deal of overlapping membership) is the United States Industrial Council—4,600 members— which takes a broader and more explicitly antiunion stance (pro-"free enterprise"). In its earlier guise as the Southern States Industrial Council, the USIC in 1934 helped Alabama coal operators win wages for their workers below standards set by New Deal legislation. The Southeastern Legal Foundation, one of several established nationwide by the inappropriately named National Legal Center for the Public Interest, aids businesses in using the law to fight workers. In its first major victory, the Southeastern Legal Foundation recently defended an Atlanta factory owner's contention that a federal Occupational

Safety and Health Administration inspector needed a search warrant.

Further, a whole network of consulting firms, acting outside the control of the NLRA, gives the union-busters a professional structure beyond the reach of most individual employers. One such firm, the Southeastern Employers Service Corporation (SESCO), begun in Appalachia in 1943, now represents 1,500 clients across the United States (but mostly in the South) by running "union vulnerability audits," countering union campaigns and negotiating contracts. The confrontation at Sanderson Farms, a chicken processing plant in Mississippi, illustrates basic change in management tactics in the last quarter century. Rather than call on the Klan, which had played a central role in previous labor battles in the county, Sanderson Farms hired Kullman, Lang, Inman and Bee, a law firm specializing in fighting unions. The strike naturally led Sanderson into repeated "confrontations" with the NLRA and other labor laws—for bargaining in bad faith, for hiring a 13-year-old strikebreaker, for an attempt to get the union decertified (illegal while a company is charged with unfair labor practices)—confrontations in which the advice of antiunion consultants could be crucial.

Unlike workers in Northern cities, Southern workers have little contact with the activities and advantages of strong, aggressive unions. Although a few unions in the South—the miners, the Teamsters, oil workers, communications workers—successfully organized significant portions of their industries, the weak presence of Southern unions plays a major role in the plans of management tacticians. Workers' "knowledge" of unions is shaped by communications media and local power structures that publicize strikes around the world but ignore both the pressures that force a strike and the positive role that unions play in a community. Each lost strike weakens the ability of all unions to organize and strengthens management's hand. Workers lack the experience that teaches that a union could mean far more than wage increases. As the recent campaign at Sanderson Farms showed, by playing on the negative image of unions, the bosses can effectively bid for workers' loyalty. Scab labor, often sympathetic to union demands but unaware or skeptical of the need for solidarity, let Sanderson keep on producing its Miss Goldy chickens in spite of the strike.

Fiber Industries made use of a similar strategy against the Teamsters in Salisbury, North Carolina, but with the added touch of distributing a slick recording which dramatized a losing strike—replete with the sounds of gunfire, corrupt union officials, statements by Salisbury church leaders, and more. The union lost that election, but the results were thrown out on the basis of the recording and presence of armed guards at a meeting just before the election. (At a new election held March 29, 1980, the union won by a vote of 1002 to 990. Twelve votes are now being contested by the company.)

Significantly, the textile industry remains virtually untouched despite repeated union initiatives and many violent battles. With that failure to organize the dominant industry, workers naturally hold the concept of unions at arm's length, treating claims of imminent success with suspicion. Even the most aggressive and dedicated organizing attempts often face a united front of church, industry, community, and even worker hostility rarely equalled in the North. Challenged by these obstacles and with their members elsewhere demanding service for their dues, unions have often been forced to limit the resources they could commit to Southern organizing. Limited money (regardless of company propaganda vilifying rich unions) forced both the AFL and the CIO to abandon post–World War II plans to bring the Southern textile industry—20 percent organized—up to Northern levels—70 percent organized. The AFL campaign lasted about a year, while the CIO drive sputtered along underfinanced until the early 1950s. Management was quick to multiply each blemish in the image of unions, each retreat no matter how strategic, manipulating sectional controversies against "outside agitators" who they claimed enlisted Southern members solely to enrich their personal coffers.

The resulting picture today is not one over which workers can rejoice. In 1964, 2,067,000 Southern workers belonged to unions—16 percent of the nonagricultural work force. In 1976, 3,076,000 workers belonged to unions—only 14 percent of the nonagricultural work force. Election statistics carry a similarly dismal message. Nationally, the total number of elections for union representation rose only slightly in the past decade, from 12,957 in 1967 to 14,358 in 1977. Meanwhile, decertification elections called for by the companies rose from 125 to 305. As the corporate offensive against established

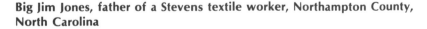

Big Jim Jones, father of a Stevens textile worker, Northampton County, North Carolina

unions mounts, the latter figure can be expected to rise dramatically in the next decade.

WHILE THE BOSSES HAVE BECOME STRONGER, THE LAWS MORE stifling, and the union structures less vigorous over the past forty years, the outcome of the war is by no means decided. Many of the obstacles to organizing—the law, labor history, high technology—are two-edged swords that can and will be wielded with great impact by workers as well as by management. The threat to workers throughout the nation that a nonunion South now poses can force unions to settle in for the long and hard but necessary task of bringing Southern workers into the mainstream of the American labor movement. History demonstrated two decades ago the South's critical role in the future of the labor movement. At the very time when the Textile Workers Union of America and the Amalgamated Clothing Workers finally dragged contracts out of the New England mills in the 1940s, those unions lost most of their membership, their war treasury, and their power when the textile jobs moved to the nonunion South. Unions in industry after industry today confront a fate textile workers suffered first: they all face a similar slow death unless they put their best effort into organizing Dixie. But organizers do realize—and can use to their advantage—the large investments that corporations now make in their Southern plants: in labor costs and, more importantly, in expensive high technology used to circumvent and defuse labor. Ironically, by making these investments, corporations have limited their freedom to run away from a union campaign. They, too, must stand and fight.

Runaways are not the only reason that unions with their power base in the North must crack the nonunion South. Companies in the North and West use the same antiunion literature, and often the same consultants, to break or keep out a union. Threats to abandon a plant, as in the steel industry, hold even more power in the ailing industrial cities of the North than in the still expanding Sunbelt. And communities everywhere vie in providing companies with the friendly, antiunion atmosphere pioneered in New England's nineteenth century mill towns. Northern workers get stereotyped as staunch unionists, but given their inability to stop plant closings, unions actually face the same skepticism throughout the nation as occurs, albeit more extremely, in the South.

As a result of this "creeping Southernism," though election losses in the South have been significant, unions actually lost a higher percentage of decertification elections in highly unionized Northern regions in 1978. Only in the South did the unions' record in decertification elections improve over the previous year. While the unions' rate of success in warding off decertifications declined from 38 percent to 34 percent nationally, it rose from 37 percent to 48 percent in the South. The lesson is clear: the labor movement needs new steam, and that steam can come from Southern workers.

Though handicapped in their resources, unions realize the importance of winning in the South and have on the whole increased their commitment to organizing the South. In textiles, much of the money to fight J. P. Stevens—one campaign often seen as a key to current Southern organizing—comes from nontextile AFL-CIO unions and the AFL-CIO's Industrial Union Department. The UAW picked up the lesson of runaways even earlier: when its organizers in Hartwell, Georgia, were assaulted and thrown out of town in 1963, they kept coming back until a union and a contract were finally won in 1978. Also in 1978, the UAW set up a permanent Southern Regional Organizing Office in Nashville; that presence quickly contributed to UAW victories from Texas to Virginia.

Recent victories by the United Rubber Workers in LaVergne, Tennessee, and the Teamsters in Winston-Salem, North Carolina, while due to many factors, grew at least in part out of the unions' previous wins in the North, a long-term commitment by the organizers to stay in town, and the new willingness of the unions to back up their organizers and Southern workers. Even after being defeated by Firestone in LaVergne four times, the URW kept up the pressure and finally won an NLRB election—held in the midst of a strike—by a four-to-one margin. The URW's announced intention to vigorously organize the South got a boost when Firestone, Goodrich, Uniroyal, and Armstrong pledged in 1979 national negotiations not to oppose such organizing. But GM had previously made a similar "neutrality" pledge which union officials believe was ineffective; the UAW achieved a major advance in its 1979 contract when it forced GM to agree that virtually all new plants will be union shops. In the Teamsters case, the union had maintained a highly visible district office in Winston-Salem for thirty years, and could therefore be on hand when workers at Hanes Dye and Finishing, angered over a shipment of material from India contaminated with lice, organized themselves into a union in less than a month.

Just as GM's original neutrality pledge proved of small value in actual practice, so too must pledges by the URW, the UAW, and other unions to stay in the South be tested by time. These successful unions have shown that traditional organizing tools can still be effectively brought to bear, including wide use of the media, good organizers, identity within the community, strong national support, and long-term commitments. They have yet to prove that they can not only win elections but also represent their members: the lack of this has been one cause of recent decertifications.

Legal warfare is also available to both sides, and unions can use existing though imperfect labor laws to win valuable gains for members. In 1979, the Oil, Chemical and Atomic Workers Union won for its workers in Marrero, Louisiana, what will amount to a $20 million back pay suit against American Cyanamid. The award was made because union workers, who had struck for nine months, were then locked out for three years while the company notified the union that it intended to replace the workers with outside contract employees (a tactic now being widely used to break public employee unions). The award would have been far greater had the Labor Reform Act been passed, with back payments made on the basis of three times lost wages.

On the other hand, barriers to union strength today arise out of changes in the labor force, changes in what kinds of jobs exist. Most organizing in the past focused on industrial work—work dominated by white male workers—such as coal mining. Industrial jobs are shrinking today; in the case of coal mining, 275,000 (mostly union) jobs disappeared in the fifteen years following World War II. Conversely, nonmanufacturing work—in hospitals, offices, government agencies— has been expanding rapidly. While this presents opportunities for organizing, it also presents new problems and demands different organizing skills than have been developed in the past, and which unions have yet to consistently handle successfully. As city hospital workers in Charleston, South Carolina, found, a state law prohibiting public employees from joining unions gave management the deciding tool in a long struggle. In North Carolina, public employees can join a union, but that union cannot engage in collective bargaining! Nine Southern states have similar laws. In Atlanta, where almost a quarter of the work force has clerical jobs, no unions appear to be actively organizing this sector. Three unions active nationally in organizing clerical workers have a total of 5,300 members in Atlanta.

Moreover, unions in the South still often face workers who apparently do not want to be organized. Much more so than Northern workers, Southerners seem to hold to the American myth of the individual's ability to "get ahead" and "make it." The widely heralded Sunbelt boom and isolated but publicized individual success stories lead workers to expect to leave the plant—and the working class— soon, making the sacrifices demanded by a union struggle seem not worthwhile. In many cases, a first-generation industrial working class is still recruited to work in rural factories. With their consciousness shaped by the mass media, little contact with the benefits of unions, and no factory experience with which to compare working conditions, these workers enter the plant already prejudiced against unions. Union organizing in the South can no longer depend on an explosion of outrage among the workers: to win the fight, unions must convert both skeptical *and* hostile workers to see that labor—even represented by today's bureaucratized unions—and management still have different and *opposing* interests.

THE QUESTION THEN BECOMES HOW TO CONVINCE WORKERS THAT unions are the best option: in political words, that a class struggle exists.

The process can start at ground level by encouraging unorganized workers to push aggressively at an early stage on those grievances, both far-reaching and mundane, that occur daily in any workplace. Issues can range from the arbitrary behavior of a foreman to longer coffee breaks to instances of discrimination and safety hazards. By acting on those complaints, workers gain in several ways. First, they may—and often will, especially when a union campaign threatens the employer—get a positive response from a management anxious to protect its paternalistic image or avoid government intervention. Second, any demand resisted reveals the limits of corporate generosity and the fact that paternalism aims to control. Third, and most important in the long run, each small skirmish gives workers experience in cooperative action, standing up to the bosses, challenging paternalistic control, and winning improvements in their lives. Each battle reinforces the knowledge that management strives to win in order to make more money, while a union strives to win to help the workers.

The experience of working collectively can be the bridge over which antiunion workers come to adopt organized labor as their servant. But this strategy carries obvious dangers. The iron fist still exists, and workers without unions run great risks of simply being fired. Issues must be chosen with care, and unions must be prepared to give full support, both personally and through the courts, to workers who suffer in even the earliest stages of organizing. It calls for a commitment to training leaders, both in the plant and in the union, and unions have yet to use this method wisely on a widespread basis.

Going beyond wage issues has proved to be another method of reaching, involving, and, eventually, organizing workers who would never have touched a union on their own initiative. As the black lung movement in Appalachia and the Carolina Brown Lung Association demonstrate, the most successful issue in the South is health and safety in the workplace, aided by and capitalizing on the establishment of OSHA and related state and federal agencies. The black lung movement formed the lever with which to prod to action a recalcitrant UMWA; while the CBLA, often working parallel to ACTWU and other AFL-CIO departments, built twelve chapters directly representing 3,000 active and retired textile workers, and advocating the needs of all textile workers. These movements effectively pushed OSHA and the

U.S. government—not to mention the textile and coal industries—into recognizing and acting upon crippling occupational diseases. Similarly, the loyalty of the UMWA membership in the 1950s, '60s, and early '70s grew to a great extent out of its cradle-to-grave health care program which served not only the miners but also their communities. Many workers are now pessimistic about the immediate future of the UMWA, in part because it has abandoned much of this program in the most recent national contract.

Other points of conflict exist between workers and bosses on which workers' organizations can and should be heard, both to win unions and to represent worker interests, two aims that should be identical. Progressives often warn that racism divides workers from each other, and unfortunately the history of unions on the issue of discrimination has not been much better than that of American society in general. Yet there have been bright spots, achievements which stand as models for new programs for labor. UMWA success in the 1930s was a reward for its policy of organizing all miners regardless of race or ethnic background, a policy duplicated by many CIO unions until the cold war. The United Cannery Agricultural Packinghouse and Allied Workers of America-CIO succeeded in organizing Reynolds Tobacco in Winston-Salem in 1943 because, unlike earlier union efforts at Reynolds, it focused on the black, unskilled men and women who formed the bulk of the work force.

Since the modern civil rights movement began in the 1950s, unions, especially at the national level, have been recognized as crucial partisans—and beneficiaries—of the struggle to end racial discrimination. The connection between the civil rights movement and the labor movement hit the front pages with the murder of Martin Luther King, Jr., in Memphis in 1968 while he was supporting the city sanitation workers' strike. The next year, the coalition among Charleston hospital workers, the union they called in to represent them, and the Southern Christian Leadership Conference brought a measure of victory against a powerfully entrenched local elite. Black workers in the Sanderson Farms strike sang "We Shall Overcome." As one of the women on strike stated, "We really feel it's a question of human dignity."

Throughout the South, the civil rights movement has opened up jobs previously reserved for whites, and black workers have taken the lead in organizing new unions and pushing old ones to be more militant. Election victories against J. P. Stevens in Roanoke Rapids and High Point, North Carolina, grew directly out of the increasing number of blacks the company hired, coupled with the union policy of nondiscrimination. One antiunion consultant drove the point home in a seminar for furniture, textile, and other manufacturing executives: "It is my strong finding that blacks tend to be more prone to unionization than whites. . . . So don't be heroes about the whole goddamn thing and fill up the work force with blacks. If you can keep them at a minimum you're better off." He added: "I feel the same way about Indians that I do blacks. . . . Stay the hell away from Puerto Ricans."

On the negative side, the CIO was not immune to the postwar wave of anticommunism that swept the United States and often resorted to its own witch hunts to prove its Americanness. In 1949, the United Steelworkers-CIO employed racism and red-baiting to replace a mostly black, radical union of Mine Mill and Smelter Workers in Birmingham, Alabama. To its credit, the USW then duplicated the progressive contract of its predecessor, but, like even the best unions, the USW national leadership does not include a significant number of minority workers. UCAPAWA lost at Reynolds in the early 1950s when Reynolds mounted a similar attack against a union weakened by racism within the CIO. These steps backward stand today as a warning, as labor is again on the defensive in a conservative climate.

Nor can unions take the support of black people for granted. Maynard Jackson rose to the mayoralty of Atlanta partly because of his identification with the organizing struggles of city sanitation workers; but, as mayor, he switched sides and refused to bargain with the same sanitation workers' union in 1976. A losing strike in 1978 dealt a major blow to the American Federation of State, County, and Municipal Employees, the only public sector union with any noticeable presence in Atlanta. In Mississippi, Charles Evers, brother of murdered civil rights activist Medgar Evers, attained a national reputation for his antiunion stance as mayor of Fayette. Understandably, but unfortunately, many black people who have moved into middle-class comfort as a result of the civil rights movement tend, like whites who move out of the working class, to forget the struggles that made their lives better.

The labor movement will also gain greatly from allying with, and giving substantial aid to, the women's movement. Obviously, unions have been one of the bastions of male hegemony, even in industries where women hold most of the jobs, as sex discrimination suits against unions testify. The entry of women into previously all-male occupations should be credited not to unions, which by and large opposed the progress, but to the women who protested and went to court to obtain the jobs. There exist no precedents of established unions which went against the tide, consciously and voluntarily moving women into organizing and leadership roles. Just as unions and workers will benefit from realizing that the race issue is part of their own struggle, so too will using workers organizations to challenge sex discrimination take away a divisive management tool, thereby mutually reinforcing two progressive movements.

Recently, organized labor has begun to make some promising moves in this direction. Most notable is the support it gives to the fight for the Equal Rights Amendment, in spite of the opposition by some male (and female) union members to ERA. In Virginia, the International Association of Machinists, the United Food and Commercial Workers, the Boilermakers, the Communication Workers of America, the UAW, the UMWA, the USW, and the Virginia Education Association have all come together in a statewide coalition, Labor for Equal Rights Now. But these moves are being taken by white male—albeit progressive— leaders. Unions must aggressively counter racism and sexism within their *own* organizations, by training and promoting women and minority workers for top leadership positions, transforming these organizations into ones with which more workers can identify. Fortunately, national unions acknowledge this need. The newspaper of the AFL-CIO, upon Lane Kirkland's assumption of the union presidency, warned of the dangers of continuing the almost total absence of black or women workers from the AFL-CIO Executive Board.

For the Southern union members, this means not only that women and minorities will have to push in regional unions to join the leadership, but that organizers and lawyers from national union offices in the North will have to be more receptive to Southern workers, to step aside and help develop leadership among Southern workers. Obviously, this will be a politically delicate situation for entrenched union officials, but it holds the key to successful organizing in the South. Education and home-grown leadership play as key a role today as in the organizing of the 1930s, enlisting men and women who not only understand the need for unions but speak in the language of Southern workers and share their concerns.

As the growing numbers of minority and women workers suggest, changes in the labor force do not necessarily work against organized labor. While the growth of nonmanufacturing work evades traditional industrial unions, other groups take up the challenge. In Florida, the establishment in 1975 of a Public Employees Relations Commission directly contributed to a phenomenal growth of public employee unions, led by AFSCME: that sector is now the most highly organized in the state, surpassing the building trades unions. Further, increasing materialism and the slow decline of regional chauvinism—a decline that counters the older, rural consciousness—can make workers more responsive to the economic advantages of unions and less responsive to employers' promises. As one woman said in a recently organized GM plant in Monroe, Louisiana: "I can give you this personal example of how things have changed since the UAW came in: my paycheck has doubled. . . . I think the best part is the feeling of security—that we can have our rights." The entry of military veterans, especially from the Vietnam War, into the Southern work force can have the same effect: "When I got out of the Air Force, after four years' mopping floors, I said damn if anyone ever controls my life again! Then I went to work for Wolverine, and it was the same old thing." This last speaker is one of the in-plant leaders of a currently unsuccessful attempt to organize his Decatur, Alabama, factory. And young workers—usually seen as wary of unions—do learn as they grow older how few people can duplicate Horatio Alger's success. Despite the alleged regional boom, a sagging national economy further diminishes the possibility of ever rising out of the working class— leading the worker back to unionism as a realistic option.

But even the most enlightened and vigorous labor movement might not, by itself, prevail over the massive power of an international elite. Recent attempts to organize factories in the South recognize the necessity of long-term, progressive, aggressive campaigns, yet many of these attempts flounder. Long campaigns cost millions of dollars, and one reason for the rash of decertification elections is that national union resources are already insufficient to service existing locals (let alone countering vastly richer industry lobbyists in state legislatures and Congress). Thus unions are often forced into the depressing cycle of organizing new locals while losing old ones. Ultimately, challenging a corporation solely within the workplace locates the battle exactly where, under capitalism, management has the most legal power simply because it owns the property. Meanwhile, it ignores an arena that management uses as its own turf, but which rightly is the natural territory of the workers: the community. In the nineteenth century, timber workers in Texas and Louisiana held the upper hand while they had the support of the community; when the Santa Fe Railroad succeeded in separating the workers from most of their middle-class supporters—having failed to divide the races—the Brotherhood of Timberworkers was crushed. Many New South companies realize the danger of a community united behind labor, and, while they act to control that community, they also break down its potential unity by hiring employees from hundreds of miles away.

Unions today *are* learning to enlist this most powerful ally. The Duke Power Company was defeated in 1974 when a broad coalition of the UMWA, consumer groups, students, and church activists came together to win a contract for Brookside workers and block utility rate hikes for consumers. The Brookside campaign—like the United Farm Workers campaign in the Southwest; the Lucas struggle in England to convert an unprofitable munitions factory to worker-controlled alternative technology productions; and the movement in Youngstown, Ohio, for community purchase and operation of a major steel mill discarded by a conglomerate—demonstrates the only possible way to win, not just unions, but unions which effectively represent the interests of the working class in its broadest definition. The Brookside

campaign was founded on the principle that miners and consumers had a common enemy: Duke Power. Based on the commitment and organizational structure of the UMWA, forces often manipulated by management—the media, the church, politicians, even Wall Street investors—were brought into the progressive coalition.

The coalition across class and cultural lines at Brookside seems obvious in hindsight, partly because it succeeded; but other coalitions, still in their infant stages, carry even more potential for wider victories. A winning coalition increases not only the financial resources, but, equally important, the human energy available for battle. The civil rights movement, the labor movement, the women's movement, and the antinuclear movement all can and should be on the same side, particularly as these "social" movements have been at least as successful in recruiting Southerners as has organized labor.

In the past, it took a crisis to force divergent progressive movements to cooperate. The Great Depression in the 1930s and the Vietnam War in the 1960s sparked movements which initiated the formation of a politically progressive majority. Today, the confluence of stagflation plus the energy crisis plus the continuing vitality of social activism could finally harden that majority coalition. The issues will be complex, but the extent of the crisis might drive all the now very separate activist streams, including explicitly labor organizations, together. Already, the once impassable barrier between antinuclear protesters and workers in the nuclear industry shows signs of cracking, with the protesters supporting the right of atomic workers to a safe and healthy workplace. Even more surprising, a prison guard union in northern Virginia has allied conditions for the prisoners with its own struggle.

Unions have often seen the value in returns of participating in broader campaigns, both with money and—as Selina Burch organized telephone workers to support various candidates for public office— with the time and effort of union members. The defeat of labor law reform points to the need for broadening the prolabor coalition into a political front to change laws that now inhibit organizing into laws to make corporations socially responsible. Such a coalition could put a brake on an inflation bred by corporate greed. The government can be forced to be an advocate of justice rather than an additional hurdle for human rights activists.

Naturally, a broad-based coalition and the type of labor movement it implies call for greater flexibility within unions than has often, *but not always,* been the case. Unions will have to build on their best traditions of democracy and nondiscrimination, recognizing the need to act on grievances outside the factories as well as within. They will have to take a more active role in and be more responsive to local needs, while mobilizing national power on national issues. Workers need to learn that the union *is* a social movement, not just a push for higher wages; for too long, unionism has seemed synonymous with middle-class life-styles and privileges that ignore those still outside the American dream.

In the end, worker organizations, like all progressive groups, must recognize a basic fact: only one struggle exists, the struggle to create a just society controlled not by corporations but by the people.

For notes on sources, see pages 374–75.

Notes on Sources

THE BROTHERHOOD

The following were the most important primary sources used in this article: The Commission on Industrial Relations Papers, Dept. of Labor, Record Group 174, National Archives; J. H. Kirby Papers, University of Houston; various articles by Covington Hall in the *International Socialist Review,* vols. 13–14 and, most importantly, Hall's unpublished manuscript, "Labor Struggles in the Deep South," in Tulane University Library and Wayne State Labor Archives (Detroit). Also the following newspapers: *Industrial Worker* (Wisconsin); *Lumberjack* and *Voice of the People* (Louisiana State University, Baton Rouge) and *The Rebel* (University of Texas, Austin). A full list of footnotes can be found in a much longer version of this article published in the British journal *Past & Present,* no. 60 (August 1973).

The most important published studies consulted included the following: Ruth Allen, *East Texas Lumber Workers* (University of Texas Press); Vernon Jensen, *Lumber and Labor* (Arno); *The Autobiography of Big Bill Haywood* (International Books); Melvyn Dubofsky, *We Shall Be ALL: A History of the IWW* (Quadrangle); Joyce Kornbluh, ed., *Rebel Voices: An IWW Anthology* (University of Michigan Press); Roger Shugg, *Origins of Class Struggle in Louisiana* (Louisiana State University Press); Sterling D. Spero and Abram Harris, *The Black Worker* (Atheneum); and C. Vann Woodward, *Origins of the New South* (Louisiana State University Press).

In addition, the following articles were useful: Ken Lawrence, "Roots of Class Struggle in the South," *Radical America,* vol. 9, no. 2; H. M. Baron, "The Demand for Black Labor: Notes on the Political Economy of Racism," *Radical America,* vol. 5, no. 2; Paul Worthman and James R. Green, "Black Workers in the New South, 1865–1915," in N. I. Huggins, ed., *Key Issues in the Afro-American Experience,* vol. 2 (Harcourt, Brace); George Morgan, "No Compromise–No Recognition: J. H. Kirby and Unionism in the Piney Woods," *Labor History,* vol. 10; Philip Foner, "The IWW and the Black Worker," *Journal of Negro History;* vol. 55; Merl Reed, "Lumberjacks and Longshoremen: The IWW in Louisiana," *Labor History,* vol. 13; Grady McWhiney, "Louisiana Socialists," *Journal of Southern History,* vol. 30.

MASSACRE AT GAULEY BRIDGE

West Virginia Department of Mines, *Annual Report,* Charleston, 1930.
Bureau of National Affairs, *Occupational Safety and Health Reporter,* October 4, 1979.

Chicago Area Committee for Occupational Safety and Health, *Health and Safety News,* January 1979.

Davis, Morris E., "The Impact of Workplace Health and Safety on Black Workers: Assessment and Prognosis," keynote address, Minority Workers Conference on Occupational Health, Memphis, Tennessee, August 18, 1979.

Lloyd, J. W., et al., "Long-term Mortality Study of Steelworkers: Respiratory Cancer in Coke Plant Workers," *Journal of Occupational Medicine,* February 1971.

Marcantonio, Vito, *I Vote My Conscience,* New York, 1956.

New York State Workmen's Compensation Board, *Report on the Feasibility of Compensating for Partially Disabling Dust Diseases,* June 1966.

Page, Joseph A., and Win-O'Brien, Mary, *Bitter Wages,* New York, 1972.

United States, House of Representatives, Special Subcommittee of Committee on Labor, "An Investigation Relating to Health Conditions of Workers Employed in the Construction and Maintenance of Public Utilities," 1936.

United States, Department of Health, Education and Welfare, National Institute of Occupational Safety and Health, "Criteria for a Recommended Standard . . . Occupational Exposure to Crystalline Silica," 1974.

United States, Departments of Labor and Health, Education and Welfare, *President's Report on Occupational Safety and Health,* 1972.

STRIKE AT DAVIDSON-WILDER, 1932–33

Crabtree, Fount W., "The Wilder Coal Strike of 1932–33," unpublished thesis, Peabody College, Nashville, Tennessee. Includes quotes from strikers and mine owners, but generally not very helpful.

Greenway, John, *American Folksongs of Protest,* University of Pennsylvania Press, 1953. Contains an account of the strike along with the songs. Strike description in many places is not true to the recollections of people we interviewed.

Highlander Research and Education Center files, State Historical Society of Wisconsin, Milwaukee, Wisconsin. A very helpful source. Files contain drafts of press releases and articles sent to various labor papers, letters, papers by Wilder young people later students at Highlander, and reports concerning the relocation of strikers in late 1933 and early 1934.

Horton, Zylphia, unpublished papers in the possession of Myles Horton. Notes and anecdotes for a Highlander play on the Wilder strike, done with the help of young people from Wilder.

Newspaper sources include: the Knoxville *News-Sentinel,* Knoxville *Journal,* Nashville *Tennessean,* Nashville *Banner,* Nashville *Labor Advocate,* and the papers of Overton and Fentress, Tennessee, counties. The county papers in the Tennessee State Archives are not complete. Best coverage was found in the Knoxville *News-Sentinel* and the Nashville *Tennessean.*

Perry, Vernon, "The Labor Struggle at Wilder," unpublished thesis, Vanderbilt University, 1934.

Tennessee Valley Authority Library and files, Knoxville, Tennessee. Files have some scant information on Wilder strikers who went to work for TVA. The Library staff is very friendly and helpful.

United Mine Workers of America files, UMWA Headquarters, Washington, D.C. Contains correspondence related to the role of the union in the strike.

West, Hedy, *Old Times and Hard Times,* Folk-Legacy Records, Sharon, Connecticut. Contains two songs from the Wilder strike with some remarks by Hedy West and A. L. Lloyd.

We would also like to thank the following people for their generous help: Mike Clark, Mr. and Mrs. Jim Crownover, Bessie and Isom Davis, Mart Dishman, Fentress Low Income People's Coop Store, Hobart Gibson, Myles Horton, Edna and Tom Lowry, Jesse Mills, Mr. and Mrs. Marvin Murphy, Fletcher and Viola Norrod, Mr. and Mrs. Early Padgett, Mr. and Mrs. Jim Randolph and family, Florence and Sam Reece, RESIST, Jane Roth, SAM, Mr. and Mrs. Harlan Smith, Arthur Stultz, Mary Jane Threet, Bradford, Nancy, Ed, Rich, Lucy, Bingham, Bill, Elizabeth, Bill, Jim, Joe, and the Institute for Southern Studies.

THE SOUTHERN TENANT FARMERS' UNION

For further reading, see the following:

Will Alexander, Edwin Embree, and Charles Johnson, *The Collapse of Cotton Tenancy,* University of North Carolina Press, 1935.

Jerold S. Auerbach, "Southern Tenant Farmers: Socialist Critics of the New Deal," *Labor History,* vol. 7, no. 1, Winter 1966. (Also reprinted in the Bobbs-Merrill reprint series in black studies.)

Donald Grubbs, *Cry from the Cotton,* University of North Carolina Press, 1971.

Howard Kester, *Revolt Among the Sharecroppers,* Covici-Friede, 1936. This book was written while Kester was working actively with the union.

H.L. Mitchell, *Mean Things Happening in this Land,* Allanheld, Osmun & Co., 1979. This is the autobiography of Mitchell. Available from STFU Association, Box 2617, Montgomery, Alabama 36105.

Mark Naison, *The Southern Tenant Farmers' Union and the CIO.* Originally published in *Radical America,* vol. 2, no. 5, September–October 1968, now available from the New England Free Press, 791 Tremont Street, Boston, Mass. A valuable and analytical account of the union's short lived affiliation with the CIO/UCAPAWA. See also article by Naison in the *Journal of Ethnic Studies,* "Black Agrarian Radicalism in the Great Depression: The Threads of a Lost Tradition," vol. 1, no. 3, Fall 1973.

The papers of the Southern Tenant Farmers' union are housed at the Southern Historical Collection, University of North Carolina, Chapel Hill, and are also available from the Microfilming Corporation of America. For a complete listing of Southern libraries that have purchased the papers on microfilm write to H. L. Mitchell, P. O. Box 2617, Montgomery, Alabama 36105.

Additional oral interviews with members of the union have been conducted by Kate Born of the Department of History, Memphis State University.

IT'S GOOD TO BE HOME IN GREENVILLE

Sources for this article include dozens of interviews conducted by the authors; newspaper articles and unpublished papers in the Greenville Public Library's

South Carolina Room, including Malcolm Cross's speech "Textile Pioneers of Greenville" and such articles as "Alester Furman Called 'Man of Great Vision,' " Greenville *News,* November 12, 1961, and "South Has Come Long Way Since Day When Mills Family Owned," by Alester Furman and Ted Shelton, Greenville *News,* October 14, 1962.

Books include Broadus Mitchell, *Rise of Cotton Mills in the South* (Baltimore: Johns Hopkins Press, 1921); Guy A. Gullick, *Greenville County: Economic and Social Conditions* (Columbia: University of South Carolina Press, 1929); James M. Richardson, *History of Greenville* (Atlanta: A. H. Cawston, 1930); George S. Mitchell, *Textile Unionism in the South* (Chapel Hill: University of North Carolina Press, 1931); William P. Jacobs, *The Pioneers* (Clinton, S.C.: Jacobs & Co. Press, 1935); William H. Simpson, *Southern Textile Communities* (Charlotte, N.C.: Dowd Press, 1948); Kenneth Marsh & Blanche Marsh, *The New South: Greenville, South Carolina* (Columbia, S.C.: R. L. Bryan, 1965); George Tindall, *Emergence of the New South* (Baton Rouge: Louisiana State University Press, 1967); Melton McLaurin, *Paternalism and Protest* (Westport, Conn.: Greenwood Press, 1971); Jack Bass, *Porgy Comes Home* (Columbia, S.C.: R. L. Bryan, 1972); and Neal R. Pierce, *Deep South States in America* (New York: W. W. Norton, 1974).

Other sources include census data, including Census of Manufactures, City & County Data Book, and County Business Patterns; and materials from Greenville city, county, and Chamber of Commerce offices, the South Carolina State Development Board, the South Carolina Appalachian Council of Governments, and other government agencies.

LABOR ON THE MOVE: THE FUTURE

A number of people at the Institute for Southern Studies contributed to this article, but especially Jim Overton and Bob Hall. In addition, Pete Brandon, Chris Scott, Chip Hughes, and Bill Barry contributed valuable insights and criticisms based on their experiences organizing Southern workers. The basic written sources were the newspapers of the AFL-CIO, the UAW, the UMWA, ACTWU, the UE, the IUE, the URW and OCAW, and the continuing labor coverage of *In These Times.* Other information came from Ray Marshall, *Labor in the South* (Cambridge, Mass.: Harvard University Press, 1967); *Wall Street Journal;* Peoria *Labor News;* Andrew Kopkind, "The Politics of Survival," *Working Papers for a New Society,* July-August 1979; Horace Huntley, "The Rise and Fall of Mine Mill in Alabama," *Journal of the Birmingham Historical Society* 6 (January 1979); Scott Deiks, "Unions Turning Them Out," *South* 6 (November 1979); Stephanie Coffin, "Organizing Clericals: The Outlook in Atlanta," unpublished ms., 1979; and the U.S. Bureau of Labor Statistics. And, of course, eight years of *Southern Exposure.*

Bibliography

This bibliography is based on a survey compiled by Ray Faherty for the Southern Oral History Program at the University of North Carolina–Chapel Hill. Special thanks are extended to Peter Wood for additions on slave labor, and to Jim Overton, Jacquelyn Hall, Page McCullough, and Pam Farmer for bringing the list up to date.

BOOKS

Adams, Frank. *Unearthing Seeds of Fire: The Idea of Highlander.* Winston-Salem, 1975.

Adams, Samuel H. *Sunrise to Sunset.* New York, 1950.

Agee, James. *Let Us Now Praise Famous Men.* New York, 1939.

Alinsky, Saul. *John L. Lewis.* New York, 1949.

Allen, Ruth A. *Chapters in the History of Organized Labor in Texas.* Austin, 1941.

———. *East Texas Lumber Workers: An Economic and Social Picture.* Austin, 1961.

———. *The Labor of Women in the Production of Cotton.* Austin, 1931.

Anderson, Sherwood. *Beyond Desire.* New York, 1932.

Appalachian Movement Press, Box 8074, Huntington, West Virginia 25405. (Pamphlets available include: Tom Bethell, *Conspiracy in Coal;* David Corbin, *The Socialist and Labor Star;* Tom Bethell and Davitt McAteer, *The Pittston Mentality: Manslaughter on Buffalo Creek;* Paul Nyden, *Coal Miners Struggle in Eastern Kentucky;* Don West, *A Time for Anger: Labor Songs from Appalachia.*)

Aptheker, Herbert. *American Negro Slave Revolts.* New York, 1943.

Armes, Ethel. *The Story of Coal and Iron in Alabama.* Birmingham, 1910.

Arnow, Harriet. *The Dollmaker.* New York, 1954.

Auerbach, Jerold S. *Labor and Liberty: The La Follette Committee.* Indianapolis, 1966.

Baratz, M. S. *The Union and the Coal Industry.* New Haven, 1955.

Beal, Fred E. *Proletarian Journey.* New York, 1937.

Beecher, John. *Collected Poems.* New York, 1974.

Belfrage, Cedric. *South of God (Claude Williams).* New York, 1941.

Berglund, A., Starnes, G. T., & DeVyver, F. T. *Labor in the Industrial South: A Survey of Wages and Living Conditions in Three Major Industries of the New Industrial South.* Institute for Research in Social Science, Charlottesville, 1930.

Berlin, Ira. *Slaves Without Masters: The Free Negro in the Antebellum South.* New York, 1974.

Bernstein, Irving. *The Lean Years.* Boston, 1960.

————. *The Turbulent Years.* Boston, 1970.

Bethell, Thomas N. *The Hurricane Creek Massacre.* New York, 1972.

Blassingame, John W. *The Slave Community: Plantation Life in the Ante-Bellum South.* New York 1972.

Blauner, Robert. *Alienation and Freedom: The Factory Worker and His Industry.* Chicago, 1964.

Bontemps, Arna. *Great Slave Narratives.* Boston, 1969.

Boskin, Joseph. *Into Slavery: Racial Decisions in the Virginia Colony.* New York, 1976.

Botkin, Benjamin A. (ed.). *Lay My Burden Down: A Folk History of Slavery.* Chicago, 1945.

Brooks, Robert R. *The United Textile Workers of America.* New Haven, 1935.

Brown, Virginia. *The Development of Labor Legislation in Tennessee.* Knoxville, 1945.

Cahn, Bill. *Mill Town.* New York, 1954.

Cantor, Louis. *A Prologue to the Protest Movement: The Missouri Sharecropper Roadside Demonstration of 1939.* Durham, 1969.

Cantor, Milton (ed.). *American Workingclass Culture: Explorations in American Labor and Social History.* Westport, Conn., 1979.

Cash, W. J. *The Mind of the South.* New York, 1941.

Caudill, Harry M. *Night Comes to the Cumberlands: A Biography of a Depressed Area.* Boston, 1963.

Cayton, Horace & Mitchell,George. *Black Workers and the New Deal.* Chapel Hill, 1939.

Chapman, H. H. et al. *The Iron and Steel Industries of the South.* Tuscaloosa, 1953.

Coleman, McAllister. *Men and Coal.* New York, 1943.

Coles, Robert. *Migrants, Sharecroppers, Mountaineers.* Boston, 1967.

Cone, Sidney M. *Aim for a Job in the Textile Industry.* New York, 1969.

Conrad, David E. *The Forgotten Farmers: The Story of Sharecroppers in the New Deal.* Urbana, 1965.

Dacus, Joseph A. *Annals of the Great Strikes in the United States.* Chicago, 1877. Reprint Arno Press, 1969.

Davidson, Elizabeth. *Child Labor Legislation in the Southern Textile States.* Chapel Hill, 1939.

Dollard, John. *Caste and Class in a Southern Town.* New Haven, 1937.

Douty, H. M. (ed.). *Labor in the South.* Washington, D.C., 1946.

Dunbar, Tony. *Hard Traveling: Migrant Farm Workers in America.* New York, 1976.

Dunn, R. W. & Hardy, J. *Labor and Textiles.* New York, 1931.

Dunne, William F. *Gastonia, Citadel of the Class Struggle in the South.* New York, 1929

Earle, John R. *Spindles and Spires.* Atlanta, 1976.

Federal Writers' Project. *These Are Our Lives.* Chapel Hill, 1939.

Fetherling, Dale. *Mother Jones—The Miner's Angel: A Portrait.* Carbondale and Edwardsville, Illinois, 1974.

Fine, Nathan. *Labor and Farmer Parties in the United States,* 1828–1928. New York, 1928.

Fink, Gary M. (ed.). *Biographical Dictionary of American Labor Leaders.* Westport, Conn., 1974.

Fink, Gary M. & Reed, Merl E. (eds.). *Essays in Southern Labor History: Selected Papers, Southern Labor History Conference,* 1976. Westport, Conn., 1977.

Finley, Joseph. *The Corrupt Kingdom: The Rise and Fall of the United Mine Workers.* New York, 1972.

Foner, Philip. *History of the Labor Movement in the United States.* 4 vols., New York, 1947.

———. *Organized Labor and the Black Worker, 1619–1973.* New York, 1974.

Foost, James D. *The Yeoman Farmer and Westward Expansion of U.S. Cotton Production.* New York, 1968.

Genovese, Eugene D. *The Political Economy of Slavery: Studies in the Economy and Society of the Slave South.* New York, 1965.

———. *Roll, Jordan, Roll: The World the Slaves Made.* New York, 1974.

Gilman, Glenn. *Human Relations in the Industrial Southeast: A Study of the Textile Industry.* Chapel Hill, 1956.

Goodrich, Carter. *The Miner's Freedom: A Study of the Working Life in a Changing Industry.* Boston, 1925.

Goodwyn, Lawrence C. *Democratic Promise: The Populist Moment in America.* New York, 1976.

Graebner, William. *Coal-Mining Safety in the Progressive Period.* Lexington, 1975.

Grant, Douglas. *The Fortunate Slave: An Illustration of African Slavery in the Early Eighteenth Century.* New York, 1968.

Green, Archie. *Only A Miner.* Urbana, 1972.

Greene, L. J. & Woodson, C. C. *The Negro Wage Earner.* Washington, 1930.

Greenhut, J. L. & Whitman, W. T. (eds.). *Essays in Southern Economic Development.* Chapel Hill, 1964.

Grubbs, Donald. *Cry from the Cotton: The Southern Tenant Farmers' Union and the New Deal.* Chapel Hill, 1971.

Hackney, Sheldon (ed.). *Populism: The Critical Issues.* Boston, 1971.

———. *Populism to Progressivism in Alabama.* Princeton, 1969.

Hagood, Margaret J. *Mothers of the South: Portraiture of the White Tenant Farm Woman.* Chapel Hill, 1939.

Hair, William I. *Bourbonism and Agrarian Protest: Louisiana Politics, 1877–1900.* Baton Rouge, 1969.

Halasz, Nicholas. *The Rattling Chains: Slave Unrest and Revolt in the Antebellum South.* New York, 1966.

Hardy, Jack. *Labor and Textiles.* New York, 1931.

Haynes, Robert V. (ed.). *Blacks in White America Before 1865: Issues and Interpretations.* New York, 1972.

Heer, Clarence. *Income and Wages in the South.* Chapel Hill, 1930.

Herring, Harriet. *History of the Textile Industry in the South.* Ms. in Southern Historical Collection, University of North Carolina.

———— et al. *Part-time Farming in the Southeast.* Washington, 1937.

————. *Passing of the Southern Mill Village.* Chapel Hill, 1949. Reprint 1977.

————. *Southern Resources for Industrial Development.* Richmond, 1948.

————. *Welfare Work in the Mill Village: The Story of Extra Mill Activities.* Chapel Hill, 1929.

————. *Worker and Public in the Southern Textile Problem.* Greensboro, 1930.

Hertz, Eric & Sherman, Jerry. *Women Power in Textile and Apparel Sales.* New York, 1978.

Hudson, Hosea. *Black Worker in the Deep South: A Personal Account.* New York, 1972.

Jacobson, Julius (ed.). *The Negro and the American Labor Movement.* New York, 1968.

Jamieson, Stuart M. *Labor Unionism in American Agriculture.* Washington, 1945.

Johnson, Josephine. *Jordonstown.* New York, 1937.

Jones, Mary. *Autobiography of Mother Jones.* Chicago, 1925.

Kahn, Kathy. *Hillbilly Women: Mountain Women Speak of Struggle and Joy in Southern Appalachia.* Garden City, N.Y., 1973.

Kelly, Richard. *Nine Lives for Labor.* Introduction by Emil Rieve. New York, 1956.

Kennedy, Stephen. *Profit and Losses in Textiles: Cotton Textile Financing Since the War.* New York, 1930.

Kester, Howard. *Revolt Among the Sharecroppers.* New York, 1935.

Killens, John Oliver (ed.). *The Trial Record of Denmark Vesey.* Boston, 1970.

Killion, Ronald & Waller, Charles (eds.). *Slavery Time When I Was Chillun Down on Marster's Plantation: Interviews with Georgia Slaves.* Savannah, 1973.

Kohn, August. *The Cotton Mills of South Carolina.* Charleston, 1907.

Krueger, Thomas A. *And Promises to Keep: The Southern Conference on Human Welfare, 1938–1948.* Nashville, 1967.

Lahne, Herbert. *The Cotton Mill Worker.* New York, 1944.

Lander, Ernest M. *The Textile Industry in the Ante Bellum South.* Baton Rouge, 1969.

Lantz, Herman R. *People of Coal Town.* New York, 1958.

Leifermann, Henry P. *Crystal Lee: A Woman of Inheritance.* New York, 1975.

Lemert, Ben F. *Cotton Textile Industry of the Southern Appalachian Piedmont.* Chapel Hill, 1933.

Lerner, Gerda. *Black Women in White America: A Documentary History.* New York, 1972.

Lewis, Sinclair. *Cheap and Contented Labor.* Asheville, n.d.

Lipsky, David (ed.). *Union Power and Public Policy.* Ithaca, N.Y., 1975.

Lumpkin, Grace. *A Sign for Cain.* New York, 1935.

————. *To Make My Bread.* New York, 1932.

Lumpkin, Katherine. *The South in Progress.* New York, 1940.

Marshall, Ray. *Labor in the South.* Cambridge, 1967.

————. *The Negro and Apprenticeship.* Baltimore, 1967.

————. *The Negro and Organized Labor.* New York, 1965.

————. *The Negro Worker.* New York, 1967.

———— & Godwin, Lamond. *Cooperatives and Rural Poverty in the South.* Baltimore, 1971.

———— & Perlman, Richard. *An Anthology of Labor Economics.* New York, 1972.

Mason, Lucy Randolph. *Standards for Workers in Southern Industry.* N.p., 1931.

————. *To Win These Rights: A Personal Story of the CIO.* New York, 1952.

McCoy, A. D. *Thoughts on Labor in the South: Past, Present and Future.* New Orleans, 1865.

McCracken, Duane. *Strike Injunctions in the New South.* Chapel Hill, 1931.

McCrea, Joan. *Texas Labor Laws.* Houston, 1978.

McDonald, David T. *Coal and Unionism.* Indianapolis, 1939.

McDonald, Lois. *Southern Mill Hills: A Study of Social and Economic Forces in Certain Mill Villages.* New York, 1928.

McLaurin, Melton A. *The Knights of Labor in the South.* Westport, Conn., 1978.

————. *Paternalism and Protest: Southern Cotton Mill Workers and Organized Labor, 1875–1905.* Westport, Conn., 1971.

McMahon, T. F. *United Textile Workers of America.* New York, 1926.

McMath, Robert C. *Populist Vanguard: History of the Southern Farmers Alliance.* Chapel Hill, 1975.

McWilliams, Carey. *Ill Fares the Land: Migrants and Migratory Labor in the U.S.* New York, 1976.

Meiklejohn, Kenneth & Nehemhis, Peter. *Southern Labor in Revolt.* New York, 1930.

Meista, Richard & Loftis, Anne. *A Long Time Coming: The Struggle to Unionize America's Farm Workers.* New York, 1967.

Miller, Elinor & Genovese, Eugene D. (eds.). *Plantation, Town, and County: Essays on the Local History of American Slave Society.* Urbana, 1974.

Miller, Randall M. *The Cotton Mill Movement in Antebellum Alabama.* New York, 1978.

Mims, H. N. & Arthur, G. B. *Analysis of 31 Southern Textile Labor Contracts.* Toccoa, Ga., 1949.

Mitchell, Broadus & Mitchell, George. *Industrial Revolution in the South.* Baltimore, 1930.

————. *The Rise of Cotton Mills in the South.* Baltimore, 1921.

————. *Textile Unionism and the South.* Chapel Hill, 1931.

————. *William Gregg: Factory Master of the Old South.* Chapel Hill, 1928.

———— & Cayton, H. R. *Black Workers and the New Unions.* Chapel Hill, 1939

Morgan, Edmund S. *American Slavery, American Freedom: The Ordeal of Colonial Virginia.* New York 1975.

Morland, John K. *Millways of Kent.* Chapel Hill, 1958.

Mullin, Gerald W. *Flight and Rebellion: Slave Resistance in Eighteenth Century Virginia.* New York, 1972.

Myers, James. *Field Notes: Textile Strikes in the South.* New York, 1929.

National Advisory Committee on Farm Labor. *Farm Labor Organizing, 1905–1967: A Brief History.* New York, 1967.

National Committee for the Defense of Political Pressures. *Harlan Miners Speak: Report on Terrorism in the Kentucky Coal Fields.* New York, 1932.

Noland, E. William & Bakke, E. Wight. *Workers Wanted: A Study of Employers' Hiring Policies, Preferences, and Practices in New Haven and Charlotte.* New York, 1949.

Northrup, Herbert R. *The Negro in the Tobacco Industry.* Report No. 13 of the Racial Policies of American Industry. Philadelphia, 1970.

————. *Organized Labor and the Negro.* New York, 1944.

Novak, Daniel A. *The Wheel of Servitude: Black Forced Labor after Slavery.* Louisville, Ky., 1978.

Nugent, Tom. *Death at Buffalo Creek: The 1972 West Virginia Flood Disaster.* New York, 1973.

Nyden, Paul. *Black Coal Miners in the United States.* New York, 1974.

Osofsky, Gilbert (ed.). *Puttin' on Ole Massa: The Slave Narratives of Henry Bibb, William Wells Brown, and Solomon Northrop.* New York, 1969.

Owens, Leslie Howard. *This Species of Property: Slave Life and Culture in the Old South.* New York, 1976.

Page, Dorothy M. *Gathering Storm.* New York, 1932.

————. *Southern Cotton Mills and Labor.* New York, 1932.

Painter, Nell I. *The Narrative of Hosea Hudson.* Cambridge, Mass., 1979.

Pang, Sam F. *A Case Study of Latin American Unionization in Austin, Texas.* New York, 1976.

Parker, Glen Lawhon. *The Coal Industry: A Study in Social Control.* Washington, D.C., 1940.

Perdue, Robert E. *Black Laborers and Black Professionals in Early America, 1750–1830.* New York, 1975.

Pflug, Warner W. (ed.). *A Guide to the Archives of Labor History and Urban Affairs.* Detroit, 1974.

Pope, Liston. *Millhands and Preachers: A Study of Gastonia.* New Haven, 1942.

Potwin, Marjorie A. *Cotton Mill People of the Piedmont: A Study in Social Change.* New York, 1927.

Raper, Arthur F. *Preface to Peasantry.* Chapel Hill, 1936.

———— & Reid, Sara. *Sharecroppers All.* Chapel Hill, 1940.

Rawick, George P. (ed.). *The American Slave: A Composite Autobiography.* Westport, 1972–76, 19 vols.

Ray, Victor K. "The Role of the Labor Union." In Leland DuVall (ed.), *Arkansas: Colony and State.* Little Rock, 1974.

Record, Wilson. *The Negro and the Communist Party.* Chapel Hill, 1951.

Rhyne, Jennings J. *Some Cotton Mill Workers and Their Villages.* Chapel Hill, 1930.

Ritlenouse, R. Lynn. *Black Employment in the South: The Case of the Federal Government.* Austin, Texas, 1976.

Rochester, Anna. *Labor and Coal.* New York, 1931.

Rogers, William W. *The One-Gallused Rebellion: Agrarianism in Alabama, 1865–1896.* Baton Rouge, 1970.

Rogin, Lawrence. *Making History in Hosiery: The Story of the American Federation of Hosiery Workers.* Philadelphia, 1970.

Rose, Willie Lee (ed.). *A Documentary History of Slavery in North America.* New York, 1976.

―――. *Rehearsal for Reconstruction: The Port Royal Experiment.* New York, 1964.

Rosengarten, Ted. *All God's Dangers: The Life of Nate Shaw.* New York, 1975.

Ross, M. H. *Machine Age in the Hills.* New York, 1933.

Rowan, Richard L. *The Negro in the Textile Industry.* Philadelphia, 1970.

Saloutos, Theodore. *Farmer Movements in the South, 1865–1933.* Berkeley, 1960.

Seagrave, Charles Edwin. *The Southern Negro Agricultural Worker: 1850–1870.* New York, 1975.

Senate Committee on Labor and Public Welfare. *Labor-Management Relations in the Southern Textile Industry.* Washington, D.C., 1952.

―――. *Labor-Management Relations in the Southern Textile Manufacturing Industry.* Pts. 1 & 2. Washington, D.C., 1950.

Sheppard, Muriel E. *Cloud by Day: The Story of Coal and Coke and People.* Chapel Hill, 1947.

Shriver, Donald W. et al. *Spindles and Spires.* Atlanta, 1976.

Simon, Charlie. *The Share-Cropper.* New York, 1933.

Simpson, William H. *Southern Textile Communities.* Charlotte, 1948.

Smith, Robert S. *Mill on the Dan.* Durham, 1960.

Spero, S. D. & Harris, A. L. *The Black Worker.* New York, 1931.

Stampp, Kenneth M. *The Peculiar Institution.* New York, 1956.

Starnes, George T. & Hamm, J. E. *Some Phases of Labor Relations in Virginia.* New York, 1934.

Starobin, R. *Industrial Slavery in the Old South.* New York, 1970.

Taber, Gladys B. *A Star to Steer.* Philadelphia, 1938.

Tany, Anthony M. *Economic Development in the Southern Piedmont, 1860–1950.* Chapel Hill, 1958.

Terrill, Tom E. & Hirsch, Jerrold. *Such As Us: Southern Voices of the Thirties.* Chapel Hill, 1978.

Theodore, Rose. *Union Agreements in the Cotton Textile Industry.* Washington, D.C., 1946.

Thompson, Holland. *From Cotton Field to Cotton Mill: A Study of Industrial Transition in North Carolina.* New York, 1906.

Thompson, Kenneth. *Labor Unions in Louisiana.* Baton Rouge, 1959.

Tindall, George B. (ed.). *A Populist Reader.* New York, 1966.

―――. *Emergence of the New South, 1913–1945.* Baton Rouge, 1967.

Tippett, Thomas. *Mill Shadows: A Drama of Social Forces in Four Acts.* New York, 1932.

―――. *When Southern Labor Stirs.* New York, 1931.

Tragle, Henry Irving. *The Southampton Slave Revolt of 1831: A Compilation of Source Material Including the Full Text of the "Confessions" of Nat Turner.* Boston, 1971.

TWUA. *Almost Unbelievable: The Story of an Industry, a Union and a Law.* New York, 1961.

————. *Building a Textile Union.* New York, 1931–48.

————. *Half a Million Forgotten People: The Story of the Cotton Textile Worker.* New York, 1944.

————. *Taft-Hartleyism in Textiles with Special Reference to Conditions in the Southern Branch of the Industry.* Washington, D.C., 1953.

United States Department of Labor. *Labor in the South.* Washington, D.C., 1950.

————. *Union Agreements in the Cotton-Textile Industry.* Washington, D.C., 1947.

UTWA. *The AFL Textile Workers.* Washington, D.C., 1950.

Wade, Richard C. *Slavery in the Cities: The South, 1830–1860.* New York, 1964.

Walker, James L. *Economic Development and Black Employment in the South.* Austin, Texas, 1975.

Ward, Robert & Rogers, William. *Labor Revolt in Alabama: The Great Strike of 1898.* University, Ala., 1965.

Webb, Elizabeth Y. *The Development of Textile Industry in North Carolina.* Washington, D.C., n.d.

Wesley, Charles H. *Negro Labor in the United States.* New York, 1927.

Wien, Sadye with Marszalek, John F. *A Black Businessman in White Mississippi, 1886–1974.* Jackson, Miss., 1977.

Wilson, Theodore B. *The Black Codes in the South.* Tuscaloosa, 1965.

Wolfbein, S. L. *The Decline of a Cotton Textile City.* New York, 1944.

Wolters, Raymond. *Negroes and the Great Depression: The Problem of Economic Recovery.* New York, 1970.

Wood, Peter H. *Black Majority: Negroes in Colonial South Carolina from 1670 through the Stono Rebellion.* New York, 1974.

Woodman, Harold D. *King Cotton and His Retainers: Financing and Marketing the South's Cotton, 1800–1925.* Lexington, Ky., 1968.

Woodward, C. Vann. *Origins of the New South.* Baton Rouge, 1951.

————. *Tom Watson, Agrarian Rebel.* New York, 1938.

Woofter, T. J. & Winston, Ellen. *Seven Lean Years.* Chapel Hill, 1939.

Working Conditions of the Textile Industry in North Carolina, South Carolina, and Tennessee: Hearings before the Committee on Manufacturers, U.S. Senate. 71st Cong., 1st Sess., May 8, 9, and 20, 1929. Washington, D.C., 1929.

Yetman, Norman R. *Life Under the "Peculiar Institution": Selections from the Slave Narrative Collection.* New York, 1970.

Zugsmith, Leone. *Summer Soldier.* New York, 1938.

ARTICLES, DISSERTATIONS, AND THESES

Abernathy, J. H. "The Knights of Labor in Alabama." Dissertation, Samford University, 1956.

Appel, J. C. "The Unionization of Florida Cigarmakers and the Coming of the War with Spain." *Hispanic American Historical Review* (February 1956).

Aronowitz, Stanley. "Miners for Democracy." *Liberation* (January 1973).

Ashbaugh, Carolyn & McCurry, Dan. "Gastonia 1929: Strike at the Loray Mill." *Southern Exposure: No More Moanin'.* (Winter 1974).

Averback, Jerold S. "Southern Tenant Farmers: Socialist Critics of the New Deal." *Labor History* (1966).

Bailey, Hugh C. "Edgar G. Murphy and the Child Labor Movement." *Alabama Review* (January 1965).

Baldwin, Jesse A. "Evils of Southern Factory Life." *Gunton's Magazine* (April 1902).

Barksdale, O. D. "Organized Labor in Etowah County, Al." Dissertation, Samford University, 1956.

Baron, Harold M. "The Demand for Black Labor: Historical Notes on the Political Economy of Racism." *Radical America* (1971).

Barry, D. Marshall & Kinnirey, Sister Ann. "The Acid in Florida's Citrus." *Southern Exposure: America's Best Music and More* (Spring 1974).

Bauer, Raymond A. & Bauer, Alice H. "Day to Day Resistance to Slavery." *Journal of Negro History* (October 1942).

Becnel, T. A. "With Benefit of Clergy: Catholic Church Support for the National Agriculture Workers Union in Louisiana, 1894–1958." Dissertation, Louisiana State University, 1973.

Beecher, John. "The Share Cropper's Union in Alabama." *Social Forces* (October 1934).

Bishop, Charles E. "Underemployment of Labor in Southeastern Agriculture." *Journal of Farm Economics* (May 1954).

Blackwell, Gordon W. "The Displaced Tenant Family in North Carolina." *Social Forces* (October 1934).

Blanshard, Paul. "One Hundred Per Cent Americans on Strike." *The Nation* (May 8, 1929).

———. "Communism in Southern Cotton Mills." *The Nation* (April 24, 1929).

Bloch, Herman D. "Craft Unions and the Negro in Historical Perspective." *Journal of Negro History* (January 1958).

———. "Labor and the Negro, 1866–1910." *Journal of Negro History* (July 1965).

Born, Kate. "Organized Labor in Memphis, Tennessee, 1826–1901." *West Tennessee Historical Society Papers.* (1967).

Bowen, Margaret. "The Story of the Elizabethton Strike." *American Federationist* (June 1930)

Boycott Begins to Hurt at Farah." *Business Week* (June 2, 1973).

Boyte, Harry. "The Textile Industry, Keel of Southern Industrialization." *Radical America* (March–April 1972).

Bragaw, D. H. "Status of Negroes in a Southern Port City in the Progressive Era: Pensacola, 1896–1920." *Florida Historical Quarterly* (1973).

Breen, T. H. "A Changing Labor Force and Race Relations in Virginia, 1660–1710." *Journal of Social History* (1973).

Brennan, C. W. "A Study of Workmen's Compensation Laws in Alabama." Dissertation, Samford University, 1952.

Brewer, Thomas B. "State Anti-Labor Legislation: Texas—A Case Study." *Labor History* (Winter 1970).

Briggs, Cyril. "The Negro Question in the Southern Textile Strikes." *Communist* (June 1929).

Brooks, Robert R. "The United Textile Workers of America." Dissertation, Yale University, 1935.

"The Brookside Mine, 1974." *Southern Exposure: America's Best Music and More* (Spring 1974).

Bubka, Tony. "The Harlan County Coal Strike of 1931." *Labor History* (Winter 1970).

Burdine, Francis B. "Regional Economic Effects of Petroleum Industry Developments in Texas, 1900–1970." Dissertation, University of Texas, 1976.

Cannon, B. M. "Social Deterrents to the Unionization of Southern Cotton Textile Mill Workers." Dissertation, Harvard University, 1951.

Carlson, Oliver. "Southern Labor Awakes." *Current History* (November 1934).

Carlton, David L. "Mill and Town: The Cotton Mill Workers and the Middle Class in South Carolina, 1880–1920." Dissertation, Yale University, 1977.

Carpenter, Charles G. "Southern Labor and the Southern Urban Continuum, 1919–1929." Dissertation, Tulane University, 1973.

Cassity, Michael J. "Southern Workers and Social Change: Concepts and Prospects." *Georgia Historical Quarterly* (Fall 1978).

Clapp, Thomas C. "The Bituminous Coal Strike of 1934." Dissertation, University of Toledo, 1974.

Cleghorn, Reese. "Black Breakthrough in Textiles." Raleigh *News and Observer* (November 11, 1969).

Cobb, William H. "Commonwealth College: A History." Dissertation, University of Arkansas, 1962.

———. "From Utopian Isolation to Radical Activism: Commonwealth College, 1925–1935." *Arkansas Historical Quarterly* (1973).

——— & Grubbs, D. H. "Arkansas' Commonwealth College and the Southern Tenant Farmers' Union." *Arkansas Historical Quarterly* (1966).

Cohn, David L. "Sharecroppers in the Delta." *Atlantic Monthly* (June 1937).

Collins, Herbert. "Idea of a Cotton Textile Industry in the South, 1870–1900." *North Carolina Historical Review* (July 1957).

Cook, Clair M. "Boyd Paxton: Saintly Scapegoat." *Christian Century* (June 14, 1961).

Cramer, Richard M. "Race and Southern Workers' Support for Unions." *Phylon* (December 1978).

Cullison, William E. "An Examination of Union Membership in Arkansas, Louisiana, and Oklahoma." Dissertation, University of Oklahoma, 1967.

Cuter, Douglas. "Labor's Long Trial in Henderson, N.C." *The Reporter* (September 14, 1963).

Cutler, Addison T. "Labor Legislation in 13 Southern States." *Southern Economic Journal* (1941).

Dallas, Sherman & Schaffer, Beverly. "Whatever Happened to the Darlington Case?" *Labor Law Review* (1973)

Davidson, Chandler. "Stalking the Southern Working Class." *Dissent* (1972).

Davidson, Elizabeth H. "Child-Labor Problem in North Carolina, 1883–1903." *North Carolina Historical Review* (April 1936).

————. "Child-Labor Reforms in North Carolina Since 1903." *North Carolina Historical Review* (April 1937).

————. "Early Development of Public Opinion Against Southern Child Labor." *North Carolina Historical Review* (July 1937).

Davis, John P. "A Survey of the Problems of the Negro Under the New Deal." *Journal of Negro Education* (January 1936).

DeVyver, Frank T. "The Present Status of Labor Unions in the South—1948." *Southern Economic Journal* (July 1949).

————. "Southern Textile Mills Revisited." *Southern Economic Journal* (April 1939).

Dew, Charles B. "David Ross and the Oxford Iron Works: A Study of Industrial Slavery in the Early Ninetenth-Century South." *William and Mary Quarterly* (April 1974).

Dewey, Donald. "Four Studies of Negro Employment in the Upper South." Case Study No. 2 in *Selected Studies of Negro Employment in the South,* edited by the National Planning Association, Committee of the South. Washington, D.C., 1953.

Dombrowski, James et al. "Miners' Insurrections/Convict Labor." *Southern Exposure: No More Moanin'* (Winter 1974).

Douty, H. M. "Development of Trade Unionism in the South." In *Labor in the South.* Bureau of Labor Statistics, Bulletin No. 898 (Washington, D.C., 1946).

————. "Early Labor Organization in North Carolina." *South Atlantic Quarterly* (July 1935).

————. "Labor Unrest in North Carolina, 1932." *Social Forces* (May 1933).

————. "The North Carolina Industrial Worker, 1880–1930." Dissertation, University of North Carolina, 1936.

Draper, Theodore. "Communists and Miners, 1928–1933." *Dissent* (Spring 1972).

————. "Gastonia Revisited." *Social Research* (Spring 1971).

Dyson, Lowell K. "The Southern Tenant Farmers' Union and Depression Politics." *Political Science Quarterly* (1973).

Eastman, Phineas. "The Southern Negro and One Big Union." *International Socialist Review* (1912–13).

Eckel, Edwin C. "The Iron and Steel Industry of the South." *Annals of the American Academy of Political and Social Science* (January 1931).

Eckert, Edward K. "Contract Labor in Florida During Reconstruction." *Florida Historical Quarterly* (1968).

Eisterhold, J. A. "Lumber and Trade in the Lower Mississippi Valley and New Orleans, 1800–1860." *Louisiana History* (1972).

————. "Mobile: Lumber Center of the Gulf Coast." *Alabama Review* (1973).

————. "Savannah: Lumber Center of the South Atlantic." *Georgia Historical Quarterly* (1973).

Ellis, Leonia B. "A New Class of Labor in the South." *Forum* (May 1901).

————. "A Study of Southern Cotton Mill Communities." *American Journal of Sociology* (March 1903).

Elmore, Nancy Ruth. "The Birmingham Coal Strike of 1908." Dissertation, Samford University, 1966.

Ethridge, Mark. "The South's New Industrialism and the Press." *Annals of the American Academy of Political and Social Science* (1931).

Evans, Mercer G. "Are Cotton Mills Feudalistic?" *American Federationist,* vol. 35, part 2.

———. "History of the Organized Labor Movement in Georgia." Dissertation, University of Chicago, 1929.

Fairfield, W. S. "The Southern Textile Industry: Union Man's Nightmare." *Reporter* (July 22, 1952).

"Farah Settles, Ending Long Strike." *Monthly Labor Review* (April 1974).

"Farah: The Union Struggle of the 1970s." *American Federationist* (June 1973).

Fickel, James F. "Management Looks at the 'Labor Problem': The Southern Pine Industry During World War I and the Postwar Era." *Journal of Southern History* (1974).

Filiatreaw, John. "White Worker in the South." *Dissent* (Winter, 1972).

Finger, Bill. "Textile Men: Looms, Loans, and Lockouts." *Southern Exposure: Facing South* (Winter 1976).

Finney, J. D. "A Study of Negro Labor During and After World War I." Dissertation, Georgetown University, 1967.

Fish, John O. "The Christian Commonwealth Colony: A Georgia Experiment, 1896–1900." *Georgia Historical Quarterly* (1973).

Flynt, Wayne. "Alabama White Protestantism and Labor, 1900–1914." *Alabama Review* (July 1972).

———. "Florida Labor and Political Radicalism, 1919–1920." *Labor History* (Winter 1968).

———. "Organized Labor, Reform, and Alabama Politics, 1920." *Alabama Review* (July 1970).

———. "Pensacola Labor Problems and Political Radicalism, 1908." *Florida Historical Quarterly* (1965).

Foner, Philip S. "An Additional Note on the Alabama State Federation of Labor." *Labor History* (Winter 1977).

Fox, Harry D. "Thomas T. Haggerty and the Formative Years of the United Mine Workers of America." Dissertion, West Virginia University, 1975.

Fox, Joseph A. "Rayon, Riot and Repression: The Lovington Sit-Down Strike of 1937." *Virginia Magazine of History and Biography* (January 1976).

Frederickson, George & Lasch, Christopher. "Resistance to Slavery." *Civil War History* (December 1967).

Gard, Wayne & Thomas, Norman. "Decline in the Cotton Kingdom." *Current History* (April 1935).

Garner, Lucy P. "An Educational Opportunity for Industrial Girls." *Journal of Social Forces* (September 1923).

"The Gastonia Strikers Case." *Harvard Law Review* (May 1931).

Goldstein, H. J. "Labor Unrest in the Birmingham District." Dissertation, University of Alabama, 1951.

Goodwyn, Lawrence, C. "Populist Dreams and Negro Rights: East Texas as a Case History." *American Historical Review* (December 1971).

Green, Archie. "The Death of Mother Jones." *Labor History* (Winter 1960).

———. "A Discography of American Coal Miners' Songs." *Labor History* (Winter 1961).

Green, George. "The ILGWU in Texas, 1930–1970." *Journal of Mexican-American History* (Spring 1971).

Green, James. "The Brotherhood of Timber Workers, 1910–1913." *Past and Present* (August 1973).

Greene, Lorenzo J. (ed.). "Negro Sharecroppers." *Negro History Bulletin* (February 1968).

Griffin, R. W. & Standard, D. W. "Cotton Textile Industry in Ante-Bellum North Carolina" (Origin and Growth to 1830). *North Carolina Historical Review* (January 1957).

―――. "Cotton Textile Industry in Ante-Bellum North Carolina" (An Era of Boom and Consolidation, 1830–1860). *North Carolina Historical Review* (April 1957).

―――. "Poor White Laborers in Southern Cotton Factories, 1789–1865." *South Carolina Historical Magazine* (January 1960).

Grob, G. N. "Organized Labor and the Negro Worker, 1865–1900." *Labor History* (Spring 1960).

Gross, Jimmie F. "Strikes in the Coal, Steel, and Railroad Industries in Birmingham from 1918 to 1922." Dissertation, Auburn University, 1962.

Gross, Judith M. "Union-Nonunion Wage Differentials in the Construction Industry." Dissertation, Princeton University, 1976.

Grubbs, Donald H. "Gardner Jackson, That 'Socialist' Tenant Farmers' Union, and the New Deal." *Agricultural History* (1968).

―――. "The Southern Tenant Farmers' Union and the New Deal." Dissertation, University of Florida, 1963.

Gulick, Charles A. "Industrial Relations in Southern Textile Mills." *Quarterly Journal of Economics* (August 1932).

Gunton, George. "The South's Labor System." *Gunton's Magazine* (March 1900).

Gutman, Herbert G. "Black Coal Miners and the Greenback-Labor Party in Redeemer, Alabama, 1878–1879." *Labor History* (Summer 1969).

―――. "The Negro and the UMWA." In *The Negro and the American Labor Movement,* edited by Julius Jacobson. New York, 1968.

Hall, Covington. "Revolt of the Southern Timber Workers." *International Socialist Review* (July 1912). Also, ms., "Labor Struggles in the Deep South." Tulane University Library.

Hamburger, Robert. "Stranger in the House." *Southern Exposure: Good Times and Growing Pains* (Spring 1977).

Hammett, Hugh B. "Labor and Race: the Georgia Railroad Strike of 1909." *Labor History* (Fall 1975).

Hancock, Faye E. "Occupational Opportunity for Southern Women: A Descriptive Picture of Women at Work in the South in 1940." Dissertation, University of North Carolina, 1946.

Hawley, Langston T. "Negro Employment in the Birmingham Metropolitan Area." In *Selected Studies of Negro Employment in the South,* edited by the National Planning Association, Committee of the South. Washington, D.C., 1953.

Haywood, A. S. "We Propose to Unionize Labor in the South." *Labor and Nation* (April–May 1946).

Head, Holman. "Development of the Labor Movement in Alabama Prior to 1900." Dissertation, University of Alabama, 1954.

Heberle, Rudolf. "The Mainsprings of Southern Urbanization." In *The Urban South,* edited by Rupert B. Demerath and Vance N. Demerath. Chapel Hill, 1954.

Herring, Harriet. "The Industrial Worker." In *Culture in the South,* edited by W. T. Couch. Chapel Hill, 1934.

―――. "Selling Mill Houses to Employees." *Textile World* (May and June 1940).

―――. "The Southern Mill System Faces a New Issue." *Social Forces* (March 1930).

Hewitt, C. M. "Some Aspects of the Development of Labor Law and Legislation in Alabama." Dissertation, University of Alabama, 1949.

Higgs, Robert. "Patterns of Farm Rental in the Georgia Cotton Belt, 1880–1900." *Journal of Economic History* (1974).

Hodges, James A. "Challenge to the New South: The Great Textile Strike in Elizabethton, Tennessee, 1929." *Tennessee Historical Quarterly* (December 1964).

―――. "New Deal Labor Policy and the Southern Cotton Textile Industry, 1933–41." Dissertation, Vanderbilt University, 1963.

Holmes, W. F. "The Arkansas Cotton Pickers Strike of 1891 and the Demise of the Colored Farmers' Alliance." *Arkansas Historical Quarterly* (1973).

―――. "The Leflore County Massacre and the Demise of the Colored Farmers' Alliance." *Phylon* (1973).

Hood, Robin. "The Loray Mill Strike." Dissertation, University of North Carolina, 1932.

Howell, D. "The Right-to-Work Law: An Investment for Social Control of the Union Security Program." Dissertation, University of Alabama, 1963.

Hudson, Hosea. "Struggle Against Philip Murray's Racist Policies in Birmingham." *Political Affairs* (September 1974).

"IAM History Preserved in Southern Labor History Archives." *Machinist* (May 1974)

Jackson, Albert. "On the Alabama Front." *Nation* (September 18, 1935).

Jeffrey, Julie Roy. "Women in the Southern Farmers' Alliance: A Reconstruction of the Role and Status of Women in the Late Nineteenth-Century South." *Feminist Studies* (Fall 1975).

Johnson, Oakley. "Starvation of the 'Red' in Kentucky." *Nation* (January 8, 1932).

Jolley, Harley E. "The Labor Movement in North Carolina, 1880–1922." *North Carolina Historical Review* (July 1953).

Jones, A. D. "The Child Labor Reform Movement in Georgia." *Georgia Historical Quarterly* (1965).

Kann, Kenneth. "The Knights of Labor and the Southern Black Worker." *Labor History* (Winter 1977).

Kendrick, A. "Alabama Goes on Strike." *Nation* (August 29, 1934).

Kennedy, John W. "The General Strike of the Textile Industry, September 1934." M.A. thesis, Duke University, 1947.

―――. "A History of the Textile Workers Union of America, CIO." Dissertation, University of North Carolina, 1950.

Kessler, S. H. "The Organization of Negroes in the Knights of Labor." *Journal of Negro History* (July 1952).

King, J. J. "Durham Central Labor Union." Dissertation, Duke University, 1938.

———. "Durham Central Labor Union." *Southern Economics Journal* (July 1938)

Knighton, D. R. "A Special Case of Union Influence on Wages: The TWUA." Dissertation, University of North Carolina, 1972.

Kundahl, George G. "Organized Labor in Alabama State Politics." Dissertation, University of Alabama, 1967.

"Labor Drives South." *Fortune* (November 1946).

Lacey, Fred. "Memphis Workers Fight: The City Sanitation Workers' Strike." New England Free Press pamphlet, n.d.

Larkin, Margaret. "The Tragedy in North Carolina." *North American Review* (December 1929).

Latham, Huey. "A Comparison of Union Organization in Two Southern Paper Mills." Dissertation, Louisiana State University, 1961.

Lawrence, Ken. "The Roots of Class Struggle in the South." *Radical America,* vol. 9, no. 2.

Lea, Arden J. "Cotton Textiles and the Federal Child Labor Act of 1916." *Labor History* (Fall 1975).

Lewis, Nell Battle. "Anarchy vs. Communism in Gastonia." *Nation* (September 24, 1929).

Lewis, Ronald. "Race and the UMW's Union in Tennessee: Selected Letters of William R. Riley." *Tennessee Historical Quarterly* (Winter 1977).

Long, Durward. "Labor Relations in the Tampa Cigar Industry, 1885–1911." *Labor History* (Fall 1971).

———. "The Open-Closed Shop Battle in Tampa's Cigar Industry, 1919–1921." *Florida Historical Quarterly* (1968).

Mandel, Bernard. "Anti-Slavery and the Southern Worker." *Negro History Bulletin* (February 1954).

———. "Slavery and the Southern Worker." *Negro History Bulletin* (December 1953).

Marcus, Irvin M. "The Southern Negro and the Knights of Labor." *Negro History Bulletin* (March 1967).

Marks, George P. "The New Orleans Screwmen's Benevolent Association, 1850–1861." *Labor History* (1973).

Marshall, Ray. "The Negro in Southern Unions." In *The Negro and the American Labor Movement,* edited by Julius Jacobson. New York, 1968.

———. "Union Racial Problems in the South." *Industrial Relations* (May 1962).

———& Jones, Lamar. "Agricultural Unions in Louisiana." *Labor History* (Fall 1962).

Martin, Charles H. "White Supremacy and Black Workers: Georgia's 'Black Shirts' Combat and the Great Depression." *Labor History* (Summer 1977).

Matison, S. E. "The Labor Movement and the Negro During Reconstruction." *Journal of Negro History* (October 1948).

Matthews, John Michael. "The Georgia 'Race Strike' of 1909." *Journal of Southern History* (1974).

McKenzie, Robert H. "Reconstruction of the Alabama Iron Industry, 1865–1880." *Alabama Review* (July 1972).

McLaurin, Melton A. "Early Labor Union Organizational Efforts in South Carolina Cotton Mills, 1880–1905." *South Carolina Historical Magazine* (January 1971).

———. "Knights of Labor in North Carolina Politics." *North Carolina Historical Review,* vol. 49, no. 3.

———. "The Southern Cotton Textile Operative and Organized Labor, 1880–1905." Dissertation, University of South Carolina, 1967.

McMath, Robert C., Jr. "Agrarian Protest at the Forks of the Creek: Three Subordinate Farmers' Alliances in North Carolina." *North Carolina Historical Review* (1974).

———. Southern White Farmers and the Organization of Black Farm Workers: A North Carolina Document." *Labor History* (Winter 1977).

McWhiney, Grady. "Louisiana Socialists in the Early Twentieth Century: A Study of Rustic Radicalism." *Journal of Southern History* (August 1954).

Meyers, Frederic. "The Knights of Labor in the South." *Southern Economic Journal* (April 1940).

"Mill Life is Tough Again." Charlotte *Observer* (June 7, 1970).

Miller, C. G. "A Study of the New Orleans Longshoreman's Unions from 1850 to 1862." Dissertation, Louisiana State University, 1962.

Miller, F. J. "Black Protest and White Leadership: A Note on the Colored Farmers' Alliance." *Phylon* (1972).

Milton, George Fort. "The South Fights the Unions." *New Republic* (July 10, 1929).

Mitchell, Broadus. "The Broad Meaning of the CIO Organizing Drive in the South." *Labor and Nation* (April–May 1946).

———. "Growth of Manufacturing in the South." *Annals of the American Academy of Political and Social Sciences,* vol. 153.

———. "The Present Situation in the Southern Textile Industry." *Harvard Business Review* (April 1930).

———. "Southern Quackery." *Southern Economics Journal* (January 1936).

———. "Why Cheap Labor Down South?" *Virginia Quarterly Review* (October 1929).

Mitchell, George S. "The Negro in Southern Trade Unionism." *Southern Economics Journal* (1936).

———. "The Cotton Mills Again." *The Survey* (July 15, 1927).

Mitchell, H. L. "Founding and Early History of the Southern Tenant Farmers' Union." *Arkansas Historical Quarterly* (1973).

———. "The Cropper Learns His Fate." *Nation* (September 14, 1935).

———& Kester, Howard. "Sharecropper Misery and Hope." *Nation* (February 12, 1936).

Moger, Allen W. "Industrial and Urban Progress in Virginia from 1880 to 1900." *Virginia Magazine of History and Biography* (July 1958).

Moore, Howard. "Black Labor: Slavery to Fair Hiring." *Black Scholar* (February 1973).

Morgan, George T. "No Compromise, No Recognition: John Henry Kirby, the Southern Lumber Operators Association, and Unionism in the Piney Woods." *Labor History* (Spring 1969).

Morris, R. B. "Labor Militancy in the Old South." *Labor and Nation* (May–June 1948).

Mosley, Donald C. "A History of Labor Unions in Mississippi." Dissertation, University of Alabama, 1965.

Mullenix, Grady L. "A History of the Texas State Federation of Labor." Dissertation, University of Tennessee, 1954.

Muller, Phil. "Populism in North Carolina." Dissertation, University of North Carolina, 1971.

Murray, Hugh T. "The NAACP versus the Communist Party: The Scottsboro Rape Case, 1931–1932." *Phylon* (1967).

Myer, Gordon L., Jr. "The Missouri Small Farm Program: An Analytic Evaluation." Dissertation, University of Missouri, 1976.

Myers, Frederic. "Knights of Labor in the South." *Southern Economic Journal* (April 1940).

Myers, John B. "The Alabama Freedman and the Economic Adjustments During Presidential Reconstruction, 1865–1867." *Alabama Review* (1973).

Naison, Mark. "Claude and Joyce Williams." *Southern Exposure: No More Moanin'* (Winter 1974).

———. "The Southern Tenant Farmers' Union and the CIO." *Radical America* (September–October 1968).

Nelson, Daniel. "A CIO Organizer in Alabama, 1941." *Labor History* (Fall 1977).

Nichols, Jeanette P. "Does the Mill Village Foster Any Social Types?" *Social Forces* (March 1924).

Northrup, Herbert. "The Negro and the United Mine Workers of America." *Southern Economic Journal* (April 1943).

———. "New Orleans Longshoremen." *Political Science Quarterly* (1942).

———. "The Tobacco Workers International Union." *Quarterly Journal of Economics* (August 1942).

Oates, M. J. "Role of the Cotton Textile Industry in the Economic Development of the Southeast, 1900–1940." *Journal of Economics History* (March 1971).

Palmer, Paul C. "Servant into Slave: The Evolution of the Legal Status of the Negro Laborer in Colonial Virginia." *South Atlantic Quarterly* (1966).

Parker, Robert V. "The Bonus March of 1932: A Unique Experience in North Carolina Political and Social Life." *North Carolina Historical Review* (1974).

Pearce, Arthur R. "The Rise and Decline of Labor in New Orleans." Dissertation, Tulane University, 1938.

Pierpont, Andrew Warren. "Development of the Textile Industry in Alemance County, North Carolina." Dissertation, University of North Carolina, 1953.

Polakoff, Murray. "The Development of the Texas State CIO Council." Dissertation, Columbia University, 1955.

Porrett, Edward. "The Cotton Mills of the South." *New England Magazine* (July 1895).

Potwin, Marjorie A. "Cotton Mill People of the Piedmont." *Studies in the History of Economics and Public Law* (1929).

Pride, Nancy. "Incidents Preceding the Louisiana Child Labor Law of 1912." *Louisiana History* (Fall 1978).

Prior, John. "Study of Three Textile Strike Communities and Unions." Dissertation, University of North Carolina, 1972.

Quinney, Valerie. "Textile Women: Three Generations in the Mill." *Southern Exposure: Facing South* (Winter 1976).

Rankin, Carl E. "The University of North Carolina and the Problems of the Cotton Mill Employee." Dissertation, Columbia University, 1938.

Ratchford, Benjamin. "Economic Aspects of the Gastonia Situation." *Social Forces* (March 1930).

Reed, Merl E. "The Augusta Textile Mills and the Strike of 1886." *Labor History* (Spring 1973).

———. "Lumberjacks and Longshoremen: The I.W.W. in Louisiana." *Labor History* (1972).

Reese, James V. "The Early History of Labor Organizations in Texas, 1838–1876." *Southwestern Historical Quarterly* (1968).

———. "The Worker in Texas, 1821–1876." Dissertation, University of Texas, 1964.

Reinders, Robert C. "The Free Negro in the New Orleans Economy, 1850–1860." *Louisiana History* (1965).

Rhee, Jong Mo. "The Redistribution of the Black Work Force in the South by Industry." *Phylon* (1974).

Rice, John Donald. "The Negro Tobacco Worker and His Union in Durham, N.C." Dissertation, University of North Carolina, 1941.

Richards, Paul D. "The History of the Textile Workers Union of America, CIO, in the South, 1937 to 1945." Dissertation, University of Wisconsin, 1978.

Rieve, Emil. "TWUA-CIO." *Labor and Nation* (September–October 1947).

Robert, Joseph C. "The Tobacco Industry in Ante-Bellum North Carolina." *North Carolina Historical Review* (April 1938).

Rogers, M. D. "Collective Bargaining in the Tennessee Valley Authority: The Trades and Labor Experience." Dissertation, University of Tennessee, 1973.

Rogers, William W. "The Agricultural Wheel in Alabama." *Alabama Review* (1967).

———. "Negro Knights of Labor in Arkansas: A Case Study of the 'Miscellaneous' Strike." *Labor History* (Summer 1969).

Rony, Vera. "Bogalusa—the Economics of Tragedy." *Dissent* (May–June 1966). Reprinted in *Poverty: Views from the Left,* edited by J. Larner and I. Howe. New York, 1968.

———. "Labor Drives to Close the South's Open Shop." *The Reporter* (November 18, 1965).

———. "Poor Whites and the Unions." *Dissent* (March–April 1967).

———. "Sorrow Song in Black and White." *New South* (Summer 1967). Reprinted by Southern Regional Council as pamphlet and included in *The Underside of American History,* edited by T. Frazier. New York, 1978.

Rosengarten, Theodore & Rosen, Dale. "Shoot-out at Reeltown: The Narrative of Jess Hull, Alabama Tenant Farmer." *Radical America* (November–December 1972).

Ross, M. H. "Court Decisions Involving Trade Unions in North Carolina: A Bibliography." *North Carolina Historical Review* (October 1953).

Sanford, D. W. "Congressional Investigation of Black Communism, 1919–1967." Dissertation, State University of New York at Stonybrook, 1973.

Scarpaci, J. A. "Immigrants in the New South: Italians in Louisiana Sugar Parishes, 1880–1910." *Labor History* (Spring 1975).

Schubert, Richard & Cooper, Jean S. "The Florida East Coast Railway Case: A Study of Governmental Decision-Making." *Labor Law Journal* (1974).

Schwenning, G. T. "Prospects of Southern Textile Unionism." *Journal of Political Economy* (December 1931).

Segal, Robert M. & Teague, John E. "Some Comments on the Right of an Employer to Go Out of Business: The Darlington Case." *Boston College Industrial and Commercial Law Review* (Spring 1963).

Seidman, Joel et al. "Knitting Mill Workers: The Impact of an Organizing Strike." In *The Worker Views His Union.* Chicago, 1958.

Seltzer, Curtis I. "The United Mine Workers of America and the Coal Operators: The Political Economy of Coal in Appalachia." Dissertation, Columbia University, 1977.

Shaffer, E. T. H. "The Southern Mill People." *Yale Review* (December 1929).

Shapiro, Harold. "The Labor Movement in San Antonio, Texas." *Southwest Social Science Quarterly* (September 1955).

Shofner, J. H. "The Labor League of Jacksonville: A Negro Union and White Strikebreakers." *Florida Historical Quarterly* (January 1972).

———. "Militant Negro Laborers in Reconstruction Florida." *Journal of Southern History* (1973).

Shugy, Roger Wallace. "The New Orleans General Strike of 1892." *Louisiana Historical Quarterly* (April 1938).

Siceloff, John. "Tobacco in Transition." *Southern Exposure: Facing South* (Winter 1976).

Sizer, Samuel A. " 'This Is Union Man's Country': Sebastion County, Arkansas, 1914." *Arkansas Historical Quarterly* (1968).

Skelton, Billy Ray. "Industrialization and Unionization in North Carolina and South Carolina: An Economic Comparison." Dissertation, Duke University, 1964.

Smith, Abbott E. "Colonists in Bondage: White Servitude and Convict Labor in America, 1607–1776." Dissertation, University of North Carolina, 1947.

Snowden, Yates. "Notes on Labor Organizations in South Carolina, 1742–1861." Bulletin 38, Part 4, University of South Carolina, 1914.

"Southern Campaign, 1946." *Labor and Nation* (April–May 1946).

Spier, William. "We Was All Poor Then: The Sub-Economy of a Farming Community, 1900–1925." *Southern Exposure: Our Promised Land* (Fall 1974).

Spillane, Richard. "Striking Facts About Southern Cotton Mills and Cotton Mill Employees." *Manufacturers Record* (December 11, 1924).

Sproggins, T. L. "Mobilization of Negro Labor for the Department of Virginia and North Carolina, 1861–1865." *North Carolina Historical Review* (April 1947).

Stachel, Jack. "Lessons of Two Recent Strikes." *Communist* (June 1932).

Stark, Louis. "The Meaning of the Textile Strike." *New Republic* (May 8, 1929).

———. "The Trial at Marion, North Carolina." *American Federalist* (January 1930).

Starobin, Robert. "Disciplining Industrial Slaves in the Old South." *Journal of Negro History* (1968).

Stephens, Oren. "Revolt on the Delta." *Harpers Magazine* (November 1941).

Stillman, Don. "The U.M.W.: Historic Breakthrough for Union Democracy." *New Politics* (1973).

Stokes, Allen H., Jr. "Black and White Labor and the Development of the Southern Textile Industry, 1800–1920." Dissertation, University of South Carolina, 1977.

Stone, Olive. "Agrarian Conflict in Alabama: Sections, Races and Classes in a Rural State from 1800 to 1938." Dissertation, University of North Carolina, 1939.

"Strike of Longshoremen on the Gulf Coast." *Monthly Labor Review* (February 1946).

"The Strikes at Marion, North Carolina." Federal Council of Churches of Christ in America, Department of Research and Education, Information Service (December 28, 1929).

"Struggles of Textile Workers Depicted by Labor Cartoonists." *Textile Labor* (February 1973).

Stuckey, Sterling. "Through the Prism of Folklore: The Black Ethos in Slavery." *Massachusetts Review* (Summer 1968).

Taft, Philip. "A Short Note on the Alabama State Federation of Labor." *Labor History* (Summer 1975).

Tamburro, Frances. "The Factory Girl Song." *Southern Exposure: America's Best Music and More* (Spring 1974).

Taylor, P. S. "Power Forming and Labor Displacement in the Cotton Belt." *Monthly Labor Review* (March–April 1938).

Taylor, Richard W. "Unionizing Activity and Unionization Potential in Hired Agricultural Labor Markets in the United States." Dissertation Louisiana Polytechnic Institute, 1976.

Thomas, Dione. "Diary of a Woman Reporter." *Southern Exposure: Focus on the Media* (Winter 1975).

Tilley, Nannie M. "Agitation Against the American Tobacco Company in North Carolina, 1890–1911." *North Carolina Historical Review* (April 1947).

Tower, J. Allen. "The Industrial Development of the Birmingham Region." *Bulletin of Birmingham Southern College* (1953).

Trepp, Jean Carol. "Union-Management Cooperation and the Southern Organizing Campaign." *Journal in Political Economy* (October 1933).

Troy, Leo. "The Growth of Union Membership in the South, 1939–1953." *Southern Economic Journal* (April 1953).

Tsong, Peter Z. W. "Changing Patterns of Labor Force Participation Rates of Nonwhites in the South." *Phylon* (1974).

Turner, R. V. & Rogers, W. W. "Arkansas Labor in Revolt: Little Rock and the Great Southwestern Strike." *Arkansas Historical Quarterly* (1965).

Van Osdell, John G. "Cotton Mills, Labor and the Southern Mind, 1880–1930." Dissertation, Tulane University, 1966.

Venkataramani, M. S. "Norman Thomas, Arkansas Sharecroppers, and the Roosevelt Agricultural Policies, 1933–1937." *Arkansas Historical Quarterly* (1965).

Wadley, Janet K. & Lee, Everett S. "The Disappearance of the Black Farmer." *Phylon* (1974).

Wagstaff, Thomas. "Call Your Old Master—'Master': Southern Political Leaders and Negro Labor During Presidential Reconstruction." *Labor History* (Summer 1969).

Washington, Booker T. "The Negro and the Labor Unions." *Atlantic Monthly* (June 1913).

Watters, Pat. "Workers, White and Black in Mississippi." *Dissent* (1972).

Webb, Bernice L. "Company Town—Louisiana Style." *Louisiana History* (1968).

Whatley, Larry. "The Works Progress Administration in Mississippi." *Journal of Mississippi History* (1968).

Williamson, Gustavaus G. "South Carolina Cotton Mills and the Tillman Movement." *Proceedings of the South Carolina Historical Association* (1949).

Willis, William S., Jr. "Divide and Rule: Red, White, and Black in the Southeast." *Journal of Negro History* (July 1963).

Wimberly, Jack. "Labor and Collective Bargaining in the Louisiana Lumber Industry." Dissertation, Louisiana State University, 1960.

Wolfe, Lee M. "Radical Third-Party Voting Among Coal Miners, 1896–1940." Dissertation, University of Michigan, 1976.

Woodward, C. Vann. "Industrialism and the New South." In *Past Imperfect: Alternative Essays in American History,* edited by Blanche W. Cook et al. New York, 1973.

Worthman, Paul B. "Black Workers and Labor Unions in Birmingham, Alabama, 1897–1904." *Labor History* (Summer 1969).

———. "Working Class Mobility in Birmingham, Ala., 1800 1914." In *Anonymous Americans,* edited by Tamara K. Hareven. Englewood Cliffs, N.J., 1971.

Yabroff, Bernard & Herliky, Ann. "History of Work Stoppages in Textile Industries." *Monthly Labor Review* (April 1953).

Zeichner, Oscar. "The Transition from Slave to Free Agricultural Labor in the Southern States." *Agricultural History* (1939).

Zeisel, Rose N. "Technology and Labor in the Textile Industry (c1945–1966)." *Monthly Labor Review* (February 1968).

Photography Credits

Grateful acknowledgment is made to the following for supplying or allowing us to use photographs:

T. E. Armitstead, Museum of the City of Mobile Collection, University of South Alabama Photographic Archives: pages 20–21
Edward L. Bafford Photography Collection, University of Maryland Baltimore County Library: page 51 (bottom right)
Franklin Blechman: page 107
Earl Dotter: pages 46, 261, 267, 303–9, 317, 333, 336, 355, 359
Mary Frederickson: pages 158–59, 163
Greenville County Library; photograph published in *A Greenville County Album: A Photographic Retrospective,* 1977: page 233
Historic Mobile Preservation Society, E. Wilson Collection: page 55 (bottom)
Lewis Koch: pages 59, 60
Labor Unity/ACTWU: pages 207, 344, 350, 368
The Library of Congress: pages 63, 82–83, 102
David Moberg, *In These Times:* pages 295, 299
National Union of Hospital and Nursing Home Employees, District 1199: page 256
Erik Overby/Mobile Public Library Collection, University of South Alabama Archives: pages 50 (bottom), 51 (top), 52, 53, 54 (bottom left), 55 (top), 167
Groesbeck Parham: page 41
Press Picture Service: page 278
The Soil Fuel Administration, National Archives: pages 66, 93, 113–19, 264–65, 269
Len Stanley: page 330
STFU Papers, Southern Historical Collection, UNC Library, Chapel Hill: pages 130, 133, 141, 170
UMW Journal and Earl Dotter: page 261
The United States Forest Service: pages 6, 26
Workers in Our Field, pamphlet published by Rural Education and Welfare Association, Inc., Memphis: page 122

Index

About the Contributors

Fran Ansley is completing law school at the University of Tennessee and lives in Knoxville with her family.

Carolyn Ashbaugh is a farmer, writer, and photographer currently working with the Arizona Farmworkers Union and with Centro Adelante Campesino, a service center for farm workers in El Mirage, Arizona. She is the author of *Lucy Parsons: American Revolutionary.*

John Beecher was a chicken farmer, professor, sailor, novelist, New Deal administrator, sheepherder, historian, printer, and lecturer. His *Collected Poems, 1924–1974* was published by Macmillan.

Brenda Bell is the coordinator of the Knoxville, Tennessee, area "Threads" program, a joint project of the Amalgamated Clothing and Textile Workers Union and the National Endowment for the Humanities.

Tom Bethell is former research director of the United Mine Workers of America and former editor of the newsletter *Coal Patrol.* He is the author of *The Hurricane Creek Massacre,* published by Harper & Row.

Mimi Conway is the author of *Rise Gonna Rise: A Portrait of Southern Textile Workers,* published by Anchor Press/Doubleday. The research for her article was made possible by a grant from the Fund for Investigative Journalism.

Sean Devereux is a lawyer in Asheville, North Carolina.

Earl Dotter specializes in labor subjects and is currently the photographer for the American Labor Education Center.

Mary Frederickson received her doctorate from the University of North Carolina, after completing a dissertation on the Southern Summer School.

Eric Frumin is acting director, Department of Occupational Safety and Health, Amalgamated Clothing and Textile Workers Union of America.

Jim Green teaches history at the College of Public and Community Service, University of Massachusetts at Boston, and is an editor of *Radical America.* He is the author of *Grass-Roots Socialism: Radical Movements in the Southwest, 1895–1943,* published by Louisiana State University Press.

Herbert Gutman is a professor of history at the Graduate Center of the City University of New York, and the author of *The Black Family in Slavery and Freedom* and *Work, Culture, and Society in Industrializing America.*

Bob Hall is the editor of *Southern Exposure* and the director of the Institute for Southern Studies.

Neill Herring is an Atlanta, Georgia, carpenter and freelance writer.

Steve Hoffius is a freelance writer living in Charleston, South Carolina, and a frequent contributor to *Southern Exposure.*

Chip Hughes is a writer and organizer concerned with labor and occupational health issues in the South

Clement T. Imhoff teaches history and economics in high school in Columbus, Georgia.

Bob Korstad is a historian working on a larger study of the union at Reynolds.

Margaret H. Martin is a freelance writer living in Roanoke Rapids, North Carolina.

Melton McLaurin teaches history at the University of North Carolina–Wilmington.

Dan McCurry, a rural community organizer and writer, comes from a family of western North Carolina textile workers.

Marc S. Miller is associate editor of *Southern Exposure.*

David Moberg is associate editor of *In These Times.*

Groesbeck Parham, a native of Fairfield, Alabama, still lives in the Birmingham area, where he is a medical student.

Valerie Quinney teaches history at the University of Rhode Island. Both her parents worked in North Carolina textile mills.

Gwen Robinson has taught history in Dartmouth's Black Studies Program and directed a research project in Chicago on minorities in the construction industry.

Cliff Sloan conducted research on Greenville, J. P. Stevens, and related matters for his senior thesis with the support of a Summer Research Award from Harvard University's John F. Kennedy Institute of Politics.

Len Stanley helped found the Carolina Brown Lung Association and worked with them for five years. She is also involved with other occupational health issues in the South.

Don Stillman is the editor of *Solidarity,* the United Auto Workers 1.8 million–circulation magazine.

Michael Thomason teaches history at the University of South Alabama.

Sue Thrasher, a founder of the Institute for Southern Studies, was on the staff of *Southern Exposure.* She is at present on the staff of the Highlander Research and Education Center.

Joanie Whitebird is a poet living in Houston, Texas.

Leah Wise is a mother, steel fitter, veteran activist, and oral historian. Formerly on the staff of the Institute for Southern Studies, she has been in the South gathering records and recollections of black people's struggles for the past twelve years.